Children's Writer.

Guide to 2006

Writer's Institute
Publications ™

Editor: Susan M. Tierney

Contributing Writers:

Lizann Flatt
Pegi Deitz Shea

Judy Bradbury
Pamela Holtz Beres
Joan Broerman
Jan Burns
Heather Burns-DeMelo
Kristi Collier
Marjorie Flathers
Leslie Davis Guccione
Christina Hamlett

Lisa Harkrader
Mark Haverstock
Louanne Lang
Suzanne Lieurance
Joanne Mattern
Mary Northrup
Cindy Rogers
Susan Sundwall
Katherine Swarts
Leslie Wyatt
Carolyn Yoder

Contributing Editor: Marni McNiff

Copy Editor: Meredith DeSousa

Production: Joanna Horvath

Cover Art: Melanie Williamson

Publisher: Prescott Kelly

Table of Contents

Book Publishing

The Alchemy of Concocting *The List*

By Pegi Deitz Shea

The 12 months of 2005 should be known as the Year of the Leaping Editors. More than 20 prominent children's book editors changed publishing houses or landed promotions. These transitions mean good news for authors and illustrators for 2006 and beyond. Like medieval alchemists, editors have new opportunities to mix the work of their most reliable authors and illustrators with fresh talent. The cauldrons must produce, twice a year, a list of books people will buy.

Editor transitions have an impact on publishers' lists in several ways:

▥ An editor joining a different company may now work with known talent who wouldn't have fit in a former publisher's list.

▥ A publishing company may hire an editor because of contacts, to help transform an established list.

▥ An editor who could not bring his contacts must look for new talent who can add fizz to the list.

▥ Books contracted at a house by a former editor may be inherited by an editor whose taste differs. If there are changes, a book can be postponed to a future list, where it may fit better.

▥ Occasionally, contracted books can lose their support at the former house and be dropped from the schedule—orphaned. This happens in reverse as well. An incoming editor may not care for an inherited book, and might be able to drop it. In either case, the author is usually free to sell it to a different publisher.

Before the recession in the early 1990s, most authors and illustrators bonded for life to their editors. Consider Natalie Babbitt with Michael DeCapua; Patricia Polacco with Patricia Lee Gauch; Shel Silverstein with Ursula Nordstrom; and David Macaulay and Lois Lowry with Walter Lorraine.

Then came a different period, one that took its measurements more at the bottom line. Corporate sensibilities, mergers, economics, and, well, healthy competition created the concoction of a freer market for authors and illustrators. For the better, this market made room for new, perhaps less expensive, talent. For better or worse, less loyalty now exists all around—publisher to editor, editor to author, author to publisher. This mobility of talents has turned list-building into alchemy—part science, part magic.

While most editors interviewed for this article don't divulge details of "who's bringing whom," they do weigh in on the permutations. "Many times authors (and sometimes books) follow an editor to a new house. Conversely, many times existing house authors are assigned to a new editor," explains Yolanda LeRoy, Editorial Director at Charlesbridge Trade Division. "These days authors tend to publish at more than one house, too. While an author may follow an editor, that person may also continue to publish with a new editor at the old house. Part of what a house is getting in a seasoned editor is his or her contacts. It's beneficial for a house to allow an editor to work with his or her former authors and illustrators."

Cecile Goyette, who leapt from Dial Books for Young Readers to become Executive Editor at Alfred A. Knopf, a division of Random House, says, "An editor taking over for a departing editor will likely inherit some projects and authors. Some editors are able to bring authors with them to their new house, but contracts and other scenarios can prevent that, at least for a time. Moving to a new house also presents a nice opportunity to look for new talent. If there's a *house specialty,* that will likely contribute to what an editor will be sent and acquire."

A house specialty is exactly what Adriana Dominguez hopes to create at Rayo, HarperCollins's fledgling Spanish language children's imprint. Hired recently as Executive Director, she plans to take the number of books on Rayo's list from 5 up to between 15 and 20 annually. That means more opportunity for Latino writers and artists.

Similar opportunities are available at multicultural publisher Lee & Low Books, according to Senior Editor Jennifer Fox. (Fox didn't change houses, just her name, from Frantz.) "In 2006, we are putting an increased emphasis on the distribution of our Spanish language books, ARCOIRIS imprint. We publish one or two Spanish language titles each list and have done so for the past several years." Lee & Low is holding steady with the number of new books, six in the spring and six in the fall. "We aim to have a variety of titles representing people of different cultural and ethnic backgrounds on each list," Fox says.

Dorling Kindersley's specialty has always been lively nonfiction illustrated with a blend of photography and artwork. That is not changing, according to Alisha Niehaus, DK Associate Editor of Children's Books. "We have similar numbers of books coming out. These totals

The Arithmetic of a Word Industry

The Association of American Publishers (AAP) reported high increases in net sales in children's and young adult publishing last year, particularly in hardcover sales. A representative monthly year-to-date figure late last year showed an increase of about 118 percent. Paperback sales were up 2 percent. Elementary and high school publishing was up 6.6 percent.

Veronis Suhler's 2005 *Communications Industry Forecast* projected that American communications would be the fourth fastest-growing sector of the economy over the next five years, reaching $1.109 trillion in 2009.

Teen consumer spending is approximately $150 billion a year. One of the largest sales categories among teens is media, from magazines to books to mobile devices. In the U.S., the number of teens will increase by 0.2 percent a year for the next several years. (www.marketresearch.com)

Publishing industry leader R.R. Bowker estimated that the number of new U.S. titles, published in the last year for which data was available, increased by 14 percent. That amounted to about 195,000 new titles and editions.

Profits increased at the largest U.S. publishers last year, according to reports in *Publishers Weekly*. At last report, Random House profits were up 55 percent worldwide, and Penguin Group's were up 44 percent. At HarperCollins, income was up 2 percent.

Scholastic distributed 350 million children's books in 2005, according to *Publishers Weekly*. The total circulation for the company's classroom magazines was 8.3 million. Based on record sales of *Harry Potter and the Half-Blood Prince,* Scholastic predicted revenues of about $2.3 billion in its next fiscal year.

include everything we publish: Eyewitness, readers, reference, sticker books, kits, reissues, a Spanish list, etc." The total for 2006 will be about 250, spread out over three seasons rather than two.

Niehaus is looking forward to 2007 and 2008, as DK has a new CEO, Gary June, former President and CEO of Pearson Technology Group. "I am not aware of any particular initiatives at this point, although that is likely to change once our new CEO has had a chance to settle in. I know our U.S. program is going to be given a focus in the company, so watch for new series, formats, ideas. If you have an innovative idea that you think might work in DK style, send it along!"

New talent and ideas are also

welcome at Abrams Books for Young Readers, which is expanding. Executive Editor Susan Van Metre, who arrived at Abrams late in 2002, states, "I left Dutton after 12 years and was able to work with some of the same authors here, after they had honored their contracts with Dutton. I also acquired new talent for this list."

Also expanding is Walker Books, which was purchased by Blooms-

bury Publishing in December 2004. (Another move saw Walker Editor Timothy Travaglini jump to Putnam.) Publisher Emily Easton is excited about Walker's future. "We'll have 40 new hardcovers on our list, up from 30. In 2007 we're slated to increase the number of titles to 50 new hardcovers. This planned growth is a direct outcome of the merger with Bloomsbury." Easton says Walker is looking to expand its middle-grade and YA fiction list even further.

Bloomsbury itself is diving head-first into the future. Victoria Wells Arms, Associate Publisher and Co-Editorial Director, reports, "We have about 60 front list books on our 2006 list, up from maybe 50 in 2005; 2007 will be yet again larger. We have more U.S.-originated books than ever before, and more for the young chapter and middle-grade set. We have added an editor—Jill Davis—plus promoted another to editor—Julie Romeis—so now have four acquiring editors." Walker also added an editor in Mary Gruetzke, formerly of Scholastic's Cartwheel Books and Little, Brown.

Walker and Bloomsbury complement each other well, says Easton. "Walker's list is more picture book-oriented, while Bloomsbury's is more fiction-oriented. Walker has more of a presence in the school and library market, particularly because we publish nonfiction titles, and Bloomsbury is particularly strong in the fantasy genre."

While most expansions are into markets for older children, Walker is heading south as well. "We'll be adding a small toddler/preschool presence, with some novelty board books and young picture books," Easton explains. "Most of our picture books fall in the four- to seven-year-old age group, and our illustrated nonfiction tends to fall into the grades two to five age level."

Mixed Loyalties

All these editorial and corporate changes cause alarm among authors and illustrators, because there are no rules about whether to stay or go. Should an author remain loyal to the publisher or the editor?

When asked if an editor is usually free to work with former authors and illustrators, Scholastic Vice President and Associate Publisher Kenneth Wright says, "It really depends on the circumstances under which he or she left his or her previous job."

Van Metre agrees. "I am hugely fond of Dutton, which was a home for me as a young editor. I respect the publishing they do there and wanted to leave on good terms. At the same time, I wanted to continue to work with all the great authors and illustrators I had helped develop there. Some authors and illustrators stayed, some came along to Abrams, and some are publishing with both, but this was amicably worked out."

Authors and illustrators were intrigued with, and perhaps cheered by, one of the biggest shuffles of the year: Anne Schwartz, who had her own imprint at Simon & Schuster, returned—after almost ten years—

to Random House, where she had previously published Apple Soup Books. She was followed shortly after by Lee Wade, formerly Simon & Schuster Vice President and Creative Director, and by Associate Editor Ann Kelley. *Publishers Weekly* reported that Schwartz was hired to beef up picture books, a market that is trying to bounce back from soft sales in the past few years. But how many writers and illustrators could she bring from Simon & Schuster? Schwartz had edited Ian Falconer's enormously successful Olivia (the pig) picture books, among other projects by well-known authors and illustrators. Would she be searching for new talent?

An announcement of the new imprint's debut, Schwartz & Wade, answered some of the questions. The spring 2006 list has four picture books and touts forthcoming talent, including Falconer, Nancy Carpenter, Patricia McKissack, Jerry Pinkney, Paul O. Zelinsky, and Barbara McClintock. Schwartz says, "Our goal is to publish approximately 20 titles a year."

Schwartz's move illustrates that publishing executives usually deal with editorial transitions on a case-by-case basis. Rick Richter, President of the Simon & Schuster's children's division, assigned Schwartz's published books to Atheneum. "Books in production stayed at Atheneum," Schwartz reports. "Other authors and illustrators that asked to be released from their contracts followed me to Random House."

Faced with additional editor

transitions, Simon & Schuster reorganized. Richter promoted Emma Dryden to Vice President, Associate Publisher of Atheneum books for Young Readers. Dryden would continue to oversee the imprint, Margaret K. McElderry Books, which now is led by Executive Editor Karen Wojtyla. Ginee Seo launched her eponymous line, Ginee Seo Books, as an imprint of Atheneum/Simon & Schuster.

Top executives leapt about at Scholastic as well. After 22 years with the company, Vice President and Publisher Jean Feiwel announced she was leaving. Barbara Marcus retired, and Lisa Holton jumped from Disney to replace her as President of Scholastic Children's Book Publishing and Distribution. Scholastic looks to improve its sales from the 15 percent decline it took a year earlier. Trade sales dropped 44 percent, to $181 million. The summer release of *Harry Potter and the Half-Blood Prince*, however, was sure to boost the company's trade sales, specifically those of the Arthur A. Levine imprint.

Speaking of multi-title publishing, Walker's Easton maintains that authors should respect the relationship forged with a company to launch a series. "If an author or illustrator has had a successful series or character at the previous company, that character and series should remain in the home that launched it because of all the time, effort, creativity, and money invested in getting the books off the ground."

Lists at educational nonfiction publishers such as Thomson Gale's Lucent Books and KidHaven Press imprints aren't affected by editorial transitions. Lori Shein, Managing Editor of Lucent Books and KidHaven Press, explains, "At our company, individual editors don't build their own lists. Everything we do is on a work-for-hire basis and all books are done in series formats. So, we build lists for each imprint through consultations with librarians, sales staff, editors, and others. These are the lists used by everyone on staff. We get many word-of-mouth referrals for authors (and some illustrators) from many different sources, including in-house editors."

More New Imprints

Most publishers have a slightly larger list in 2006 than in 2005, 5 to 10 extra titles, suggesting cautious optimism. Dollar figures may be unclear signs, but the number of imprints and expansions seems a clear indicator of an industry poised to grow even more.

The Book Industry Study Group projects a slight dip in children's book net sales at roughly $21.5 million for 2006. The numbers climb modestly to about $22 million in

2007, and to $22.5 million in 2008. Editors keep these figures in mind today, as they represent the sales of many of the manuscripts they're contracting for right now. Scholastic's Wright, for example, says the company will have about 5 percent fewer books published in 2006 and again in 2007. That doesn't sound drastic until you do the math with Scholastic's expected annual total of 610 titles. The 30 books fewer represents more than many imprints' yearly lists.

Yet editorial transitions from the last couple of years have resulted in the launch of numerous imprints. Most of the growth is taking place in the middle-grade age group and older.

Ginee Seo Books debuted with four titles last fall. "I will have about 15 books in 2006. I expect to publish between 15 and 17 titles in 2007," Seo says. While she publishes for a range of ages, "I tend to concentrate on the novels. Most of my list is middle-grade and young adult fiction."

Charlesbridge Publishing is hoping to lead their picture book readers into new lines of chapter books. LeRoy indicates that Charlesbridge is excited to launch Bridge Books. "This initiative, headed by Executive Editor Judy O'Malley, is geared toward independent readers," says LeRoy. "These early readers, chapter books, and novels bridge the transition between picture books and successful, more sophisticated independent reading. Bridge Books offers a range of fiction and non-

fiction topics and invites kids at various stages of their reading experience to tackle a book on their own."

Abrams busily expanded Amulet Books, an imprint begun the year before with paperback reprints. Now, new novels are hitting the shelves, including *ttfn* by Lauren Myracle, author of the *New York Times* best-seller *ttyl*, and books by O.R. Melling, author of The Chronicles of Faerie, an international best-selling series of fantasy novels.

In addition, Van Metre says, "Abrams is launching an imprint called Abrams Image, of visual books for the hip, older teen and 20- and 30-something reader. The first list includes a satiric travel 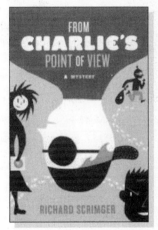 guide to Afghanistan and an award-winning graphic novel, *Mom's Cancer*, by Brian Fies."

New at the Penguin Young Readers Group is Sleuth, an imprint of middle-grade and young adult mysteries, according to Stephanie Owens Lurie, President and Publisher of Dutton Children's Books/ Penguin Young Readers Group. Interestingly, all the imprints or divisions of Penguin—Putnam, Dial, Viking—can publish into the line, and profit by it. "All mysteries are supposed to be placed on the Sleuth list," Lurie explains. "They actually carry two imprint names, Putnam/Sleuth or Dutton/Sleuth, etc. The profit goes to the imprint that acquired the book."

Heavy hitters at Little, Brown have come together to launch LB Kids, a line of novelty and interactive books. Publisher David Ford, Associate Publishers Bill Boedeker and Megan Tingley, and Executive Editor Liza Baker plan to sell these books through mass-market venues, specialty or niche markets, as well as through traditional bookstores.

Chronicle Books now has more to offer traditional bookstores, according to Melissa Manlove, Editorial Assistant. Known for picture books, Chronicle is "launching an early chapter book series in 2006." Overall, Chronicle has upped its titles from 80 to 98.

No Perfect Formula for Balance

Authors and illustrators frustrated by rejection letters saying their work is "not right for our list" wonder exactly what that means. Most publishers can readily give breakdowns of how many picture book, novel, and nonfiction titles they will release as part of the answer. For instance, Dutton's Lurie says, "We try to be responsive to market trends when we balance the list. Picture books used to make up 75 percent of our list; now the balance is about 50 percent picture books and 50 percent novels, both middle-grade and YA."

Of 68 forthcoming titles from

Knopf, Goyette says the list is balanced evenly among picture books, middle-grade fiction, and YA. If you're a professional writer, you keep up on this information. To get a good idea of a company's list, editors recommend studying the recent catalogues, which usually specify imprints—a Wendy Lamb Book or a Richard Jackson Book. You can get a good idea of an editor's taste and submit accordingly.

"The actual number of titles published on each list in a given season and in a given year are not at all random," explains Dryden of Simon & Schuster. "Each list has set title count goals and each editor also has general title count goals for themselves." Lists are looked at with the cold eye of finance, she says, and with the "warmer eye of creativity," which might, for instance, select a variety of art styles and palettes.

Dryden says, however, that the most fun and most magical element in building a list is surprise, and that editors are prepared to handle all kinds—"winning an auction for a book we didn't know we needed but absolutely have to have; an author's or illustrator's family emergency; a writer's writer block; an illustrator's pregnancy that delays the artwork for nine months; the boss saying we have a huge financial hole to fill; a favorite author coming in for lunch and offering you a manuscript you didn't know they were writing, *anything*!"

The lists of educational or institutional (school and library) publishers are less prone to surprises. Still, they strive to remain flexible. "We are continually evaluating our list and adjusting as needed," reports Thomson Gale's Shein. "We try to expand our list in areas that seem to be in high demand by school and public librarians, and weed out titles and series where demand seems to be flagging. We try hard to respond to the needs of our customers on an ongoing basis, and this should be reflected in our list. Each year we add new series to keep our list fresh and (we hope) to reach more customers. We continually add titles to series that are selling well. We also try to respond to important world and national events and hot topical issues by adding titles on these subjects wherever possible."

The Cats in Krasinski Square

By KAREN HESSE ~ Illustrated by WENDY WATSON

Danger of Homogeneity?

These days, however, the trade publishers' emphasis on marketing, combined with the movement of editors and talent, has made year-old catalogues out of date, and future lists less predictable. How can an editor tell you what the publisher wants when it may merge with another company or discontinue an imprint the very next day? How can you know that an editor is going to take her quirky sensibility elsewhere? Does the house she left still want *quirky*? Or will these mergers and editorial movements result in homogeneity?

"Yes," says LeRoy, "and that is why I choose to work for a smaller independent house [Charlesbridge]. I believe that our kind of publishing represents an alternative to that homogeneity. There is a void being created by the bottom-line conscious, conglomerate-driven houses, and the smaller presses are stepping into that gap and keeping publishing alive and well."

"To some degree, I'm sure [homogeneity] happens," concedes Bloomsbury's Arms, "but each house does have a personality, and many editors change to some degree to suit their new environment. As long as individual editors are finding (and encouraged to find) great new voices, I don't think the consumers really care who published the books—big or small, homogenous or not."

Knopf's Goyette admits, "Publishers tend to hire someone who will complement their aims, or add variety, if that's a goal. Mergers do tend to mean that the big publishers publish a broad spectrum of books and formats. Smaller, independent houses may have a more focused identity. But neither has to lead to 'interesting versus homogeneous' publishing. Publishing is a venture for risk-takers and visionaries, of any size."

"Actually, publishing is just one big risk, isn't it?" asks Van Metre. Even though Abrams is expanding, "we're continuing to publish to our core market, the art and museum worlds."

"Every large house must cover all bases, but that doesn't mean lists are homogeneous," says Amy Burton, until recently a publicist at Harper-Collins. She explains, "HarperCollins Children's Books tries to reflect the

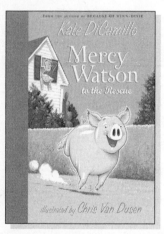

strengths of the overall house and support them through publishing children's titles within the major house imprints. For example, both general books and children's books publish in the Rayo (Hispanic), Amistad (African-American), and Eos (Sci-fi/Fantasy) imprints."

"I think the large houses are doing some of the best and most innovative publishing," says Wright. For example, the literary imprint Scholastic Press publishes Karen Hesse, easily one of the top risk-taking authors."

Dutton, part of the huge Penguin Group, which in turn is part of the huge Pearson Publishing company, carves out its own niche inside the company. "We acquire books that have both retail and institutional appeal," Lurie says. "We don't publish mass-market or merchandising books. We leave that to our sister imprint, Grosset & Dunlap." But outside the group, Dutton's mission—to publish high-quality entertainment with immediate child appeal—is echoed by editors around the industry.

Book by Book

Karen Lotz, President and Publisher of Candlewick Press, explains that the company's location in Cambridge, Massachusetts, rather than in a publishing center like New York cuts down on editorial transitions and mergers. A few miles away in Watertown, Charlesbridge's LeRoy feels the same way. (Although Little, Brown and Houghton Mifflin—both in Boston—haven't been immune to changes.) Candlewick's and Charlesbridge's missions seem to remain undiluted.

Lotz says Candlewick is "a trade house; we have a philosophy of publishing book by book rather than genre by genre. That means we work collaboratively in-house and with our authors and illustrators to bring each book to the highest level of quality it can attain, in text, illustration, design, and production values. This often leads us back to our maxim: Publish no book on the basis of *good enough*. We do not look at our lists from the perspective of slotting titles, although we do strive for a generous mix of ages and genres on each list. Although many of our books have a broad appeal and sell into channels that are considered mass-market, we do not pursue mass-market publishing per se. We do publish the occasional movie tie-in book when one of our titles lands on the silver screen!" A recent Candlewick title includes *Operation Red Jericho,* a YA novel of intrigue by Joshua Mowll, and Newbery Winner Kate DiCamillo's chapter book, *Mercy Watson to the Rescue,* illustrated by Chris Van Dusen.

Charlesbridge's main focus is still quality nonfiction for the trade market, but it has been publishing more and more fiction recently, according to LeRoy. "The only real guidelines we use for our yearly publishing plan are to keep a ratio of about one-third fiction to two-thirds nonfiction, and about four-fifths picture books to approximately one-fifth Bridge Books."

She elaborates, "There's a nice mix of science, nature, social studies, math, diversity, and concept books on our list along with our fiction and Spanish translations. We publish many first-time authors, but we're also excited to have many well-known children's authors on our list as well. Some recent additions to our list include Martha Alexander, Bill Martin Jr., Kathryn Lasky, Jane Yolen, Eve Bunting, April Pulley Sayre, and Sandra Markle. We also work with several illustrators who we think will be big

names in the industry: Paul Estrada, Megan Halsey and Sean Addy, Robin Brickman, Paul Carrick, Mitch Vane, and Kelly Murphy, to name a few."

Among recent nonfiction titles from Charles-bridge are Sneed B. Collard III's *A Platypus, Probably,* illustrated by Andrew Plant; *A Mother's Journey,* by Sandra Markle and illustrated by

Alan Marks; and Cynthia Chin-Lee's *Amelia to Zora, Twenty-six Women Who Changed the World,* illustrated by Megan Halsey and Sean Addy.

In the larger houses, imprints allow for diversification. "The Knopf group is committed to publishing great literary books for all ages. Beyond that, the tastes and talents of our editors and designers are what define the list," says Goyette.

"I'm interested in literary work of lasting merit," Seo asserts, "and I do publish *name* authors, such as E.L. Konigsburg, James Howe, Chris Lynch, and Marc Aronson. My imprint is part of Atheneum Books for Young Readers. My imprint reflects my own peculiar editorial tastes— what these are will, I hope, become apparent, but in general I think I'm interested in unique, sometimes quirky books with a real point of view and strong writing. This is no doubt what every editor says, so I'm afraid people will just have to read the books [I've edited] and figure me out."

Seo continues, "As for Atheneum in general, we are the boutique imprint at Simon & Schuster. We've had enormous literary and critical success with awards, most notably this year's Newbery Award. I would say overall our editors take creative risks and enjoy pushing the envelope of children's literature, be it with the literature itself or with new formats." The latest titles include Chris Lynch's *Inexcusable*, and Marc Aronson's *Witch- Hunt: Mysteries of the Salem Witch Trials.*

Atheneum also places a special emphasis on new authors, says Dryden. She comments on the two other Simon & Schuster hardcover imprints. The children's division's flagship imprint, Simon & Schuster Books for Young Readers, consists of "titles that are commercial, high profile, celebrity, etc.," such as *Eloise*. Margaret K. McElderry Books, the smallest imprint, publishes a "balance of fiction, picture books, collections, and poetry, with an eye to bringing English and European design and voice to an American audience," says Dryden.

"Homogeneity comes not from editors' tastes, but from the kinds of books that are succeeding in the retail marketplace and the fact that we are all chasing profit," Lurie frankly concludes.

Maybe Candlewick has it best.

Lotz explains: "We are creatively affiliated with our parent company, Walker Books of London, and we jointly benefit from the ownership of the company worldwide, which is held by a trust whose members include all the staff in the U.S., U.K., and Australia/New Zealand, as well as invited authors and illustrators. This means that in addition to being employee-owned, we also are completely independent, and thus can continue to be creatively led."

Once Upon a List, Then What?

"Fabbity fab, your story is accepted! Congratulations on your cleverosity!" Georgia Nicholson would say. "But are you full-frontal list? Or are you middley?"

Basically, the terms *front-list*, *mid-list*, and *back-list* describe the physical layout of publishers' catalogues. In the front (or on the top of a Web page) are the newly released titles, and usually the books that garner the most promotion money. HarperCollins's Burton says, "Our front list always reflects the changing needs of the consumer. Right now, we are publishing a lot of fantasy, trilogies, teen girl fiction and movie/TV tie-in books."

In the back of the catalogue are older titles that continue to make money. Goyette calls them "the economic backbone" of the list. At HarperCollins, those include "classic titles, school and library-focused books, and best-selling celebrity books," reports Burton.

It's that area in the middle that concerns authors and illustrators

Give Your Mid-List Book Front-List Treatment

To get more promotion money from your publishers and hopefully become a back-list regular, you need to help your book perform well. In many cases, all you need to do is *ask*. They want your book to succeed too.

- First, make friends with the publicity department.
- Draw up your own marketing plan and share it with the publicists. Tell them what you can do on your own, and ask them to accomplish other ideas.
- Write up and post teachers' guides on both your own website and the publishers'. Have your publisher print them as handouts or inserts with your book at conventions.
- Link with organization sites, such as the Children's Book Council.
- Research awards, and ask to be submitted to applicable ones.
- Propose presentations for teacher conferences. Sometimes the publisher cannot afford to *sponsor* you (pay your travel, lodging, and registration) at a conference, (because they're usually sponsoring a front-list author); but the publicity department may be able to set you up for school visits in the area of the conference to make the trip profitable. Have the publicist schedule you for a book signing at conferences, and be ready to hand out your own brochure.
- It's hard for authors—especially novelists—to get visual items such as bookmarks and posters. Timing helps. Before the book's illustration or cover goes to its first printing, ask your editor to have bookmarks or post-cards designed in the press sheets' extra spaces. So, eventually when the book goes to press for 10,000 copies, you'll have 10,000 bookmarks automatically.

On the Best-Seller Lists

The following are among the many books that appeared on best-seller lists in Publishers Weekly, *the* New York Times, *or in the American Bookseller's Association's* Book Sense *last year.*

▓ *Beyond the Valley of Thorns (*Land of Elyon, Book 2*)*, Patrick Carman (Orchard). A middle-grade fantasy.

▓ *Chasing Vermeer,* Blue Balliett, illus., Brett Helquist (Scholastic). Middle-grade mystery about a stolen painting, in the spirit of E.L. Konigsburg's *From the Mixed-up Files of Mrs. Basil E. Frankweiler.*

▓ *Eldest,* Christopher Paolini, book two in the Inheritance Trilogy (Knopf). YA fantasy.

▓ *Fairy Dust and the Quest for the Egg,* Gail Carson Levine, illus., David Christiana (Disney). The history of Tinker Bell and the fairies of Never Land, for ages 5 to 8.

▓ *Flush,* Carl Hiaasen (Knopf). An adventure story for readers 10 to 13 centering on an environmental issue. The author's *Hoot* was also on recent lists.

▓ *Inkspell, Inkheart, Dragon Rider, The Thief Lord,* Cornelia Funke (Chicken House). By a best-selling German author of fantasy, for ages 9 to 12.

▓ *Kira-Kira,* Cynthia Kadohata (Atheneum), 9 to 12. Newbery winner about a Japanese-American family in the 1950s.

▓ *Mercy Watson to the Rescue,* Kate DiCamillo, illus., Chris Van Dusen (Candlewick). First in a chapter book series for ages 4 to 8. Other DiCamillo books that appeared on best-seller lists last year were *The Tale of Despereaux* and *Because of Winn-Dixie.*

▓ *Ready or Not, An All-American Girl Novel,* Meg Cabot (HarperCollins). Young adult sequel to *All-American Girl* by the author of the Princess Diary books, with more mature themes.

▓ *Rebel Angels,* Libba Bray (Delacorte). YA fantasy, a sequel to *A Great and Terrible Beauty,* also on the best-seller's list last year.

▓ *Runny Babbit: A Billy Sook,* Shel Silverstein (HarperCollins). Post-humously published, and written over a 20-year period.

the most. If your brand-new book is on page 14 of the catalogue with a half-page layout, you may only get a handful of reviews, no starred ones, no awards, no posters, no bookmarks. Within two years, your book may be remaindered.

Mid-list is a fuzzy term, too, because it means different things in different houses. At Abrams, Van Metre says, "Mid-list are books for which there are moderate sales expectations (no editor or author thinks of a book as mid-list, though)." Chronicle's Manlove says mid-list books are "the real bread and butter for a company, books that sell well and steadily. If they're in the catalogue, they're being actively marketed."

"Positioning a book is more of an art than a science," Goyette says. "In general, front-list are the books you expect to sell the most or to gain great critical acclaim. Mid-list are those with a more modest forecast, such as those by less well known authors, or ones that are on their way up." Seo says, "Mid-list books tend to be quieter, to find their own way."

Dutton describes placement differently. "We use the terms *lead title* and *make book*," Lurie explains. "We aim to have a lead picture book and a lead novel in every given season. We would hope to sell more than 20,000 copies in hardcover of any lead title. A *make book* is a less obvious book. For instance, it might be a first novel that the company decides to make successful by using extra marketing money to create

word-of-mouth and to promote sell-in to bookstores. Mid-list is any book that isn't a lead or make book." Lurie adds that the average amount of promotion money spent on mid-list books is 6 percent of that book's projected net receipts.

At Bloomsbury, a book's position on a list is fluid. "Often a book will push itself right out of the middle of the list because so many in-house people love it so much," Arms exclaims. "When we editors first shape the list we guess which books will be easiest to get publicity coverage on, which the sales group will respond to most enthusiastically, which are the most unusual, groundbreaking, etc. Then it shifts as more people read the books, as starred reviews highlight other titles, as authors find sudden fame or success in other areas, and sometimes if the jacket seems to set it apart. Nothing is set in stone at Bloomsbury and because we're small, we can focus on a much bigger percentage of the list than other houses."

While promotion money seems to go to books that don't need it— books by celebrities, noticeably— editors maintain that it isn't always tied to a book's position on the list. It's also not a finite figure; authors and illustrators can work harder to get more promotion money.

"Those designations [front-list vs. mid-list] aren't absolute forecasters of how much money or promotion a given title will receive," Goyette asserts. "Many other factors contribute to those decisions. We don't have a specific dollar amount for each mid-list title, but every book on the list will get a significant amount of marketing. There are no *left-behind* books! A supposed mid-list title may make a bigger splash than anticipated, and we will of course respond accordingly. Sometimes the book tells us what it needs as it makes its way into publication."

Wright agrees. The amount of promotion money allocated at Scholastic "truly depends on the book, its channels, the cooperation of the author. It's tough to attach a dollar amount."

Candlewick takes a similar approach. "Marketing resource is driven by the channels we are supporting; we work in partnership with our accounts to achieve the right mix of title-by-title spending, co-op, and grouped promotions," Lotz explains. "We budget our marketing money by theme and author as well as by title."

Van Metre and LeRoy concur about the case-by-case process. "We do not decide our marketing efforts based on mid-list versus best-seller projections," LeRoy states. "We tailor our marketing strategies for each book and its individual needs."

It's inevitable that some books won't perform up to expectations and will not even make the back-list, much less stay on it for a long time. When asked if there is a threshold of sales a book must make annually to be kept on back-list, Wright says, "Yes, we have thresholds, and they vary depending on format, market, and genre.

But we do look closely at back-list performance and make decisions to reprint accordingly."

Bloomsbury doesn't have a hard and fast threshold either. "We make a judgment call when a book's sales have effectively stopped and there's nothing more we can do for it," Arms explains.

Goyette says, "To stay in print as a back-list title, a book must be reasonably profitable and consistent, out-earning the cost of things such as warehousing. There are also those books that are simply important to keep in print, and so we do."

Van Metre says that a threshold of 1,000 to 1,500 sold annually is typical in the industry, though not necessarily at Abrams. "We're very proactive. We are always looking for ways to extend the life of a book by keeping it in the thoughts of its audience. This can mean repromoting the back-list in our catalogue or creating teachers' guides, etc."

Now more than ever, publishers are trying to get the most out of every book, by aggressively marketing their back-list with teacher guides and themed packages. Generally, the smaller the publisher, the longer it will keep your book alive.

"We just keep trying to sell," states Shari Dash Greenspan, Editor at Flashlight Press. This Brooklyn, New York, company publishes two trade children's illustrated books each year. "We try pushing them as new for the first year or two, as it takes a while to penetrate different parts of the market."

As a small independent publisher,

Flashlight doesn't budget for promotion, "especially after the initial launch period where the bulk of publicity money goes," Green-span explains. "Nonetheless, even for back-list we continue to send out books for review and award applications."

"We work to keep books in print as long as we can; this is particularly important for us in servicing our school and library customers," says Lotz. Candlewick prefers to do small overstock sales when necessary to reduce inventory rather than sell off all stock and put a title out of print.

"We have many back-list-specific promotions," Chronicle's Manlove says. "We have a paperbacks promotion in the spring 2006 catalogue that applies to all paperbacks in print. We create sell sheets and special promotions around a particular theme (bilinguals, award winners, SeeMore Readers, Halloween books, holiday books, etc.). When we exhibit at educational, library and other trade shows we bring much of our back-list."

"One of the ways we're continuing to invigorate our key back-list titles," says Burton, "is through Harper's Backlist + program, for which we've gathered teams of Harper staff to study our core properties and create new ways to keep them in the forefront of the consumer's mind."

"We make a concerted effort to market all of our titles each list," states Fox of Lee & Low. "Nothing gets lost in the shuffle. In addition to our new titles, we continue to market our older titles, regardless of how long they've been in print. That's one luxury of having a small back-list: You can continue to give all the books attention through the years."

Perhaps more so than any publisher, Scholastic is always in the forefront of readers' minds, with its ubiquitous book clubs, book fairs, and summer reading programs. "One of our strategies is to build authors over time, so each year we publish authors from previous seasons and years," says Wright. "So, the front-list helps the back-list, and vice versa. We have some back-list titles that can sell 100,000 copies or more each year, while a new front-list title might only sell 10,000 (as planned)."

Charlesbridge has grown so much that it's been only recently— still infrequently—that it has had to put books out of print. "We believe in doing all we can for our back-list, including changing covers, changing titles, creating new marketing plans, or even re-illustrating a book. Also, we often create special catalogues that target a specific market, such as a nature catalogue. We like to build on themes so that many of our books work well together," says LeRoy.

Marketing is a little different for a non-trade, educational publisher. "At Lucent Books and KidHaven Press, we put most of our marketing money on front-list (or new) titles. With promotional mailers and other tools, we try to show our customers how our books support curriculum," Shein says. "We do essentially the same thing with our back-list, although more resources go into selling the front-list."

In addition to teachers' guides and themed collections of back-list books, Lotz says Candlewick publishes "a small but solid list of *big books*, targeted to classrooms, activity kits, and discussion group guides for our titles. We also continually review the needs of the institutional market when making our paperback decisions."

In addition to the publishers' efforts to keep back-list titles fresh, Walker's Easton says, "It is the authors and illustrators who do many appearances, mostly in schools, that really help to drive back-list titles. We support these authors' efforts by bringing them to conventions and producing brochures and promotional material whenever appropriate."

Authors and illustrators are discovering that, not only is it hard to fight your way onto a publisher's list, you also have to fight hard to stay on a publisher's list.

At a Glance:
New & Growing Imprints & Lines

Abrams Books for Young Readers started **Abrams Image**, visual books for teens and up. It also expanded **Amulet Books**, which published its first new titles, rather than reprints.

Charlesbridge Publishing launched **Bridge Books,** under Executive Editor Judy O'Malley. Its audience is newly independent readers and its focus is early readers, chapter books, and novels bridging picture books and higher reading levels.

Chronicle Books is in the process of launching an early chapter book series, and has increased its titles from 80 to nearly 100 a year.

LB Books is **Little, Brown**'s new line of novelty and interactive titles.

Rayo is the expanding Spanish language children's imprint of **HarperCollins**. The list is growing from 5 titles to 15 to 20 a year.

Schwartz & Wade is a new **Random House** imprint, publishing picture books, middle-grade and YA nonfiction.

Ginee Seo Books debuted as an imprint of **Atheneum/Simon & Schuster**.

Sleuth is the new mystery line at **Penguin**. The audience is middle-grade and young adult.

Walker Books is expanding, after being purchased by **Bloomsbury Publishing**. Hardcovers will jump to 40 from 30, and the following year Walker will publish 50 new hardcovers.

Anne Schwartz: Picture Books & the Marriage of Text & Art

By Judy Bradbury

In February 2005, Anne Schwartz left her position as Vice President and Editorial Director of Anne Schwartz Books at Atheneum Books, a division of Simon & Schuster, to head up an imprint at Random House. She was joined in the spring by Lee Wade, formerly Creative Director and Vice President at Simon & Schuster. They worked feverishly to put together their first list, published in spring 2006. They had the help of Ann Kelley, who also left the ranks of Simon & Schuster to become an Associate Editor for the Schwartz & Wade imprint, and with designer Rachael Cole. Their goal is to publish 20 books a year. The Schwartz & Wade list will be predominantly picture books, "with some innovative nonfiction, middle-grade and young adult."

Schwartz, the editor who brought readers *Olivia,* by Ian Falconer; *Ben Franklin's Almanac* and *Our Eleanor,* by Candace Fleming; and many Patricia McKissack titles, including *Goin' Someplace Special,* is energized by this new direction in her career. Collaborating with Wade, her colleague for nine years at Simon & Schuster, "is wonderful," Schwartz says, "and I am thrilled with the freedom Random House has given us."

Although the picture book market is currently on the back burner at many publishing houses, Schwartz is not bothered. "I know picture books and love the genre, and I won't abandon publishing them just because the market is quiet." She explains further, "I have always been intrigued by the marriage of text and art. I love that as the editor I get to choose an illustrator, go over dummies, have a hand in the word play— all the stages that go into the making of a picture book are so appealing. There's a piece of me in every book I edit." As to the market, "it's cyclical," Schwartz notes, pointing to young adult literature as an example. "Just a few years ago, nobody was interested in buying books for teens. Now look at the YA market!" Schwartz is convinced, "Picture books have to come back. In fact, they have never not been back. The top 10 percent have always sold well. The difference now is that it's hard to sell the mid-list book."

The reason for this, says Schwartz, is because "a lot goes into making picture books." They're expensive to produce, and they have been overpublished for a while. What this means, Schwartz believes, is that publishers have to be "smarter, more creative, and more focused." Authors who hope to be successful in today's tough picture book market should heed Schwartz's advice. "Be tough on yourself. Be focused on your work, not on

Anne Schwartz: Picture Books & the Marriage of Text & Art

writing a winning cover letter or following a specific manuscript format. In the end, the only thing that matters is voice. Create something original."

When asked about celebrity books, which sometimes seem to take more than their share of marketing budgets and shelf space in bookstores, Schwartz does not hesitate to offer her opinion. "Most," she says, "are published for the wrong reasons. Publishers want to slap a big name on the cover of a book. It's cynical, and it's a disservice to children." Having said that, however, Schwartz admits to having edited one celebrity book. She is proud of the picture book she worked on with James Carville, entitled *Lu and the Swamp Ghost,* co-written by Patricia C. McKissack and illustrated by David Catrow. "It turned out well," says Schwartz, of the book/CD package.

It's clear when talking with Schwartz that she loves the business she's in. She credits Janet Schulman, former Publisher of Knopf/Random House and now Editor at Large, with helping her snag her first job in children's publishing. "Later, when I came back to Random House, I worked under Janet. She is an amazing publisher. I picked up so much from her." Regina Hayes, currently President and Publisher at Viking Books "taught me how to edit a picture book when I was her editorial assistant at Dial," recalls Schwartz, who also credits Amy Ehrlich with teaching her much about the editorial process.

When asked what she loves most about her role as editor, Schwartz begins by saying, "I love a lot about it." She then adds, "I love when something crosses my desk that is not like anything I have ever seen before. It may be rough at the edges, but I can tell it has something special. It needs me to help realize its potential. And when it does, it's satisfying to be able to get the finished book out and into the hands of children."

Currently, Schwartz & Wade is not accepting unsolicited submissions, "although that may change in the future. At this time, we are not equipped to handle large numbers of manuscripts," says Schwartz.

A Peek At What's to Come from Schwartz & Wade

▧ *Duck & Goose,* Tad Hills. A young picture book about sharing, in which a duck and a goose find what they think is a ball, but really is an egg.

▧ *Mama, I'll Give You the World,* Roni Schotter, illustrated by S. Saelig Gallagher. A slightly older picture book about a girl and her relationship with

(continued on next page)

Anne Schwartz: Picture Books & the Marriage of Text & Art

her single mom who works in a beauty parlor. "Touching and beautifully illustrated," says Schwartz.

Porch Lies: Tales of Slicksters, Tricksters, and Other Wiley Characters, Patricia McKissack. A collection of stories, and a companion volume to *Dark Thirty: Southern Tales of the Supernatural.*

Toys Go Out, Emily Jenkins, with black-and-white line art by Paul O. Zelinsky. A young chapter book reminiscent of *Winnie the Pooh* about three toys who are friends. "Brilliant and completely captivating," says Schwartz.

Magazine Publishing

Magazines Make It in the Digital World

By Lizann Flatt

No one can doubt half a decade into the millennium that we live in a digitalized society, or that the technocultural trend shows no sign of slowing. From computers with wireless access to cell phones to GPS, *connected* is the operative word. With all manner of information available from your home computer, on the road with your PDA or mobile phone, at the corner Internet cafe or community library, where does that leave print-on-paper magazines? Far from being left behind, magazines are embracing digital technology and using it to engage their readers anew.

Some magazines mix print and online editorial, crossing the boundaries of the two media by reprinting in part and creating new copy and artwork in part. Other magazines have distinct editorial content for onscreen and on paper. Many have different publications schedules—perhaps weekly upgrades online, monthly for print. Some provide online information about the business, writers' guidelines, and contact information but leave editorial content largely to print. Whatever the online/print profile, publications are expanding and optimizing how the media work together.

In print, the *National Directory of Magazines* reports that the total number of consumer magazines published is up for the second consecutive year. New titles appeared in the teen, children's, and babies categories. The category with the largest number of new publications was regional, especially parenting—good news if you like to write family-oriented articles with a local, statewide, or regional twist.

Ever narrower topics or target audiences seems to be another trend, if new adult titles such as *CityDog* (for dog owners living in Seattle) or *Geezer Jock* (for those over 40 who want to stay fit and active) are examples. New publications for young readers include science magazines such as *KNOW*; newsmagazines *Loud* and *Accent on*

Read on, for 100 More Years

The Magazine Publishers of America (MPA) launched a $40 million, three-year campaign to show advertisers that magazines are more effective at getting across advertisers' messages than other forms of media. Magazines such as *Seventeen, Nick Jr., CosmoGirl!,* and *Parents* participated in the Read On campaign, producing mock covers complete with futuristic cover lines for the year 2105.

"While this campaign is targeted at advertisers," says Nina Link, President and CEO of the MPA, "we're interested in communicating our message as widely as possible about the strengths of magazines. We want to show the enduring power of magazines to captivate readers. We also want to illustrate that in an increasingly complicated high-tech, digital world characterized by media interruption, consumers—including teens—continue to choose magazines."

Seventeen's Special Projects Director Sabrina Weill says, "The MPA does such a terrific job of talking about magazines and how important they are. People love their magazines, especially teenage girls. They tear out pages and put them up in their room and their locker, they read us in their pajamas, they bring us to the beach."

The futuristic issue of *Seventeen* carries cover lines such as "Read His Mind (Machines that Work!)" and "Oops . . . I Vaporized My Parents! Could this Happen to You?"

Says Weill, "It was a thrill to support the MPA and show readers that magazines are a really exciting place now and will be an exciting destination in 2105 and beyond. It was fun to brainstorm what it will be like then and remain true to the brand."

The MPA wants to get out the message that the appeal of magazines, the ability to engage readers by connecting with them, and the lasting power of their brands will continue decades into the future. Visit www.magazine.org/readon to see more.

News; the hip-hop *Tha Block DVD Magazine* and *Rap-Up; Justine* and *Y:L,* just for girls; regional classroom magazine *KidTimes;* and other magazines focusing on subjects from games to exchange students to training for high school athletics.

A measure of the health of the magazine industry has long been the number of advertising pages sold. According to *Media Life*, out of 20 magazine categories last year, 14 saw increases in their ad pages. Total ad pages for consumer titles saw a 2.1 percent increase in the first half of the year. Magazines for teens showed the strongest performance, with an increase of 9.6 percent. Teen publishing, simply put, is flourishing in bytes and in ink.

Teens Rule at 20 Million Strong

The teen market is getting lots of advertiser attention these days. Nina Link, President and CEO of the Magazine Publishers of America, says that is because "8 out of 10 teens read magazines, which translates into almost 20 million readers. Our research shows that teens trust magazine advertising more than advertising in other media, and they do not multitask when reading magazines."

Link says young adult magazine readers are out and about and involved. "Generally, teens read about their leisure pursuits, which is why many of the titles that are popular among teens are enthusiast titles," she explains. "Research indicates that teens who read magazines are engaged in more activities—ranging from sports to music to organized interests—than teens who do not read magazines."

Jan Fields confirms the high level of teen interest, as well as an increase in specialized or niche publications for young readers. Fields is a veteran magazine writer and Editor of *Kid Magazine Writers e-zine.*

"Most of the newer print magazines I've seen (*Justine, Y:L*, etc.) are for girls, generally tweens and teens," she says. "Even when something comes along for boys, like *Riot*, the market is tweens. I think publishers are recognizing that tweens and teens have money to spend on entertainment and are marketing accordingly."

Teen magazines for girls often focus on fashion and beauty. A title such as *Seventeen* has had decades-long appeal. "Girls come to *Seventeen* because it's an all-inclusive package—fashion, style, beauty—it's got everything they want to read," says Sabrina Weill, Special Projects Director. "Because we are a huge brand name and so well known and have a fantastic entertainment director, we are able to get perfect content for *Seventeen* readers. In our celebrity section, we talk to the celebrities our readers are most interested in; we ask the questions they most want to know. It's really customized for our reader."

Other established publications that include a mix of celebrity coverage and fashion are *Teen*, and teen versions of adult magazines: *Teen People, CosmoGirl!, ElleGirl,* and *Teen Vogue.* Some newer entries in the

teen fashion field have put a distinctive spin on their coverage. *Justine*, finishing its first year of publication, offers a more modest approach to fashion, beauty, and celebrity content for teens but also focuses on positive self- esteem and helping readers achieve their goals.

Last September, *Y:L* launched its premier issue for urban African American teens, ages 13 to 18. The title initials stand for *young lady, your look, your life, young love, your language,* and *young leaders*. The magazine is published quarterly in print and monthly online. "My magazine is for the Baby Phat or Rockaware girls," says Editor Quia Querisma. "On the newsstand, I felt, there aren't any magazines that apply expressly to African American

girls. There are African American models in other magazines, but I didn't really feel they represented all the girls in the hip-hop culture. I didn't see any styles that looked like anything my friends and I wore."

Querisma is looking for writers who can help her magazine reach its audience. "I have editorial guidelines on the website, so submit a query according to the guidelines," she says. "I really think the easiest section to get into would be the young leaders section—finding and profiling someone in the community who's doing a good job of community service and volunteering."

A start-up like *Y:L* can be a strong market for writers. "If you have a good idea and you can convey it well," says Querisma, "and it would fit with the tone of my magazine, then I'm always willing to listen, as opposed to large magazines who may have already been there, done that."

Debuting late last year was *FGBG Magazine, For Girls by Girls.* It takes its own approach to reaching 13- to 25-year-old females. "We are one hundred percent readership participation, a coast-to-coast network of friends!" says Editor in Chief Tammie Figlinski. "Our readers can promote their talents, become our models, role models, writers, volunteer staff, and much more." The publication can offer adult writers insight into the lives, interests, and thoughts of teens today.

An online magazine that is also published quarterly in print, *FGBG* invites readers to sign up through its website to become official *FGBG* girls, and to help build the pages of the magazine. "We're looking for stories written in the first-person, as experienced by that individual writer, the *FGBG* girl. We also look for stories as-told-by writers—*FGBG* girls who do the interviews and research to create a great story that has universal appeal and interest," Figlinski says. "Suggestions are posted via the website; however, we encourage girls to think about what matters to them and the voice from within their hearts. We believe that's what makes a great story, someone who has passion about something."

The teen market is overflowing with new niche titles. *Loud* targets Generation Y teens as a newsmagazine, with content on teen rights, technology, college, and profiles of teen entrepreneurs. Fashion-conscious teens in Canada now have *Vervegirl*, featuring fashion, beauty, and style. *Shout* strives to reach aboriginal youth in Saskatchewan.

YGA, Young Gay America addresses young gays and lesbians in their teens and 20s, across North America. Here, first-time writers have the best chance at acceptance with short music or film reviews. *YGA* is not currently looking for advice submissions but they are very open to contributions. The magazine is bi-monthly, with plans to go monthly this year.

Other titles for teens making their debut this year have a music twist. One innovative title is *Tha*

Block DVD Magazine, which claims to target 12- to 50-year-olds. It is delivered in DVD format. The magazine focuses on the entertainment industry for an urban, hip-hop audience. *Rap-Up* is also about hip-hop and rap, with reviews of the newest artists. It targets ages 14 to 28.

Putting a collegiate spin on lifestyle are several new publications that bridge the gap from the teens to the twenties. They include *World Scholar*, for international students living in the U.S. *DMP Access* covers college life, sports, music, entertainment, modeling, and life after college. *Accent on News* is a digital newsmagazine that moves to print this year. It covers news, economics, science, the arts, health, career, entertainment, industry, and more and was started by an economics student at the University of Chicago. The *New York Times*'s New England Media Group launched an event guide for college students, *Boston Uncovered*.

Athletes and sports enthusiasts can look for *Stack* ("For the Athlete, by the Athlete") to give high school athletes health information and training ideas. *ASX* ("Action, Adventure, Lifestyle") provides coverage of an outdoor lifestyle and sports such as snowboarding, mountaineering, surfing, skiing, and paddling. Readers 18 to 26 are the target here. From *Tennis* magazine comes *Smash*, directed at 14- to 21-year-old tennis enthusiasts. The premiere issue included fashion, celebrity news, and product information, as well as sports coverage. This is not to be

Selected New Magazines

Accent on News: Digital news-magazine for college age and 20s. www.accentmag.com

AfterSchool: Published by Scholastic for after-school educators and professionals. By the editors of *Instructor*. http://teacher.scholastic.com/products/instructor/afterschool.htm

ASX: Outdoor lifestyle magazine, covering snowboarding, surfing, rock-climbing, mountain biking, mountain climbing for ages 18 to 26. www.asxmagazine.com

BabyCenter Magazine: Content by Babycenter.com about specific stages of pregnancy, exactly when moms need it. www.babycenter.com

Being Family: The new incarnation of *Babies Like Me* and *Kids Like Me,* for African Americans. www.beingfamiliymagazine.com

Boston Uncovered: College and lifestyle for students in Boston, and associated with Boston.com.

Bundle: The newest products available for newborns and moms; articles on parenting and pregnancy. From Harris Publications. http://bundle-magazine.com

Co Ed: Student writers cover college life, music, fashion, dating, and sports from four different college campuses. www.coedmagazine.com

Cookie: Fairchild Publications magazine for upscale parents who want to outfit their children in the latest fashions; also covers home, health, travel, entertainment. www.cookiemag.com

DMP Access: College lifestyle magazine; dorm life, music, entertainment, sports, modeling, health. www.dmpaccess.com

Dragonfly Spirit: An e-zine that highlights creativity for children. www.dragonfly spirit.com

FGBG, For Girls by Girls: Young adults, 13 to 20, submit their ideas, photos, and stories on fashion. www.fgbgmagazine.com

Freeskier: "Skiing's independent magazine" about freesking, published by Storm Mountain Publishing. www.freeskier.com

Justine: For teen girls, a choice between the "clean-cut" and the "cool" magazines. www.justinemagazine.com

Kids on Wheels: For young wheelchair users and their families; covers stories of people facing physical challenges. www.kidsonwheels.us

KidTime: San Diego, elementary-school-based educational and "recreational" publication. www.kidtimemagazine.com

KNOW: A new science magazine for ages 6 to 9 from the publishers of Canada's *YES Mag*. www.knowmag.ca

Knucklebones: For families that love non-electronic card, board, strategy, and dice games. www.kbones.com

Selected New Magazines

Loud: Subtitled "news of the next generation," it provides news via "a magazine that treats teens as reasonable people with something to say." www.loudmagazine.com

Mississippi Mom: A regional lifestyle bimonthly to promote family life and togetherness. www.mississippimom.com

Mom and Baby: Fitness, nutrition, and other aspects of new motherhood for first-time moms, from Weider Publications, the publisher of *Fit Pregnancy*. www.fitpregnancy.com

MotherVerse: A literary magazine for mothers with articles on parenting as well as politics and social issues.

Rap-Up: Hip-hop and rap; reviews of newest artists and their CDs. Targeted to ages 14 to 28. www.rap-up.com

Real Dad: Practical advice for fathers from fathers, from Gibbs Media Group. www.realdadmagazine.com

Shout: A Saskatchewan magazine for aboriginal youth, ages 14 to 18, on fun, health, education, positive role models.

Ski Time: Aimed at aspiring competitive and professional skiers. Covers music and culture as well as skiing. www.skitimemag.com

Smash: Youth counterculture publication on music and sports. www.smashmagazine.com

Smash: From *Tennis* magazine, for ages 14 to 21, and covering the sport, fashion, entertainment. www.smashtennismag.com

Southern Baby: Published by specialty magazine publisher Hoffman Media to serve families with children to age four, with a Southern flair. www.hoffmanmedia.com

Stack: Gives high school athletes health information and training ideas—"For the athlete, by the athlete." www.stackmag.com

TAP Magazine: For parents of autistic children, persons with autism, and professionals. www.theautismperspective.org

Tha Block DVD: Bimonthly DVD entertainment magazine that focuses on "the streets." www.thablockdvdmag.com

Vervegirl: Canadian publication on fashion, beauty, and style. www.vervegirl.com

World Scholar: For international students. Topics include scholarship, immigration, living accommodations, jobs, understanding American culture. www.theworldscholar.com

YGA, Young Gay America: For gays and lesbians in their teens and 20s. Covers news, pop culture, life and love, fun, politics, role models, advice, music, film. www.ygamag.com

confused with the *Smash Magazine* that arises from the youth counter-culture and covers rock music, biking, and skateboarding; it was launched in 2004.

Younger News

New titles for younger readers range from general to specialized interest. With a March 2006 debut, *Kids on*

Wheels is putting a different spin on things. This quarterly for young wheelchair users has stories of people facing physical challenges and enjoy-ing life. It is meant to be read in conjunction with a book and used regularly alongside the website.

New educational magazine *Kid-Time* is taking a tightly focused ap-proach to its audience, but its topics are wide-ranging. "Our mission is to provide an educational, fun maga-zine free of charge to children in San Diego," says Producer Tania O'Donnell. "The magazine will be delivered in grades two to five in three school districts in San Diego."

For those interested in writing for *KidTime*, O'Donnell reveals that "Adding a sidebar or a follow up activity is desired, but the manu-script needs to be lively and fun." Its pilot issue offers fiction; poetry;

nonfiction on nature and inven-tions; a science column; opportuni-ties for play, art, and experiments; local activities; and a puzzle. *Kid-Time* begins manuscript reviews in May. "By selecting the best of the best manuscripts instead of assign-ing topics to hired writers, the mag-azine will be able to keep the best articles," says O'Donnell.

The fields of science and nature for kids seem evergreen. A new—or transformed—magazine for ages 8 to 12 is *Cousteau Kids*. Put out by Weekly Reader and the Cousteau Society, which formerly published *Dolphin Log*, this bimonthly ex-plores the global water system. It includes facts, a *creature feature*, expedition information, interviews with Cousteau Society divers, comics, art, games, and puzzles—all about the sea and life within it.

KNOW's January 2006 debut gives Canada's *YES Mag* a younger sibling. "We launched a new sci-ence magazine for readers ages 6 to 9. *KNOW* is subtitled 'the science magazine for curious kids,'" says Jude Isabella, Managing Editor of *YES Mag,* which covers science for ages 9 to 14. *KNOW*'s Managing Ed-itor Adrienne Mason says, "Our magazine is a fun-filled and fact-filled way to explore the world of science. I hope to decompartmen-talize science in the minds of our readers. Science is all around us and it is endlessly fascinating. Just about everything is fair game to us, from hockey sticks to bubble gum, space travel to saliva." Both *YES Mag* and *KNOW* are themed. Past themes for *YES* include the Vikings, cruise ships, animal intelligence, the science of sport, and the periodic table.

"I am interested in seeing clips from published nonfiction writers or being directed to a writer's website. All nonfiction is assigned," says Mason. "We do accept unsolicited submissions of fiction and poetry loosely based on the theme. Emerging or experienced writers with a strong science background, particularly in fields other than biology, are welcome to get in touch with me." Mason stresses that she does not want to be phoned but writers can e-mail her. "In each issue we are looking for writers to write in the *KNOW* News department (science and technology news), and departments on human biology, animals, and technology."

At *YES Mag,* "We cover the sciences—all the sciences—not just cute, fluffy animals," Isabella says. "We provide the latest research written for kids whose knowledge of science is at the higher elementary to middle-school grades. Each issue also covers a scientific theme. This ranges from basic stuff, such as simple machines, to the more complex and current, such as viruses."

Isabella recommends, "The best way to break in to *YES Mag* is through the Science/Technology Watch section. We rarely go with a new writer for the theme section or a feature unless they have a proven track record and really wow us with their query."

The magazine generally prefers topics that are currently in the news, but it does not cover science fairs. "The science doesn't have to be Canadian, although it helps," says Isabella. "The sidebars for an upcoming feature on the ivory-billed woodpecker, recently rediscovered in the Arkansas bayou, concern the northern spotted owl (found in British Columbia) and the sage-grouse (found in Alberta and Saskatchewan)."

Still on the subjects of nature and Canada, Hilary Bain is Editor in Chief of *Chirp, ChickaDEE,* and *OWL* magazines at the OWL Group, owned by Canadian publisher Bayard Press. She says all remains as it was: Good, new writers and ideas are welcome, but unsolicited manuscripts are not. "We do not ac-

cept unsolicited fiction submissions for any of the magazines. Although we are open to receiving pitches for nonfiction, for the most part we generate story ideas in-house and call upon writers we know to write them. I don't expect that to change anytime soon," Bain says. "Nevertheless, we are happy to receive writing samples of authors and journalists who have written for children, and if it fits we would try to find a place for them in one of the magazines."

Although the OWL Group has been publishing for almost three decades, Bain continues, "Our magazines have adapted to the speed of images in video games and TV that kids are used to by including more visuals, more color, and more quick captions."

Everything Old Is New Again

Like the OWL magazines or *Seventeen*, *Highlights for Children* has been publishing for decades with great success. It remains well-read because it is dynamic and continues to evolve.

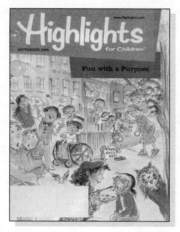

"We've been around a long time, and people—both writers and subscribers—feel that we are very familiar to them," says *Highlights* Editor Christine French Clark. "We often hear 'you haven't changed a bit.' But while it's true the magazine hasn't changed in mission, character, and tone, it's also true that the way we present our editorial package is changing."

If you haven't picked up an issue lately, it's time. "Savvy writers who want to be published in *Highlights* definitely need to study current issues," Clark says. "They should note that we cut our maximum word count from 900 to 800 words a few years ago, and we're firm

about that. They should also be aware that we're working to provide more multiple entry points into an article or story—more subheads, sidebars, pulled quotes, and expanded picture captions. We're very aware of how these *display elements* work like hooks to draw kids into a story. An article that includes these little extras stands a better chance of acceptance."

One of the qualities that has always distinguished *Highlights* from other popular and successful publications for children is its wide audience age range, from 2 to 12. That is still true, but the magazine is shifting its balance some, says Clark: "A content analysis on recent issues will also reveal that we're including more material targeted to our core readership—kids about 6 to 9. In the past, we published more articles intended for kids in the upper end of our age range, about 9 to 12. We still do that, of course, but we'd prefer more articles that are interesting to our oldest readers but that don't require so much previously acquired knowledge so that the 6- to 9-year-olds can also enjoy them. We're also publishing more one-page stories and articles."

As a staple market for fiction, writers may not like to hear that *Highlights* has added a series:

"Fiction writers will find it a little tougher, as we're regularly publishing a new story series, 'Ask Arizona.' This series, which features a continuing character named Arizona, is finding a loyal audience among our readers, but publishing it means that we publish one less fiction story each month from a freelancer." But being adaptable to what readers want has kept *Highlights* publishing for 60 years.

Bridges

At the similarly venerable Carus Publishing, and its Cricket Magazine and Cobblestone Publishing divisions, the changes take a different form. Many of their magazines find themselves building new bridges—to educational requirements, to authors, and to books.

For the history and culture publications of Cobblestone Publishing, and for educators and the students who read them, the No Child Left Behind Act continues to be a factor. Cobblestone Editorial Director Lou Waryncia says, "My feeling based upon talking to various people—teachers, librarians, and such—is that the greatest impact is on material designed for history or social studies. No Child Left Behind focuses on reading only. People have said if there's a choice between reading and history content, for example the history content of *Cobblestone*, they're apt to choose general fiction over history. The reality is a good teacher or parent could teach two things at once by offering children content reading in history or

social studies, or science. There is much discussion of this in the educational press. History especially is being de-emphasized by many schools because kids aren't tested on it." Cobblestone Publishing's titles include *Appleseeds*, on history and culture for ages 6 to 9; *Calliope*, world history for ages 9 and up; *Faces*, anthropology for 9 and up; and *Footsteps*, on African American heritage.

Paula Morrow, Executive Editor of *Ladybug* and *Babybug*, comments about No Child Left Behind, "This unfunded mandate has left too many schools scrambling for money, and when funds are tight, magazine subscriptions are one of the *frills* to be cut. Because of this, the Cobblestone Group has begun publishing more nonfiction books for the school market. Subscribers to Cricket's *bug* magazines (*Babybug, Ladybug, Spider, Cricket,* and *Cicada*) are predominantly homes rather than schools, so we've been less affected, but school subscriptions do seem to be down across the board."

Cobblestone Publishing's book series are on the Civil War and on animals. "Most material has been in the magazines in various stages," reveals Waryncia. "We rewrote and refocused and updated where needed." He sees this as a benefit to writers. "Their material is getting out into a different environment. It will have a bit more longevity. Some of these stories are seeing new light."

While these books are somewhat of a new direction, the magazine

Internet Interaction:
Computer & Print as Partners

While the ability to access information from all over the world with a few taps of a keyboard might seem to spell the end of ink-on-paper publishing, that hasn't turned out to be the case. "Magazine publishers have learned that the Internet—and all digital platforms—is an effective and efficient way to not only sell subscriptions but to communicate with readers on a daily basis," says Nina Link of Magazine Publishers of America (MPA).

"Roughly 9 percent of all new subscriptions are generated from publisher websites," says Link. "The Internet is also an excellent way for magazines to extend their brands and reach new readers. It helps magazines engage their readers in new and exciting ways. Magazines can communicate with readers on a 24/7 basis now."

Publishers also use the Internet to improve reader satisfaction. "We can add moving images and sounds in imaginative ways that enhance our core content. Magazines can personalize information so that only the most relevant information will be sent to readers," says Link.

Paula Morrow, Executive Editor at the Cricket Group, explains that at Carus Publishing (which incorporates Cricket and Cobblestone Publishing): "Marketing offers free e-newsletters to anyone who requests them—free e-mail teacher guides to the themed Cobblestone magazines, for example. There's an *e-Cricket* sent to those who request it. Our website also offers special prices on many of our products." Morrow continues, "The editorial content on our website supplements the print magazines. *Ladybug* offers an online parents' companion with parenting articles, book lists, activity suggestions, and so on, all related to themes in each issue."

Enhancing core magazine content with a website is important to most kids and teen magazines. "*Seventeen*'s website is hugely popular," says Sabrina Weill, Special Projects Director. "On every page of the magazine, we alert readers to a complementary website component. Whenever a new special project or a new and exciting feature is in the magazine there's always a Web component."

The same is true for *Pockets*. "Our website supplements the magazine and also provides information for parents and other adults who work with children, and for potential writers," says Patricia McIntyre, Assistant Editor. Editor Lynn Gilliam elaborates: "There is some duplication of content between the website and the magazine. We use the same recipes and jokes, for instance. Other features—-a question of the month, poll questions, and all of the content aimed at adults—are just for the website."

The Internet helps magazines stay current in another way. McIntyre ex-

Internet Interaction:
Computer & Print as Partners

plains: "Our print production schedule is such that we begin work on an issue almost a year before publication. It is difficult for the magazine to address disasters in the news. Later, we may mention it, perhaps on the anniversary of the event if it fits the theme in some way." A website can be more timely. "After 9/11 we had a special story on a child dealing with fears and listed resources for adults helping children cope with crisis. For other disasters, we may post special prayers on our *prayer wall* or encourage children to submit their prayers. Whether in print or on the website, we try to present a caring, loving God who is always with us."

"Although our online content is linked to the magazine, it is not the same every month," explains Hilary Bain, Editor in Chief of *Chirp, Chick-aDEE,* and *OWL.* "The coloring, joke, and art sections are original online material." Web links may function as abbreviated sidebars for print articles. "We always recommend high-quality websites to our readers, especially when we want to offer them more information on a particular topic and we don't have the space to run it," says Bain.

Links have proven successful for *Ladybug* as well. "I find the Internet most useful when there's something for which further information is interesting but not vital," says Morrow. "We recently featured a story about a child visiting a sculptor's studio. The story stands alone, but it's based on a real artist, so we added a link and posted info and photos of the real person and his work."

That ability to find out more, or to participate in a discussion, is one of the strongest Internet features for magazines. "For the older *OWL* audience, we have monthly polls where they read an article in the magazine and then go online to vote for where they stand on the issue. Online-only viewers can vote, but they won't have had the benefit of reading the article," says Bain.

"We get e-mail every day from girls telling us what they want," says *Seventeen's* Weill. "They see something on MTV and write us that same hour. Bam! It's here. They can say this is what I saw and I'm so interested in it. We react to that." Similarly, Morrow says, "*Cicada,* our young adult magazine, has 'The Slam,' where aspiring teen writers can submit their work for other teens to critique." Weekly Reader Corporation gives readers something to think about every day now that it has started a blog in conjunction with its magazines *READ* and *Writing.*

Through polls, discussions with editors, and reader forums, print magazines are finding new ways to interact with readers to ensure that their magazine's community continues growing.

titles, including *Odyssey, Cobblestone, Calliope, Appleseeds, Faces, Dig,* and *Footsteps,* will capitalize on their own strengths too. "We're continuing to produce high-quality reading, but in a contextual learning environment. If you want to give kids something of substance to read, why not check us out?" Waryncia says. "We value good writing and we like to have a good relationship with our authors that can often lead to a long-term relationship. In most cases, if someone writes for us and we feel it's a successful debut that writer will generally have a return engagement, often over and over again. We're a great place to have your writing featured."

Guidelines and theme lists are available at the company's website. "If you have a great idea and write a great query, and we like the way you present it to us, most likely you're going to get an article published," says Waryncia. "Almost every month, in every magazine we publish a new writer. We publish 59 individual magazines; most of them are published nine times during the school year."

At the Cricket Group, Morrow says they also carry on with their strengths: "First, the best in literature and art for children. Second, a sense of community. Our readers identify with us and with each other, as their letters to the magazine clearly show. We'll continue to offer the very best stories, articles, poems, and artwork for children. Good quality is good quality whether you're 2, 12, or 20."

Purely Digital

For established magazines, new, blockbuster publishers, or small presses, it's close to essential to have an online presence today. Readers may still love to curl up in a chair with a good magazine, but they also like to check out the latest from their favorite publications on the computer. The interaction of print and screen is perhaps the biggest publishing news of all.

Yet the purely digital—e-zines— are increasing in number. Heidi Fraser, Assistant Editor for the new online magazine *Dragonfly Spirit*, muses, "I think that there is a current trend toward everyone putting more content online. Most magazines, books, TV shows, and movies have official websites with excerpts or ways to download content. Even books on tape are now available for download at most mp3 sites (iTunes, Napster, Limewire, etc.), thus increasing exposure to yet another literary market through the Internet."

Fraser sees this as a good development for the relatively new online magazine community. "This trend toward literature and entertainment on the Internet can only be a benefit to small online magazines like ours. This kind of exposure is changing the way people think about where they want to find their children's magazines. Once the public develops a taste for this sort of thing, they will want more. They will go looking for magazines that entertain and educate them, and they will find us. I believe that big-name magazines increasing their online content will strengthen the market to the benefit of all."

Building a bigger reader base is what established e-zine *Wee Ones* is all about. "My goal is to find more people to visit our site each year and make *Wee Ones* a better magazine," says Jennifer Reed, Editor and Publisher. "Many sites geared for kids try to get their attention by putting games and polls on their sites. But we're all about reading and making it fun, so we don't put that kind of material on our online magazine."

Reed's magazine is one of the success stories. "Each year our hits increase. The more people find out about our magazine, the more hits we receive. It's very hard to keep an online magazine running, but 2005 was a good year for *Wee Ones*."

Fields, of *Kid Magazine Writers,* says: "An online magazine can make a nice home for fiction that has been passed over by the print magazines for being too . . . *something.* For example, it's virtually impossible to sell a short story about Santa to any print children's magazine—but you can find an online magazine that would love it."

She cautions writers about jumping in blindly when submitting to online magazines. "If anything, I think many writers aren't quite reluctant enough. You really need to read the magazine and after looking at everything in this magazine, ask yourself: Is this someplace I want my work? If the editorial oversight is good and the content is impressive, then it's a good clip. If the

magazine seems to print anything, it's not going to be a good clip."

Dragonfly Spirit spotlights creativity in pursuing its quality. "Where we differ is that our focus isn't only on reading for the sake of entertainment or education, we combine creativity with it. Our view is that reading is simply one way of unleashing your imagination," says Editor Gisele LeBlanc. "Creativity in a child's world is so important, and we want kids to realize that all they need to weave their own magic is to pick up a pencil or pen—the power is right there at their fingertips."

LeBlanc says at *Dragonfly Spirit,* "We enjoy stories with unique characters; that have a concrete beginning, middle, and end; and have a focused goal or obstacle followed by a distinct resolution. We are fans of tight writing. When it comes to poetry, we like authors who think outside the box, who write poetry that is fun, original, and catchy. Poetry that uses descriptive language, evokes strong imagery, and leaves a smile on our face will stand out from the norm. What doesn't captivate us is poetry that is wordy or contains forced or near-rhymes."

She also likes to work with authors who are flexible and willing to revise. "We don't mind putting in a little extra time on pieces that we know are special but may still need a little work," LeBlanc says. "This doesn't mean that you shouldn't make sure your submission is as perfect as it can be, only that we are very receptive to diamonds that may still need to be polished a bit."

Parenting Publications

The parenting and family magazine market continues to innovate. Niche title *Knucklebones* focuses boldly on games. "*Knucklebones*'s audience includes adults who like to play games, spend time with family and friends, and enjoy brainteasers and puzzles," says Editor Sarah Gloystein Peterson. "We are the only print games magazine out there that is editorially driven, bringing reviews, strategy, game history, game designer and company profiles, and information about new products to game players." The first of the bimonthly issues came out at the end of August.

"A good and interesting story idea or proposal is the best way to get started," Gloystein reveals. "We also look for articles that cover topics the magazine hasn't touched upon yet." Since the magazine is so new, is it more open to new writers? "Being a start-up magazine in a field we haven't covered before, we are basically starting from scratch and have to find writers, reviewers, and puzzlers. This makes it a little easier for potential writers who want to contribute to the magazine."

Families are fun, but of course also take work. Many magazine titles aim to help with the job. *Being Family*, a quarterly for African Americans, is the new incarnation of former titles *Babies Like Me* and *Kids Like Me*. Plans are in the works for *Wondertime*, a new publication from *Family Fun* and its publisher, Disney Worldwide Publishing. It will focus on the joy of raising children, not the work, from birth to age six.

In terms of specific material, LeBlanc offers this tip: "We would like to see more stories geared toward our younger and older audiences, namely the 4-to-6 and 10-to-14 age groups. It would also be great to see more fantasy, mystery, and science fiction submissions."

Reed is blunt about why writers submit to *Wee Ones*. "At first we didn't pay our contributors and the quality of material we received was pretty bad. Once we started paying, tons of writers began submitting. That was about a year after being online and not paying contributors. That's the only reason I think writers are more open to us. We receive about 200 submissions a month."

The quality of submissions to *Wee Ones* is high. "I expect a high degree of professionalism from all contributors," says Reed, "which means read our guidelines and follow them. Submit appropriate material and write me a cover letter. If an author won't take the time to write a short letter about a submission, I will reject it."

At *Dragonfly Spirit*, LeBlanc says, "We're happy to report that our submission volume is steadily increasing and the quality of the writing we see leaves nothing to be desired.

Parenting Publications

The general magazine industry boom in regional publications continues often in the form of parenting publications, many of which are regionally focused. Joining a long list of established titles, *Mississippi Mom* is a new free bimonthly lifestyle magazine that promotes family life and togetherness. The quarterly *Southern Baby*, from Hoffman Media, addresses parents and grandparents of newborns to four-year-olds.

Mothers and mothers-to-be will find a host of new titles this year. *MotherVerse* is an online literary magazine for mothers. It publishes short fiction, poetry, and articles on parenting, politics, and social issues. For women who have left a career to raise their family, *Total 180!* features articles on physical and emotional health. *Baby Center,* created for pregnant women and new moms, has an innovative slant: The content in each issue is geared to a specific stage of pregnancy, providing information for the reader at exactly the time she needs it. *Mom and Baby,* sister publication to Weider Publications's *Fit Pregnancy,* covers fitness, nutrition, and other aspects of new motherhood for first-time moms. Titles for parents looking for information on what to buy their new offspring include *Bundle* and *Cookie,* which is subtitled "the magazine for sophisticated parents."

Dads are not to be left out. *Real Dad* bills itself as a magazine that helps fathers with "what really matters in life." It includes advice for fathers from fathers in all phases of parenting.

We were pleasantly surprised to see so many seasoned authors submitting. I think people see that we are running a quality publication and want to be a part of it."

Online magazines aren't all that different from their print cousins. Indeed, LeBlanc says, "The work that goes in to prepare the publication is the same. Submissions must be reviewed and edited, and artwork must be assigned. The end product is similar except publications in print format are tangible and easily accessible, whereas e-mags can only be viewed online. But many e-mags are free, which makes them an appealing and practical literacy tool in many classrooms."

"We work with test publishers who buy our material," says Reed, explaining how *Wee Ones* generates income. "Not only does the author make more money, but so do we. Although we don't break even and our staff is all volunteer, we are always looking for new ways to generate revenue. We also sell the magazine on a CD and are promoting it to schools."

Marketing & Manuscripts

The proliferation of magazines can only be good for writers. While the days of writing an article for one magazine and selling it with no changes to another may be gone now that so many publications insist on putting their own spin on the information they publish, writers can easily rework an article to fit different markets.

Fields offers an example: "If you want to write about a refuge for retired circus elephants, that could be general interest, or it could be for a science magazine, or a career magazine, or a social consciousness magazine—with just a little futzing with the slant. I think that means writers have to be very savvy about marketing. We have to know the magazine, its specific niche, and how to address it."

These days editors are very directly telling writers what they want. "Many magazines are putting guidelines online to try to save some money on fielding writer requests," says Fields. "Magazines really would prefer writers to know what the editors want because getting so many inappropriate submissions is costly. Even when editors do the bare minimum of stuffing paper back in an envelope with a form rejection letter, that's time and effort that could have been spent making the magazine money."

Having guidelines and theme lists online "makes these items more readily accessible to writers and saves us some cost in postage and printing," says Patricia McIntyre, Assistant Editor of *Pockets*.

"It has reduced the stack of mail requests, which saves a lot of staff

time," agrees Morrow. Waryncia puts it in numbers: "We used to get thousands of letters requesting guidelines and theme lists. We still get some and we honor those, but now it's only one or two, because now people know the information is on the Web."

Besides guidelines, many magazines post sample content online from their print magazines. This type of content on the Internet makes researching a market easier for writers. "I would love to see all children's magazines, even the smallest, with an online presence, because the better I am informed about the magazine as a writer, the more successful I will be with my marketing," says Fields.

Morrow offers a cautionary note. "Sample pages are not enough for the aspiring writer to peruse as the *only* market research before sending submissions. It's still important to look at a complete issue—or preferably several issues—to know what works for us."

Some magazines pursue their editorial needs even more directly on the Internet. At *Seventeen*, Weill says, they have used listservs to find writers. "The Casey Journalism Foundation is a fantastic organization. They do a fantastic newsletter. They're really helpful if you're reporting on kids and family issues." Recently, the magazine was looking for someone to profile a girl affected by Hurricane Katrina and they put out a call over the Internet. Weill says of the result, "We got a great response from writers local to the area and we got good leads for writers for the future."

Current news used to be difficult for monthly magazines to cover because of the long production schedules. Weill says, "Previously, monthly magazines might think they couldn't cover news because it's too timely. Now we're more competitive. We now have the ability to give reporters assignments quickly and ask for a short turnaround. Writers' assignments can be e-mailed back. It's much faster."

Highlights also started circulating a *wants list* over the various writing listservs. Clark says, "The special calls that we send to writers and listservs do seem to reach receptive people. These calls have increased the number of submissions we receive and, happily, are giving us more manuscripts on subjects and themes we need. The technique has also introduced us to writers we hadn't heard from before." So it seems to work, and they'll likely do it again. "When we started this, we wondered if these manuscripts would be of higher quality than those we receive in other ways, but, generally speaking, that hasn't been the case. But the simple fact that the technique is giving us more to choose from makes it worth doing, and we expect to continue these mailings from time to time."

At *YES Mag*, Isabella says, "Electronic submissions have become the norm and we encourage it. It's cheaper for the writer, easier, and more immediate. It saves everyone a lot of time." At the Cricket Group,

Morrow says, "Some editors like to use e-mail when working with authors. But this is a personal preference." For now, writers should be careful of the ease of Internet communication. Don't e-mail an editor unless you're invited to do so.

Fields suggests writers become more electronically proficient in general. "I think it is becoming increasingly important for magazine writers to be Web-savvy and to understand how to use e-mail safely and efficiently. I think good market research will become even more important to sales in the future and that is going to depend upon knowing your way around online."

Forecasts

Is it likely that one day magazines will abandon paper and only publish digitally? "We definitely don't have any plans to do so; there are many advantages to print. But I wouldn't rule it out as a possibility," says Lynn Gilliam, Editor of *Pockets*. "It definitely depends on how the technology develops and what would best meet the needs of our readers or potential readers."

No matter how fast technology has changed, those needs are rather difficult for digital technology to meet in its current form. "What comes through your browser doesn't feel like tangible goods, but a paper magazine does," says Fields. "You can hold it, fold it, read it in the bathroom, stuff it in your purse. Buying it feels more natural."

Those thoughts are echoed by many magazine editors. "We still

Publisher & Organization Websites

▓ ***Accent on News:*** www.accentmag.com

▓ ***AfterSchool:*** http://teacher.scholastic.com/ products/instructor/afterschool. htm

▓ ***ASX:*** www.asxmagazine.com

▓ **Baby Center:** www.babycenter.com

▓ ***Bayard Press:*** *Chirp, ChickaDEE, OWL,* www.owlkids.com

▓ ***Being Family:*** www.beingfamilymagazine.com

▓ ***Boston Uncovered:*** www.Boston.com

▓ ***Bundle:*** http://bundle-magazine.com

▓ **Carus Publishing:** *Cricket, Ladybug, Babybug, Cicada,* www.cricketmag.com

▓ **Casey Journalism Foundation:** www.casey.umd.edu

▓ **Cobblestone Publishing:** www.cobblestonepub.com

▓ ***Co Ed:*** www.coedmagazine.com

▓ ***Cookie:*** www.cookiemag.com

▓ ***Cousteau Kids*** www.cousteaukids.org

▓ ***Disney Publishing Worldwide:*** http://disney.go.com/disneybooks/

▓ **DMP Access:** www.dmpaccess.com

▓ ***Dragonfly Spirit:*** www.dragonflyspirit.com

▓ ***Family Fun:*** http://familyfun.go.com

▓ ***FGBG:*** www.fgbgmagazine.com

▓ ***Freeskier:*** www.freeskier.com

▓ ***Highlights for Children:*** www.highlights.com

▓ ***Justine:*** www.justinemagazine.com

▓ ***Kid Magazine Writers:*** www.kidmagwriters.com

▓ ***KidTime:*** www.kidtimemagazine.com

▓ ***Kids on Wheels:*** www.kidsonwheels.us

▓ ***KNOW:*** www.knowmag.ca

▓ ***Knucklebones:*** www.kbones.com

▓ ***Loud:*** www.loudmagazine.com

▓ **Magazine Publishers of America:** www.magazine.org

▓ ***Mississippi Mom:*** www.mississippimom.com

Publisher & Organization Websites

Mom and Baby: www.fitpregnancy.com

Mother Verse: www.motherverse.com

Pockets: www.pockets.org

Read On Campaign: www.magazine.org/readon

Real Dad: www.realdadmagazine.com

Scholastic www.scholastic.com

Seventeen: www.seventeen.com

Ski Time: www.skitimemag.com

Smash: www.smashmagazine.com

Smash: www.smashtennismag.com

Southern Baby www.hoffmanmedia.com

Stack www.stackmag.com

TAP Magazine: www.theautismperspective.org

Tha Block DVD Magazine: www.thablockdvdmag.com

Total 180!: www.total180mag.com

Vervegirl: www.vervegirl.com

Wee Ones: www.weeonesmag.com

Wondertime: www.wondertime.com

World Scholar: www.theworldscholar.com

YES Mag: www.yesmag.ca

YGA: www.ygamag.com

Y:L: www.yl-mag.com

believe strongly in the value of books and magazines a reader can touch," says Morrow. "There's no substitute for actually holding the issues in your hands, reading through them at your leisure, and saving favorites to return to again and again. We have *Cricket* readers who tell us they still read their parents' early issues from the 1970s and 80s, and *Babybug* readaloud parents who tell us they are saving all their issues for their grandchildren. You can't do that with a digital download."

Bain of Bayard Press agrees. "I never foresee a day when computers will replace the printed word. There are still too many kids and adults who appreciate the experience of holding something in their hand while reading it, something they can curl up with on the couch, something they can put down and pick up at any time."

Perhaps there is middle ground. "As far as digital, Zinio.com is a way to get magazines on CD," suggests Weill. (Zinio.com offers digital services to publishers.) "In terms of storing huge amounts of info that's past, digital can be great. In terms of current info, you want your magazine. Girls want their magazine. They want to feel it in their hands and turn down the pages and interact with it."

Exactly what should be available online and what will remain print only, what is free and what costs, is still in transition. But while there are still a few bumps to be worked out on this technological road, it's clear that magazines are determined to go onward, doing what they do best whatever the vehicle.

"Print is our primary platform and will remain so for the foreseeable future," says Link. "Magazines—ink on paper—have existed for 264 years. We have an illustrious past and our future is bright because of the strength of our content."

From Editors' Lips to Your Ears: A Revealing List of Picture Book Favorites

By Judy Bradbury

"I've felt sort of down in the dumps about picture books lately . . . . But this bright, beautiful Monday your beautiful book . . . reminds me that I love creative people and love to publish books for creative children."

Editor Ursula Nordstrom, in a letter to Maurice Sendak about *Where the Wild Things Are,* from *Dear Genius: The Letters of Ursula Nordstrom*

Children's book editors are asked at every turn the kind of picture book manuscripts they are looking for. A typical response is silence, a deep sigh, a teeth-locked-in-jaw semi-smile, or an exasperated wave of the hand. "I'll know it when I see it," is a standard, frustrated and frustrating, response.

The same editors will readily list three favorite picture books. Witness the enthusiasm, the ear-to-ear grin, and the rubbing of palms together. Note the abundant eagerness to respond. "What fun it is to talk about my favorites!" exclaims Lauri Hornik, Vice President and Publisher at Dial Books for Young Readers, when asked. "Thank you for thinking of me," responds Associate Publisher and Editorial Director of Philomel Books, Michael Green.

This list of favorite picture books compiled from a dozen seasoned, stellar editors actively acquiring children's books can guide you as you decide where to send your story. Is your teddy bear tale more likely to suit this editor or that one? Who will warm to the wacky custodian in your story about a school for parents who have flunked Sportsmanlike Behavior for Soccer Matches 101? Tuck this list in your pocket when you head to the library or bookstore for a session of "reading research" of the amazing, vibrant field of children's literature.

The Titles, the Reasons, the Excuses

"Here are four favorite picture

books. I tried, but three was impossible," claims Green at Philomel. "I chose to focus on contemporary books only, because I don't think I could narrow my selections down to three (okay, four) if I included favorites from my childhood."

Difficulty narrowing choices was echoed by many of the editors cited here. Some chose only classics. Others aimed at selecting one title from the classics, one from those books they had personally edited, and one from those they wish they had edited. Others preferred not to select titles from their personal list so as not to offend any of their other authors. But all the editors seriously considered their choices and explained why they chose those books, allowing a peek at their personal tastes and insight into their preferences in style, delivery, tone, and theme.

Green lists *Monster Mama,* written by Liz Rosenberg and illustrated by Stephen Gammell, as "the perfect metaphor for parenthood. This book, edited years ago by Paula Wiseman, combines concise storytelling, fun language, a gentle undercurrent of humor, and brilliant artwork. The result is a poignant, visually stunning book that is a joy to read aloud."

Falling for Rapunzel, written by Leah Wilcox and illustrated by Lydia Monks stands out for Green. "Every page has a legitimate laugh on it for young readers, making it a natural for reading aloud. The art is bright, childlike, and pops off the page. It's a wonderful book I wish I had edited."

Stick Kid, by Peter Holwitz, "tells the simple story of a stick figure who begins as an infant and grows to adulthood, and features art equally simple—black-and-white stick illustrations that children love to draw on their own," says Green. "Like the classic *The Giving Tree,* it is a story about sacrifice and love, and it works on multiple levels. I cried the first time I read the dummy book, as did my wife. My child, on the other hand, was nothing but smiles." Finally, Green says, *Bark, George,* by Jules Feiffer, is, "in three words: clever, clever, and clever. And yet so simple. It's pure fun and a favorite of children."

Like Green, Emily Brenner, Vice President and Publishing Director of HarperFestival at HarperCollins couldn't limit herself to just three favorite picture books. Her top four choices were *Eloise,* written by Kay Thompson and illustrated by Hilary Knight; *Goodnight Moon,* written by Margaret Wise Brown and illustrated by Clement Hurd; *Where the Wild Things Are,* by Maurice Sendak; and *The Sneetches and Other Stories,* by Dr. Seuss.

Of *Eloise* Brenner says, "I love this book for three very important reasons. The first is that I read it when I was a child, and absolutely *knew* that I was Eloise. Never mind that I was living in Long Island and not the Plaza Hotel, and never mind that I didn't have a private tutor, or a pug dog, or a nanny. That character was alive and living right in my little six-year-old brain. The second reason is that when I was working at Doubleday Book Shop on 57th Street and Fifth Avenue in New York City, I sold *Eloise* more than any other children's book because it's a great book—and we were a block away from the Plaza Hotel. The third reason is that my daughter loved the book when she was little, which gave me the opportunity to read it another hundred times."

Goodnight Moon made the list, she says, and her husband's as well, "because it became part of my daughter's nightly bedtime ritual. We called it 'old reliable,' and we never tired of its simple poetic tone." Brenner voices a popular sentiment when describing *Where the Wild Things Are:* "This is one of the best children's books ever, and the book I always recommend to aspiring children's book writers."

In referring to her final pick, *The Sneetches and Other Stories,* by Dr. Seuss, Brenner says, "In this collection of stories, the Sneetches were my favorite because the subject of conformity was fascinating to me as a child. When I shared the book with my daughter, she found the Zaxes were her favorite because of the theme of stubbornness. I guess there are all kinds of personality traits that you are just beginning to fathom as a child, and there's probably no better guide to character traits than Dr. Seuss."

Sweet Justice & Subversiveness
Also unable to honor the request to choose just three favorites, Deborah Wayshak, Editor at Candlewick Books, chose six titles, two series,

and one author. "This sort of narrowing down is a challenge for me," she jokes. "As a kid I loved *The Five Chinese Brothers*, written by Claire Huchet Bishop and illustrated by Kurt Wiese, and when I was older, I discovered Margaret Mahy and Mousien Tseng's *The Seven Chinese Brothers* and liked that just as much. It is so clever and suspenseful and satisfying. Those wry asides about the emperor still delight me. John Burningham's *Cannonball Simp* and Dr. Seuss's *Horton Hatches the Egg* are dear to my heart. Both are love stories that feature underdogs. There's sweet justice in these books; they make the world seem right."

Wayshak continues: "A very young picture book I think of as nearly perfect is *We're Going on a Bear Hunt,* written by Michael Rosen and illustrated by Helen Oxenbury. It is so dramatic and comforting. A great favorite I discovered as an adult (though its subversiveness would have thrilled me as a kid, too) is *The Shrinking of Treehorn,* written by Florence Parry Heide and illustrated by Edward Gorey." Wayshak also lists "anything by James Marshal—what a cutup!—and the early Rotten Ralph books, written by Jack Gantos and illustrated by Nicole Rubel. I was mesmerized by Dare Wright's *The Lonely Doll* books too."

Anne Gunton, Associate Editor of Viking Children's Books, says it is "incredibly difficult" to pick favorite picture books, particularly since her favorites change with each new publishing season. Gunton finds that "even choosing classics proves problematic." Nevertheless, this daughter of a children's librarian lists her childhood favorites as "those that were filled with details and had satisfying endings. The most tattered and well-loved of this set was *The Island of the Skog,* by Steven Kellogg. The miniature ship, the mice warming their hands by waffle iron, the Skog himself—I never tired of re-reading this gem."

As an adult, says Gunton, her favorite picture books are "those that have a sense of humor." At Viking, one of Gunton's current favorites is one that she edited, *Henry's 100 Days of Kindergarten,* by author and illustrator Nancy Carlson. "Nancy does a lot of school visits and really gets what makes kids laugh. Throughout the story she hides a little runaway spider who got loose during show-and-tell. You know young readers are going to love looking for and finding that spider on every spread," says Gunton.

Another of her favorites is one that Viking Publisher Regina Hayes edited, the best-seller *Science Verse,* written by Jon Scieszka and illustrated by Lane Smith. "Jon is incredibly clever and based most of the laugh-out-loud funny poems on well-known poems and songs.

Lane's illustrations are the perfect complement to the text: They are simultaneously gorgeous and humorous. Another unique thing about *Science Verse* is that Jon and Lane prank-called Regina Hayes and then put that hilarious conversation on the CD that comes with the book." Recalls Gunton, "We all must have listened to the 'A Call to the Editor' (track 23!) a dozen times, and never failed to giggle." What's great about all three of these books, believes Gunton, is that "you can tell the authors and illustrators are having fun. It comes through in the warmth—and winning details—of the text and illustrations."

At Orchard Books, Editor Lisa Ann Sandell "agonized" over choosing just three favorite picture books. She selected two classics and one recent publication. Topping her list is *Make Way for Ducklings,* by Robert McCloskey. "This book has been my all-time favorite for as many years as I can remember. It endures because Mr. McCloskey's illustrations are sweet, filled with tenderness and care—yet, never sentimental—while the seriousness with which he treats his ducks belies a warm and incredibly rich humor. The spunkiness of the ducklings, coupled with Mrs. Mallard's pride in her family and protectiveness of her beloved Jack, Kack, Lack, Mack, Nack, Ouack, Pack, and Quack, are rendered so perfectly, that every time I go back to this book, I find myself giggling over the ducklings' escapades, worrying over the Mallards' safe passage, cheering for Police Officer Michael, and praying for the family's happy reunion."

Her second choice is *Clotilda,* by Jack Kent. "Though it's now out of print, this story of a fairy who has no friends was my favorite readaloud as a small child. Jack Kent's vivid and fanciful illustrations brought the cynical brother and sensitive sister who stumble upon Clotilda, the lonely wishgranting fairy, to life."

Sandell calls *Giraffes Can't Dance,* written by Giles Andreae and illustrated by Guy Parker-Rees, "jaunty and whimsical." The book makes her short list because "Guy Parker-Rees's art is filled with an energy that rollicks along with the rhyming text and evokes Gerald the Giraffe's love of music and movement. I adore this story. It's inspiring, but it's also wacky and just plain fun."

Top Two

Some editors at the top of their field struggled to whittle their choices to two titles each.

The picks of Emma Dryden, Vice President and Associate Publisher of Atheneum Books for Young Readers and Margaret K. McElderry Books at Simon & Schuster, were both McElderry publications. *Bear Snores On* was written by Karma Wilson

and illustrated by Jane Chapman. *We're Going on a Bear Hunt* was written by Michael Rosen and illustrated by Helen Oxenbury. Of *Bear Snores On* Dryden says, "I edited this best-selling picture book and love it for many reasons. The text is a perfectly balanced rhythmic readaloud that I don't tire of reading over and over. The story has a funny twist ending that makes me laugh. The adorable illustrations that complement the story are rich and playful while being completely accessible and warm. To read this book and look at the pictures is a completely satisfying experience."

Of *We're Going on a Bear Hunt,* Dryden says, "I love the stylistic blending of black-and-white artwork alternating with full-color artwork to propel this energetic story along. The story is a great readaloud. It's a game, and it's about a big, bubbly family with a dog—just the kind of family I, as an only child without a pet, always wanted. One can experience the book on many levels and it is a joy to read over and over again."

Larry Rosler, Editor at Boyds Mills Press, chose Maurice Sendak's *Outside Over There,* which he describes as "the creation of an original mind," and as an "odd, eerie, and disturbing picture book that draws you into its own enchanted world." His second choice is *Mr. Gumpy's Outing,* by John Burningham, which he terms "a perfect picture book from start to finish, with its simple, repetitive language and elegant illustrations. Spending a day on the river with the unflappable Mr. Gumpy and his friends never fails to please."

Abigail Samoun, Editor at Tricycle Press, says, "The first one I have to list is *Little Bear's Visit,* by Else Holmelund Minarik with illustrations by Maurice Sendak. I adored this book when I was a kid. The illustrations are done in vignettes and spots and printed in just two colors. What's amazing about it is the richness of emotion and atmosphere that's conveyed within that simple layout. Sendak's characters are wonderful, of course—the tenderness of the grandmother bear, the twinkle in the eye and humor of the grandfather bear (who reminded me so much of my French grandfather), and Little Bear himself. But what sets this book apart for me is the way Sendak used props in the illustration to convey the atmosphere of the grandparents' house, at once exotic and familiar. It was the little details, unusual and unexpected, that captured my fancy as a child. The trend in picture books seems to be toward more aggressive visuals— full-bleed spreads, fancy production work, bright colors. As an editor, I have to catch myself sometimes and remember *Little Bear's Visit*

and how its power lay in simple presentation and small, unexpected details."

Turning toward more recent books, Samoun speaks of *Mountain Dance,* by Thomas Locker. "The book is unusual in that it has no characters and no plot, yet it's entirely captivating. It's a poem about different types of mountains, from shield volcanoes to fault blocks to folded mountains, and the way they're created, the way they wear, the way they fade away. The paintings were done in oil on canvas and not only are they masterfully rendered, but the mountains actually have a real sense of presence. They grow and evolve just like animals. The text and illustrations elicit a sense of wonder at the grace and beauty of our planet. It's one of the most successful books I've seen that combines poetry and natural science."

Unrestrained Imaginativeness

Timothy Travaglini, Senior Editor at G.P. Putnam's Sons, chose one classic, one book he wishes he had edited, and one he did edit, in compiling his list of three picks. "One of my favorites from childhood is *In the Night Kitchen,* by Maurice Sendak," he says, "which I still have, with my name written on the front endpaper in my mother's handwriting. For all I know it's a first printing! I'm certain that the reason I read it over and over and over again was its unrestrained imaginativeness. Mickey's experience is as completely unbound by the mundane laws of the natural world as he is unbound by his clothes. I can't tell if I was so imaginative as a child that the book struck a special chord with me, or if the book itself helped transform me into the child I became."

One book Travaglini wishes he had edited is *Good Night, Gorilla,* by Peggy Rathmann. "While I have dozens of favorite picture books, *Good Night, Gorilla* never fails to stand out as the ideal example, the archetype perhaps, of how to tell a story through pictures, with just a modicum of text that provides a perfect accent to the enterprise."

Travaglini admits, "Choosing among the books I have edited is a bit like telling someone who your favorite child is. You can imagine how all your other children will feel when you announce it. However, rather than ducking the question, I will offer up *One Witch,* by Laura Leuck and illustrated by S.D. Schindler, as a shining example of one of my favorites. Laura's counting rhyme is the closest to pitch perfect that I have had the pleasure to edit so far in my career. It rolls off the tongue and commits itself to one's memory almost at the first reading. S.D. Schindler's illustrations, using his most sophisticated and labor-intensive style, are like Edward Gorey's best work, but in Technicolor. And the jovial humor infused throughout the art makes it more appealing and better suited to young audiences than the classics the illustrious Mr. Gorey is famous for."

Julie Strauss-Gabel, Senior Editor at Dutton Children's Books, also chose to list a classic, a current title, and a book she edited. "*Corduroy,* by Don Freeman, a childhood favorite, has always held a special place in my heart, perhaps because I remain convinced to this day that stuffed animals have feelings. It's a perfect package: beautiful illustrations, the secret mysteries of a department store at night, and an endearing and enduring story of love and dedication with the message that everyone is most special to someone."

Strauss-Gabel chooses *The Happy Hocky Family* by Lane Smith for its "irreverent humor, reinvention of children's lit conventions, and unique art. *The Happy Hocky Family* came into my life just as I was first starting to think about children's books in a new way and imagining myself with a future in the business. It opened my eyes to a whole new world of possibilities and extended the way I thought about picture books, beyond the titles with which I'd always been familiar. And it always makes me laugh out loud."

The Milkman, written by Carol Foskett Cordsen and illustrated by Douglas B. Jones, "was my first Dutton picture book acquisition to hit the shelves," Strauss-Gabel says. "I love the melodic, lilting readaloud text that's both lovely to read and invigorated by a playful subplot about a runaway puppy—perfect to actively involve even the youngest children. Douglas B. Jones's delightfully retro illustrations are awash in the glow of early morning and have the warm and whimsical feel of classic picture book titles."

Hornik at Dial puts Kevin Henkes's *Owen* on the list of favorites. "To me, this is an example of a perfect book. The text is carefully constructed but comes off effortlessly, with a cozy, breezy style; the artwork expresses so much character and mood in deceptively simple images; but most of all, the book conveys a typical kid experience—nothing flashy, no overblown fantasy element or intricate plot, but instead an enriching, entertaining story about a universal stepping stone of childhood."

Contrast that with *The Sea Chest,* written by Toni Buzzeo and illustrated by Mary GrandPré, says Hornik. "This is one of my favorite books I have edited. I love the lyrical storytelling that is more sophisticated than the typical picture book but still manages to be accessible. I love the story itself, which is so full of heart and provides elements of adventure, wish fulfillment, and history from within an intimate family tale. And I love the artwork, which sweeps and glows and matches the text style so gloriously."

Last, but not least, Hornik points to *The Monster at the End of This Book,* written by Jon Stone and illustrated by Michael Smollin. "This *Sesame Street* book brings me right back to my own childhood when Dad would read it to me over and over again, and now that I have a daughter, I'm tickled by how satisfying it is for the parent as well as for the child. It's a book that instantly draws in the reader through its in-teractive approach, and it's a sure giggle-provoker. I suspect that Mo Willems was inspired by this book when he created *Don't Let the Pigeon Drive the Bus!*"

Learn What You Yearn to Know

Writers wise enough to study the titles admiringly discussed here stand to learn what they yearn to know. The editors reveal in their responses the types of manuscripts that would send them dancing down the hallway to colleagues' offices, or set them spinning in their chairs. That knowledge can give more insight than an answer to "What's hot, what's not?"

So grab the list and let's meet at the library. We've got some reading to do. When we get there, we'll read as writers, with an eye toward looking at what makes these books so special that acquiring editors in today's competitive market chose them as one of their top three (okay, four) all-time favorites.

Key Picture Book Elements

These qualities were mentioned by the editors describing their favorite picture books.

- concise storytelling
- fun language
- gentle humor
- brilliant artwork
- a joy to read aloud
- bright, childlike art
- simple
- story works on many levels
- clever
- fun
- poetic tone
- suspenseful
- satisfying
- wry humor
- makes the world feel right
- comforting
- dramatic
- filled with winning details
- satisfying endings
- warmth
- wit
- sweet and tender
- jaunty
- whimsical
- rollicking
- wacky
- rhythmic
- twist ending

- playful
- accessible
- joy to read again and again
- energetic
- rich emotion
- simple layout
- unexpected details
- simple presentation
- a sense of wonder
- unrestrained imagination
- pitch-perfect rhyme
- endearing
- enduring
- irreverent humor
- unique art
- melodic text
- involves the young listener
- cozy
- breezy style
- deceptively simple
- enriching
- entertaining
- universal childhood experiences
- lyrical
- full of heart
- interactive
- giggle-provoker

Emerging Needs: Writing for Early Readers

By Pamela Holtz Beres

From the time they enter the world, children are fascinated with language. Infants gaze at their parents' faces, watching as their lips form words, often responding with a smile, a wiggle, or a giggle. Toddlers snuggle on laps, ready to hear their favorite story for the third, fourth, or fortieth time. It's no wonder that by the time children approach the age of five, they search for stories they can read on their own, either in book form or in magazines. As children strive for independence, the desire to read by themselves enters a natural phase.

When my children were young, a battered rummage-sale copy of Syd Hoff's *Danny and the Dinosaur* landed on our bookshelf. I winced when my daughter selected this book night after night, despite my offers to read just about any other book in the house. One night, we were about halfway through the story when she bounced up and down, giggling, as I turned the page. "I want to read that," she cried. She indeed read the page and I realized what was going on. After hearing the same few words read night after night, listening to the rhythm and the beat, comparing what she heard to how the words looked on the page and then connecting the words to the pictures, she was learning to read. I no longer tried to hide this I Can Read classic from HarperCollins, but left it out where my daughter could sample the pleasures of independent reading whenever she chose.

Despite the fact that children outgrow these easy-to-read books quickly, setting them aside in favor of more challenging stories once the book is mastered, these books play a huge role in a child's reading development.

Kathryn Heling and Deborah Hembrook are educators who write beginning readers collaboratively. They say that with an easy-to-read book, even the youngest child can be active in learning the concepts of print—what a book is, how to hold it, how to look at the pictures and turn the pages in the right direction. "Early readers are patterned and predictable, which helps the child to

61

be successful and independent as a reader."

"Early reader books aim to make reading and learning curriculum topics fun," says Stephanie Hedlund, Managing Editor at educational publisher ABDO Publishing Company.

Anne Hoppe, Executive Editor at HarperCollins, thinks that teachers and parents guide the child through the reading process. The company's I Can Read Books aren't designed to teach reading, she says, but instead "are meant to be enjoyed and to validate the child's reading skills."

by Dori Chaconas
illustrated by Lisa McCue

Hoppe offers advice that reminds writers that not all easy readers can or should be lumped together. She says, "Writers should be aware of the differences between houses, and especially the rather large differences between trade publishers such as Viking and HarperCollins and the world of educational publishers," and their goals in producing early readers.

Guidelines for Success

Keeping reading goals in mind, editors and writers adhere to numerous guidelines when writing for this audience. Book publishers place their books in levels, with each level presenting new challenges for the reader. Pay attention to the distinctions between houses, however. Random House, for instance, has five levels in its Step Into Reading program. Level 1, called Ready to Read, draws in children who know their alphabet and are eager to begin reading. A Level 2 book introduces short sentences and simple stories, while Level 3 books have engaging characters with easy plots. Level 4 introduces paragraphs, and Level 5, chapters.

According to Hedlund, ABDO's Sandcastle early reader books are leveled in a four-tier system. "Each level is based on topics, word choice, and punctuation," says Hedlund. "These levels provide stepping stones for teaching language arts to early readers."

Strictness of these guidelines, however, varies from publisher to publisher and depends on whether the company is a mass-market, trade, or educational publisher like ABDO, with specific teaching goals in mind.

Viking, a trade publisher, says Senior Editor Catherine Frank, works with experts who evaluate manuscripts to determine which words or sentences are too advanced for their three-level system of Easy-to-Read Books. "We don't have our authors work from a vocabulary list, but they are all familiar with the basic requirements for an easy-to-read."

Dori Chaconas, whose *Cork & Fuzz* was published by Viking as a

Level 3, confirms that she was not restricted by many guidelines. "I did read a lot of Easy-to-Read books and picked up the rhythm—short sentences, no contractions, words that are easy to read or easy for a young reader to decode, and content that is age-appropriate."

Heling and Hembrook say that the guidelines for early readers like *Mouse Makes Words, Mouse's Hide-and-Seek Words,* and *Mouse Makes Magic,* published by Random House, were very specific. "They stipulate such things as the number of characters per line, the number of lines per page, the acceptable range for total number of words, the number of pages the book must have, etc. They are also very restrictive as to the use of contractions and multi-syllabic words, with very limited use of these allowed in the lower level books."

HarperCollins stipulates the maximum number of characters per line, including spaces and punctuation. "While we do offer parameters on length, the guidelines themselves are as broad as possible to give writers the room they need to be creative," says Hoppe. Page counts range from 24 for My First I Can Read Books to a maximum of 64 pages for Level 4, Advanced Reading.

At ABDO, writers do use a word list to determine appropriate readability. For their Buddy Books imprint, which features nonfiction biographies and other research materials for early readers, glossary words are bolded in the text to point out words that are above the reading level.

In magazine writing, the guidelines are looser. The child uses the magazine as entertainment and as a supplement to their learning experience. Marileta Robinson, Senior Editor at *Highlights for Children*, explained her preferences in a chatroom interview at the Institute of Children's Literature. "We don't use a graded word list, but generally you would want to use words that a young child would be familiar with. The challenge is to write simply but vividly."

Writer Kathryn Lay, whose early reader magazine stories have appeared in *Spider* and *Wee Ones,* uses short sentences and words that younger kids can read. When revising her story "Cave-a-Phobia" for *Spider*, she split complicated sentences into two. In cutting for length, she deleted much of the inner dialogue and clever phrases. "I never want to write *down* to kids," says Lay, "but I did want to keep the reading level age appropriate so even the kids who had difficulty reading at their own level would be able to enjoy the stories."

Jennifer Reed, writer and Editor of *Wee Ones*, keeps word count, target age, sentence structure, and subject matter in mind. "The simpler the sentence, the shorter the story, the more relevant the theme or subject matter, the better," she says.

Beyond the Guidelines

While publishers' guidelines for early readers are important, writers should remember not to let vocabulary lists and other restrictions overpower their ability to relax and create a story the reader will enjoy. One handy tool is fun word play.

When she wrote "The Birthday Tooth" for *Wee Ones,* about a young girl who desperately wants to lose her first tooth, Lay wanted above all for the story to be fun. "Throughout the story, I had the girl afraid to pull it out, but wiggling it, so I used 'WIGGLE! WIGGLE! WIGGLE!' throughout."

Heling and Hembrook's *Mouse Makes Magic,* a Level 1 Step into Reading, begins like this:

Mouse is magic.
Mouse is quick.
Changing letters is his trick.

The illustrations on this two-page spread show Mouse waving his wand. The word *pin* becomes *pen, ten* becomes *tin,* and *bug* becomes *bag.*

Humor is useful, too. Lisa Stenger, Director of Sales and Marketing at Kaeden Books, says most of their books have humor with some kind of surprise twist at the end. Hoppe cites *Minnie and Moo,* a pair of funny, adventurous cows, as popular characters, and Frank mentions *Pirate Pete and Pirate Joe* and its two silly characters.

Chaconas says her characters Cork and Fuzz were inspired in part by Abbott and Costello and Lucy and Desi, two of her favorite comedy teams: "Abbott and Costello," she explains, "for their ability to turn a common situation into something unexpected and hilarious, and Lucy and Desi for their balance of common sense versus wackiness."

Although the importance of plot increases as the reading level goes up, most early reader stories are character-driven. "The key," says Frank, "is finding a character kids want to keep reading about."

Jean Little has written a series of books about a girl named Emma, who is shy, says Hoppe. In *Emma's Magic Winter,* the character makes a new friend and in the process gains confidence and learns to trust herself.

In a series of books by Alyssa Satin Capucilli, Biscuit is a little yellow puppy who is sweet, always means well, but gets into binds. Another HarperCollins series character, Mittens, is a kitten who is curious about the world and has adventures with his owner, Nick.

Chaconas's Cork and Fuzz characters are richly developed. "Cork, who is a muskrat, is very sensible, an average, play-by-the-rules kind of guy. Fuzz is a possum. He's unpredictable, daffy, and makes up the rules as he goes," she says. In *Cork & Fuzz: Short and Tall,* the friends' differences are further defined. "Cork eats a healthful diet of roots and seeds while Fuzz eats beetles and worms . . . and pancakes and gum wrappers and hamburger buns and anything else he can find that vaguely resembles food."

In magazine stories for early readers, character remains key. "I like character-driven stories," says

Two Authors, One Goal

Early in 1997, co-workers Kathryn Heling, a school psychologist, and Deborah Hembrook, a kindergarten teacher, casually discussed New Year's resolutions and discovered that each of them shared a goal: to write for children. Nine years and four published books later, they each can claim it's a goal they've reached together.

Although Heling had made an attempt at publishing in the 1970s, she had never gotten farther than the personal-rejection (rather than form-rejection) phase, so each of them were clueless when they began combining their talents and efforts toward writing books for children. "We met regularly, gathered writers' resources, attended conferences, and submitted manuscripts that came right back with form rejections," says Heling. "We began to appreciate the magnitude of what we needed to learn."

Their first success came with the publication of a story called "Listen to the Night Lullaby" in the 1998 Half Price Books Say Good Night to Illiteracy contest. Then, in April 2000, they attended a conference and met an editor from Random House who invited attendees to submit manuscripts. Heling and Hembrook took advantage of that opportunity and in August 2000, they were offered a contract for their book, *Mouse Makes Words,* an early phonics reader.

Heling and Hembrook are diligent in their efforts and meet at least once a week for work sessions that last several hours. Hembrook is the idea generator, often inspired by her young students, while Heling has the stronger knack for rhyming and general writing mechanics. Otherwise, the writing is a real collaborative effort. They often schedule an extra work session on Saturdays and exchange voice mails and e-mails almost daily. "Working together keeps us disciplined and provides us with a built-in support system for each other when we might otherwise become discouraged," says Heling. "Writing is usually such a solitary endeavor—writing with a partner has proven to be great fun!"

With the success of their first three books, including a 2004 Oppenheim Toy Portfolio Gold Award for *Mouse's Hide-and-Seek Words,* and several more books contracted and sold, young readers will benefit by Heling and Hembrook's New Year's resolution for years to come.

Satisfying Young Bilingual Readers

Dawn Jeffers, Publisher of Raven Tree Press, knows that not all young readers are the same. As the number of Spanish-speaking and bilingual households increases, so does the need for the young children in these families to have books they can learn from, relate to, and enjoy. Established in 2000, Raven Tree published its first four bilingual titles in fall 2001. Currently, the company has 20 titles in print, all focused on readers in kindergarten through third grade.

Jeffers says that earlier Raven Tree Press titles were full-text English and Spanish. Their newest titles, however, reflect their attempts to reach different children with different learning styles and reading needs. For example, *Tito the Firefighter/Tito, el Bombero* features embedded text. The majority of the text is in English, with a few key Spanish words embedded. The child learns the Spanish words through repetition and context. There is also a bilingual vocabulary page at the back of the book. *Alien Invaders/Invasores Extraterrestres* features a full-text translation. On each page, the words appear in English followed by the Spanish translation. To help signal the reader that something different is coming up, the Spanish text is printed in a different color and an icon separates the two texts.   Bilingual readers can compare and translate.

Finally, *Ocean Whisper/Susurro del océano* is a wordless picture book. It includes an instruction page for adults, in both English and Spanish, with tips on helping the child move through the book and tell the story in different ways.

Writing bilingual easy readers presents different challenges because the reading levels don't always translate equally. To compensate, Jeffers says the writer must bring the word count and vocabulary down to equal levels. "It's an uphill battle," she says, "trying to get them to mirror one another."

Overall, the approach has been successful. The books allow multicultural enjoyment, language development, and a unique learning experience.

Reed, "where the main character stands out and is guided by right and wrong. I like to see the characters challenged." She says that topics for early readers can include problems with school, bullies, friends, family issues and pets. "However," she adds, "I am always looking for something different because we see a lot of these types of stories."

Lay says, "When writing for young readers, the story ideas need to be ones they can relate to." She names the loss of pets, loss of friends, and fears as topics that are at their level. "In 'The Remembering Game,' an early reader story I sold to *The Friend*, young Sammy plays a game with his mother while they run errands. Mother promises Sammy an ice cream cone if he helps her remember all the places they need to go. After finishing the errands, Mother claims to have forgotten the way home, so it's up to Sammy to retrace their route. Remembering things in sequence, coupled with the surprise twist in the end, makes this story appealing to children."

What it Takes

Working successfully in this genre, Hoppe says, takes "an author who is willing to work very, very hard and has read lots of easy-readers. Also needed is a good sense of how to tell a successful story for this age group." Stenger says most of Kaeden's authors are teachers and Hedlund says ABDO works with specialists in the education field as well.

Reed had this advice for writers: "Start by writing for magazines. Build up your credits." This seems particularly wise because the market for early reader books is tight. Frank stresses that Viking is not accepting easy-reader manuscripts, agented or otherwise, and Hoppe says that even though their list is growing, they strive to find the right number of titles. "There's more competition for shelf space," she says, "since more publishers have jumped on the bandwagon in the last five to ten years."

Reed secured her first contract with Chelsea House after selling 50 stories and articles to magazines. "Magazine writing experience can and will open up doors in other areas of writing," she says.

Despite the hard work, early reader authors find the effort worth it. Chaconas says there's satisfaction in knowing you've written a good story, having an editor buy it, and then holding the book in your hand. "But the thrill doesn't end there," she says. Reading the story with a group of second graders, hearing them laugh in all of the right places, and knowing that they *get it* sends a thrill right to your middle. "And that," she says, "is the ultimate satisfaction."

The Specialty of Middle-Grade Writing

By Marjorie Flathers

When Denise joined our critique group, she was upset because some members suggested she immerse herself in as many children's books as possible. "I have little enough time to write as it is," she said. "Why should I waste it reading what somebody else wrote, instead of concentrating on what I want to write?"

Unfortunately, although she wrote every day and sent out manuscripts regularly, Denise never realized the success that could have been hers. What was missing? The answer, of course, was her reluctance to become familiar with children's books, especially those written for the audience she wanted to reach.

Reading established writers is especially necessary when writing for the middle grades, usually defined as grades 3 to 6 or ages 8 to 12. Many writers are drawn to this audience, perhaps because at first glance it seems like an undemanding group. After all, they don't have the limitations of early readers, but they're not ready for reading about those edgy teen issues.

Writing for the middle grades is rewarding and creative, but it is as specialized as any other. It is also the chronological center of children's publishing and so the competition, particularly in writing fiction, can be daunting. Tim Travaglini, Senior Editor at G.P. Putnam's Sons, maintains that the middle-grade audience is "underserved," however, and that there is a "solid, steady demand for middle-grade fiction."

Confusing Feelings, Exciting Challenges

Middle-graders are at a unique time in their lives, especially today, when the actual childhood years seem to be getting shorter and shorter. Peer pressure escalates, and life becomes complicated by issues that range from making sports teams and succeeding at science fairs to taking standardized tests and living with the fears that compel school security.

Catherine Lee, Publisher and founding Editor of the tween magazine *Discovery Girls*, speaks of the middle grades as "a time of many, many changes," when young people are facing "confusing feelings and exciting challenges. They want to laugh, to learn, to think."

These same challenges can make starting points for great stories, or inspire subplots for others. Middle-graders might read fiction about how a student lacking in science proficiency came up with a winning project. Perhaps a lighthearted non-fiction look at peer pressure (without diminishing its importance in any way) would help a girl or boy deal with this daily problem. A subplot showing how increased school security hinders daily life could add drama and intensity to a story.

Middle-graders are looking for books that address their concerns and problems, their hopes and dreams. They look, too, for stories that offer escape to other times and places, that ignite the imagination. Many prolific writers have written for this audience: Phyllis Reynolds Naylor, Beverly Cleary, Roald Dahl, and Judy Blume are classics. More recent middle-grade masters include Donna Jo Napoli, Pam Muñoz Ryan, and Sharon Creech.

"The most successful books," says Julie Romeis, Editor at Bloomsbury Publishing, "stand out because their authors find a way to share something new. We receive so many submissions that are frighteningly similar to many books that have already been published or that claim to be the next Harry Potter. It's easy to jump on the latest bandwagon, but it's much more interesting to find a story that travels off the beaten path."

"Focusing more on the market than on the story itself," says Jennifer Wingertzahn, Editor at Clarion Books, "is a mistake writers often make. A well-told, engaging story with believable, memorable characters and timeless themes will always get an editor's attention."

Distinctions

In recent years, the category of young adult publishing shifted as it divided more into writing directed at younger teens and that for older teens. While a similar distinction may not crystallize for the middle grades, consider the large range in reading and interests between an 8-year-old third grader and a 12-year-old sixth grader, as well as the differences in interests between boys and girls at those ages.

Throw in the maturity issues in any given 8- or 12-year-old population and it becomes clear why there are variations in audience targeting among the numerous magazines that address middle-grade boys and girls. *Guideposts for Kids* targets ages 8 to 12; *Highlights for Children* embraces ages 2 to 12. Girls 8 to 12 read *American Girl* and *Discovery Girls,* while *New Moon*'s readership is girls 8 to 14. Middle-grade boys fall into the middle of the age range for *Boys' Life,* ages 6 to 18. Other audience spans include *Cricket,* 9 to 14; *My Friend,* 7 to 12; *Nature Friend,* 6 to 12; and *Sports Illustrated For Kids,* 8 to 14.

All are directed at least in part to elementary school age children, some move toward junior high, but even given crossover ages, each middle-grade magazine has it own particular focus. Among those with the most clear-cut concentration are the publications of the Children's Better Health Institute (CBHI), including *Jack And Jill, Children's Playmate,* and *U*S*Kids,* which are targeted to younger middle-grade readers. Every submission for these magazines must have a healthy living slant. The editors also caution that stories must be written from a child's perspective, not as an adult talking to children.

Guideposts for Kids, an online magazine, is published by the spiritually-based *Guideposts* but it decidedly does not want overt religion in the stories they publish. Editor Mary Lou Carney has repeatedly said she gets far too many "I prayed and I got" stories, and these are never publishable for her.

Other magazines do. *My Friend, the Catholic Magazine for Kids* always wants a spiritual theme woven into a story, and *Clubhouse* and *Clubhouse, Jr.,* published by Focus on the Family, require literature that promotes Biblical thinking.

Highlights for Children demands very high quality fiction that is fresh, imaginative, and child-friendly. Its subject range is wide, but its specifications are precise. The monthly needs 500-word stories for the very young and longer works for older children. Judy Burke, Associate Editor, says, "The best way that authors can prepare to submit their work to *Highlights* is to study our guidelines." Burke also recommends that authors "study the most current issues" of the magazine.

Commonalities

Whether you are trying to place short stories with magazines or are working on a book-length manuscript, and whether your audience is 8 or 18, many of the same principles apply. They can be particularly important to the middle-grade audience. Young as they may be, this can be a very discriminating audience: They know how to flush out the false.

First and foremost, tell the story you need to tell. Any story, long or short, that comes from your heart, your emotions, your experience, has a much better chance of being accepted than one that tries to capitalize on trends or hopes to copy someone else's success.

Writers can generate ideas and address middle-grade readers by getting in touch again with the sensibilities of the age. Noted author Graham Salisbury, whose middle-grade novels include *Under the Blood-Red Sun* and *Island Boyz,* says, "Think about specific words from your own childhood," he says, "and write about those words for ten minutes, nonstop. This will unleash ideas and plots that are unique to you." Times change, but feelings and emotions don't, and doing this exercise can put you in touch with your inner middle grader. Salisbury grew up in Hawaii, in a family of journalists, and he uses his own history to explore and create his novels.

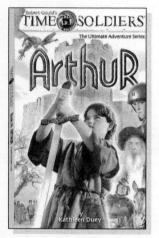

Kathleen Duey is the author of numerous middle-grade books, including the Unicorn's Secret series, and with photographer Robert Gould, the Time Soldiers series. She says, "When you know your main character as a person, the plot will develop." But Duey cautions, "Avoid pushing and pulling your characters around. This is the sign of a weak plot. If you continue to struggle with your plot, try coming at it from a different angle."

Expiration Dates

Editors and authors agree that you must capture your middle-grade reader on the first paragraph of a story or article or the first page of a book. Once your story or book is written, it's a good idea to rework this first part, changing and replacing dialogue and word structure. The same is true for nonfiction, where your lead and language and energy must connect with the young, sharp audience.

Putnam's Travaglini knows this audience and he identifies an overriding truth that writers for this age must recognize: Middle-graders don't like quiet or slow; they lose patience with too much description. The writer needs to "draw the middle-grade reader into the scene, allowing that reader to care about the character right away." He adds that readers in this age group like to recognize themselves in the protagonist and want that person to be "engaged, in motion."

Realistic dialogue is a sharp tool in keeping a middle-grader's attention, but don't resort to slang, which is quickly dated and therefore boring. If possible, listen to words and phrases young people use, perhaps as a volunteer at an elementary school, but don't get caught in it. Use the energy and the rhythms, but don't focus on select words or you'll pass an expiration date quickly.

Bruce Hale, author of the popular Chet Gekco mystery series, advises writers not to make things too easy for the protagonist. "Always ask 'how can I make this worse before it gets better?'" he says. Hale also believes editors and young readers want a satisfying, but not necessarily

Wisdom to Make a Good Story Great

Author and illustrator Rosemary Wells believes that each person sees life through the colors of a "rose window," as one would view the changing colors in a kaleidoscope. When a writer brings a personal rose window to a story, she says, it heightens the intensity and adds an important personal touch.

Award-winning children's author Graham Salisbury sees particular feelings that won't go away as "diamonds." They are the choices we've made and consequences that followed, the life lessons that we learned, he says. These ideas can effectively be put to use in developing characters.

Popular author and speaker Bruce Hale recommends "playing a grace note." A grace note in music, he explains, is an extra passage that is not essential to the melody or harmony, but gives the listener a quiet moment of beauty. In literature, this short addition needs to be organic to the plot, but doesn't move it forward. Still, finding a way to incorporate a grace note into a story gives the reader a moment to savor what he or she is reading.

happy, ending. What's most important, he says, is a conclusion that gives "a sense of hope."

Go Away, Mom & Dad!

Because of the fierce competition, rejections are an unavoidable part of submitting when writing for the middle grades. Writers have even been known to call them *reverse acceptances* to take away the sting. Rejections can be kept to a minimum, however.

All the editors interviewed for this article agreed that poor writing skills and lack of professionalism—such as not following accepted format requirements and not including an SASE—are the two major reasons for rejection.

Rosanne Tolin, Managing Editor at *Guideposts for Kids,* says, "It's immediately obvious which writers have been studying our website and are familiar with the flavor of our stories. By not reading guidelines and studying current back issues, authors often misunderstand our audience. Some stories are too heavy-handed while other writers simply miss the point altogether, thinking that this publication is for adults needing advice on topics that apply to raising children."

Bloomsbury's Romeis says that manuscripts are rejected "if the writing isn't cohesive, rhythmic, and eloquent."

"Many times," says Clarion's Wingertzahn, "I'm not convinced that the writing or the premise of a book is strong enough to attract attention in today's marketplace."

Burke, at *Highlights*, agrees. "Often a story is good, but not great," she says. "There's a lot of competition, and we're looking for the stories that stand out." To make a good story great, veteran children's writers have learned to add special little extras that help their stories rise to the top of the acceptance pile. (See sidebar on page 73, "Wisdom to Make a Good Story Great".)

It can be too easy to fall into errors in writing for middle-graders or other children's markets, however. Burke says that even stories that have an interesting plot and strong characters can turn "too preachy or teach a lesson in an obvious way. They'll always be returned."

Some writers have trouble distinguishing this from a quality that is very important to put into writing for children. The issue of a lesson or moral seamlessly woven into the plot, the take-away, requires a balancing act. Editors want to see that a change has taken place within the main character in the course of a story, that the protagonist sees things in a different way, and ideally, is a better person. Julie Strauss-Gabel, Senior Editor at Dutton Books for Children, states clearly that she is "always looking for a good take-away."

The problem, says Burke, can be identified within the motto of *Highlights*—Fun with a Purpose. But, she says, "We often have to return manuscripts that have too much purpose, not enough fun." Burke clarifies strongly that the take-away should serve the basics of "plot, conflict, and resolution" and not the other way around.

A more apparently subtle, yet telling consideration is the role of parents or other adults in a story. Almost without exception, editors do not want adults to figure into a middle-grade story in any significant way. Some don't want to see the adults at all. Many otherwise well-written stories are rejected because adults help, even in a small way, with solving the main character's problem.

At *Highlights*, Burke says simply, "We like it when the child protagonist thinks up a clever solution to whatever problem he or she is facing. That's empowering." Even mild sentences such as "Mom whispered an idea to me," or "Dad went with me," can cause a story to be unacceptable. This is definitely a fine line since, in reality, adults are still arguably the most important influences in a middle-grader's life.

Study real life, look at books and magazines, and note how often, in a page, a chapter, or a whole book, adults appear and what their roles are. Familiarize yourself with the language other writers use when adults are remotely in the picture. Words such as *suggested* (instead of *told me*) and *did it by myself* (instead of *Uncle Jim helped me*) can make a difference.

Continually being aware of how other writers cope with changing times and publishing requirements will help you capture the essence of what editors and readers want to see and read will cut down on those "reverse acceptances." It's why Denise's rejection of the writing group's wisdom couldn't overcome her rejections.

Sometimes, when reading the works of accomplished authors, writers can feel as if all worthwhile ideas have already been used and the best books already written. There's always room for more, especially when stories say "something old in an new way," according to Romeis. "I like a story that I can't put down, something that takes me somewhere new and unexpected, whether it's ancient China, a California school, or another world."

"A fresh voice, an engaging plot and memorable characters" sell a story to *Highlights*, says Burke. "Great writing, believable and memorable characters, and timeless themes" stand out for Wingertzahn. *Guideposts'* Tolin says, "It's refreshing to read a new twist on an old theme."

Middle-grade readers are perhaps the core of the juvenile audience, and good writing for them is always in demand. Studying other writers, knowing the personalities and needs of publishers, and exploring childhood with authenticity will help you capture the elusive writing that touches the 8- or 10- or 12-year-old of today, as the work of other authors rings still in your middle-grade heart.

Fantasy Makes Anything Possible

By Mark Haverstock

Fantasy is a means of making wishes come true, allowing readers to escape to worlds where magical adventures and fantastic characters or creatures are only a page turn away. "It's a genre that inspires the imagination and sparks creativity—and what child doesn't adore many of its recurrent motifs, including dragons, magic, and fairies?" says Adam Oldaker, Associate Editor of *Cricket* and *Cicada*. "Our *Cricket* readers, who are between 9 and 14, write us letters of praise all the time for their favorite fantasy authors, including Tamora Pierce, Brian Jacques, and Philip Pullman."

According to Oldaker, contemporary authors of teen fantasy are also doing amazing things, and their books tend to be grittier than those written for *Cricket*-age readers. "Among my favorite recently published titles are *Gifts,* by Ursula K. Le Guin; *Sabriel* by Garth Nix; *A Fistful of Sky,* by Nina Kiriki Hoffman; and *Tithe,* by Holly Black."

With the exception of recent blockbusters like J.K. Rowling's Harry Potter or the revival of J.R.R. Tolkien's Lord of the Rings trilogy, fantasy still remains somewhat of a niche market.

"Fantasy will never be accepted fully by the mainstream and it shouldn't be, because if it is, it's doing something wrong. In commercial fiction, most of what the books are doing is reinforcing your worldview," says Gordon Van Gelder, Editor of *The Magazine of Science Fiction and Fantasy.* "However, fantasy draws more on mythology and I don't think it's inherently as radical as science fiction."

Writing fantasy requires a good knowledge of its best works, as well as a love of the genre. "We receive a lot of submissions from writers who don't read fantasy but are trying to capitalize on the popularity of the genre," says Oldaker. "There are many different approaches to fantasy writing, which writers can't know without reading the masters and contemporary authors. We're seeing, too, more and more knockoffs of famous books or series, which are sure to receive impersonal rejection slips."

Characterization

Stories are about people. Whether your story is fantasy or another variety of fiction, characters are the centerpiece—your first and most

Kate Elliott

important consideration in writing a successful piece. "Your characters have to be believable, even if the world itself may be fantastic," says Debra Euler, Managing Editor at DAW Books. "That's what people are looking for, characters they can relate to."

Author and Publisher J. Royce Adams agrees. "Even though a fantasy character may not be human, it's important for the characters to have some weaknesses or traits that allow us to identify with, root for, or connect to on a human level," he says. "If we can't feel for or with them, we aren't really interested in what happens to them."

Most fantasy characters should somehow mirror the human condition. They should also have struggles, frailties, hopes, and dreams. "That way, readers will identify with and care about them," says

Oldaker. "For example, if a teen character has come of age and is leaving her region to enter the larger fantasy world, her experience should reflect that of real people."

Don't be afraid to base fantasy characters on human models. For starters, think of the personalities that appear on your favorite soap opera or reality show: the backstabber, the naive soul, the long-suffering saint, and the manipulator. "To give an example from my own work, the primary villain in the Crown of Stars fantasy series really strikes a chord with readers," says author Kate Elliott. "They write all the time asking me to make something horrible happen to this character." Readers dislike him because he is very closely based on the model of an abusive, controlling spouse. "I think they respond to this particular character because they know people like that exist, or they have known someone like that. They respond to him because he feels right, he feels true as opposed to the stereotype character."

Writers at times have reasons for using stereotypical characters in fantasy. In some cases, readers read for comfort and come to a book with certain expectations that it will be familiar and come out a certain way. "If a writer is doing that kind of book, they'll tend to go with a more stereotypical character. Either that's the way they want to write it or to please the audience they're targeting," says Elliott. "But I think writers need to be careful not to use the default because of laziness or

Speculative Fiction

Sometimes it's difficult to classify fiction neatly, something major book chains have been trying to do for years. When you've come across a story that both is and isn't fantasy, science fiction, and/or horror, then you've discovered speculative fiction. This term, attributed to writer Robert Heinlein, is used collectively to describe works that don't neatly fit into the genres of fantasy, science fiction, and horror.

So why do we need to confuse the issue with yet another genre description? Because speculative fiction addresses fiction that includes weird tales, amazing stories, and the paranormal. It also may include other genres, such as mysteries, alternate histories, and historical fiction. The term becomes a catchall to describe works of science fiction, fantasy, and horror and also addresses works that are not strictly science fiction, fantasy, or horror—but don't rightly belong to the other genres either.

One example of speculative fiction for tween and YA audiences is Jeanne DuPrau's *The City of Ember,* which includes some features of fantasy and science fiction, yet can't be neatly placed in either camp. It takes place on what appears to be a post-apocalyptic Earth, with a society that's been sheltered underground for almost 250 years. Though it specu-lates on a possible future, a science fiction trait, the idea is solidly rooted in the past. "One of the influences was my experience growing up in the 1950s during the Cold War. I was very aware of the possibility of global devastation," says DuPrau. "People were building underground bomb shelters in their backyards."

The City of Ember has no elves or wizards, magic, or people unlike you or me. Yet main characters Lina and Doon embark on a quest, a staple in fantasy stories, to find a world outside Ember.

lack of imagination."

People are never totally good or totally evil; neither should characters be. They all may at times be moti-vated by greed, revenge, altruism, or a love of cuddly puppies. Hitler probably didn't think of himself as evil, but one who nurtured mastery and purity. John F. Kennedy cer-tainly did many positive acts in his lifetime, yet he also succumbed to the temptations of fame and poli-tics. Writers should take care not to perpetuate the stereotypical good guy or bad guy.

Nothing attracts most editors more than a good story that begins with strong, real characterization. "It's the kind where you know the protagonist well by the end of page two," says Van Gelder. "Stories that turn me off are the ones that feel like they really have to grab my at-tention from word one with people

Staging Fantasy

Fantasy is a popular genre for the theater. Pioneer Drama Service does adaptations of traditional fantasy stories like *Alice in Wonderland,* as well as new material. "We try to offer material that's simple to stage, but one of the problems you get into with fantasy is special effects," says Lori Conary, Assistant Editor. "Our customers will steer clear of something with a lot of special effects because they're generally on limited budgets. We work mostly with schools: Drama settings for them can be anything from a cafeteria to a stage." Some special effects are fine. However, the simpler the staging requirements, the greater chance of success their customers will have.

The same applies to scene changes in a fantasy world. "One of the things we do when we work with authors who write a lot of scene changes is to make the recommendation to convert to area staging," says Conary. What works best is if plays "have two or three major sets, and the plays are condensed into an area staging that works a lot better with groups."

Writers who incorporate flexible casting—in number and gender—and field test their work have the best chance of acceptance at Pioneer. "Having a play staged by a group or done in a reader's theater setting gives the author a way to refine the work—see it on stage, do some blocking," says Conary. "Plays don't always come out like they look on paper."

breaking in, guns blasting, and non-stop action all the way. As a reader, I would prefer character driven more than plot-driven."

Unless the main character is likeable, the reader isn't going to be interested in following the story. "We get some books with unattractive characters. Fantasy is escapism and who wants to escape into a world of unpleasant people?" says Peter Stampfel, Associate Editor of DAW Books. "There have to be some redeeming traits."

Exercise care when bestowing powers, talents, and special abilities on fantasy characters. "There's a part of me that reacts to exceptional powers: Why is the author incorporating them into the character? If there's a good reason in the story, then I can understand it," says Elliott. "Some people have gifts, like John Nash in *A Beautiful Mind,*" and that exceptional quality made the story of his human struggles interesting. The same is true, says Elliot, "when I read about successful characters who just happen to have exceptional abilities, like the *X-Men.* One of the things these young characters still had to do was struggle with adolescence." Readers identify with these kinds of characters because they face the same struggles as most people, but they also have

Small Press/Self Press

Among the science fiction publishing giants such as DAW, Tor, and Del Rey are numerous small presses that specialize in science fiction, fantasy, and horror. They're certainly worth a look in your search for a publisher, and many pay modest advances and royalties. Several listings and links can be found at: www.locusmag.com/Links/Publishers.html. Locus is also a great source for magazine and e-zine listings, as well as the latest news on the fantasy, science fiction, and horror markets.

Is DIY more your style? If you're willing to take the hands-on approach with marketing and publishing, you can enlist the help of a print-on-demand (POD) or short-run press. W. Royce Adams both writes and publishes his Rairarubia series, noting that there are pluses and minuses to his mom and pop press. "The benefit is being in total control from manuscript to book, both in product and in time. Once a manuscript is finalized, it can take less than one to two months to get the book in print as opposed to taking two years with a major publisher," he explains. "The pitfalls are the number of books being published each year, lack of a budget comparable with a major publisher's for marketing and publicity, and lack of respect. We'll never get rich, but we're having fun, especially when we receive the enthusiasm our young readers show."

special powers that no one else has.

Just like us, story characters are also products of their environment. "When creating fantasy characters, it's important to bear in mind how their way of relating to the world would differ from our own," says Oldaker. "For example, a human raised in Fairyland would surely have different values and attitudes than the rest of us, as would someone raised in a primitive community of people with special powers."

Welcome to My World

Whether the manuscript takes place in a nonexistent fairyland or in a hidden setting within our own, real world, a fantasy writer needs to create certain rules and abide by them. "The rules, too, must be explained in a subtle way, without interrupting the prose with lumps of information, and they have to make sense," says Oldaker. "We see many fantasy submissions where the authors clearly haven't thought them through."

Also, these rules shouldn't be introduced whimsically or to shore up weaknesses in the story itself. "In our fantasy submissions, we sometimes see new elements plunked in for the sake of furthering the plot," explains Oldaker. "All of a sudden, for example, the reader learns that a dragon hates water, which explains why a wizard is safe from attack on

Catching an Editor's Eye

Don't forget the conventions of manuscript submissions and presenting a professional package. "A lot of what comes may be dismissed pretty quickly just because of improperly formatted manuscripts, poor cover letters, or subject matter we don't publish," says Michael Metzler, Publisher of Action Publishing. "The main issue you deal with as a small publisher is how much time can you spend looking at manuscripts. Generally, I admire anyone who wants to write and create something and is willing to send it out. If I had unlimited time, I'd be as encouraging as I could to everybody."

Memorable characters, believable worlds, and fresh plots, as well as a thorough knowledge and love of the genre, are key to a successful story or novel. "People should write what they care about, they shouldn't try to read the market," says Managing Editor of DAW Books, Debra Euler. "They should write what they enjoy reading, which will be ultimately be their best effort. It's much more real and genuine, and comes out in the work."

a ship. If this facet of the dragon's character isn't clearly established from the beginning, it should at least be foreshadowed."

Remember that what the poet Samuel Taylor Coleridge called the *willing suspension of disbelief* is key in fantasy: Your reader must mentally take the journey to your alternate world. "For fantasies that take place in nonexistent lands, their settings should be brought to life, so much so that the reader never questions that such places could exist," says Oldaker. "Still, too much description can bog down a narrative, so there's a delicate balance to be achieved."

While you do your world-building, consider keeping a notebook to help you maintain consistency throughout your current manuscript—and future sequels. Elliott kept a notebook and a detailed glossary for the Crown of Stars series, which now contains seven titles. Even with her current project, which has the working title *Crossroads,* Elliott continues to track the details carefully, listing even the seemingly insignificant. "I always use my glossary. I have lists of plants and what they're used for. I have the names of constellations, and the calendars used, and so on," she says. "If you have a good notebook, you can always refer back to it when you forget. I often do."

Books allow the room to establish your fantasy world, but for short stories, it's important to be choosy with details because of length considerations. "Keep it simple. You really don't need to build an entire world for a short story; you only need to build one community within that world," says Edward Knight, Editor of *Amazing Journeys.* "Narrow it down to a town, region, or some geographical area within your world, so you aren't trying to cover so much." Character development should take precedence over world-building, especially in magazine fiction.

Yet don't assume that because you're writing a short piece you can cut corners. "In terms of the actual craft, just because you're doing a 1,000-word short-short story doesn't mean you won't put in the same amount of work developing your setting as in a novella," explains Van Gelder. "There's more of a challenge getting it into a shorter piece."

Van Gelder suggests that an underlying level of world creation is assumed in most short science fiction and fantasy. Ninety percent of a story is submerged, like an iceberg. You still need to put in the effort on that short story to get that hidden 90 percent.

Fresh Perspectives

It's hard to write a totally original plot, but always look for a different perspective or twist. Sure, it's all been done before, but writing is often about new wine in old casks. "Sometimes it's just a matter of providing a modern perspective," says Van Gelder. "I bought a frog prince story last year and the twist was that it involved a computer dating match-up and featured a transgender character. The magic in the story was that kissing the frog turns him into the woman he wants to be."

While it is unlikely that many editors for children and teens will take

on that twist, the point remains. Distinguish your story. "Make sure if you submit vampire story number 811, it has something to distinguish it from the other 810 vampire stories I've seen recently," says Van Gelder. "I just bought a YA fantasy. It's a parable about school kids but it's from the viewpoint of a goblin schoolteacher who teaches a mixed class of goblins and humans. I almost never buy goblin stories, but it was very refreshing, something that stood out."

Look beyond the well-known European myths and explore other cultures for ideas. "It seems that a lot of the material we receive is based on the medieval knight-in-armor scenarios, which if well-written, I'll still buy," says Knight. "But we need to broaden our

horizons a little." He notes that lately he's been reading many stories that are based on myths from other peoples.

Euler looks for something that isn't the usual retread. "People have a habit of looking at what's popular and write their own version of it," she explains. "We seem to get many not-so-good versions of Harry Potter. "The trick is to write something that is familiar enough to the readers, yet different enough to interest them." Imitation may be a sincere form of flattery, but it won't get you published.

"We really aren't looking for any more quest novels with your mixed bag of elves, dwarves, and other traditional characters," says Stampfel. "There are so many that have the same stock plots that are done to death. We'd like to see more original ideas."

Cliché Check

Do your heroes, evil overlords, and elves sound a bit too familiar? Are your characters bearing a close resemblance to Xena, Hercules, or Harry Potter? Do readers say "It's déjà vu all over again" about your writing? Check out these websites for an exhaustive list of clichés to avoid:

- **Risus Fantasy Clichés:** http://codepoet.org/~markw/risus/fantasy.html
- **The Grand List of Fantasy Clichés:** http://www.geocities.com/Area51/Labyrinth/8584/stuff/cliche.html
- **The Not-So-Grand List of Fantasy Clichés:** http://amethyst-angel.com/cliche.html
- **Peter's Evil Overlord List:** www.eviloverlord.com/lists/overlord.html

History in the Works: Truth & Fiction

By Jan Burns

Historical fiction is packed with adventure, tragedy, triumph, personal stories, and grand events. Characters set out on quests, perform acts of exploration or daring, or struggle valiantly against fascinating backdrops. Children love to read these books to travel along with the characters through time and place.

Writers of historical fiction strive to make their characters, stories, and settings so real that nothing jars readers out of fictional realms and back into the present. They want children to enter fully into the worlds they have created. For historical fiction, thorough research is the indispensable first step.

In its Time

While each book or magazine story has its own unique requirements, the first law for writers of this genre may be: "All in its proper time." That is, historical fiction must have no anachronisms, be fully accurate, and use the right details of people, places, words, and things in their proper times to create an evocative atmosphere and intriguing story appropriate to a particular epoch.

The more specific the information—the more tiny details—the richer the story, says Carolyn Yoder, Senior Editor of History at *Highlights for Children* and Editor of Calkins Creek Books. Yoder recommends that authors stay away from general reference books and search out the rich and specific. Local historical societies, state museums, and state libraries are wonderful places to explore and Yoder finds newspapers, in particular, to be strong sources.

"Regarding research for historical fiction, we like authors to include a bibliography and photocopies of sources that verify the facts and events mentioned in their story," says Judy Burke, Associate Editor of *Highlights for Children*. "We prefer primary sources as opposed to encyclopedias, Internet sources, and children's books. We also encourage authors to ask an expert to review their story for accuracy before submission and to include a photocopy of the expert's response."

Every manuscript sent to Yoder at *Highlights* or Calkins Creek requires a detailed bibliography. She recommends that authors send annotated bibliographies, which she says show how serious an author is about research, and she wants to see authors use a wide variety of resources. "At Calkins Creek, history needs to be front and center in historical fiction manuscripts," Yoder says. "I look for stories that shout the times and are firmly placed in a well-defined historical and cultural context. I am not looking for stories from any particular period in U.S. history. Most of the historical fiction manuscripts that I do receive highlight the American Revolution and Civil War periods."

Historic language is one of the elements that must ring true, but not be stilted or awkward to the ears of modern children. Reading a manuscript over several times can help to find any passages that need to be rewritten because they seem unnatural. It also helps to read widely in children's historical fiction, to see how others have handled the unique requirements of the genre.

A delightful example is the Newbery winner *Crispin: The Cross of Lead,* by Avi. Set in fourteenth-century England, it is a well-crafted story filled with details of medieval life and packed with mystery, adventure, and plot twists. The back-of- the- book glossary, author's historical note, and author interview offer additional information to the reader about the time period in which the book is set. From the first page, readers will feel sympathy for the main character as he and the village priest carry his dead mother's body to the village church. The penniless lad seems destined for a life of abject poverty, until he runs away to seek a better life. During the journey he discovers that there is a way to change his life, if he can achieve it.

The Unexpected

Some writers prefer to do the bulk of their research before they start writing. Lila Guzmán first explores many aspects of a time period, including language, clothing, hairstyles, food, customs, culture, taboos, voice, sports, dance, entertainment, religion, flora and fauna. No matter how well you research a time period, however, Guzmán says, "unexpected questions will pop up as you write."

Although she had already done a considerable amount of research for her most recent book, *Lorenzo's Turncoat,* cowritten with her husband Rick Guzmán, she had to stop writing and investigate whether umbrellas were in common use during the American Revolution. She discovered that British men did not use them in the 1770s, but that the French did.

Writer Veda Boyd Jones agrees that the details can trip you up in historical fiction. In her book *Maureen the Detective: The Age of Immigration* (Barbour), she originally put a zipper in a purse and then fact-checked to make sure that zippers were in handbags during the time of the story. They were not, so she changed that detail.

It can be a professional weakness to over-research, however. Writer Susanna Reich says that she loves historical facts and has "to be careful not to get carried away." Know your subject, do a solid amount of research, but be careful how many details you pack into a story. Reich believes it's important to use only what you need because too many facts can be a distraction. Among Reich's titles are *Penelope Bailey Takes the Stage* (Marshall Cavendish), which is set in San Francisco in 1889 and features a character based on the dancer Isadora Duncan; *José! Born to Dance, the Story of José Limon* (Simon & Schuster/Paula Wiseman Books); and *Clara Schumann, Piano Virtuoso* (Clarion Books).

Jodi Goldberg, Editorial Director of Pleasant Company Publications, says, "The more an author thoroughly researches the subject, the more a character and their circumstances are believable. If the character isn't coming to life in the initial submission, I'm not likely to take an interest." She says that bibliographies aren't requisite, although they are helpful and show the thoroughness of an author's research. Goldberg wants compelling historical fiction featuring strong 7- to 12-year-old girls in any period in American history; send a synopsis of the story idea and a sample chapter.

Crucial Conflict

While your story may be taking shape during research, it may not be until late in the process that you have a good idea of the well-known people and events of the time period and can truly flesh out the initial story idea. You cannot change the historical facts, but you can weave your plot around them to create an exciting story. As a plotting strategy, ask yourself what-if questions. Ask what kinds of conflict might have existed, specific to that time or universally human. Balance the historical framework with the story line and characters.

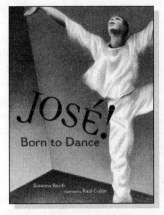

Guzmán believes that the story should always come first, before the dimension of history, especially when writing for children. "If you don't have interesting characters doing interesting things," she says, "children will stop reading." Guzmán weaves the history into the story by using cleverly placed details to make her readers feel like they are there.

She often asks herself, what will interest young readers? Children know about getting shots, for example. General Washington required all of his soldiers to be inoculated against smallpox. The British planned to send infected people into camp and decimate the Continental Army. In a small scene in the Guzmáns' *Lorenzo's Revolutionary Quest*, a young cook named Molly in Washington's camp is inoculated. Guzmán believes if the novel is well-written, young readers will learn history without realizing they are.

Lynn Polvino, Associate Editor at Clarion Books, looks for stories that are relevant to the lives of the children who will read them, stories that create a genuine connection with the reader and make them think, long after the final page has been turned. She says an ideal submission is a well-crafted story with a compelling plot, a rich, interesting setting, and fully developed characters.

Burke says, "Strong plots, engaging characters, and a central conflict—preferably solved eventually by the child protagonist—are crucial, as with any fiction submitted to us."

Links of Interest

■ **Do History:** www.dohistory.org. This website uses a case history to explore how to put together the fragments of the past. Essays are on such topics as how to organize your research project and how to use primary sources.

■ **American Association for State and Local History:** www.aaslh.org. This website provides links to regional museum groups, state associations, national resource organizations, and state historical societies.

■ **PRNewswire for Journalists:** www.profnet.com. This site is a collaboration by information officers to give journalists and writers free, convenient access to expert sources.

Personal Past & Future

Even though dramatic events may be taking place in your story, young readers are likely to be most interested in reading about the kids in the story. All children share certain traits, regardless of the time period in which they live. They wonder what their futures hold, what their lives will be like. They are hurt when something bad happens to their family. They want to be loved. Whether your characters live today, on the American frontier, or in ancient Egypt, these remain the same.

The main character of historical fiction is often a rebel or a pioneer of one sort or another, involved with an event that is intriguing and unexpected. A character like this brings adventure and conflict into your story, propelling the action. Rebellion also makes readers want to keep reading, to find out what happens as your character battles the status quo or takes on large challenges.

Polvino is partial to edgy young adult and middle-grade novels, including books with strong, quirky central characters dealing honestly with kids' emotions, and books about young people's relationships (with each other, with adults, with siblings), and about those who don't fit in for one reason or another. In addition, she likes stories involving sports (particularly girls playing sports), music, the performing arts, and science and nature all appeal to her.

As a child, writer Dorothy Leland always enjoyed stories about pioneers and covered wagon journeys, and as an adult, she has lived in an area rich with Gold Rush history. She wrote a couple of nonfiction books about the region, which fueled her enthusiasm for writing historical fiction. Her first novel, *Sallie Fox: The Story of a Pioneer Girl,* was based on a real child. In the course of that research, she happened across the remarkable true story of a San Francisco newsboy in 1853. That became the basis for her second novel, *The Balloon Boy of San Francisco.*

Leland's goal is always to put as much "real stuff" in the book as possible, but she points out that historical records usually don't supply the child's point of view. Basing her books on actual people and events, she found out as much as she could about what really happened but her goal was to write a book that children could identify with. That's where imagination must take over, while remaining supported by historical documentation. For instance, while working on *Sallie Fox,* Leland came across a brief notation that the family's dog had died during their wagon journey to California.

Because she knew how important the death of a pet can be to a child, Leland created a story line for the dog, even though she had little actual information to go on. Many young readers have since told her the dog was one of their favorite parts of the book.

Good historical fiction should be "truly child-centered and age-appropriate" for Maureen Sullivan, Executive Editor at Dutton Children's Books. The main character should be about two years older than the target readership and "active in his or her own transformation." The story should feel immediate and fresh, be firmly grounded in a time and place, have universal themes, and hopefully help the reader to see themselves or the world in a new way.

Don't fall into selecting the same old times and places, either. According to Tracy Schoenle, Senior Editor at *Cricket, Cicada,* and at Cricket Books, they've received manuscripts set in ancient Egypt, Greece, and Rome, which *Cricket* readers love, but also desirable are less familiar time periods and places, such as South America or pre-industrial Europe. They're also very much interested in contemporary stories set in Africa or Asia. Cricket Books accepts only agented book manuscripts, but for the magazines, quality historical fiction is always welcome.

While there is no magic formula for writing successful historical fiction, there are a few things writers can do to increase the chances of selling their work. First, find a time

period that you know you will love
to research and write about. This
will help you maintain a high interest level in your project. Then, try to
create a compelling story with sym-
pathetic characters who struggle to
solve their problems to reach an important goal. Weave enough historical information into your work to
give it an authentic feel, but not so
much that it overwhelms the story.
Put all of these things together and
you should have a story that children will be eager to read.

At Their Leisure: Magazines Target Kids' Spare Time

By Pamela Holtz Beres

Leisure time breaks monotony, eases stress, and adds enjoyment to the busy lives of adults. For kids, leisure can serve similar purposes, but even more, it provides imaginative, creative, learning time. Play is the work of children. Hobbies and special interests help them explore the world and themselves. Leisure time can be full of unscripted educational experiences especially suited to the individual child. For adults and kids alike, down time is a vital ingredient in the recipe for a healthy life.

Countless leisure magazines for young people nestle among the general interest magazines on bookstore and library shelves. Between *Highlights for Children, Boys' Quest,* and *Cricket* you might see *BMX Plus, Nickelodeon,* and *Nintendo Power.* The first three might include articles that target a child's recreation in a general way, but the three latter magazines and others like them concentrate on readers interested in particular spare-time activities. That's what sets leisure magazines

apart from others on the shelf: their sharp focus on one, entertaining subject. It could be animals or electronics, stamps or skateboards, the outdoors or dancing. The list of subjects, and of possible markets for writers, is long.

Kids & Pets, a Natural Fit

A slogan spotted on a child's t-shirt says it all: "LOST: 1 Sister, 1 Dog. Reward for Dog." Almost every child has a pet at some point. Attachment to a pet develops a child's sense of responsibility and compassion, but above all, animals represent fun for children.

Magazines targeted to pet owners abound. *Cat Fancy, Dog Fancy, Dogs for Kids, Reptiles, Young Rider, Horsepower, AKC Family Dog,* and *I Love Cats* are a few of the titles you'll find, some aimed at middle-grade readers and others at young adult and adult readers. Editors of these magazines have a common goal: to share information and educate in a fun and inviting way.

"Our audience is kids who own

91

dogs," says Roger Sipe, Managing Editor of *Dogs for Kids*. Each issue contains five or six features that discuss caring for dogs, showing dogs, and even ideas for play. "We give kids ideas on what to do with their dog," Sipes says. They might be "seasonal ideas, like take your dog to the beach or things to do with your dog in the snow." He also likes to profile kids who are doing things to help dogs, such as raising money for dog shelters or for bullet-proof vests for police dogs.

While magazines provide readers with specific tips on pet care, some of their articles also broaden reader knowledge on breeds or species, or on products or upcoming events of interest to animal owners. An issue of *Reptiles,* for example, featured an article on scorpion geckos and a species profile on the blunt-headed tree snake. *Dogs for Kids* has a regular column called Cool Jobs, which introduces children to dog-related careers, such as veterinarian or dog groomer. An issue of *Cat Fancy* informed readers about how Egyptians popularized the love of cats, and an issue of *Horse Illustrated* instructed readers on how to teach their horse to handle water crossings.

Action!

Leisure for adults often means kicking back and relaxing, but for kids it almost always means getting busy and moving. From skateboarding to dancing, baseball to hunting, if it's an action-oriented activity, there's a magazine to cover it.

Junior Baseball is for kids 7 to 17

for whom baseball is a way of life. *Gball* is an e-zine targeting girls who play and are passionate about basketball. *Slap* and *Thrasher* reach kids who skateboard, and Young-BucksOutdoors.com addresses those whose adventures are in field, forest, and stream.

Mitchell Lavnick, Editor of *Kick-Off*, says his football publication for middle-grade readers differs from other sports magazines in that it is participatory. "It contains instructional articles on

how to play better and improve skills," says Lavnick. The magazine also features news items and profiles of professional players. The profiles "focus on when they were kids—how they got interested and started and what kind of player they are today."

Sarah Keough, Editor of *Young Dancer,* says her middle-grade readers take a variety of dance instruction—jazz, ballet, tap. The publication also covers world dance, modern dance, and hip hop. Keough includes profiles of young dancers and seasoned professional dancers, and articles on technique and health and nutrition. Every issue of *Young Dancer* also provides information on competition. "But not all readers dance competitively," says Keough. Many are "just interested in dance."

While YoungBucksOutdoors.com was launched as a newsletter nearly 15 years ago, it has been in its electronic format for several years. The purpose for the change, according to Managing Editor Dockery Austin, was to reach more kids in a financially feasible manner. Hunting is the e-zine's focus, but it also covers camping, fishing, scavenger hunts, and other outdoor activities. "It's all fair game," says Austin, "and can expose the child to activities that they may not have a chance to participate in otherwise." Austin says the audience is "about 60 percent boys and 40 percent girls."

The most popular features of the e-zine are those that let kids share personal stories or photos showcasing outdoor adventures they've had. How-to and informational articles are also an essential component of YoungBucksOutdoors.com. Articles that show how to build a fire or how to identify and treat poison ivy include a safety slant whenever possible. "Safety can never be stressed too much," says Austin.

Entertaining Moments

Frank Sinatra, Marilyn Monroe, the Beatles, Bruce Willis, Julia Roberts, —a fascination with the stars of our youth never ends. Is it any wonder then that teens want to know about the celebrities of their generation? Entertainment publications remain staples of the publishing world. *Teen People* alone has a circulation of

about 1.5 million. About a quarter million girls between the ages of 10 and 16 read *Tiger Beat* and another 200,000 read *Bop*.

Leesa Coble, Editor of *Bop* and *Tiger Beat,* confirms how fascinated kids are with celebrities and with reading about them. "It takes them away to another world that seems more exciting than their own." Coble says 99 percent of the audience for her magazines is female. The median age is 13 for both *Bop* and *Tiger Beat*. "The voice for each is young, hip, and celebrity-obsessed. Readers look to us for celebrity news, quizzes, contests, and pages of full-color images."

Meeting audience needs is of primary importance. "Our magazines thrive because we listen to what our readers tell us. We log hundreds of direct-feedback surveys a week, so we are right on top of who is hot and who is not. Unlike nearly all other tween-targeted magazines, we maintain celebrity information in a realm of innocence. Rather than focusing on celebrity scandal and criticism, our mission is to be positive and uplifting. We don't want our readers to grow up too fast."

Coble explains that *Bop* has recently had a change in editorial direction, targeting the same age as *Tiger Beat*. "You will find similar faces on the covers, but neither exact content or images are repeated between the magazines. We distinguish each title mainly through design. While *Tiger Beat* uses a lot of saturated colored pages, *Bop* uses more white space

Selected Leisure Markets

AKC Family Dog: American Kennel Club, 260 Madison Ave., New York, NY 10016. www.akc.org

American Cheerleader, American Cheerleader Junior: 23rd floor, 110 William St., New York, NY 10038. www.americancheerleader.com

Beckett Publications: Baseball Card Monthly, Beckett Basketball Monthly, Beckett Football Monthly, Beckett Hockey Monthly, 15850 Dallas Pkwy., Dallas, TX 75248. www.beckett.com

Bop, Tiger Beat: Suite 700, 6430 Sunset Blvd., Hollywood, CA 90028. www.bopmag.com, www.tigerbeatmag.com

Camping: 5000 State Road 67 North, Martinsville, IN 46151. www.ACAcamps.org

Canoe & Kayak: Suite 3, 10526 NE 68th St., Kirkland, WA 98033. www.canoekayak.com

Cat Fancy, Dog Fancy, Dogs for Kids: Fancy Publications, 3 Burroughs, Irvine, CA 92618. www.catfancy.com, www.dogfancy.com, www.dogsforkids.com

Chess Life: Suite 200, 3068 US Route 9W, New Windsor, NY 12553. www.uschess.org

Classic Toy Trains, Dollhouse Miniatures: 21027 Crossroads Circle, Waukesha, WI 83187. www.classictoytrains.com, www.dhminiatures.com

Coins: 700 East State St., Iola, WI 54990. www.collect.com

Creative Kids: P.O. Box 8813, Waco, TX 76714. www.prufrock.com

Dance: 11th floor, 333 7th Ave., New York, NY 10001. www.dancemagazine.com

Dragon: Suite 110, 3245 146th Place SE, Bellevue, WA 98007. www.paizo.com/gragon

FineScale Modeler: 21027 Crossroads Circle, P.O. Box 1612, Waukesha, WI 53l87. www.finescale.com

Gball: 2488 North Triphammer Road, Ithaca, NY 14850. www.gballmag.com

Horsepower: P.O. Box 670, Aurora, Ontario L4G 4J9 Canada.

I Love Cats: 16 Meadow Hill Lane, Armonk, NY 10504. www.iluvcats.com

Inside Kung-Fu: 4201 Vanowen Place, Burbank, CA 91505. www.cfwenterprises.com

Jam Rag: Suite 240, 22757 Woodward, Ferndale, MI 48220. www.jamrag.com

Junior Baseball: P.O. Box 9099, Canoga Park, CA 91309. Submit to: editorial@juniorbaseball.com.

Selected Leisure Markets

■ *Keyboard:* 2800 Campus Dr., San Mateo, CA 94403.
www.keyboardmag.com

■ *Kick-off:* 23rd Floor, 110 William St., New York, NY 10038.
www.kickoffmag.com

■ *Kid Zone:* 450 Benson Building, Sioux City, IA 51101.
www.kidzonemag.com

■ *Model Airplane News, Radio Control Boat Modeler, Radio Control Car Action:* Air Age Publishing, 100 East Ridge Road, Ridgefield, CT 06877.
www.modelairplanenews.com, www.rcboatmodeler.com,   www.rc-caraction.com

■ *The Numismatist:* 818 North Cascade Ave., Colorado Springs, CO 80903. www.money.org

■ *Pack-O-Fun:* Suite 375, 2400 Devon, Des Plaines, IL 60018.

■ *Quilt It for Kids:* 741 Corporate Circle, Golden, CO 80401.
www.quiltersnewsletter.com

■ *Racquetball:* 1685 West Uintah, Colorado Springs, CO 80904.
www.racqmag.com

■ *Recess Time:* P.O. Box 20, Lupton, MI 48635.
http://mieastsidepubs.com/recess.html

■ *Reptiles:* P.O. Box 6050, Mission Viejo, CA 92690.
www.reptilesmagazine.com

■ *Scott Stamp Monthly:* P.O. Box 828, Sidney, OH 45365.
www.scottonline.com

■ *Slap, Thrasher:* High Speed Productions, 1303 Underwood Ave., San Francisco, CA 94124.
www.slapmagazine.com, www.thrashermagazine. com

■ *Teen People:* Time Life Building, 35th Floor, Rockefeller Center, New York, NY 10020. www.teenpeople.com

■ *Toy Farmer:* 7496 106th Ave. SE, LaMoure, SD 58458.
www.toyfarmer.com

■ *WaterSki:* Suite 200, 460 North Orlando Ave., Winter Park, FL 32789.
www.waterskimag.com

■ *YoungBucksOutdoors.com:* P.O. Box 244022, Montgomery, AL 36124.

■ *Young Dancer:* 11th Floor, 333 7th Ave., New York, NY 10001.
www.youngdancer.com

■ *Young Rider:* P.O. Box 8237, Lexington, KY 40533.
www.youngrider.com

for ultra-bright color combinations. Each has their unique look and design elements." Coble continues: "Having two titles on the stands allows us to have more market share. A reader initially bonds to the magazine that speaks to her and through it, we introduce her to its sister magazine."

Just for Fun

Crafts, hobbies, and activities just for fun come in all shapes and sizes. Teens who are serious collectors might read *Coins* or *Dollhouse Miniature*. Model enthusiasts might read *Finescale Modeler,* while other hobbyists might enjoy *Quilt It for Kids* or *Radio Control Car Action.* All of these magazines focus on one subject and cover it in depth.

For the younger crowd, magazines such as *Pack-O-Fun* help kids create with paper, scissors, and glue. *Kid Zone* features games and puzzles, brain teasers, and theme-party ideas. Their Zone section offers entertaining information on topics such as animals, different cultures, food, and nature. Craft projects accentuate the fun. An article highlighting facts about the American flag, for example, included a sidebar on making a flag placemat. An article about strawberries had simple

recipes for pie, jam, and smoothies.

New to the scene is *Recess Time,* a regional publication serving kids in Michigan. According to Editor Tina Musial, *Recess Time* publishes almost anything that interests 7- to 12-year-olds. "We are trying to stick with being educational (without being obvious) and still keep it fun and light." She avoids clothing and fashion articles and focuses instead on career exploration, road trips kids would like, easy recipes, outdoor activities, sports, hobbies, crafts, video games, and puzzles. "We also have three contest sections where readers write to us to win savings bonds—photography, essay writing, and drawing," adds Musial.

The Write Opportunity

As wide-ranging as leisure magazines for children, teens, and families are, the writing styles and opportunities are equally varied. *Teen People* offers little for freelancers. Coble says writers for *Bop* or *Tiger Beat* have the best chance if they live in an area where large celebrity events are held often. But writers will find their queries and articles welcome at many of the other leisure markets.

Keough says that a background in dance might be helpful but is not necessary when writing for *Young Dancer.* Her advice is "Don't talk down to children; make sure it's short, fun, solid information; and try to include quotes from interview sources."

Lavnick says writers for *Kick-Off's*

instructional articles should have a football background—experience in coaching and playing football. Articles about professional players are usually written by professional sports writers. "But new writers should feel free to query with an article idea," Lavnick says. "The best chances to break in are in writing for the news section at the front of the magazine." For Sipes at *Dogs for Kids,* the key is "Query, and write with a tight focus."

Opportunities are more abundant at publications that focus on simpler activities. Writer Shari Lyle-Soffe found success in writing craft how-to's for publications such as *Pack-O-Fun*. Her ideas often come by looking at a bunch of recyclables and trying to figure out what they look like. A pile of creamer bottles once looked like bowling pins, so Lyle-Soffe created *gnome bowling*. In her cover letter, she mentions her experience in selling home-crafted items in local malls. She pays close attention to the specific format each magazine uses for arts and crafts and follows it carefully. She says trying the project herself before submitting the article is absolutely necessary. "Sometimes a concept seems simple, but you try it and find it doesn't work."

For *Recess Time,* Musial says some of the submissions she receives are on a topic kids would enjoy, but the writing is geared toward parents. "The words might be too big or the reading level way too high for them to comprehend. I need articles written directly for the kids," she says. Writer Kevin Scott Collier matched that formula and sold Musial two articles, one on sandboarding and one on skimboarding. To enhance the appeal of the article, to the editor and to the reader, Collier says the article "even described how to make an inexpensive sandboard out of skateboard deck."

Pets, sports, outdoor activities, crafts, hobbies, and entertainment: It seems kids actually have little spare time in their lives. Savvy writers can cash in on this market and then take a little R & R for themselves—at their leisure!

Amen! Religious Fiction Gets Respect

By Judy Bradbury

Kathleen Long Bostrom, the author of nearly two dozen books, has been publishing in the Christian market for 12 years. "When I first started trying to market my children's stories, it was a tight market," recalls Bostrom. "At that time, for example, Tyndale House was receiving about 5,000 submissions and publishing only three. Since then the market has boomed. A lot more books are being published. This doesn't mean it's easier to get published," Bostrom is quick to clarify. "It just means there are more options."

Exciting, Challenging, Happening

Etta Wilson of March Media has been a literary agent for children's authors since 1994. She finds the market for religious fiction for children exciting and challenging. "At this time," she reflects, "children's publishers in the Christian market seem torn between two distinct ends. Some want to publish sweet, reassuring, nurturing products that undergird a child's faith, while others publish dark fantasy and edgy fiction depicting the reality of evil." As examples of the latter, Wilson points to Frank Peretti's most recent titles from Tommy Nelson in hardcover and trade paperback: *Hangman's Curse* and *Nightmare.* "Perhaps to offset these books, Nelson has also released a series of audio, video, and CDs by Peretti entitled *Wild and Wacky Totally True Bible Stories.*"

Graphic Bibles, such as those by Rebecca St. James and those published by Nelson, are another example of what speaks to contemporary Christian youth. To meet the needs of today's market, Wilson finds, "Writers are beginning to understand that simplistic or memory-based picture books rarely work now."

Kar-Ben, a small press that is part of the Lerner Publishing Group, publishes books on Jewish themes for children. According to Editorial Director Judye Groner, Kar-Ben "is seeking fiction that reflects where the Jewish community is today."

Groner is interested in stories about intermarriage, adoption, single parents, and gay and lesbian themes, in addition to the more traditional Hanukkah and Passover stories. "There is very little of those subjects crossing my desk," says Groner.

"The Jewish community is multicultural within our culture, and we're looking for contemporary stories to meet the needs of our readership," she says. Representative titles on Kar-Ben's upcoming lists include *Rebecca's Journey Home,* by Brynn Sugarman, about a Jewish family that adopts a Vietnamese baby.

Middle-grade fiction is a new direction Kar-Ben is exploring since joining forces with Lerner Publishing, which also publishes middle-grade fiction under the Millbrook Press imprint. "We are joining forces with the Millbrook editors in producing these novels," notes Groner. Among Kar-Ben's middle-grade titles are *Boy of Seville,* about Jewish life in post-Inquisition Spain, written by Dorit Orgad and translated by the Institute for the Translation of Hebrew Literature in Ramat Gan. Another middle-grade novel, *All-Star Brother,* by Tovah Tavin, is a contemporary story "about brotherly competition and baseball with a Jewish backdrop," reveals Groner.

Christmas, Hanukkah and More

In the preschool realm, Kar-Ben continues to be successful with its Sammy Spider series, about an arachnid that learns about the Jewish holidays by celebrating them with his human neighbors, the Shapiros. Now in its seventh installment, all books are written by Sylvia Rouss.

In picture books about Hanukkah for older children, Groner looks for stories that "tackle the issues of the experience of being a Jewish child in the midst of Christian holidays."

General publishers of books for children also continue to seek out strong Hanukkah and Christmas stories. But these days it goes beyond these two well-known holidays. Books with a range of religious themes are also crossing over into the secular market. "Mainstream publishers are more open now," believes Bostrom. "It used to be if you wrote for the Christian market, you didn't do both. Now there's an openness, a feeling that books with a religious message are acceptable and perhaps even sought out in the general market."

Wilson agrees. "We've seen a number of Thanksgiving stories with religious content recently, as well as some Easter stories about more than bunnies and eggs." One example is Mary Manz Simon's Halloween board book, *The Pumpkin Gospel: A Story of a New Start with God!,* published by Standard Publishing. In addition to fiction with Christian and Jewish perspectives, other world religions are also being represented in recent releases.

Boyds Mills Press is the publisher of *My Name Is Bilal,* written by Asma Mobin-Uddin and illustrated by Barbara Kiwak. It is a story about religious prejudice toward Muslims set in present-day America.

Dorling Kindersley has published *A Faith Like Mine: A Celebration of the World's Religions through the Eyes of Children,* written by Laura Buller. This accessible guide to religions, and their traditions and festivals, includes insights from children and color photographs of elements related to each religion. Simon & Schuster recently published *The Secret of Saying Thanks,* written by Douglas Wood and illustrated by Greg Shed, which reflects on the benefit of giving thanks and appreciation for everyday things without ascribing to one particular faith.

Magnificent Art

In addition to representing a wide spectrum of faiths, the quality of art in children's books published for the religious market has matured. Bostrom's picture book, *Josie's Gift*

the Secret of Saying Thanks
Douglas Wood
the author of Old Turtle
Greg Shed

(Broadman & Holman), illustrated by Frank Ordaz, was featured on the cover of *Publishers Weekly.* Ordaz has worked on such classic films as *E.T.* and *Return of the Jedi,* and won an ECPA Gold Medallion Award for his illustrations in *The Very First Christmas.*

Bostrom reflects that since she first entered the market in the mid-1990s, illustration in religious children's books has grown up. "The art is magnificent. There are full-color illustrations on every page, and the artwork is amazing!"

Unfortunately, as with mainstream publishing, the picture book market for religious themes is quiet. Jan Axford, Senior Acquisitions Editor at Tyndale House, sees "a decrease in the number of Christian picture books making it into the market. Instead, the focus seems to be on building youth and preteen products."

Teach Me

Of the picture books that are being published, Wilson finds, "The Christian market as a whole is turning more and more to books with a teaching component. Publishers are decreasing the number of trade picture books in favor of books with activities, comment pages for parents, or other features that offer the possibility for faith reinforcement."

The addition of back material in many children's religious fiction books augment and extend the story. "Although the story is fiction," notes Bostrom, "the back material is not. For example, I include Scripture references in the back of my Little Blessings books." This allows the books a wider audience to use the books and helps adults to help children get the most from the story's message.

This combination meets a need for many of today's young families. Wilson cites a recent poll that suggests that young parents often lack a philosophy of Christian parenting. "Many are not well-equipped, due to their having grown up in a home without much attention to religious matters. Consequently, they look to the church or to the religious school to provide their children with a faith-based foundation," she notes.

Today's parents often want material that "makes clear the elements of their faith and supports the teachings of their church." They look to publishers such as Tyndale House, which "specializes in products that will help parents pass on their faith to their children," according to Senior Editor of Children's Books and Bibles, Betty Free Swanberg. "We publish one-year devotional books for all ages, illustrated Bible storybooks, fiction for preteens, and some picture books that focus on Bible-based topics."

Wilson also sees a "disparity between parental emphasis on the more classical and biblical faith, perhaps as a means of insuring security in the face of war and calamity, and the impact of exposure to new technologies and new ideas." She goes on to say, "While technology can impart beliefs through enticing formats (other than the written word), it can also diminish the basic truth with bells and whistles or even present a radically alternative view."

The Market

Religious publishers are not unlike mainstream publishers in seeking out consumers. The home school market is one venue where religious children's books, including fiction, are actively sought out and purchased. More than 200 home school conventions take place in the U.S. every year, and religious publishers find growth in this market to be 5 to 10 percent a year, according to Wilson.

Like the trend in general publishing, many well-known authors of adult Christian books are now writing books for children. Francine Rivers, the award-winning author of historical fiction and romances, penned a Christmas picture book, *The Shoe Box: A Christmas Story* (Tyndale House).

Christian music and book company Integrity Publishers has released *On the Farm with Farmer Bob,* with the voices of Vince Gill, Amy Grant, and Randy Travis. Accompanying the video are novelty board books.

Jerry B. Jenkins, author of the Kids Left Behind series (Tyndale),

A Closer Look

Kathleen Long Bostrom's books for children have been nominated for the Evangelical Christian Publishers Association (ECPA) Gold Medallion Award, given to outstanding books in Christian publishing, and the People's Choice Award, and have sold more than one million copies since 1997. A co-pastor with her husband at Wildwood Presbyterian Church in Wildwood, Illinois, Bostrom earned a Master of Arts in Christian Education and a Master of Divinity from Princeton Theological Seminary, and a Doctor of Ministry in Preaching degree from McCormick Theological Seminary in Chicago.

Her most recent picture book, *Why Is There a Cross?* is the sixth in a question-and-answer series written in verse and published by Tyndale House. Although meant for preschoolers and beginning readers, each book includes a listing of Bible references at the back. Bostrom's editor at Tyndale, Betty Free Swanberg, says, "We make sure the stories are biblically accurate and easy for little ones to understand, but they are also fun!" This also serves to extend the readership of Bostrom's books to parents and teachers who want help in finding passages in the Bible. "I've been told they've been used as devotionals for adult Bible study, too," says Bostrom.

For Zonderkidz, Bostrom has penned a number of books, including an Easter story, various board books, and a picture book that tells the story of the origins of the Advent calendar. Her picture book *Papa's Gift* is meant to help children cope with the loss of a loved one. *When Pete's Dad Got Sick* and *The Day Scooter Died* are two titles in the Helping Kids Heal series meant to aid children dealing with divorce, loss, loneliness, and other difficult issues. At the back of the book are "guidelines written by a child psychologist for parents on how to help children understand what they are going through," explains Bostrom. In today's religious market, "values, integrity, and morals are a big trend," Bostrom is pleased to report.

recently released the Red Rock Mysteries series (Tyndale), which targets middle-grade boys.

Probably the biggest name currently in the Christian children's book market is Max Lucado. For some time, his children's books have been published by Tommy Nelson and Integrity, but recently he endorsed Little Simon Inspirations, where numerous books for young children are written by his associate, Karen Hill.

Little Simon Inspirations is an imprint of Simon & Schuster Children's Publishing that debuted in February 2005. The line of faith-based but nonsectarian novelty mass-market books has a "lighter touch" and intended for "every child every day."

Valerie Garfield, formerly of Sesame Workshop Book Group, is Vice President and Editorial Director of Little Simon. According to Lucado, "Little Simon Inspirations is an enriching new line of faith-based books that introduce, strengthen, and celebrate a child's relationship with God and prayer. Karen Hill's books . . . encourage children to learn more about Jesus and how He is presented in their everyday lives."

Eerdmans Books for Young Readers is a good example of an independent publisher of children's books that emphasizes spiritual themes. It offers picture books to young adult fiction and nonfiction for the general trade, school, and library markets. Eerdmans's guidelines say it seeks manuscripts that "celebrate the wonders of our physi-cal and spiritual world, the joys and beauty, but also the challenges. We seek stories that are honest, wise, and hopeful; but we also publish stories that delight us with their storyline, character, or good humor."

Recent Eerdmans releases include *The Jesse Tree,* written by Geraldine McCaughrean and illustrated by Bee Willey, an anthology of Bible retellings; and *The Song of Francis and the Animals,* written by Pat Mora and illustrated by David Frampton, which offers poems celebrating the popular saint.

HarperCollins imprint Laura Geringer Books has also released a picture book, *Saint Francis and the Wolf,* about the talents of this beloved hero whose words could work wonders. Another religious title on their list is *Music from Our Lord's Holy Heaven,* a collection of spirituals, psalms, and hymns written by Gloria Jean Pinkney and illustrated by Jerry Pinkney, Brian Pinkney, and Myles C. Pinkney.

Dial Books has offered the popular spiritual *He's Got the Whole World in His Hands,* by Kadir Nelson, and Random House published *Jerusalem Sky: Stars, Crosses and Crescents,* a book about the sacred city, by Mark Podwal.

The Package

In addition to mainstream book publishers, packagers seem to be more interested in the religious market of late, as evidenced by their attendance at major Christian bookseller events such as the annual International Christian Retail

Show (formerly the Christian Booksellers Association show).

"They are often creating more than books for publishers. Authors need to think when writing not just about words on a page, but also about the possibility for story development in other formats," advises Wilson, who encourages authors to consider such possibilities. "Videos, plush toys, and computer-related products are just some of the things publishers are examining to develop interest in their book product."

Zonderkidz, the children's division of Christian publisher Zondervan, publishes "developmentally appropriate, biblically based books, bibles, gifts, and videos" for children 12 and under. Anticipating the release of the feature film of *The Lion, the Witch and the Wardrobe,* based on the book from the Chronicles of Narnia series by C.S. Lewis, Zonderkidz developed an extensive array of tie-in products. Nearly 12 pages of its fall catalogue were devoted to related merchandise. In addition, Wilson reports that Tyndale House collaborated with Focus on the Family to distribute an elaborate CD set of the classic fantasy.

What's An Author to Do?

Those who publish religious fiction look first for "an enticing story," says Wilson. "Be clear about the story you want to tell, and avoid didacticism."

Swanberg at Tyndale explains, "Religious fiction must have the same appeal and quality that a parent or child would expect from secular fiction. Topics and vocabulary need to be age-appropriate. The writer needs to display a knowledge of what's cool for today's kids, how they interact, how they talk, and ways they might realistically respond to a variety of situations. In addition, the writer of religious fiction must be able to convey biblical truths in a way that kids will accept. That doesn't mean the writer has to sneak in the Christian values and truths. It does mean that the text must not have a sermon or two buried in it."

Groner says, "Your story should be concise, have interesting, believable characters, and action that holds the reader's attention. Good prose is far better than tortured verse." For Kar-Ben, she adds, "Be accurate regarding Jewish holidays and traditions, and," she cautions, "be original."

Wilson counsels, "In deciding about story content, the problem for writers becomes identifying what they themselves believe and then being free enough to create something really exciting and affirming for children." Once your story is the best it can be, endeavor to "seek publishers most suited to your story," she says.

"Look for a publishing house that creates the types of products you think you would buy for your own children," Axford recommends. "With that approach, you are sure to find a house that would be a good fit for your writing style and content."

Swanberg illustrates what she

Submission Guidelines

Boyds Mills Press is a publisher of picture books, fiction, nonfiction, and poetry for children of all ages. It accepts queries and unsolicited manuscripts. The website explains, "Fiction should tell a good story in good prose. We're looking for middle-grade fiction with fresh ideas and subject matter, and young adult novels of real literary merit." As for nonfiction submissions, they "should be fun and entertaining as well as informative" and include a detailed bibliography. "We recommend that authors rely on the most up-to-date and classic references—adult and children's. Primary sources are highly recommended. We also stress that authors should seek expert reviews as part of their research."

Send manuscripts and queries to Jeanna DeLuca, Manuscript Coordinator, Boyds Mills Press, 815 Church Street, Honesdale, Pennsylvania 18431. Include a self-addressed stamped envelope. Publisher Kent L. Brown has pledged that authors will hear at least a preliminary word on the fate of their manuscripts within 30 days of their receipt at Boyds Mills Press. General Note: If you have had writing or art published in *Highlights for Children, Teaching Pre K-8,* or Zaner-Bloser textbooks, please note that when you get in touch. For more information visit their website at www.boydsmillspress.com.

Eerdmans Books for Young Readers publishes 13 to 16 books yearly, including picture books, middle readers, and YA fiction and nonfiction for the general trade, school, and library markets. Open to unsolicited submissions, the editors prefer complete manuscripts for picture books and middle readers under 200 pages. For longer books, send a query and 3-4 sample chapters. Inform of simultaneous submissions and include a SASE. Turnaround time is 2 to 5 months. For additional guidelines, visit www.eerdmans.com/youngreaders/submit.htm. The address for submissions is Eerdmans Books for Young Readers, 255 Jefferson SE, Grand Rapids, MI 49503.

Kar-Ben publishes 8 to 10 new titles each year. Unsolicited fiction and nonfiction manuscripts are accepted, for preschool through high school. Kar-Ben is interested in reviewing holiday books, life-cycle stories, Bible tales, folk tales, board books, and activity books. In particular, "we are looking for stories that reflect the ethnic and cultural diversity of today's Jewish family." Kar-Ben does not publish games, textbooks, or books in

Submission Guidelines

Hebrew. Flat fee and royalty. Enclose a SASE. Send manuscripts to Kar-Ben Publishing, 11430 Strand Drive #2, Rockville, MD 20852-4371. The guidelines are available at www.karben.com.

Little Simon, of which Little Simon Inspirations is a part, is the mass-market imprint of Simon & Schuster Children's Publishing. It accepts agented submissions only.

Tyndale House Senior Editor of Children's Books and Bibles, Betty Free Swanberg says, "Because we were receiving an ever increasing flood of unsolicited manuscripts of which we published less than one percent, we have adopted the following policy: We accept only solicited manuscripts or proposals from agents."

Zonderkidz does not open and review any envelope or package that is not addressed to a particular individual or that does not come from an identified, recognized source. Any such packages are returned to the sender unopened; if there is no return address, packages are discarded.

Zonderkidz encourages authors to submit book proposals electronically to First Edition, the Evangelical Christian Publishers Association (ECPA) Manuscript Service on their website (www.ECPA.org). Book proposals posted on this website are available for review by all the member publishers of the ECPA, and Zonderkidz has assigned an editor to review all new proposals posted on First Edition. If you feel you must submit your book proposal directly to Zonderkidz, you may do so by faxing your proposal. Include the book title; table of contents, a two or three sentence description of each chapter; a brief description of the proposed book, including the unique contribution of the book and why you feel it must be published; your intended reader; and your *vita*, including your qualifications to write the book. The proposal should be no more than five pages. If Zonderkidz is interested in reviewing more material from you, they will respond within six weeks. Fax proposal to: Book Proposal Review Editor, 616-698-3454. E-mail proposals are not accepted.

looks for in an author by describing her working relationship with Bostrom. "Kathy Bostrom and I have worked together on a number of Little Blessings books. She is truly an editor's dream. Why? First, because her work comes in very clean. She has worked and re-worked the material until she is satisfied with it. Second, if I present some concerns to her, she is eager to work back and forth with me to make the content the best it can be for the product and the audience."

For those interested in writing for the Christian market, Wilson "heartily recommends" the recently published resource book *Imagining Faith with Kids, Unearthing Seeds of the Gospel in Children's Stories from Peter Rabbit to Harry Potter,* by Mary Margaret Keaton (Pauline Books & Media). "This book will really get a writer's mind working in several ways." And with the children's religious fiction market looking as sunny as it does, that's a very good thing.

Stage, Page, or Cinema? Choose the Best Venue for Your Plot

By Christina Hamlett

I f you've ever found yourself in the mental cul-de-sac of struggling how to start your story—or how to keep it traveling once you've begun—there's a good possibility that you're simply trying to write it in the wrong medium.

For your characters to shine, they need the spotlight of the right forum, the complement of the right frame. Just as the selection of a bad border can detract from the beauty of the painting that lies within, so can a compelling story be overlooked by potential buyers because its author didn't know the best way to frame the content.

This point is brought home on a fairly regular basis in my work as a script coverage consultant for the film industry. Many an idea that fails to ignite as a prospect for the big screen would be perfectly plausible as a stage play, novel, or short story. Making this observation to an author, however, is often akin to holding up a cross to a vampire. "But this has to be a movie!" they insist. "That's where the big money is!"

If you are faced with the decision of keeping a beloved project on the shelf indefinitely or finding an immediate and happy home for it in a market you hadn't previously considered, what is the better choice? Knowing your options—and the pros and cons inherent in each— will put you ahead of the game when it comes to embarking on a new project or rethinking one that is currently stalled.

The Limits of Your Canvas

It was Alfred Hitchcock who said that a good movie was one that could be watched without the sound. The next time you're on an airplane with in-flight movies, don't rent a headset and you'll see for yourself that this is true. Films are primarily driven by action. If one is well done, you don't have to watch it for very long to figure out who's being chased, who's doing the chasing, and who's falling in love in between.

In contrast, the measure of a good stage play is one that can be enjoyed without any visuals. (You've probably heard your grandparents talk about the good old days of radio.) Theater scripts are driven by dialogue. Even if all three acts take place in the same set, we're riveted as an audience because we care what the actors have to say and, most especially, how they say it.

Books and short stories are driven by imagination and fueled by each reader's frame of reference. Why else would they keep us up late at night, peering into dark corners for evidence of the goblins that our minds have conjured up from the printed page? Novels hold an advantage over film and theater in that they allow us to look directly into the characters' heads, hearts, and souls, as well as incorporate historical research that would be cumbersome and unrealistic to deliver in the context of dialogue.

Let's see how each of these orientations would work in the following scene (written here in screenplay format):

EXT – DESERT – DUSK
Two HORSEMEN are pursuing a third RIDER.
SFX: A single gunshot.

In only a dozen words, a picture has been painted that provides an instant hook. Put that visual up on a big screen and an audience will be hooked, too, immediately immersed in a mystery: Who are these guys? Why are they in the desert? Who fired that shot? Is someone now dead as a result?

All right, let's move this same set-up to a community theater and test its feasibility. For one thing, you're going to need a large, runway stage to accommodate those three fast-galloping horses. You'll also need a Plexiglas barrier to keep the front row from getting sand kicked in their faces. Suppose, though, you scratch the opening chase scene. Instead, you have a minor character run into the Casbah and excitedly announce to the patrons, "You'll never guess what I just saw happen out in the dunes!" Loses something, doesn't it? Each time that you tell instead of show a critical plot point, it puts the story on hold until a swift kick of action can get it rolling again. Trust me. That's not a good habit to get into.

Maybe the best option, then, is to try this as a book rather than screenplay or script. Same desert, same time of day, same trio of horsemen. Could you paint that picture for a reader if you were only allowed 12 words? The point of this, of course, is that it takes more verbiage to spell out the particulars on paper than simply to show them on a screen or stage, depending on how exact an image is desired. For instance, are the horses light or dark? If they're dark, are they brown or black? Are the riders on saddles or bareback? What are the riders wearing?

Time & Space

Literature and cinema have virtually no limits on where they can go, the latter owing much of its freedom to the advent of computer-generated wizardry. A play's parameters, however, are dictated by the physical limitations of the stage on which it will be performed. This subsequently influences the set design, size of the cast, and the feasibility of special effects (i.e., pyrotechnics, prehistoric raptors, and the supernatural).

Transitions from Point A to Point B are also handled differently in live theater. In a movie or novel, a character can walk out the door of his Chelsea flat and emerge—two frames or two paragraphs later—at a Starbucks in Cleveland. He may even have aged 20 years in the interim. In a script written for the stage, such transitions not only require a change of wardrobe and makeup, but a total redo of the set and everything in it. While some transitions can be accommodated with intermissions, you can't keep sending your audience into the lobby each time your hero walks through a door and ends up somewhere else.

On the minimalist flip side, of course, the suspension of disbelief inherent in live theater allows audiences simply to read in their theater program that a given scene is "The next morning" or "Five years later in Amsterdam," and they readily accept that a change in venue has taken place. Through the use of isolated lighting, platforms, and generically themed sets, it is the audience's imagination that fills in the blanks and minimizes the need for a complete overhaul of the existing backdrop. In the film industry, these are the very items that prove to be

the priciest and make the project more likely to garner a *no* than a *yes* from a producer with limited resources.

Time, of course, is a trickier issue to orchestrate when a performance is live. While all three media employ an accelerated pace of storytelling, books and films can flash back, fast-forward, or hover in multiple zones simultaneously. In contrast, a play is pretty much relegated to the structured increments of acts and scenes. Audiences can accept these temporal boundaries because they have already accepted the notion that 20 minutes of stage time doesn't necessarily translate to 20 minutes of real time. In fact, it probably more closely equates to dog-years; specifically, 20 minutes of theatrical dialogue would take up at least an hour and a half anywhere else.

Creating Empathy

Unless you're reading out loud in a classroom, a book is a solitary experience, one in which the reader can superimpose his or her own personality and vicariously live the plot. With a book in hand, you can skim, you can linger, you can reread favorite passages, you can envision anyone you want (including yourself) in the key roles. You can even set the whole thing aside, think about it and come back a month later to pick up where you left off.

For movies and plays, the story is being told on someone else's clock and with someone else's definition of who all the characters really are.

Jumpstart Your Imagination

The following exercise is popular in my writing workshops. (I guarantee you'll never look at a movie, play, or novel in quite the same way hereafter!) Once you've learned to identify the elements that make a particular medium work, you can apply the knowledge to an analysis of your own projects. Then play to a story's strengths, rather than trying to force it into a framework it just doesn't fit.

■ What is the most recent movie you have seen? (If you haven't been to the movies lately, pick a favorite one from the past.) List all the reasons this story is so effective or clever as a film.
■ Would this same story work as a stage play? Why or why not?
■ Would it work as a novel? Why or why not?

This exercise can also be initiated with favorite books or plays. Are they adaptable to the screen? If not, what types of changes would need to be made? Who would you cast in the lead roles? How many different locations would you need to convey the story?

There isn't as much latitude for your imagination to go wandering off to other things. This is especially true of movies, where you witness everything from just one angle and point of view: the camera's.

When it comes to stirring empathy, however, a play shares a book's capacity to engage an audience in a manner that movies cannot. Can you name a single musical, for example, that was ever made better by its adaptation to the silver screen? There's something electrifying about the presence of real bodies, real voices, real music, and real energy that even the glitziest cast-of-thousands blockbuster can't compete with. Suffice it to say, people on stage are also the same size as the people in the audience, a condition which always makes for more comfortable and immediate bonding than staring down the tonsils of a 30-foot-high face on a screen.

How deeply are we allowed to know what makes a character tick? Within the intimacy of a novel, we can literally read their thoughts and emotions at every juncture. In a play, we learn about characters gradually through the course of their conversations; we only know what they're thinking if they express it out loud to someone else or in a monologue. In a film, we tend to get more distracted by, "Oh, here's Mike Myers or Cameron Diaz in another role" than we are captivated by the background of the character they are portraying. While flashbacks and voice-overs can reveal what's on their minds, excessive use of these devices becomes confusing for audiences to follow.

Beyond the Immediate Page

If you're the type of author who likes to approach projects on the basis of a daily output quota (i.e., two pages a day no matter what), consider the following statistics in estimating how long it would take to complete your story:

- A typical screenplay is approximately 120 pages and is comprised of master scenes and dialogue. Formula: 2 pages a day equals 2 months of writing.
- A three-act play is a little shorter, with the longest act first and the balance of the show split between the remaining two (i.e., 40:30:30). Formula: 2 pages a day equals 1.6 months of writing.
- A book of about 350 pages, depending on genre, is made up of roughly 65 percent narrative and 35 percent dialogue. Formula: 2 pages a day equals 5.8 months of writing.

Since many of today's writers are looking to maximize the marketability of their plot by exploring other mediums, the question of adaptation is relevant. Right away you can see the challenge in adapting a book to a feature film; if the bulk of narrative research and inner thoughts can't be conveyed in dialogue or through the lens of a camera, out it goes. Nor can every film smoothly segue to live theater or to a paperback; the first requiring it to shrink substantially and the second demanding that it significantly expand. Clearly, the easiest transition is from a play to a film, their respective lengths and content being the most similar. Keep in mind, though, that in putting a dialogue-driven story against a bigger and more colorful backdrop, you run the risk of killing the very charm that made it accessible and unique to begin with.

News of the Year

By Heather Burns-DeMelo

Anniversaries

■ World-renowned children's book author Hans Christian Andersen was born 200 years ago. To commemorate the anniversary, his classic tales were updated. These included *Thumbelina* (Little, Brown); *The Ugly Duckling*, illustrated by Robert Ingpen (Penguin); *The Wild Swans*, translated by Naomi Lewis and illustrated by Anne Yvonne Gilbert (Barefoot Books); and *The Pea Blossom*, retold and illustrated by Amy Lowry Poole (Holiday House). Jane Yolen published the biography *The Perfect Wizard: Hans Christian Andersen*, illustrated by Dennis Nolan (Dutton).

■ Holiday House celebrated its seventieth anniversary. Its founding mission was to publish children's books exclusively; it was the first American publisher to do so. Holiday House publishes such award-winning authors and illustrators as Bruce McMillan, Paul Brett Johnson, Will Hillenbrand, Vivian Vande Velde, and Marilyn Singer.

■ Three HarperCollins imprints marked anniversaries this year. The first was Greenwillow Books, founded 30 years ago by Susan Hirschman, Ava Weiss, and Ada Shearon. They named the imprint for *Under the Green Willow*, by Elizabeth Coatsworth, a book they published together at Macmillan. The line's historic quality continues: Greenwillow published Kevin Henkes's *Kitten's First Full Moon*, the 2005 Caldecott Medal winner.

■ Laura Geringer Books, also at HarperCollins, celebrated its fifteenth anniversary. The list showcases the work of such authors and illustrators as Felicia Bond, Richard Egielski, William Joyce, Karla Kuskin, and Laura Numeroff.

▨ Ten years ago Joanna Cotler stepped down as Vice President of HarperCollins Children's Books to launch her own list of titles at the company. Cotler has worked with William Steig, Sharon Creech, Joyce Carol Thomas, Francesca Lia Block, Patricia MacLachlan, Doreen Cronin, Clive Barker, Laura Cornell, Harry Bliss, and Jamie Lee Curtis.

▨ Fifty years after Don Freeman, best known for *Corduroy*, tried to have his picture book *Earl the Squirrel* published, it was released by Viking. Plans to publish more of Freeman's work include a follow-up book in which Earl travels to Washington, DC.

▨ Children's Book Press was founded 30 years ago. Harriet Rohmer started the company when she realized that her son's schoolbooks did not represent the multicultural experiences of the students who were reading them. Children's Book Press specializes in Latino, African American, Asian American, and Native American children's literature. One of the company's titles, *Family Pictures/Cuadros de Familia*, by Carmen Lomas Garza, sold more than 420,000 copies over 15 years and was re-released this year in an anniversary edition.

▨ In honor of its fortieth anniversary, literacy organization Reading Is Fundamental partnered with Dutton Books to publish *The Art of Reading*. The book is a compilation of essays by 40 well-known children's authors and illustrators about children's stories that influenced them as artists. Original and re-imagined artwork accompanies the text.

Awards

▨ The American Library Association (ALA) John Newbery Medal was awarded to *Kira-Kira,* by Cynthia Kadohata (Atheneum), edited by Caitlin Dlouhy. The Newbery honors the author of the year's most distinguished contribution to American children's literature.

The Newbery Honor books were *Al Capone Does My Shirts,* by Gennifer Choldenko (Putnam); *The Voice That Challenged a Nation: Marian Andersen and the Struggle for Equal Rights,* by Russell Freedman (Clarion); and *Lizzie Bright and the Buckminster Boy*, by Gary D. Schmidt (Clarion).

▨ *Kitten's First Full Moon,* by Kevin Henkes (HarperCollins/Greenwillow), received the ALA's Randolph Caldecott Medal, given to the artist of the year's most distinguished American picture book for children.

Caldecott Honor books were *The Red Book,* by Barbara Lehman (Houghton Mifflin); *Coming on Home Soon,* illustrated by E.B. Lewis, written by Jacqueline Lewis (Putnam); and *Knuffle Bunny,* by Mo Willems (Hyperion).

For her lifetime contribution in writing for young adults, Francesca Lia Block received the Margaret Edwards Award from the ALA.

For excellence in young adult literature, *How I Live Now,* by Meg Rosoff (Random House/Wendy Lamb) received the ALA's Michael L. Printz Award.

The Printz Honor winners included *Lizzie Bright and the Buckminster Boy,* by Gary D. Schmidt (Houghton Mifflin/Clarion); *Chanda's Secrets,* by Allan Stratton (Annick Press); and *Airborn,* by Kenneth Oppel (HarperCollins/EOS).

The ALA Coretta Scott King Author Award was presented to Toni Morrison for *Remember: The Journey to School Integration* (Houghton Mifflin).

Honors were received by Sheila P. Moses for *The Legend of Buddy Bush* (Simon & Schuster/McElderry); Sharon G. Flake for *Who Am I Without Him? Short Stories About Girls and the Boys in Their Lives* (Hyperion/ Jump at the Sun); and Marilyn Nelson for *Fortune's Bones* (Front Street).

Kadir Nelson received the ALA Coretta Scott King Illustrator Award for *Ellington Was Not a Street,* written by Ntozake Shange (Simon & Schuster).

Illustrator Honors included *God Bless the Child,* illustrated by Jerry Pinkney, and based on the Billie Holiday spiritual (Harper/Amistad); *Jazzy Miz Mozetta,* illustrated by Frank Morrison, and written by Brenda C. Roberts (Farrar, Straus & Giroux); and *The People Could Fly,* illustrated by Leo and Diane Dillon, and written by Virginia Hamilton (Knopf).

Winners of the ALA Coretta Scott King/John Steptoe Awards for New Talent were Barbara Hathaway, author of *Missy Violet and Me* (Houghton Mifflin); and illustrator Frank Morrison for *Jazzy Miz Mozetta,* written by Brenda C. Roberts (Farrar, Straus & Giroux).

In recognition of the most distinguished informational book for children, the Robert F. Sibert Award was presented to Russell Freedman for *The Voice That Challenged a Nation: Marian Anderson and the Struggle for Equal Rights* (Clarion).

Sibert Honor Books included *Walt Whitman: Words for America,* by Barbara Kerley (Scholastic); *The Tarantula Scientist,* by Sy Montgomery (Houghton Mifflin); and *Sequoyah: The Cherokee Man Who Gave His People Writing,* by James Rumford (Houghton Mifflin).

The Society of Children's Book Writers and Illustrators (SCBWI) presented Golden Kite Awards to *Bucking the Sarge* (Wendy Lamb), by Christopher Paul Curtis, for fiction; *Dust to Eat: Drought and Depression in the 1930s* (Clarion), by Michael L. Cooper, for nonfiction; *Apples to Oregon* (Atheneum), written by Deborah Hopkinson and illustrated by Nancy Carpenter, for picture book text; and *The Mysterious Collection of Dr. David Harleyson* (Walker), written and illustrated by Jean Cassels, for best picture book illustration.

The ALA Carnegie Medal for excellence in video production for children was awarded to Paul R. Gagne and Melissa Reilly, producers of *The Dot* (Weston Woods), which was based on the book by Peter H. Reynolds.

The Shadows of Ghadames, written by Joëlle Stolz and translated by Catherine Temerson (Delacorte) won the ALA Mildred L. Batchelder Award for best work of translation. Batchelder Honors were given to *The Crow-Girl,* by Bodil Bredsdorff, translated by Faith Ingwersen (Farrar, Straus & Giroux); and *Daniel Half Human: And the Good Nazi,* by David Chotjewitz, translated by Doris Orgel (Atheneum/ Richard Jackson).

The Quill Awards are a new consumer-driven book award. Titles are nominated by booksellers and librarians and voted on by the reading public. Among the winners of the first Quills were J.K. Rowling, for *Harry Potter and the Half-Blood Prince* (Arthur A. Levine/Scholastic); Shel Silverstein, for *Runny Babbit: A Billy Sook* (HarperCollins); and Ann Brashares, for *Girls in Pants: The Third Summer of the Sisterhood* (Delacorte).

Jeanne Birdsall was the winner of the National Book Award for young people's literature, for *The Penderwicks* (Knopf). Other nominees were Adele Griffin, for *Where I Want to Be* (Putnam); Chris Lynch for *Inexcusable* (Atheneum); Walter Dean Myers for *Autobiography of My Dead Brother* (HarperTempest); and Deborah Wiles for *Each Little Bird that Sings* (Harcourt).

Winners of young readers' Edgar Awards, conferred by the Mystery Writers of America, were *Chasing Vermeer*, by Blue Balliett (Scholastic Press) for juvenile; and *In Darkness, Death*, by Dorothy and Thomas Hoobler (Philomel Books), for young adult.

Britain's Carnegie Medal was awarded to Cotrell Boyce for *Millions* (Macmillan), published by HarperCollins in the U.S. Chris Riddell received the Kate Greenaway Medal for *Jonathan Swift's Gulliver* (Walker), published in the U.S. by Candlewick.

Mergers, Acquisitions & Reorganizations

Bloomsbury Publishing, the U.K.-based publisher of the Harry Potter series, purchased Walker Publishing Company for $7 million and announced plans to expand and diversify the list. Walker President and Publisher George Gibson heads the new division and reports to Karen Rinaldi, Publisher at Bloomsbury USA. Previously a publisher of fiction primarily, Bloomsbury is growing to include children's nonfiction and school and library titles in part through its acquisition of Walker.

▧ Harcourt Children's Books consolidated and it dissolved its Gulliver Books imprint. All original children's books are now listed under the Harcourt Children's Book name. Allyn Johnston is Editor in Chief, and former Editorial Director of Gulliver Books Liz Van Doren became Editorial Director of Harcourt Books.

▧ Scholastic purchased Chicken House Publishing and formalized its four-year partnership with the British company. Chicken House publishes 20 titles per year as an imprint of Scholastic's trade book division. Chicken House founder Barry Cunningham is Publisher and Managing Director and reports to Ellie Berger, Senior Vice President of Scholastic Trade Books.

▧ Random House Ventures purchased American Reading Company, a standards-based learning system to improve students' reading and comprehension skills. Its 16,000 leveled books are read by 150,000 students. Founder Jane Hileman hopes to reach a million students in the next five years.

▧ House of Anansi Press, based in Toronto, acquired Groundwood Books from Patsy Aldana and Douglas & McIntyre. The purchase added a children's division of 600 titles and more than doubled House of Anansi's sales. Aldana remains as

head of Groundwood Books. Distribution for Groundwood and Anansi is handled by HarperCollins Canada.

▧ Facts on File, the publisher of print and electronic references owned by Veronis Suhler Stevenson, purchased Chelsea House from Haight Cross Communications. Chelsea House is now a subsidiary and has added 3,000 titles to the 1,500-title Facts on File back-list.

▧ The St. Paul, Minnesota, educational publisher EMC/Paradigm Publishing was sold to the New York City-based equity firm, the Wick's Group, for $44.1 million. It joined Delta Education, Educators Publishing, and Modern Learning Press in the group's education publishing arm. Targeting the high school and post-secondary school markets, EMC/Paradigm's focus is foreign language, literature, business, and health. Founder David Feinburg retired and former Senior Vice President at McGraw-Hill Education Stephen Van Thournout was named President and CEO.

▧ Bain Capital purchased School Specialty, a supplemental education publisher. Bain added it to McGraw-Hill's Children's Publishing unit. It was the investment firm's fifth acquisition in the education field.

In turn, School Specialty bought Delta Education from the Wicks Learning Group. Delta's materials for elementary school science curricula bolstered School Specialty's Frey Scientific line. A Publishing

Service division was also part of the acquistion of Delta Education.

▨ Random House expanded with the purchase of contemporary fantasy publisher Wizards of the Coast. Also a producer of tie-in products and role-playing games, Wizards of the Coast and its young adult imprint, Mirrorstone, published 600 titles.

▨ Scholastic partnered with the American Museum of Natural History to form a Science Exploration Program. As part of the new program, Scholastic's *SuperScience* and *Science World* magazines report on the latest museum events. The magazines reach more than 1.5 million students and teachers each month. Exclusive educational material developed by museum scientists and Scholastic is available on the publisher's website, and six special editions of the magazines feature museum exhibitions.

▨ Aspire Media acquired craft and hobby book and magazine publisher Interweave Press. The CEO of Aspire Media is Clay Hall. Founder of Interweave, Linda Ligon, remains with the company as Creative Director.

▨ Children's book publisher Shoe String Press ceased operations. Owner Diantha Thorpe decided against selling outright and sold titles off to various parties. Its refer-

ence line was acquired by EBSCO, and August House purchased several titles from Shoe String's children's imprint, Linnet Books.

▨ Computer book publisher Charles River Media became an imprint of educational publisher Thomason Delmar Learning. Charles River specializes in titles for professional game developers and brings with it a 200-title back-list. The increasing number of institutions offering courses on games was behind the purchase.

▨ WRC Media sold AGS Publishing to Pearson Learning Group. AGS Publishing's student assessment and instruction materials had netted a 20 percent increase in profits the year preceding purchase.

Launches and Ventures

Books

▨ Disney launched a new product line with the introduction of *Fairy Dust and the Quest for the Egg,* written by Gail Carson Levine and illustrated by David Christiana. The novel, which stars Peter Pan and Tinker Bell, is the first in a newly created adventure series. The book and merchandise line enjoyed an

international launch party and garnered promotion from Disney
theme parks, cruises, ABC Family,
and Disney Radio. Random House
expanded the series with tie-ins in
chapter book format.

■ HarperCollins joined forces
with the Smithsonian Institution to
create a new education imprint,
Smithsonian Books. The publisher
has also taken responsibility from
W.W. Norton & Co. for distribution
of the Smithsonian Institution
Press's 200-title backlist, which
brings with it a 158-year academic
publishing history. Formerly Director of Smithsonian Institution Press,
Don Fehr is Publisher of the new
imprint. Smithsonian Books is publishing about 100 adult titles in
2006 on science, U.S. history, natural history, Native American history, art and design, as well as biographies and popular reference
books. Plans also include adding
children's and Latino titles.

■ Holiday House launched a paperback line after 70 years of exclusively publishing hardcovers. *The
Word Eater,* by Mary Amato, inspired the line. Holiday House
hopes to increase its sales in bookstores by offering reprints and original titles in paperback.

■ *The Norton Anthology of Children's Literature,* compiled by Jack
Zipes, is a 2,471-page volume that
spans 350 years of children's literature and features 170 authors and
illustrators. It is the first ever anthology devoted solely to children's
literature. Marketed as a trade and
educational title, it carries a price
tag of just over $76.

■ Little, Brown Books for Young
Readers launched LB Kids. The new
imprint features interactive and
novelty books, including *The Cranium Big Book of Outrageous Fun,*
an activity book that follows the
Cranium board-game format.

Little, Brown also made high-
profile acquisitions from Marc
Brown, Patrick Carman, Jerry
Spinelli, and Rosemary Wells, with
all books set to be released in 2007.

■ Anne Schwartz and Lee Wade
left Simon & Schuster for positions
at Random House, where they
teamed up to head the new imprint, Schwartz & Wade Books. Its
first list comprised four picture
books, with work by authors and illustrators such as Tad Hills, Deborah
Hopkinson, James E. Ransome,
Ronnie Shotter, Giselle Potter, and
Valorie Fisher. Schwartz & Wade
Books will publish 20 hardcover
books each year.

■ Ginee Seo, former Associate
Publisher of the Simon & Schuster
imprint Atheneum Books for Young
Readers, now has an eponymous
line. Ginee Seo Books focuses on
young adult fiction. *Sign of the
Raven,* by Julie Hearn, was among
the titles on its inaugural list.

■ A healthy religious market
prompted Simon & Schuster to

launch Little Simon Inspirations for young readers. Nine spiritual-based titles were released initially; the line will publish four to six titles a season. Robin Corey is Executive Vice President, and Valerie Garfield is Vice President and Editorial Director.

Joanna Bicknell has founded the U.K.-based children's book publishing house Make Believe Ideas, which will publish 40 books a year. Its books focus on early-learning concepts appropriate for children in infancy through age eight. Bicknell was formerly Dorling Kindersley's Business Development Director. Former President of Dorling Kindersley Publishing Danny Gurr is now Director of U.S. operations for Make Believe Ideas.

Gary June is the newly appointed CEO of Dorling Kindersley (DK). He headed Pearson's computer game publisher, BradyGames, and has held several executive positions at Pearson. As CEO, he divides his time between DK's U.S. and U.K. offices.

Running Press launched Word World, a series of interactive board books and magnetic toys targeting children ages three to six. Building on the interactive nature of reading, the books create connections between letters, words, and real world objects.

Running Press also joined with PBS to co-produce a new animated television series that will air in spring 2007.

Amazon.com celebrated its tenth year in business and broadened its scope this year with the acquisition of print-on-demand (POD) and vanity publisher, BookSurge. BookSurge boasts more than 10,000 titles. Amazon also acquired the e-book company MobiPocket.

Well-known television animators are now among the artists illustrating preschool picture books for the new Random House imprint, Bolder Books for Boys and Girls, in conjunction with new animation company Bolder Media for Boys and Girls. The imprint will produce books that cross media lines from print to television and film. The first four titles are set to launch in spring 2007.

Luna Rising is the new imprint of bilingual publisher Rising Moon, which is the children's division of Arizona-based Northland Publishing. Luna Rising features picture books, including fiction and biography, and is publishing two to four titles a year.

PowerHouse Books has a new imprint, PowerHouse Kids. Its focus is self-help books that teach life skills. Children's author and human development expert Joy Berry kicked off the list with *Mine & Yours: Human Rights for Kids,* and a series that includes *Get Over It!, Work It!,* and *Go For It!* Also on the list is the Nicky the Jazz Cat series, by author/photographer Carol Friedman.

Language and travel publisher Berlitz Publishing launched a new line of educational products for children ages three and under, Baby Berlitz on Board. The line's Talk & Tunes CDs and Talking Board Books focus on cognitive skills and language development in English and Spanish. The concept was conceived by Editorial Director and mother Sheryl Olinsky Borg while on maternity leave.

Some of HarperCollins best-known children's titles are now featured in Spanish. Former children's Review Editor at *Criticas*, Adriana Dominguez is in charge of expanding the Spanish-language program. HarperCollins is tripling its annual Spanish-language titles from 5 to 15 and offering more original titles.

The nonprofit organization What Kids Can Do launched Next Generation Press, a publisher devoted to teens' commentary. *What We Can't Tell You: Teenagers Talk to the Adults in Their Lives*, by Karen Cushman, was one of three books

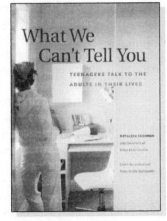

on the inaugural list. Next Generation is a grant-funded organization.

Scholastic's Spanish-language distribution unit, Lectorum Publications, is the new distributor of Fondo de Cultural Economica's children's and young adult titles. Fondo de Cultural Economica is one of Mexico's top publishers.

Magazines

Targeting parents of children from birth to age six, the Disney Family and Children's Magazine Group launched *Wondertime*, an early learning magazine targeting parents of preschoolers. It is currently published quarterly but will increase in frequency to 10 times a year. Topics include getting children ready for school, healthy eating habits, and parenting issues associated with raising three- to six-year-old children.

FGBG (For Girls By Girls) is a new magazine that provides a forum for young women between the ages of 13 and 20 to share their personal experiences and opinions about family, relationships, and emotional issues.

Outdoor adventurers between the ages of 18 and 26 are the target of *ASX*, a new lifestyle magazine featuring the latest trends, equipment, and apparel associated with outdoor pursuits such as snowboarding, rock climbing, kite boarding, and surfing. Brian Metzler is Editor in Chief.

Young Gay America is a new bimonthly for gay and lesbian teens that features articles, interviews, profiles, games, advice, and reviews on topics of interest.

Discover Media purchased 25-year-old *Discover* magazine from Disney Publishing Worldwide. Founder of Discover Media, Bob Guccione Jr. said he created the company with the intention of buying the adult science magazine. *Discover* has a circulation of 860,000 and was sold off by Disney as it hones in on publishing magazines for children and families.

The new online magazine *Rainbow Rumpus* is aimed at children 6 to 12 with lesbian, gay, bisexual, or transgender parents. The monthly features one story written for 6- to 7-year-olds, one for ages 8 to 10, and one for 11 to 12.

MotherVerse, a new quarterly literary magazine, examines motherhood from a global perspective. Articles, essays, stories, reflections, and book reviews make up the editorial content.

Professionals and executives who became stay-at-home mothers are the target audience of the quarterly *Total 180!* It features articles on new roles, identity shifts, relationships, finance, and mental and emotional issues.

Navigo is a new education magazine providing families who homeschool with information on travel, news, educational products, and family events associated with independent learning. Exclusive online content is available to subscribers at navigo-online.com.

Eclectron Publishing Group has a new online magazine for girls called *Young-Expressions*. Its mission is to foster expression, self-acceptance, and creativity in adolescents.

STACK is a new magazine for high school athletes who want to improve their athletic performance. It features information on training, nutrition, and athletic skills from coaches, trainers, and athletes.

Y.L is a new quarterly targeting African American girls 13 to 18. Its mission is to counter stereotyping by educating and inspiring readers. It offers articles on dating, school, fashion, beauty, entertainment, health/fitness, community service, and current events.

The lifestyle magazine *Cookie* showcases upscale children's toys, furnishings, and apparel. It offers information on such subjects as travel with children and themed birthday parties. Helen Schifter is Contributing Editor.

Gwinnet Parents Magazine focuses on how local issues in this Georgia county affect area parents. The bimonthly is available at local businesses and by subscription.

Riot is an online magazine that features political and satirical editorial content. Its mission is to provide free press to young people whose views, the editors believe, are not being accurately represented by other publications. The Dublin, Ireland-based editors remain anonymous.

▓ *GRAND* is a new bimonthly that focuses on practical issues associated with grandparenting. Tips on child safety, long-distance relationships, and finance are featured.

Multimedia

▓ Alloy Entertainment divided into separate operations. Its retail merchandise line is no longer part of the main company. The book publishing and packaging division remained part of Alloy, Inc.

▓ Two months after Scholastic's release of J.K. Rowling's *Harry Potter and the Half-Blood Prince,* the sixth book in the series, Apple purchased audio rights from Random House to download all six audiobooks onto iPods through iTunes. *The Half-Blood Prince* boasted a 10.8 million first printing.

▓ Fisher-Price and Scholastic became partners to create interactive DVDs for young children. The Read with Me DVD! series teaches comprehension and vocabulary to children ages three to seven by means of animated classic stories. The Ready for School: Clifford series helps preschoolers prepare for school by focusing on basic social, academic, and physical skills.

▓ More than 60 years after his debut, Curious George is making a comeback in book, film, and television. Houghton Mifflin published *The Journey that Saved Curious George,* written by Louise Borden and illustrated by Allan Drummond. The book is the true story of how Curious George authors Margret and H.A. Rey fled Paris by bicycle shortly before the Nazi invasion in 1940. An animated film starring George and featuring Will Ferrell as the Man with the Yellow Hat has a 2006 release date. In fall 2007, PBS plans to air a television series featuring George that teaches preschoolers math and science.

▓ Reader's Digest Children's Publishing released a book and DVD program aimed at children up to eight years old. Among the premier titles are Fisher-Price Flashcards and DVD, and *Elmo's Easy as ABC* book and DVD. Future plans include expanding the program from branded material to original titles.

Other News

▓ In a landmark class action settlement following the Supreme Court decision in Tasini v. *The New York Times,* more than $10 million was awarded to thousands of freelance writers. Tasini and the related class action suit focused on writers whose work was used in electronic databases without their permission.

Scholastic and its subsidiaries, Scholastic-at-Home and Grolier, paid $710,000 to settle FTC charges that it did not provide consumers with details about membership to its negative option book clubs.

People

Books

Andrea Pinkney left her position as Publisher of the Houghton Mifflin children's book group after deciding not to move with the offices from New York to Boston. Pinkney moved to Scholastic Trade as Vice President of hardcover and early childhood material.

Alan Smagler was appointed to the position of Vice President and Publisher of Houghton Mifflin's Children's Book Group. He oversees the group's three children's imprints, Houghton Mifflin Books for Children, Clarion Books, and Kingfisher Publications. Smagler's most recent position was as Associate Publisher of Simon & Schuster's Children's Publishing Division where he launched Simon Spotlight.

Lisa Holton stepped down as Senior Vice President and Publisher of Disney Global Children's Books and joined Scholastic as President of its children's book publishing and distribution. She replaced Barbara Marcus, who left Scholastic after a 22-year career. Marcus is credited with increasing the company's revenues tenfold.

Scholastic Library Publishing, which includes Franklin Watts and Children's Press, hired Amy Shields for the position of Editorial Director.

Disney Global Children's Books appointed Brenda Bowen as its new Associate Publisher and Editor in Chief. She had been with Hyperion and Simon & Schuster Kids' trade book division.

Rubin Pfeffer was named Senior Vice President and Publisher of Simon & Schuster Kids' trade publishing and acquired some of Brenda Bowen's responsibilities. Pfeffer oversees and coordinates the children's hardcover and paperback lines. He reports to Rick Richter.

Valerie Garfield was promoted to Vice President and Publisher of Simon Spotlight and Little Simon.

HarperCollins Children's Book executives Mara Anastas and Mary McAveney left the company to fill positions at Simon & Schuster. Anastas was appointed Vice President of sales and subsidiary rights, and McAveney is the new Vice President of marketing. Both report to President and Publisher, Rick Richter.

Judy O'Malley was promoted to Editor at Farrar, Straus & Giroux Books for Young Readers.

Suzanne Murphy stepped down from her position of Vice President of marketing at Simon & Schuster's Children's Publishing group and is now Vice President of trade marketing at Scholastic. Murphy reports to Senior Vice President of trade publishing, Ellie Berger.

Former Publisher of University Games and Ten Speed Press, Kirsty Melville is now Publisher of Andrews McMeel's book division. She replaced Tom Thornton, and reports to new President Hugh Andrews.

Jon Rosenberg has acquired the position of Editorial Director of the imprint Simon Scribbles.

Justin Chanda joined Atheneum Books for Young Readers as the new Executive Editor.

Susan Canavan was promoted to Senior Editor at Houghton Mifflin and is developing a list of titles.

The new Editor at Houghton Mifflin is Monica Perez. She had been with Candlewick Press.

Editor of five *New York Times* best sellers, David Hirshey has been promoted to Senior Vice President at HarperCollins.

Ellen Stamper, who previously worked for Scholastic, G.P. Putnam's Sons, and Nickelodeon Books, left her most recent position as Publisher of Paint Chip Productions and was named Editorial Director of the HarperFestival group.

Allyn Johnston was promoted to the new position of Editor in Chief of Harcourt Children's Books.

Former Editorial Director of Gulliver Books, Liz Van Doren, is the new Editorial Director of Harcourt Children's Books. Van Doren also heads the Red Wagon imprint and reports to Publisher Lori Benton.

Evan St. Lifer left a 10-year stint with *School Library Journal* to become the new Vice President and General Manager of Scholastic Library Publishing. St. Lifer oversees the editorial, marketing, and sales departments. He reports to President Greg Worrell.

Brian Kenney is the new Editor in Chief at *School Library Journal*.

Sterling Publishing hired Meredith Mundy Wasinger as Senior Editor. She is developing a list of nonfiction activity books, how-to titles, and picture books.

Kathy Dawson ended a 17-year stint at G.P. Putnam's Sons and joined Harcourt as Associate Editorial Director.

The Time Warner Book Group hired Nora Rawlinson for the newly created position of Vice President of Library Services, which will focus on children's and academic markets. Rawlinson had been the Editor in Chief at *Publishers Weekly*.

The new Executive Editor at G.P. Putnam's Sons is Timothy Travaglini. He had been Editor at Walker Books for Young Readers.

Mary E. Gruetzke left Scholastic to replace Timothy Travaglini at Walker Books for Young Readers, as the new Senior Editor.

Cecile Goyete stepped down from her position as Senior Editor at Dial Books and is Senior Editor at Knopf.

Emerson Blake stepped down as Editor in Chief of Milkweed Editions to become Editor in Chief of the literary arts magazine *Orion*. He reclaimed his position as Executive Director of the Orion Society, where he had been prior to joining Milkweed in 2003.

Sam Moore remains chairman at Thomas Nelson, but stepped down as CEO. Michael Hyatt was named the new CEO.

David Linker is the new Editorial Director at InnovativeKids.

Magazines

Lori Majewski is Managing Editor at *Teen People*. Its new Deputy Editor is Laura Morgan.

ELLEgirl appointed Christina Kelly as Editor in Chief.

Betty Wong stepped down from her position as Executive Editor at *Working Mother* and is now the Executive Editor of *Family Circle*. Linda Fears is the new Editor in Chief of *Family Circle*. Darcy Jacobs is Articles Editor.

The new Senior Articles Editor at *Parenting* is Deborah Skilnik.

Diane Debrovner was named Health and Psychology Editor of *Parents*. The new Associate Editor is Ilisa Cohen.

The new Features Editor at *Teen Vogue* is Leigh Belz.

Closings

Books

- Dandy Lion Publications
- Gulliver Books
- Harcourt Canada
- Munchweiler Press
- Riverfront Books
- Shoe String Press
- Stiles-Bishop Productions
- XC Publishing

Magazines

- *American Kids Parenting*
- *And Baby*
- *Children's Magic Window*
- *Church Worship*
- *Class Act*
- *Discovery Trails*
- *Gball*
- *In the Family*
- *Northwest Family News*
- *Parents' Monthly*
- *Pray Kids!*
- *World Kid Magazine*
- *YM*

Deaths

Teacher and illustrator Thomas B. Allen died at age 76. His illustrated books included the award-winning *In Coal Country,* by Judith Hendershot (Knopf). Allen's most recent illustrations were for *Grandma's General Store: The Ark,* by Dorothy Carter (Farrar, Straus & Giroux).

▨ Pierre Berton, Canadian-born author, journalist, and historian, died at age 84. Considered by many as Canada's best-known author, he earned more than 30 literary awards and more than a dozen honorary degrees for writing on Canada's history, people, and culture. His children's classic, *The Golden Trail,* was recently republished by Fitzhenry & Whiteside.

▨ James A. Houston, writer and illustrator of children's books, died at age 83. He is the only three-time recipient of the Canadian Library Association Book of the Year for Children Award. Houston's work portrayed Inuit art and culture and reflected his ten-year stay in the Arctic region.

▨ Trina Schart Hyman, award-winning children's illustrator, died at age 65. She was *Cricket*'s first art director and illustrated more than 150 children's books. Her *Saint George and the Dragon*, written by Margaret Hodges, won the 1985 ALA Caldecott Medal. Hyman garnered three Caldecott Honors including the retelling of *Little Red Riding Hood; Herschel and the Hanukkah Goblins,* written by Eric A. Kimmel; and *A Child's Calendar*, a book of poems by John Updike. *Goddess Stories*, written by

Hyman's daughter Katrina Tchana and illustrated by Hyman, was published by Scholastic Press posthumously.

▨ Nancy Larrick, an editor, writer, and devoted literacy advocate, died at age 93. Larrick was an editor for children's magazines, a children's book editor at Random House, and a published author. She also founded the International Reading Association, which today serves over 80,000 members in 99 countries around the world.

▨ Pioneering science fiction and fantasy author Andre Alice Norton died at 93. She authored more than 160 novels, anthologies, and collections during her 70-year career. In her honor, Fantasy Writers of America created the Andre Norton Award to recognize excellence in science fiction and fantasy for young adults.

▨ Publisher, author, and a leader in science fiction, illustrated-book, and graphic-novel publishing, Byron Preiss died at age 52. He developed books for Random House, Rizzoli, and HarperCollins and worked with such well-known authors as Arthur C. Clarke and Isaac Asimov. Many argue that *Red Tide*, written by Jim Steranko and published by Preiss, was one of the first graphic novels. From collaborations with Marvel to e-books, Preiss was a contemporary publishing pioneer.

▨ Illustrator, teacher, and co-founder of Graphic Studios, Ted

Rand died at age 89. He began illustrating children's books in his 60s and collaborated with such authors as Eve Bunting, Jean Craighead George, and Bill Martin Jr. Henry Holt published his most recent work, *A Pen Pal for Max*, posthumously.

Mystery author of 100 books, Willo Davis Roberts died at age 76. She spent the last 30 years writing for children, and her young adult mysteries *Twisted Summer* (Atheneum), *The Absolutely True Story . . . How I Visited Yellowstone Park with the Terrible Rubes* (Atheneum), and *Megan's Island* (Atheneum), received Edgar Awards. Roberts' first novel, *Murder at Grand Bay,* dates back to 1955.

Characters

Silver Spoon or Wrong Side of the Tracks?

By Kristi Collier

Rich or poor? Stable family or dysfunctional? Popular with peers or a loner? All of these considerations and more go into creating a character. Writers and editors must work to ensure that each character's social environment is not only believable, but that it contributes to the theme of the story. Social pressures impact and influence characters, and in turn, characters often shape and counterbalance social pressures.

In day-to-day life, children and teens are affected by their social situations. Shannon Barefield, Editorial Director of Carolrhoda Books, says that it's essential for an author to develop a convincing social milieu. "One of the essential struggles of being a teenager is how to define yourself as a growing, changing individual in the face of deeply powerful social forces: your friends, your family, your home."

Like real people, characters do not live in a vacuum. Their interactions with their culture, with their society, and with their friends and family contribute to the whole of the character.

"We are cultural animals," says Janet Tashjian, author of a number of social novels, including *The Gospel According to Larry, Vote for Larry,* and *Fault Line.* She explains that society's rules, and how an individual character translates those rules, impact how a character is shaped and what choices he or she makes. "Different characters in different environments will make different choices."

Know the Backstory

The life a character led before the day he or she steps foot into the pages of a novel plays an important role in shaping the fictional personality. In what type of society was the character reared? Did he confront any major life changes? What were his relationships with family and friends?

Elaine Marie Alphin's recently released novel from Carolrhoda Books, *The Perfect Shot,* introduces the reader to characters whose backstories all contribute to their current social environment and to the book's theme of determining right versus wrong.

"I put a lot of effort into backstory," Alphin writes. "I work to understand the characters' families and how they feel about their families, where they live and how they feel about living there, their friends and how they feel about their friends. I don't think many writers put enough effort into understanding the backstory."

Such effort put into understanding the characters' histories and environments and psychologies takes on major importance in *The Perfect Shot*. The characters in the novel all have different ideas of what is right and what is wrong. "Right and wrong isn't always clear, and it isn't always something people agree on," Alphin says. "Their beliefs are impacted through their backgrounds."

Different authors have different techniques for getting to know their characters. Elsa Marston, author of several novels, including *Figs and Fate* and *The Ugly Goddess,* says that she starts by deciding on a few basic facts: gender, age, where and when the character lives, type of family, and general social status. Then she begins to write. "At a later stage, when rewriting, I often think in more detail about the main character, jot down what they want, their fears, the way they see themselves, how they relate to other characters. For me, it works to do that after the characters have started to live."

Rebecca O'Connell's first novel, *Myrtle of Willendorf,* started as a writing exercise in which she began to explore the character's history. "It turned into a character sketch, and then into a character, and then into a book."

Tashjian says that getting to know a character and that character's history and backstory is almost a physical process. "I spend a lot of time writing and letting the character talk to me. Even if I have a story idea that I want to write about, I'll let it germinate for a while. I won't start it until I have a character popping."

By the time a character makes it to the printed page, the writer must have a clear understanding of how that character's past life and social situation impacts personality, beliefs, and actions.

Research

Once a character's past and present are established, it is often necessary to do extensive research to make sure that character's environment rings true. Whether the novel is set in the present day or in ancient Egypt, in America or in Lebanon, authors are unanimous on the need for research in order to depict that environment accurately.

For *The Ugly Goddess,* set in ancient Egypt, Marston needed to research the physical environment of the story as well as the social environment. One of the main characters, Meret, is a princess who is to be married to a god—not a familiar situation to any of her readers.

"Both Elsa and I wanted to show

how Meret had been groomed to feel pride and dignity in spending the whole of her adult life confined to a temple, but at the same time we wanted the idea to terrify her, as it would most any teenager today," says Carol Saller, who edited *The Ugly Goddess* and who is currently a Senior Manuscripts Editor with the University of Chicago Press.

She commends Marston's research and attention to detail. "As Elsa's editor, I felt equally responsible for the accuracy, but Elsa's an expert on ancient Egypt and I'm not. So I gave the book to an Egyptologist at the University of Chicago to read. He found the book to be remarkably accurate."

For *Figs and Fate,* a collection of short stories set in the Middle East, Marston visited the region, observed children, and interacted with local residents. "I almost never write about a place that I have not visited," Marston says. In addition, she keeps extensive journals and does secondary book research.

"When depicting foreign environments, I feel that it is very important that the author have firsthand experience with these environments," says Tara Zapp, Associate Editor and Publicist at George Braziller, which published *Figs and Fate.* "Elsa attended the University of Beirut, where she met her husband. She has since traveled extensively throughout the Middle East. I was confident in Elsa's ability to accurately depict these settings in *Figs and Fate.*"

Tashjian also believes in the

need for research into the character's social environment. "I do a ton of research," she says. "For *Fault Line,* I talked to a lot of stand-up comics, went to a ton of clubs and stayed in San Francisco."

Alphin cites the adage to "write what you know." *The Perfect Shot* is set in Indiana and focuses on basketball. "I didn't have to do a lot of nominal research about Indiana because I knew it.

I was able to depict the honest minutiae of day-to-day life because that's the environment in which I live day to day. Basketball, on the other hand, was something I remembered from my own middle school days, but I had to research the way it's played today in Indiana."

Whether a writer has experienced the social setting of a book firsthand or has traveled many miles, read countless books, and conducted numerous interviews to gain knowledge of that environment, research is necessary to describe that world accurately to the reader.

The Character's World

Once a writer has a handle on the character's backstory and has researched the story's environment, it must then be communicated to the reader. "If I know the backstory well enough and I know the characters well enough, then depicting their environment is second nature," says Alphin.

O'Connell mentions the importance of using specifics to show a character in particular surroundings and situations. "One good trick is to appeal to all the senses. When Myrtle visits Sam's restaurant, we see the décor, hear the conversation, feel and taste the food."

These physical details, used by O'Connell in *Myrtle of Willendorf* and other books, often give the reader a sense of the character's social environment as well. A description of a squalid physical setting—cramped living quarters, dirt and dust, shortages of food or other necessities—indicates to the reader that the character is living in poverty and may be worried about how to meet basic needs. Large homes, manicured lawns, and gourmet food usually indicate a life of wealth and leisure. A character's socioeconomic status shapes that character's personality and influences his or her choices.

Marston draws on her extensive knowledge of the Middle East to include important sensory details about characters' physical environments. In the *Figs and Fate* short story, "The Plan," her visits to several refugee camps allowed her to provide specifics that show the bleakness of a camp and its social, political, and economic aspects. On the other hand, Marston's relationships with members of the upper-middle class in Beirut provided the appropriate details to describe Aneesi's social situation in "Hand of Fatima."

The physical environment, a novel's setting, is often essential to the action and to a character's social situation. In *The Perfect Shot,* Barefield says that the small-town Indiana setting is seamlessly integrated into the storytelling. "Brian is a product of his environment, and a major part of his growing up is coming to terms with what he loves about it and why he may not want to leave it behind."

The work a character does also communicates information about social status. Saller emphasizes that social environment is a factor in the formation of a person's habits and opinions. "In *The Ugly Goddess,* the lower-class character Bata is perhaps most true to the historical period, dutifully sweeping the shop, longing for something that he can't articulate or realistically hope for."

Tashjian also recognizes the importance of a character's choice of work. "I come at the world of the character through their work. How the characters choose to spend their time is how I get to know them, through their jobs—be it stand-up comedy, working in a Goodwill store, or blogging."

Dialogue and interaction with other characters is another tool that writers use to show characters' social environments and how they are influenced by those environments. Barefield describes the way that Alphin showed a change in one of the characters of *The Perfect Shot* as a result of a negative social interaction experienced by that character. "Julius makes a decision to adopt a different persona, one he's absorbed mainly through media rather than personal experience. Elaine and I found that Brian's own voice was the best tool for making these changes convincing. We needed to hear Brian's shock and confusion at seeing his friend change so radically and in such a seemingly forced way. His responses function as context clues to help the reader better understand both boys."

Interaction between characters often provides a social catalyst, one that O'Connell used to depict social environment in *Myrtle of Willendorf*. "The tension between Myrtle and her roommate, Jada, is an important part of the story," says O'Connell. "If they didn't live together, and if Jada's boyfriend weren't always around (often naked) in their apartment, there wouldn't be as much tension."

A character's family and friends play an important role in the shaping of a character's personality and decisions. Those relationships are presented through dialogue, narrative, and interaction, and they cause a character to make important social decisions. Barefield says that these familial tensions are familiar to many readers. "In what ways do you want to be like your parents? In what ways do you want to be different? And can you choose to be different but still maintain strong ties to your parents?"

The Cauldron

People are social animals who live under the rules that society imposes. Take one specific but major example.

"How men are raised in the culture affects how your boyfriend treats you," Tashjian says. "What's the role of a 17-year-old in society? The rules that society puts on certain characters and the way they translate those rules impacts the choices they make. Those rules come into play in the shaping of all of the characters."

A character's growth and change throughout a book often stems from interaction with these larger social forces. "Only so much change can happen spontaneously and internally," says O'Connell. "The rest has to come from the environment, whether that be personal relationships, societal expectations, or physical setting."

"The environment is extremely crucial," says Zapp. "It is the setting that is responsible for the majority of a character's personality."

Characters often fight against the setting in which they find themselves and push against the rules and the roles that are imposed on them. It is this fight and this push that cause a character to come to a deeper understanding of what he or she really wants out of life. This understanding often leads to growth and change.

In *Figs and Fate,* Marston uses different environments in two short stories to show character growth. In "The Plan," the bleak environment of the refugee camp has a marked effect on the main character. "Rami's environment and his determination to rise above it are critical elements of the story," says Marston. His environment doesn't change his personality, but his good nature and determination allow him to strive to overcome the punishing effects of his environment. "Rami grows by trying to rise above his environment."

In "The Hand of Fatima," the main character is from a poor Syrian family and works as a maid in a wealthy Lebanese household. "Aneesi grows by trying to rise to her new environment. It offers her the chance to develop her abilities and become someone quite different from what she would likely become in her home environment," says Marston. The social and physical environments and Aneesi's desire to profit from them are vital elements of the story.

In *The Ugly Goddess,* Bata is a character from a poor background who reveres the goddess as a result of his training. "His growth and change are in keeping with his upbringing and passions," says Saller. The princess, Meret, is from a privi-

leged and educated background but also struggles with the role she is expected to take in society. She ultimately changes that role.

Characters in a novel live in a cauldron in which social forces are at work—shaping them and being shaped by them. "All of the characters are impacted by this cauldron," says Alphin. "The characters change because of the events in their lives, and in turn their changes reshape their environment."

Thou Shalt Not Moralize

By Katherine Swarts

In the early days of children's books, the nineteenth and early twentieth centuries, most writers considered it their duty to teach children good behavior. The typical children's story was a moral treatise thinly disguised as melodrama, emphasizing the values of piety, obedience, and virtue in a form only slightly removed from a lecture. Most such stories featured sweet, innocent, too-good-to-be-true heroes; some featured naughty children who got what they deserved in ways we would now consider R-rated. Side remarks to the reader, such as, "You'd never do this, would you?" were a matter of course.

While a few writers of those early days—Beatrix Potter, Lewis Carroll, and Frances Hodgson Burnett, for example—managed to turn out classics, most sweet, moralistic books have gone the way of the corset. When better books became available—books where children seemed real, neither monsters nor angels, but people who could learn and grow in the course of the story—cute and preachy books were largely forgotten. Today, such books are relegated to rare book and sociological history collections.

The moralistic tome disguised as fiction died out for the same reason weighty, preachy books don't sell to adults. Children are as fully human as adults, and human nature resents being lectured, talked down to, or exposed to know-it-alls. Children already have to put up with this on a regular basis. "Shouldn't you be in bed by now, dear?" "Isn't she just too cute?" "Biting your nails at your age, honey?" "Don't touch that, you'll break it." With a book or magazine, kids don't have to *take it* for a moment; they can easily toss *it* aside without recrimination.

A Book That Broke All the Rules—And Became a Classic

But the line between preaching and entertainment is sometimes thin. A first-rate storyteller can get away with a surprising amount of moralizing. Picture yourself in the following situation: You're a children's book editor thumbing through the day's slush pile. You open a book proposal that begins as follows:

Dear Acclaimed Editor:

I would like to send you my manuscript for a collection of short stories about a sweet little old lady who tells parents how to reform their misbehaving children.

Any editor who reads past that sentence is either altruistic, optimistic, or having an extremely slow day. A children's book written from the viewpoint of adults? A fictionalized instruction manual on how to make children "be good?" What child would want to read a book like that? What editor would be crazy enough to publish it?

Actually, publisher J. B. Lippincott took the chance, back in the 1940s. Not only did children read the book, they made it and its three sequels into classics. Reprints are still easy to find; so are modern picture book, video, and stage versions. The book was *Mrs. Piggle-Wiggle,* by Betty MacDonald.

Why did MacDonald's books succeed when the basic premise alone would have seemed to doom them to oblivion? For one thing, Mrs. Piggle-Wiggle isn't just a sweet little old lady who bakes cookies and has all the answers. She's the grown-up every child secretly would like to become—the little girl who never quite finished growing up, the woman who married a pirate (not the sinister type, but the lovable comic character who lives for parrots, sailing ships, and buried treasure), and who built her house upside down for the fun of it. She stands hardly taller than the kids, has a magic hump on her back, and can turn any chore into a game.

Best of all, Mrs. Piggle-Wiggle treats children as equals. She never criticizes childish attempts at making things, never jumps in and offers to do it for you, and never bats an eye when youngsters do typically childish things like digging for treasure in her backyard and then sitting down on her couch without washing up. She understands the difference between youthful fun and genuine misbehavior.

For the latter, Mrs. Piggle-Wiggle's treatments (chronic misbehavior is always called *disease*, and she doesn't seem to believe in *bad* kids) never involve spanking or deprivation or anything else typically called punishment. Invariably, the cure involves being eased out of one behavior into another, or learning through the natural consequences of actions.

Every story of a Mrs. Piggle-Wiggle cure is hilarious. When asked how to deal with a boy who won't share his things with anyone, her prescription runs as follows: Give him what he wants. Lock all his doors and boxes so no one can get at his things. When he has to carry something within other people's reach, label it with his name and *Don't Touch* in huge letters. At first, the boy is delighted at the prospect. Before long, however, he finds that the

Don't Touch signs have made him the laughingstock of his school. After a few days of mockery, and after locking himself out of his room, he decides sharing isn't such a bad idea.

Many of Mrs. Piggle-Wiggle's cures, especially in the later books, are fun to read about because they're literal magic and don't exist in real life. One story in *Hello, Mrs. Piggle-Wiggle* involves a girl who has hysterics over every little thing. Mrs. Piggle-Wiggle provides a medication that makes the girl literally "cry buckets." After one crying fit floods the school and leaves the girl outside in water up to her neck, that's the end of that habit.

Mrs. Piggle-Wiggle has a lesson to teach writers, too: If the characters are engaging and the story line intriguing, children will absorb moral lessons without even realizing it.

Practical Principles for Everyday Writing

This isn't to say the average writer should imitate Betty MacDonald and create a series about the funniest ways to make your kids behave. Few writers should even try to create children's stories where the primary impetus toward the solution comes from adults; only one in a thousand writers can execute such ideas smoothly. As a general rule, main characters should be the readers' age, and should work out their own problems.

Some principles hold true for virtually all writing, and are important in avoiding overly moralistic stories:

Principle 1: Make your characters human. A perfect hero is an unpopular hero, because readers can't identify with him or her. The main character should have—if not some moral flaw—at least some fault or bad habit, some character trait that gets on others' nerves, or some lack of competence that causes problems.

Dennis the Menace is a long-popular character who isn't really bad but whom adults would rather live without. He conducts messy or destructive experiments, can never sit quietly for more than a few minutes, and feels free to question adult authority.

Protagonists shouldn't be out-and-out bad guys, either; if they aren't basically likable, they should at least arouse some sympathy in the reader. The totally-evil-but-fascinating viewpoint character is best left to adult literature.

Often, unlearning a character flaw—especially if it's something the hero himself is ashamed of, such as being a coward—is a major theme of the story. A protagonist shouldn't get rid of all annoying habits or less-than-perfect traits by the end of the story, however. The timid character may gain new self-confidence by finding himself capable of courage in a crisis, but he probably won't spend the rest of his life walking into danger for the fun of it. The arrogant character can be taken down a peg or two without completely losing cockiness. The head-scratcher or tune-hummer can be allowed to keep that habit. Real people don't become perfect in a lifetime, and fictional people shouldn't either.

Even minor characters shouldn't be straight stereotypes. The doting stay-at-home mother, the totally competent or totally bungling father, the heartless school bully, and the humorless teacher have all been overdone. If you use any of these, give them some atypical characteristics to make them less predictable—a mother may greet the kids with fresh-baked cookies when they get home from school, but she may be a die-hard football fan as well. Though it should go without saying in the politically correct twenty-first century, think at least 100 times before including a character who conforms too closely to a cultural or racial stereotype. Unless it's an integral part of the story or you apply the same standard to all characters, it's best to avoid mentioning race or nationality at all.

A Fine Line Between Narrative & Preaching

Principle 2: Don't let your text wander off into long preachy paragraphs. It's best to use all physical description sparingly—include just enough to set the mood or help readers visualize the scene. Integrate description with the story line so you never lose forward momentum. Beware of philosophical analysis. Remember you aren't writing a scriptural commentary, or even a personal essay (and even those are better when mixed with story).

Most modern writers know better than to pause the story and de-liver a two-page moral treatise. Many, however, do practically the same thing by putting moral lectures into a character's mouth. While dialogue normally keeps a story moving, having the same character speak for more than two paragraphs (or more than 10 sentences) is not dialogue but monologue, effectively the same as straight narrative. And pretty much as boring.

If you must have a character deliver a lecture—usually at the conclusion of a story, where lengthy explanations may be necessary to account for loose ends—it can help to have the character deliver the speech in the heat of emotion, which makes him or her seem like a real person instead of a know-it-all. In any case, use short paragraphs, and break up the monologue with physical actions and with comments from other characters.

Principle 3: Don't play omniscient narrator nor talk directly to the reader unless you're unusually adept in the technique. If lectures from characters turn off readers, lectures from the author are even worse. The days of "now, reader" comments are long past. Today's author should remain virtually invisible. If written in the third person, a story's narrative should sound as if it were taken directly from the viewpoint character's observations, colored by that character's opinions and doubts. Using an "omniscient narrator" makes the moralizing temptation harder to resist.

Care & Moderation

Principle 4: Censor parentheses—the comments, not the punctuation marks—in fiction. Parentheses are asides to the reader and can't easily be conveyed through speech, so there's little place for them in contemporary fiction. But also do be careful of including any punctuation, such as italics, dashes, semicolons, quotation marks, and the like, that make any part of the text stand out. Emphasis is best confined to dialogue and first-person narrative, and even then best used in moderation.

Principle 5: Don't quote scripture extensively. Moderation is all the more important when writing a piece with a religious theme. Some religious fiction is so loaded with scriptural quotes that it looks like a memory verse list. Better to weave in the religious principles through characters' actions and their consequences and to save direct scriptural references for a few well-placed and extremely relevant quotes. Don't let a character quote scripture with every breath, either (unless that's a personality trait).

Principle 6: With religious stories, never assume that your audience is familiar with the scriptures in question. Gone are the days when a writer could safely assume that readers knew most of the Bible or other religious texts by heart. Even if readers are followers of the religion, that doesn't always mean they've studied or even read many sacred writings. And even if they have, that doesn't mean they understand it; cultural and even language differences may get in the way.

Story can be an excellent vehicle to explain religious principles, but only when quotes and expositions are woven smoothly into the story line. And never use references (such as *Romans 3:23*) without quoting or paraphrasing the entire verse. Annoying enough in nonfiction, this approach is the kiss of death in fiction. Who wants to interrupt the flow of the story to hunt down a Bible passage?

Speaking of Nonfiction

If moralizing and preaching are insidious temptations for the fiction writer, they're likely to be upfront concerns for the nonfiction writer. How can anyone instruct youngsters in practical living, explain scriptural passages, or discuss the lessons of history without making readers feel lectured or talked down to?

Principle 7: Remember that nonfiction can be story, too. When writing history or biography, use fiction techniques. If a nonfiction work is primarily narrative, it can be told like a story, letting events and consequences speak for themselves. You needn't invent fictionalized dialogue to make history read like story.

Principle 8: Never write a manuscript or chapter without some story in it. Even in how-to pieces, include anecdotes, complete with dialogue, about real or imaginary youngsters who were involved in the same situation. Straight advice tends to lose the reader after a while; anecdotes let readers learn by example.

If you include anecdotes about your own children, however, be careful of mentioning the relationship. The second you refer to "my son" or "my daughter," readers will think, "Oh no, she's going to talk to us as a parent!" (For the sake of harmony in your own family, get your children's permission to tell their stories. Even if you fictionalize everything, people always expect their peers to know whom you're talking about.)

Principle 9: Remember you aren't perfect, or a separate class of humanity from your readers. If you can include a story about yourself when you were roughly your readers' age, all the better. Especially if you fell on your face in the story, they'll consider you a peer and will be more likely to pay attention to the rest of your article. If you're several decades older than your readers and are afraid the anecdote may sound like ancient (read *irrelevant*) history, writer's license allows you to modernize technology, clothing, and speech in the retelling.

Principle 10: Write from the viewpoint of a peer. Even if you don't tell tales on yourself, pretend you're sharing advice—advice that worked for you—with a good friend. If you think like a teacher or consider it your duty to inform readers for their own good, it will show in the text. Readers will be bored at best and disgusted at worst.

Principle 11: Avoid such phrases as "of course you know," and "your parents will be disappointed." The former reeks of condescension. The latter is rarely sufficient motivation and makes the writer sound like another parent. Other phrases that should be censored are "for your own good," "you have to" or "you must," and "I'm going to prove to you" or "I'm going to show you."

Do *show* your readers, of course; just don't tell them you're going to show them. Besides, spending too long describing what you're going to do loses the audience before you have a chance to actually do it.

Your primary duty is to tell the story or convey the facts. If you do that effectively, the lessons will take care of themselves.

Story Structure

Four-Part Harmony

By Christina Hamlett

Beginning. Middle. End. Whether your chosen medium of expression is the page, the stage, or the cinema, the three-act structure of *conflict, complication,* and *conclusion* is one of those immutable laws of good storytelling that we learned as far back as childhood fairytales.

Simple as that rule sounds, however, it's a concept that new writers often have difficulty applying to their works in progress. The reason? Most people just aren't adept at doing the mental math when it comes to dividing by three and evenly parsing out the development of character and the build-up of suspense over the duration of their plot.The result is one or more of the following weaknesses.

The Backstory Bog
How did your protagonist arrive at this particular juncture of his or her life? Whatever the inciting incident that set the wheels of plot in motion (i.e., a chance meeting, a missed phone call, a freak acci-

dent), novice writers usually make the mistake of turning back the hands of the clock too far and launching the story in the wrong place. Too much expositional background gets a story off to a sluggish start and encumbers readers with way more preliminary detail than they need to understand the central problem.

Let's say, for instance, that you're writing a book about a teenage girl who stumbles upon an astonishing secret while her family is on vacation in Japan. If chapter one begins with her toddler years, it's going to be a very long time before she and her parents ever board that plane to Tokyo, and even longer before we ever learn what that astonishing secret is.

Even if the genre isn't a mystery, readers will soak up every name, date, and event that you provide as if it were a critical clue in solving a crime. Why cause their heads to explode with too much historical minutiae that has no bearing on the immediate conflict or quest?

The Sagging Middle

The middle of the book is the most likely place for writers to wander *off message*. Characters, conversations, and scenes that have no bearing on the protagonist's current problem impose a weight that slows the action to a dead halt.

By the time an author approaches the midway point of the plot, one of two things may have occurred. The first is the tendency to give minor characters a life of their own. It isn't enough, it seems, that the doorman is named Bob; a novice will also provide him with a wife named Emily, four children (two of whom are twins), and a secret ambition to play the saxophone. The more details, the more validation there may seem to be for Bob's ongoing presence as a character—but at the expense of the major players and the conflict itself.

The second weakening condition stems from anxiety about the book's finale. An author who hasn't thought through the resolution or is fearful that it won't be satisfying to readers may resort to delaying its arrival for as long as possible. By rehashing prior information, introducing more characters, and splintering off into a succession of subplots, the author forestalls having to tie all the elements together.

The result is story *sagosis*. Not unlike the effect of using only two end pins to hang a wet blanket on a clothesline, a heavily weighted middle makes it impossible to regain sufficient momentum for a strong finish.

The Slapdash Ending

Who among us hasn't been told that the worst crime a story weaver can ever commit is to have their characters wake up and discover "it was all a dream"? While television has provided us with excellent exceptions to this rule (the finale of *Newhart*) and blitheringly awful ones (Bobby's death in *Dallas*), novice writers often resort to hurried endings in order to meet a contest deadline, move on to a new project, or concede that their muse has run off on vacation and that they haven't a clue how to wrap things up.

The result is a story that (1) is predicated on doofy contrivances (an asteroid just happens to wipe out the enemy), (2) fails to wrap up loose ends (why did the murderer never mention he had a sister?), or (3) halts abruptly (the characters suddenly decide to abandon the past 200 pages of their quest and become pirates instead).

The expectation of readers is that the time they have invested in accompanying your characters on their journey will be rewarded with a summation that's not skimpy or weak. The payoff for the ride has to be worth all the anticipation of standing in line.

Story versus Plot

Where does a beginning officially end and a middle begin? How soon should you start setting up your ending? When do you know to stop writing after the conflict has been resolved?

What tends to trip up writers the

most in charting a roadmap for the course of their book is failing to recognize the difference between a *story* and what constitutes a *plot*. The first one inevitably leads you astray; the second one—if well constructed—is what will always bring you back.

Let's say that someone asks you what your story's about. Your answer is likely to be something along the lines of "it's about a princess who loses her kingdom" or "it's about a pig that likes to herd sheep" or "it's about a high school dropout who goes to live with his grandfather." The operative words in each case are *it's about*—a summation of the type of tale it's going to be without divulging any of the particulars on where the characters came from or where they're going next.

Assuming a listener is intrigued with your one-line premise, you'll probably be asked, "How did she lose her kingdom?" or "Where did the pig learn to do that?" or "Do the two of them get along?" Any question that queries how a situation happened or how it is going to happen in the future is answered in terms of plot.

A story needs a plot to help it open up speed and reach the finish line. A plot needs a story to give it a starting point to enter the race. This differentiation is crucial to keep in mind as you start to split the content of your book equitably among those actions and scenes that created the central conflict and those that will ultimately contribute to its resolution.

Similar to a storyboard in its placement of primary and secondary plot points, a four-act template allows you to see at a glance how you're distributing the weight of the tale you'd like to tell. Mathematically, it also provides a more clearly defined midpoint—two parts before, two parts after—than a nebulous middle that embraces the entire spectrum of a second-of-three acts complication.

Divide & Conquer: The 4-Part Technique

Once you start writing, and especially if you're not working from an outline, it's easy to lose track of just how many pages you're spending on the development of each scene and character. Before you realize it, you could find yourself halfway through a book and discover you still haven't introduced all of your players. The four-act template is a simple way not only to build the suspense in incremental steps but to avoid the tendency to linger too long on any given chapter.

This exercise begins with identifying how many words or pages you want the completed manuscript to be. Typically, a writer starts without really thinking about length in this way. Unless, for instance, a magazine publisher has specified that a short story cannot exceed 2,000 words, most writers simply scribble away until they run out of interesting things to say. They then go to the word-count feature on their computer to see if their manuscripts are in the ballpark for submission.

With a full-length book, it's much harder to cut back or pad the chapters if the target publisher is seeking material that falls within a specific range. In the quest to accommodate those parameters, writers are most likely to shorten the ending or bulk up the middle.

The four-act template eliminates that guesswork because a targeted length is identified at the outset. It also has the practicality of being able to work as well with novels as it does with theater scripts, screenplays, short stories, magazine pieces, and even speeches.

Let's say you have a contemporary young adult story about a teenage female werewolf that would be perfect for Smooch Books, an imprint of Dorchester Publishing (www.smoochya.com). The guidelines state that completed manuscripts need to be 45,000 words. At roughly 250 words per page, this equals a total of 180 double-spaced pages. Divide 180 by 4. This comes out to 45, the number of pages that you'll be allowed to devote to each *act*.

Forty-five pages? Yikes! Once you start the actual writing, you'll quickly discover how disciplined you need to become in cutting out superfluous scenes and dialogue that take away from your focus on the central conflict.

The next step is to take a sheet of paper, turn it horizontal, and fold it into four equal columns. Each of these columns will represent 45 pages of your book.

At the top of the first column, write the words Act 1, and label the

remaining columns 2, 3, and 4. You're also going to take one more step and fold the column for Act 1 in half again, and do the same for Act 4, now giving you a total of 6 columns across the page.

Label the very first column (the left half of Act 1) *Foreshadowing*. Label the next to the last column (the left half of Act 4) *Uh-oh*.

You're now ready to start filling in each column with plot points— the major scenes and developments that occur in each of the acts. The idea here is that the columns will contain equal amounts of information and that each act will escalate the suspense. All should be described in the most simplistic terms (boy meets girl, boy loses girl, boy gets girl back), just enough to jog your memory when you start writing.

Act 1 will introduce the main characters and the central conflict. The foreshadowing element (which needs to be introduced no later than 22 $\frac{1}{2}$ pages into our example of a 180-page story) is planted early so that the reader will forget about it. Foreshadowing, as we will see in the example below, is tied to the *uh-oh* that occurs in the first half of Act 4 and that is the final obstacle the protagonist must overcome.

In Act 1, write the words, "Protagonist gets chased into tree by antagonist." In Act 2, write the words, "Antagonist starts throwing rocks at tree." By Act 3, "Antagonist sets the tree on fire." Oh no! Will the protagonist burn up along with the tree or jump to the ground? Act 4 reveals

Act 1 (45 pages)	Act 2 (45 pages)	Act 3 (45 pages)	Act 4 (45 pages)
Fore-shadowing			Uh-oh
Protagonist meets quirky guy selling alligator repellent.			Protagonist crawls out on branch overhanging a pool of water.
Protagonist gets chased into tree by antagonist.	Antagonist starts throwing rocks at tree.	Antagonist sets the tree on fire.	Big alligator lives in pond.

"Protagonist crawls out on branch overhanging a pool of water."

These plot points are the primary objectives that need to be met in each 45-page block. You can introduce as many supporting points/scenes under an act's objective as you'd like, as long as a comparable number of elements are incorporated in each column for overall balance. If you are called upon to add or subtract verbiage from your manuscript, you can do it in a systematic way that doesn't skew the story's equilibrium.

It would seem in the above example that all the character needs to do to save herself in Act 4 is to jump into the water. This is where your *Uh-oh* comes in. How? On the left side of your Act 4 column, you have written the words "Big alligator lives in pond."

Fortunately, you had the foresight to deal with this back in Act 1. Specifically, somewhere in the first 22 ¹/₂ pages, the protagonist made the acquaintance of a quirky little guy selling alligator repellant. Although the protagonist didn't have any need of this product, she was nonetheless a kind person and bought a can of it just to help the salesman out. Lo and behold, that alligator repellant is now exactly what she needs to save her life and bring the story to a satisfying close.

Whether the foreshadowing is overt or subtle, it needs to be in place as early as possible. In the movie *Back to the Future,* for instance, it was the long-defunct clock tower disabled by lightning that later provided Marty and Doc Brown a clue for harnessing the power that could get Marty home. In the movie version of Tom Clancy's *The Hunt for Red October,* it was the reference to there being two Russian submarines, a situation most viewers forgot about until it appeared just before the final stretch of the film.

The difference between these two examples of foreshadowing is that the first one presents a solution while the second one presents an obstacle that throws a final monkey wrench into what seems to be a smooth ending.

Dime & Nickel

On a final note, authors should be aware that editors approach new manuscripts in much the same way that bookstore browsers decide whether to put an item in their basket or back on the shelf. Nicknamed the "Dime and Nickel," this time-saving strategy involves a skim of the first 10 pages followed by a skim of the final 5.

While this combination obviously yields a sense of the writer's expertise, voice, and ability to hold a reader's attention, the test itself goes a step further. Specifically, no amount of good writing throughout the bulk of a book can overcome the problem of straying by story's end from whatever gauntlet was flung down in the opening scenes. What determines whether a manuscript gets put in the *read now* versus the *read later* stack is this figurative 15 cents of an editor's time.

In the ideal equation, whoever was deemed to be the main character between pages 1 and 10 should either still be standing in the last 5 pages or at least still be talked about by the remaining characters. This bookend structure—readily apparent from judicious use of the template—will ensure that you'll never lose sight of your original premise and character point of view.

Audience

Hit the Target with Nonfiction

By Joanne Mattern

I s there anything in the world left to write about, for any young audience? Walk into a library or a bookstore and you're likely to be overwhelmed by the number of nonfiction titles available, on endless subjects. It might be hard to tell just from glancing through the shelves, but every successful book is aimed at a specific target audience and yes, there's much yet to be written.

Smart authors know that the key to writing success is finding the proper target and making the book hit that bull's eye. Only when authors know their target audience will they be able to score a successful project.

Age-Appropriate Writing

Readers can be divided into different groups by age, gender, interests, and reading ability. Age is probably the easiest to target. Younger children have different interests and needs than older ones, and a good writer recognizes the variations.

Janeen Adil has written non-fiction books for several major pub-

lishers, as well as articles for nearly a dozen magazines. Several years ago, Adil wrote an article about river otters that was published by *Ladybug*. Before submitting, she zeroed in on her readership. "The magazine's audience is ages two to seven, so I focused on what the otters and kids have in common: They both love to play. By using age-appropriate vocabulary and varied sentence structures, the article was accessible to beginning readers, while younger kids could follow the story as they were being read to."

Adil provides another example to show how she targeted an older audience. For a *Cricket* article, she focused on "the work done by an archaeochemist in analyzing the remains of King Midas's funeral feast. These 9-to-14-year-old readers would be able to understand the background and concepts inherent in this story. The vocabulary and sentence structure were, of course, geared toward their level, with the most challenging terms pulled out and explained more fully in a sidebar."

One of the important tasks of a writer is to identify topics of interest to readers at different age levels. Barbara Mitchell, Publisher of Mitchell Lane Publishers, directs books to specific age levels by looking at "what is studied in school at that age, or what hobbies and interests kids have. For instance, soccer has gained in popularity among young people. There was very little in the way of professional soccer biographies for a young audience. We recently introduced several books for second and third graders to fill a void in the soccer interest area."

Boys & Girls

Gender can also play a role in what a child wants to read. Although there are definitely exceptions, girls and boys usually have different interests, and these preferences are reflected in the nonfiction they like to read.

Jennifer Knoerzer, Head of Children's Services at the Suffern Free Library in Suffern, New York, sees gender preferences every day. "For boys, it's books about sharks, dinosaurs, sports, the military, and the paranormal. For girls, it's books about ballet, animals, butterflies, crafts, and cooking." She also reminds authors that some themes will always be popular for both genders: "I read every book in the 001.94s at my school library two or three times when I was a kid," Knoerzer says. "That section of the supernatural and unsolved mysteries is still extremely popular today."

Boys have a reputation for being particularly hard to please as readers. Mitchell notes that "Boys in the middle grades do not read much outside of what they are assigned in school." While girls may be interested in a greater variety of topics, writers who aim at a specific target to appeal to boys may have an advantage in selling a submission.

Tamara Britton, Editorial Director of ABDO Publishing Company, says there are definite topics that draw young male readers. "Boys respond to high-interest books, such as biographies of sports figures or books about sports cars."

Talking to children about their interests is always a great way to understand your audience. Librarians, teachers, and parents can also fill you in on what appeals to the boys and girls they know. Another way to know your audience is to see what other books have succeeded. Britton advises writers to "read book reviews in the national trade journals to find out what educators like and dislike. Reviewers will let you know what works and what doesn't."

Reluctant Readers

Many nonfiction books are aimed at reluctant readers, a term that encompasses several types of readers, not all of whom have reading challenges. Britton explains, "There is no one set of rules that defines the reluctant reader. A reader could be in this category for any number of reasons, from learning challenges to disinterest in assigned literature to just plain not liking to read."

Barbara Levadi is the President of

SuperScript, a publishing and editorial services organization that provides consulting and management expertise to clients such as Benchmark Education Company, the Wright Group, Macmillan, and Scott Foresman. She describes why some children don't like to read and how writers and publishers can attract them to books. The key is "taking into account the particular interests of a reluctant reader. It is an art to tease out of some students their personal interests, the topics that they would really like to know about. Poor readers generally do not like to read, so it is no surprise that they'd rather be on the ball field or taking dance lessons or art lessons. But these activities and interests they pursue outside of school are often the clues to what they'd like to learn about."

Other children are reluctant to read because they struggle with vocabulary they don't understand and reading skills they simply don't have. This market is often referred to as *hi-lo*, because the books have a high interest level and a low reading level. Hi-lo books feature topics of high interest such as sports, disasters, animals, or weird science facts. The text is written at a lower reading level than the age of the reader. A 12-year-old might read at an 8-year-old reading level, and a successful hi-lo book reflects that.

Knoerzer feels that nonfiction is the perfect way to get these children to open a book. "Nonfiction can grab the interest of reluctant readers more often than fiction because they can pick topics they are already interested in, and the books have wonderful pictures and photographs, so they appear more like fun than homework."

Designing for Readers

When asked to name some of the most successful nonfiction books for young readers, Knoerzer lists popular series: Eyewitness Books; Let's Read and Find Out Science series; See More readers; and the Don't Know Much About series. All feature kid-friendly designs with many photographs and illustrations to break up the flow of text.

Design plays a huge role in creating a successful, targeted book. DK, formerly known as Dorling Kindersley, pioneered the art-heavy design that is so popular among nonfiction today. Beth Hester, Editor of Children's Books, describes the company's approach: "DK uses plenty of photographic images, as well as illustrated cross-sections, computer-generated graphics, and other images to make each page instantly appealing even before a reader takes in a word of text."

Photos and graphics do more than grab the reader's attention. They also break information into manageable pieces. Hester explains, "Breaking up blocks of text into digestible chunks makes each piece of information approachable. Even if the vocabulary is simple, a page chock-full of text will be intimidating to a beginning reader."

Levadi is also a fan of good design. When asked what will make readers pick up a nonfiction book, she replies, "The photos, of course! Everyone loves to look at amazing photos and beautiful illustrations in well-designed books. The best nonfiction books being written for children today are designed to look like magazines. The writing is interesting and lively. The spreads have engaging special features, sidebars, lots of charts and graphs, and other pictorial information that makes the reading easier."

ABDO's Britton also mentions another visual. "Text and graphics can work together in sidebars. Sidebars can be used to add information in a nonthreatening way. It can be something extra in a fun box, not something difficult in the body text."

What all this means for the nonfiction writer who wants to target particular markets even more—such as hi-lo or other readers for whom visuals have a special importance—is that copy must be written to fit into successful, proven designs. Choose a topic with exciting photo or illustration possibilities, convey facts in an easy-to-understand manner, present information in chunks, include fascinating facts with lots of kid-appeal, and pull out extra information into sidebars, and you'll be well on your way to hitting the target.

Classrooms in the Crosshairs

Many nonfiction publishers target materials toward topics studied in the classroom. Mitchell of Mitchell Lane frequently works with local teachers to find out their needs and what their students respond to.

Britton reports that ABDO works "with focus groups that include parents, educators, librarians, and reading specialists to understand the reading needs of reluctant readers, both in the classroom and at leisure." Knowing what is studied at specific grade levels is a key to succeeding with nonfiction books.

Levadi notes that nonfiction takes many forms. She is a big fan of *reader's theater*. This genre features scripts that are read aloud in a classroom setting rather than being performed from memory on a stage with elaborate costumes and sets. "Reader's theater is an authentic means of getting students to practice and develop fluency with repeated readings of the same text. Some are now written with the same themes and leveling as leveled readers for small group reading instruction, and their content will enrich and extend class study on the particular social studies or science theme." Levadi also recommends multimedia items, such as CD-ROMs that are "multi-layered and multi-sensory to stretch students' learning in many directions."

Hester echoes the popularity of multimedia materials. She says that one of the most popular DK projects in recent years has been a joint collaboration between DK and Google called *e.Encyclopedia*, which combines "a traditional book format with the capabilities of the Web in a safe, monitored environment." The *e.Encyclopedia* allows students to go beyond a book by following links to explore topics on the Internet.

Targeting Tips for Success

Editors and publishers are unanimous when asked what they are looking for from nonfiction authors: writers who understand the needs of their readers, especially reluctant readers. Talking down to kids is a huge mistake. "The reluctant reader is not necessarily learning challenged," Britton points out. "Authors should communicate in a way that respects the reader's intelligence."

Writers must also be able to follow the requirements of the publisher. Publishers don't make up designs or writing specifications arbitrarily. Style guides and word counts are chosen precisely to meet the needs of readers. Levadi points out that "writers must adhere to the guidelines. It is easy to say, 'This fact or idea is so interesting, a couple of extra words or sentences on the page won't matter.' But experts and teachers know exactly what their students can handle. Two more sentences on the page can be too demanding for an emergent reader."

It is also important not to make the books so simple that they don't say anything. Mitchell complains about authors who leave out details. "Even young kids who are just learning to read like specifics. Just because a book is targeted to second graders or reluctant readers doesn't mean the book should have no information. The author needs to determine the most important information and do a good job with that."

Nonfiction writers should also be good researchers. Knoerzer won't

Jon Scieszka Gets Guys to Read

Jon Scieszka is an enormously popular author of such books as *The Stinky Cheese Man and Other Fairly Stupid Tales, Math Curse,* and *The True Story of the Three Little Pigs.* He was also a teacher for ten years. During his career, he realized that many boys simply do not like to read. Scieszka felt that a big part of the problem was that boys couldn't find books they liked. So he started a literacy-based website with an edgy, contemporary feel called Guys Read. His website lists books, authors, and illustrators who appeal especially to boys. He also invites people to submit their own choices for great books for guys. Check out www.guysread.com for some interesting background and information on what books captivate boys.

buy a book if it is not accurate and up-to-date. "You certainly don't want to be handing children books that give them information that has since been proven to be untrue!" Editors agree, and cite excellent research skills as a must for nonfiction writers.

Don't forget the importance of fun. Levadi looks for "writers whose portfolios show that they add energy and excitement to their writing, because they craft what they write. They are willing to review and rewrite until they believe they have a manuscript that a young reader will really enjoy."

A Final Word

Adil believes "everyone is born with curiosity about the world around us. The number of nonfiction writing topics with the potential to elicit 'Oh, that's so cool!' is virtually limitless. The author's own enthusiasm, coupled with good writing, will carry readers along on the adventure."

An athlete practices hitting a target over and over again until it becomes easy to achieve the goal. Writers need to do the same thing. By knowing their audience and targeting their material specifically to meet its needs, nonfiction writers will be sure to hit the ball right out of the park!

Word Choice for Bricks, Syntax for Mortar

By Susan Sundwall

I *think of novels in architectural terms. You have to enter at the gate, and this gate must be constructed in such a way that the reader has immediate confidence in the strength of the building.*
—*Ian McEwan*

You can't build a house from the sky down. Any well-constructed house is designed from the ground up. When attention is paid to every detail, the completed structure is beautiful, solid, and invites habitation. It's the same with the stories you fashion from the raw materials of your imagination, personal experience, or research. At the outset it's wonderful to contemplate the sky-bright glory of your finished masterpiece, but like the successful architect you, the writer, must hunker down and hammer out the details of your story edifice. Two of your most powerful building tools are word choice and syntax.

The Blueprint

You begin with a good understanding of the basics of writing. You know the who, what, where, and when of what it is you want to say. Only one task remains: figuring out how to put it all together. This is the blueprint stage. Here's where your scene setting and story flow are sketched out or where the structure of your nonfiction begins to be forged.

The bricks or stones for your building are the words and sentences; the mortar is the order in which they are joined. In fiction, you'll decide which words best describe the personality of your main character and what will come out of his or her mouth. You'll select the words for setting, struggle, mood. You'll work with the sentence length and rhythm to slow or speed action, convey angst or joy. Think about this in terms of the metaphor we're using: Is your story a cottage of mud and wattle or a castle with dressed stones? Get your supplies and tools right, get your parts in place, and the whole will be sturdy and pleasing.

"I always encourage authors to

delve deep into their subjects, to feel comfortable with them, so that they can construct believable and accurate worlds," says Carolyn Yoder, Editor at Calkins Creek Books.

"Every author has a different style," says Joy Neaves, Editor at Front Street Books. "Certainly sentence structures and lengths vary. The important thing is that every project have a rhythm and a flow." Rhythm and flow are aided mightily by a clear understanding of syntax.

Syntax & Voice

No, *syntax* is not another piece of financial punishment passed by the legislature last Tuesday. Syntax is the orderly arrangement of your words and sentences in relation to each other. The manner in which you structure your sentences is an essential part of your developing voice and style.

"The components of *voice* are diction and syntax," says Neaves. "Every writer achieves a certain kind of voice in their work differently. Our more successful authors follow the rule that *less is more*. They do not use two words when one word will do."

Consider the following sentences.

When Jeremy woke up the following morning, he could see that the sun was obscured by ominous clouds.

The ominous clouds obscuring the sun exactly reflected Jeremy's mood that morning.

The first sentence sets up a scene, but makes no direct connection between Jeremy and his mood. In the context of a story it could be showing and not telling, creating an image. But it is not direct and makes no overt connection. The second sentence does make that connection, and could easily be made into a simile: "Jeremy's mood that morning was like the ominous clouds obscuring the sun." Not only is the second sentence shorter, but the order and word choice changes provide information in a different manner.

No matter what is written, clarity is a goal for the writer, and a gift to the reader. Both sentences above can work. The choice is about the voice of the author, the tone of the story, its overall purpose. All is dependent on word choice, sentence length, and syntax: There are syntactical rules best followed and there are times when rules are well broken.

"I encourage writers to take chances," says one editor at the Weekly Reader Corporation. "Why not a one-word paragraph? Boom! Why not have fun with the English language? Consider giving your readers *treats* along the way. Develop your own style, just don't get too clever. The key is knowing when you are reaching too far." Attempting to pass off a cliché as an original thought, for instance, only brings out the moan-and-groan factor and does your story no service. "Give your readers some credit."

Christine Spence, former Editor of Program Books at Standard Publishing, says, "One pitfall I notice is an overuse of punctuation (exclamation points!) to make a point, rather than a good use of words."

"If rule breaking works, it works," says Neaves. "What's important is that authors convey precisely what they mean."

Above all, a writer wants a story to have meaning for the reader. Writing that is uncluttered, well-structured, and concise has the best chance of accomplishing this. Our desire for proper syntax, the right words in the right order, becomes a quest for what the nineteenth century French author Gustave Flaubert called *le mot juste*, exactly the right word.

A good example of this can be found in Lemony Snicket's A Series of Unfortunate Events. In book one, *The Bad Beginning,* after the ill-fated Baudelaire children lose their home and their parents in a tragic fire, they are sent to live with a distant relative, Count Olaf. Here we have Count Olaf meeting the three children for the first time.

> "Hello, hello, hello," Count Olaf said in a wheezy whisper. He was very tall and very thin, dressed in a gray suit that had many dark stains on it. His face was unshaven, and rather than two eyebrows, like most human beings have, he had just one long one.

Yikes! Who would want to live with this guy?

The Count does not merely *whisper*; but the author uses the modi-fier *wheezy* to begin building this creepy character. Using the intensifier *very* and the adjective *many* exaggerates his tallness and thinness. And that eyebrow! With the addition of the phrase *like most human beings have*, doubt is even cast on our assumption that the Count is human. What a beautiful layering of bricks and mortar informs our fictional image.

Getting it Right—From the Beginning

Any word is a beautiful one when it perfectly expresses the writers' intent, when it brings the vision to ground, but oh, how we often struggle to get each one right, especially in opening lines. For this is where our verbal identity, our style, is established.

Writers are told all the time they must use attention-grabbing words right from the beginning of any piece, fiction or nonfiction. The responsibility placed on those words is immense. Each one must count.

Jill Esbaum, author of *Stink Soup* (Farrar, Straus & Giroux), knew when she was writing that book that she had her story blueprint well in hand, but that her opening lines were lifeless.

"I'd begun in third person, with Annabelle and her brother getting out of the car at their grand-mother's farm, where they'd be spending the week. I'd written a bit of dialogue between the kids and their grandmother and added the requisite hugs," Esbaum ex-plains. "At this point I was the one in charge of the story. And it was a yawner."

Then in a revealing moment, Annabelle herself presented the fol-lowing 22 words to begin the story:

> Granny's chickens stood petrified, staring at my brother with shiny button eyes. He drummed on the car door again and yelled, "Buk-BAWWWK!"

"Suddenly the story had a voice," says Esbaum, "and the spark it had been lacking."

The point of view change made a big difference. Instead of a narrator relating a car trip to Grandma's farm, now there is Annabelle her-self, in the car with her brother Willie, showing us what's going on. Phrases like *shiny button eyes* enable us to *see* the fright of the chickens. Willie's drumming on the car door *again* lets us know that the car ride was a doozy and that brother Willie is going to be trouble.

Fire & Focus

Suppose your house is destined to be built on what may appear to be the dreary plain of nonfiction. Do you have what it takes to build up your writing with pizzazz equal to that in your fiction? The opportunity to impart facts in a way that kids enjoy is a delight and an awesome responsibility. And the language rules are the same.

"A good story is a good story, re-gardless of whether it is fiction or nonfiction," says the Weekly Reader editor. "Nonfiction tends to be more chronological. Good nonfiction sto-ries, like well-written fiction, require details. Our best writers use a con-versational tone in their nonfiction writing. Good nonfiction involves a dialogue between the writer and au-dience."

In *Roberto Clemente, Pride of the Pittsburgh Pirates,* author Jonah Winter reduces the great baseball player's career to carefully chosen, almost austere, but beguiling prose. The opening lines avoid dry facts such as date of birth or the name of his hometown. Instead we read:

> On an island called Puerto Rico, where baseball players are as plentiful
>
> as tropical flowers in a rain forest, there was a boy who had very little
>
> but a fever to play and win at baseball.

The language and punctuation are spare but the unconventional spacing of the sentences invites readers to have a look. When they do, they find the words have impact and meaning. Notice the syntax strategy: It's chronological, it's detailed, and the writer-reader dialogue is subtle, almost poetic, like soft drops of rain skimming those tropical flower petals on the way to the ground.

When writing for a classroom audience, every word counts. Find the one word that best communicates the thought, simply and with no ambiguity.

Nonfiction writers often gather mountains of research material and its subsequent organization can be daunting. Giving all that substance *life* is always the challenge.

"The reason that many nonfiction writers lack the qualities of their fiction counterparts has to do with a lack of research," says Yoder. "A solid research foundation leads to accurate, fair, energetic, and original stories."

Is the writer compelled to use every speck of research when constructing a nonfiction piece? Will the result be an unwieldy mass of words with the potential of scaring off the reader?

"Sometimes research *does* get in the way," Yoder says. "The writer feels that he or she has to cram in all the information gathered—as if to justify all that time spent investigating sources. When this happens, the manuscript lacks any kind of fire and focus. Strong nonfiction and historical fiction writing come from a balance of research and solid writing—the silent weaving in of the information into the story."

In *The Case of the Mummified Pigs and Other Mysteries in Nature* (Boyds Mills Press), author Susan Quinlan piques the interest of young readers by weaving in references to scientists as "nature sleuths" who investigate *cases, mysteries, puzzles,* and *disappearances*. A careful blend of simple sentences ("You have probably heard of Egyptian mummies") with compound and complex sentences (". . . asked them for dead baby pigs, but they gave him several . . .") moves the reader through each chapter. Years' worth of experiments and documentation are sifted down to essential nuggets, which are then laced with all the elements of good detective fiction.

The Experimental

When you choose to write in a particular genre, you face specific challenges associated with it. You understand that the longer the story, the more complex the blueprint. This is especially true when writing for young adults. More sophisticated devices, such as innovative language, must be used to draw in the teen reader.

"There are writers such as Adam Rapp, William Faulkner, Russell Hoban, and Anthony Burgess, who have used invented language successfully," says Neaves. "This device is particularly useful in young adult fiction because the language of adolescence is constantly changing. Adolescents establish their independence by creating a language that is cryptic enough to keep the world at bay. The invented language usually

Writing for the Spiritual Teen: Wise Words from an Editor

Writers often attempt to construct something new or edgy to capture the imagination of the teen reader. That includes those who write about the spiritual side of life. Are there ways to honor the rules and tell a good story, yet maintain the freshness or shock value that teens sometimes crave? Dale Reeves, Acquisitions Editor for Teen/Young Adult products at Standard Publishing, a Christian publisher, offers these insights on balancing good writing and good substance.

"That's often the job of a good editor. Because speaking with what I'd call a random stream of consciousness is so popular with postmodern young adults, I want to retain much of that style from a writer. Often it's simply a case of shortening run-on sentences or being creative with punctuation," Reeves says. "Lately I find myself using more em dashes and semicolons in my editing. I want the writer to sound as if he or she is speaking with a young adult in person, and the trick is to capture that feel, while still maintaining good grammar.

"Today's young adults are craving transparency and authenticity. These traits are paramount concerning what they want to pick up and read. Some young adult writers I know seem to go off on tangents, but what makes their style work is the fact that, after a great anecdote or metaphorical aside, they are able to bring the focus around full circle to the original point. Today's young adults consume good stories through

works within the confines of normal rules of usage."

Experimental fiction has great appeal for this age group, including experiments in language. A truly challenging example of invented language is found in Adam Rapp's *The Buffalo Tree*. His character Sura says things like "They'll carp you with the quickness" or "You got to keep your lungwind up to clip hoodies." A cell in the detention center is a *patch* and a cigarette is a *square*. Even within the context of the story this language may be difficult to understand—but it's purposely cryptic, enough to keep the world at bay and with both fists. That is how word choice and word use sustain and reflect story.

Another strategy that is ultimately syntactic is visual: the effective use of white space in text. The typical teen reader scans ahead and will avoid large blocks of text without breaks. In contrast, small bytes with visual appeal in between creates ongoing interest.

Writing for the Spiritual Teen:
Wise Words from an Editor

reading or watching movies, and they have no trouble tracking with a good story that eventually brings them back to the main point of an author. Some call this a *mosaic* style, as opposed to the *linear* style of the past."

It's sometimes difficult for spiritually based material to have an authentic teen voice when much of that authenticity goes against the moral voice. How can a writer use powerful language that isn't profane?

"The products we produce are culturally relevant and spiritually challenging," Reeves states. "I want what we produce to be authentic, spiritual, and God-centered; it's possible to do all three at the same time. That's what made *The Lord of the Rings* and the *Passion of the Christ* films so readily accepted. I'm convinced that today's young adults are spiritually hungry, so they resonate with this approach when they see it.

"In their nonfiction titles, authors are more willing to speak in the second person rather than in the third person because they want to speak straight to their young adult audience with cultural relevance. Other things, like ending sentences in prepositions, also seem more common because that is often how we speak. Many of the submissions I receive seem to have a more narrative, conversational tone than in the past, and I am in favor of this approach, so I'm not alarmed at all. In fact, I encourage it if it helps get more young adults reading!"

Start Building

When at last you have your idea blueprinted, your strategy developed, and your mind in focus, you begin. The style of your home will be evident in your diction and syntax. These are the bricks and mortar that will be laid upon the foundation of your story idea. Now your vision may be pulled as if from the sky and take form in the language you use to reveal it.

The best tools of the writing trade—grammar, punctuation, syntax, and rich words among them—were forged by those who have gone before you. They have helped writers give the world millions of story homes to love. Pick only the best tools for your project and prepare to count yourself among the artisans. Start building.

Language:
Let's Get Logical

By Cindy Rogers

From time to time, I review old grammar rules, if only to dust them off and apply them with renewed vigor. But old rules must also be examined to see if they retain any merit. They could be outdated, too narrow in scope, or not logical in the first place.

So which rules do we toss? And how do we decide? It's a dilemma. As William Zinsser, in *On Writing Well,* a book that's been around since 1976, says, "We have no king to establish the King's English; we only have the President's English, which we don't want." Perhaps lexicographer Samuel Johnson provided a clue back in the 1700s, when he said, "The pen must at length comply with the tongue." Common usage, it seems, is ultimately the determining factor.

It also seems that logic has everything to do with whether or not we cast aside or reinvent the rule. I've chosen a few rules that have been in debate for some time. I'll supply the logic behind the old rule, as well as the logic for taking a wider view, backed up by examples from literature.

To Split or To Not Split?

Never split an infinitive is a rule that has been traveling the countryside since the mid-nineteenth century. In a peanut shell, an infinitive is the purest, most basic form of a verb, before it has been conjugated into its various tenses. The rule suggests that if one is using this pure form— *to race, to stay, to purchase*—one does not divide the infinitive, as it is in "Harry decided to bravely stay." The rule suggests that by splitting the infinitive, the sentence becomes not only messy but confusing. In this case, it's Harry who is being brave, not the staying itself. Thus, the sentence and intent is: *Harry bravely decided to stay.* Or more simply put: *Bravely, Harry stayed.*

Yet, even William Strunk Jr. and E.B. White suggest in *The Elements of Style* that some infinitives are improved when split. It may sound more natural to insert the modifier, as in these examples: *To completely support your project, we need more data. I want to really like my mother-in-law.* Some adverbs that work well in the midst of an infinitive include *really, finally, just, actually, not, further, fully, even, completely, ever.*

Following are literary passages that use pure infinitives and split infinitives. Say the sentences aloud and hear how natural they sound and how clear the meaning is.

> But somebody, you see, had to make the connection for him. Someone had to first give him the words.
>
> *Katherine Paterson,*
> *A Sense of Wonder*

> Its continuing mission: to explore strange new worlds; to seek out new life and new civilizations; to boldly go where no one has gone before.
>
> *Star Trek*

No one stated the infinitive frustration more succinctly than George Bernard Shaw when he wrote this complaint to the *Times* of London:

> There is a pedant on your staff who spends far too much of his time searching for split infinitives. Every good literary craftsman uses a split infinitive if he thinks the sense demands it. I call for this man's instant dismissal; it matters not whether he decides to quickly go or to go quickly or quickly to go. Go he must, and at once.

Warning: Be prudent. Don't overuse the split infinitive and don't force formal correctness either. Know your intent when you write.

On Ending a Sentence with a Preposition

Never end a sentence with a preposition is another rule that's been around a long time, at least since the eighteenth century when—according to grammarphobe Patricia O'Conner, author of *Woe is I*—English clergyman Robert Lowth wrote the first grammar book. Prepositions are often small words. They show relationships between the noun or pronoun the preposition precedes and another word: The raccoon disappeared *into* the woods. Silas raced home *with* Joshua and Tameka.

The logic behind the rule is that a preposition is part of a phrase and should not stand alone, as in these examples: Where is he *at*? I want to go *with*. Here, the preposition is either extra baggage and should be dropped (Where is he?) or a clarifying noun or pronoun should be added, making it a prepositional phrase (I want to go with them.).

But, back to that rule. Common usage and logic should prevail. *Where's she from?* sounds natural, less stuffy than *From where is she?* These examples may remind you of a clever line attributed to Winston Churchill: "This is the sort of English up with which I will not put." I went in search of some examples to back up Churchill's sentiment, lines that end effectively with prepositions:

Use it up, wear it out; make it do, or do without.
> *New England maxim*

Bye baby bunting, Daddy's gone a-hunting.
Gone to get a rabbit skin, to wrap the baby bunting in.
> *Nursery rhyme*

I was always told that I should read the *Odyssey*. It popped up in small doses in English and Latin textbooks as I was growing up.
> Katherine Paterson,
> *A Sense of Wonder*

This affair must all be unraveled from within.
> Agatha Christie,
> *The Mysterious Affair at Styles*

Once again: Be prudent, don't overuse, and know your intent when you write.

And or *But* as Sentence Starters

Don't begin a sentence with and *or* but. The logic behind this rule is that two conjunctions yoke elements in a sentence but do not join one sentence with another. A conjunction—by its very term—conjoins parts. The strict grammarian suggests that a sentence should begin substantially, with something of consequence. In the examples that follow, you could delete the conjunction starter and the sentence would be both strong and acceptable.

And yet, as sentence starters, *but* or *and* provide relationship to the preceding sentence or an added emphasis to the words that follow (as this sentence just did). In this first example, note the use of the conjunction as a sentence starter, but also notice the uses of infinitives and a preposition at the end of the passage.

She had no dresses, no jewels, nothing. And she loved nothing but that; she felt made for that. She would so have liked to please, to be envied, to be charming, to be sought after.
> Guy de Maupassant,
> *The Necklace*

At first he thought it might have been some kind of animal, and it frightened him. But as the sleep cleared from his head, he realized that the noise was coming from the cot next to him.
> Louis Sachar,
> *Holes*

The author of the following example is establishing the mind of a madman. As the short story progresses, the erratic thoughts and madness are accentuated by the constant flow of sentences beginning with *and* and *but*. Here's the beginning of that build-up:

I was never kinder to the old man than during the whole week before I killed him. And every night, about midnight, I turned the latch of his door and opened it—oh, so gently! And then, when I had made an opening sufficient for my head, I put in a dark lantern, all closed, closed, so that no light shone out, and then I thrust in my head.

> *Edgar Allan Poe,*
> *"The Tell-Tale Heart"*

The conjunction precedes a philosophical nugget in this final example:

> To be a good writer, you not only have to write a great deal but you have to care. You do not have to have a complicated moral philosophy. But a writer always tries, I think, to be a part of the solution, to understand a little about life and to pass this on.
>
> *Anne Lamott,*
> *Bird by Bird*

The use of conjunctions to begin sentences has become more and more common. Don't fall into the pattern of it too often. It's too easy and less effective with frequency, as any stylistic device is.

Active or Passive?

Always use an active voice; avoid the passive. The active voice puts the doer in charge of the verb and the sentence: *The north wind swept the field bare. The Oliver twins won the race. His mother made his lunches.*

In the passive voice, the subject does nothing but instead has some-thing done to it: *The field was swept bare. The race was won by the Oliver twins. His lunches were made by his mother.* These passive examples create distance, whether that was the intent or not. The passive voice creates wimpy, weak narrative. Switch the sentence around, place the doer in the action seat, and you've created more intimacy and immediacy. An added bonus is a shorter, clearer sentence.

The passive does have its place. While it's true that this sentence—*John Wilkes Booth assassinated Abraham Lincoln*—is more straightforward and active than this arrangement—*Lincoln was assassinated by Booth*—the latter may be preferred. Because the facts are historical in nature and *Lincoln* itself carries power at the beginning of the sentence, the passive and more distant voice works just fine.

Technical, historical, medical, and scientific data often use the passive voice because the subject is acted upon (literally passive). Here are several examples from literature:

> Its walls had been lined with human remains, piled to the vault overhead, in the fashion of the great catacombs of Paris. Three sides of this interior crypt were still ornamented in this manner. From the fourth the bones had been thrown down, and lay promiscuously upon the earth.
>
> *Edgar Allen Poe,*
> *"The Cask of Amontillado"*

In some cases, the dead were left in their homes for days. Private undertaking houses were overwhelmed and some were taking advantage of the situation . . . Complaints were made that cemetery officials were charging fifteen dollar burial fees and then making the bereaved dig graves for the dead themselves."

Gina Kolata,
Flu, The Story of the Great
Influenza Pandemic of 1918

Sometimes, the passive verb serves up the element of surprise in a better way than an active verb could: *The winning poem was written by a third-grader!*
Here's the same usage from a middle-grade novel:

He was awakened one night by a strange noise.

Louis Sachar,
Holes

Determine when the instance calls for passive and when for active and take your stand.

There Is No Way to Start
Do not start a sentence with there. Nine times out of ten, the sentence starter *there* is another weak, inarticulate way to write. It's weak because the word has no meaning, just stands in for something else: *There are too many kids standing around. There is a hockey game underway.* Simply delete that ineffec-

tual opener in both examples and the sentences are stronger: *Too many kids are standing around. A hockey game is underway.*

Yet, literature is full of examples in which that inarticulate sentence starter does an excellent job of creating a maxim, starting a story, making a generalization, or offering a description:

There was an old woman who lived in a shoe, she had so many children . . .

Nursery rhyme

There are no second acts in American lives.

F. Scott Fitzgerald,
Notebooks

And when you close Homer, there are the books of Jane Austen and Joseph Conrad, and great fat volumes of Tolstoy. There is the Bible, perhaps the most overprescribed and least taken of any. There is Flannery O'Connor and Anne Tyler. There is William Shakespeare and Jacob Bronowski. There is *The Yearling* and *A Tale of Two Cities.* There is . . .

Katherine Paterson,
A Sense of Wonder

There is no lake at Camp Green Lake. There once was a very large lake here, the largest lake in Texas. That was over a hundred years ago.

Louis Sachar,
Holes

There were crisp husks of beechmast and cast acorn cups underfoot in the russet slime of dead bracken where the rains of the equinox had so soaked the earth that the cold oozed up through the soles of the shoes, lancinating cold of the approach of winter that grips hold of your belly and squeezes it tight.

> *Angela Carter,*
> *"The Erl-King"*

Repetition equals Redundancy?

Avoid repeating the same word in a passage; repetition is redundancy. This particular rule suggests that a writer get out a thesaurus and find synonyms to replace a word that has been overused:

Olaf went to the store to look for his favorite snack. He went down every aisle, looking for Frostios. He even went to the checkout and looked in customers' baskets.

The verbs *went* and *look* could and should be replaced with more interesting, descriptive verbs or the reader will want to snap at Olaf.

Yet, fear of repetition can result in what we might call *creative reaching,* which often results in painful reading:

Harry loved his football and would run for the pigskin whenever Billy or Stewart appeared in his backyard. Even on rainy days, when he was trapped inside, Harry would toss around the elliptical leather ball.

In some cases, a repeated phrase makes for weak writing. But repetition is also a powerful tool. The echo of a word or phrase or sound creates memorable rhetoric. Remember Martin Luther King Jr.'s "I have a dream" speech, in which he repeated those very words over and over. That speech is often quoted, not just for content, but for its superb rhetoric, as is an example from Abraham Lincoln's *Gettysburg Address*: ". . . and that government of the people, by the people, for the people, shall not perish from the earth."

Look back also at the Katherine Paterson example, in which repetition builds on the fact that there is no end to the reading possibilities.

The author of the next passage uses repetition to help the reader understand how profound a role the sky plays in the life of the main character, who is aboard a tiny raft in the middle of the ocean. By the time the passage ends, many sentences later, the reader is as engulfed by the sky as the narrator.

The sky was completely cloudless . . . The sky was a heavy, suffocating blanket of grey cloud . . . The sky was thinly overcast. The sky was dappled with small, white, fleecy clouds. The sky was streaked with high, thin clouds that looked like a cotton ball stretched apart. The sky was a featureless milky haze. The sky . . .

> Yann Martel,
> *Life of Pi*

That same kind of emphasis occurs in this final example:

One realizes that there are two breeds in Turkey: those who carry and those who sit. No one sits quite so relaxedly, expertly, beatifically as a Turk; he sits with every inch of his body; his very face sits. He sits as if he inherited the art from generations of sultans in the palace above Seraglio Point. Nothing he likes better than to invite you to sit with him . . .

> V.S. Pritchett,
> *A Cab at the Door*

Fragments? Yes, by Gum!

Use complete sentences with a subject and predicate. Fragments have no place in good writing.

This rule has long been overruled, but every English teacher enforces it to establish good writing practices among new writers. Yet, even the youngest readers and writers know that dialogue often uses the single word fragment: *No! Yes. Maybe. Okay.*

If applied well, a fragment can create a measured emphasis, not only in dialogue but in narrative. Here are a few fine examples to back up the case for fragments,

fragments that work far better than complete sentences. Note that the length of the sentence has no bearing on the definition of a fragment.

Lolita, light of my life, fire of my loins. My sin, my soul.

> *Vladmimir Nabokov,*
> *Lolita*

There was a change in the weather. For the worse.

> *Louis Sachar,*
> *Holes*

Eye of newt, and toe of frog, wool of bat, and tongue of dog.

> *William Shakespeare,*
> *Macbeth*

This wimpled, whining, purblind, wayward boy, this senior-junior, giant-dwarf, Dan Cupid, Regent of love-rimes, lord of folded arms, the anointed sovereign of sighs and groans, liege of all loiterers and malcontents.

> *William Shakespeare,*
> *Love's Labour's Lost*

Everybody has at least one ugly secret, and mine is as ugly as they come. I square-dance. With my mother.

> *David LaRochelle,*
> *Absolutely, Positively Not*

In the final passage, note the repetition of words, a repetition that builds and adds power to the fragments:

171

Memories crash against her.
Memories of being bare to the
sun. She wonders what it will
be like. Not to have to go to a
job. Not to work in a sewing
plant. Not to worry about
learning to sew straight seams
in a workingman's overalls, . . .

Alice Walker,
"Roselily"

Finally, once again: Be prudent.
Don't overuse. Know your intent
when you write. Above all, be clear.
Be logical.

End of Story

By Christina Hamlett

Coming up with a good ending is not unlike trying to say goodbye to dear friends after a party. There you are, hovering in the doorway for a final round of hugs. The night is getting late. You know that you should've been on your way hours ago but something keeps triggering one more anecdote, one more hug, one more reason to linger.

Your host asks you (and perhaps not for the first time) if you'd like to come back inside. "No, no, it's late. I really shouldn't," you decline, nonetheless sufficiently energized to keep right on chatting until the cows come home.

While our friends can be forgiving of our reluctance to bring an enjoyable evening to a close, the buyers of your book won't be as tolerant of a tale that either takes too long to make its exit or rings false in its summation of the events preceding. Although many writers insist that a story's beginning is the hard part, the greater challenge is in orchestrating a finish that will not only end exactly when it's supposed to, but leave a reader looking forward to the next encounter.

If saying goodbye to your characters often has you flummoxed and tongue-tied, the following advice—paralleled in the workings of successful films—will help make the parting less painful.

Start Late, Finish Early

The party analogy with which this article began is one of the first rules of crafting a story that stays tight from start to finish. Just because the invitation states that the soiree will run from six until midnight doesn't mean you should be ringing the doorbell at 5:59 and parking yourself next to the buffet table until you turn into a pumpkin. To paraphrase the etiquette books, your presence should be long enough to invite intrigue but not so much as to induce boredom.

The same can be said of the characters in your book, story, or script. The majority of them will not have been born interesting but, rather, evolved into compelling persons based on a progression of events. Accordingly, you wouldn't start a story with little Wilma's childhood and follow her through high school, college, marriage, divorce, etc. if, in fact, Wilma's life didn't get exciting until she turned 62 and bought herself a Harley. While reference can be made in dialogue or flashback to incidents in her tamer youth, she needs to be introduced to your audience at the point when she will be her most fascinating to them: 62.

Unlike real life, a novel or movie is conveyed in a series of ellipses. These time-jumps allow you to fast-forward through pregnancies, adolescence, and career struggles and cut to the chase of the central conflict. This abbreviated structure also enables you to set the pace that will prevail throughout the story, ensuring that your characters won't overstay their welcome. Consider an example from the movies that works.

Example: Miss Congeniality. Gracie's tomboy qualities and ineptitude with the opposite sex as a child are set forth in the prologue, allowing us to leap ahead with her to adulthood as a policewoman. Her journey in between is immaterial because we already have enough information to glean what it was like.

Know Your Destination

"You don't often hear about the beginning or the middle of a film being re-shot or rewritten," says Jennifer Wynne Farmer, Executive Director/Producer of Pumpkin Pictures. "You do, however, hear a lot about endings being redone. Why? Because the ending of a film will absolutely make or break a story in terms of its success and appeal." She compares a film's ending to "what the final crescendo is in music, what the closing arguments are in law, and what the gallery exhibition is in visual art. It's literally the moment we've all been waiting for." The same is true for any fiction.

Unfortunately, many writers either rush that moment with a slapdash, implausible leap of faith or engage in the literary equivalent of a taffy pull to stretch the denouement out for as long as possible.

The first offense—contrivance— is often borne of author desperation and reflected in the actions of characters. It's a scenario played out time and again. A protagonist is suddenly boxed into a position of jeopardy from which all avenues of escape have been eliminated. We frantically root for the hero's survival but, alas, really can't see how it is possible as the remaining seconds of his life tick away. But wait! Isn't that an AV-8B Harrier II now hovering over the balcony?

Once you resort to a flimsy, quickie save predicated on coincidence, luck, or previously unrevealed talents (i.e., the power suddenly to render oneself invisible), you instantly diminish whatever affection and respect you spent building up for your endangered characters. "I call these the 'I got 90 pages, so let's end this thing' ending," says independent filmmaker James Tucker. "They just stop or get tired and throw in something from completely out of nowhere."

A second flawed ending—overt elucidation—is the result of a writer's angst that maybe *happily ever after* leaves too much room for ambiguity. Like an English mystery in which former suspects gather in the parlor to have the entire crime neatly explained to them, the intent of all the analysis and replay is to ensure that no one goes home confused. Unfortunately, it also removes the readers' enjoyment of engaging in further speculation.

Peter Dimond, Publisher of *Plays, The Drama Magazine for Young People,* offers this observation: "For an ending to be believable, it must be satisfying yet leave room for readers to interpret events as suits them. A lot of new writers beat you over the head with an ending, especially with dialogues heavy-handedly drawing conclusions that audiences can come up with pretty well on their own."

Both of these closing *faux pas* can be avoided if the author just takes time to answer two questions before the plot gets underway: (1) what is the protagonist's quest, and (2) what resources are available to make that quest a reality?

Let's say that the teen heroine of your YA novel is kidnapped in a case of mistaken identity. To accomplish her goal (freedom), she needs to rely on whatever attributes and personal effects she possessed prior to the kidnapping (a sense of

humor, an ability to climb trees, and a half roll of breath mints). Likewise, if her only chance of rescue depends on external intervention (a nosy neighborhood kid), that device needs to be introduced or foreshadowed early enough for readers to forget about its existence until its reappearance as a plausible exit strategy. Once that goal is satisfactorily met, nothing further need be explained.

Example: Back to the Future. In this time-travel comedy, it's the hero's knowledge of forthcoming events (the clocktower, the lightning, and the school dance) that allows him to exert influence on the past in which he is trapped.

Putting Bookends to Best Use

Does your pulse ever go into race mode when you're reading an autobiography? Even if the chapters contain life-threatening adventures at every turn, you're never detached from the fact that the author lived to tell about them. The same can be said of the *bookend* approach, a device in which a plot's entire middle is comprised of flashback.

As younger readers, would we have been as swept up in the mischief of Tom and Huck, the determination of Velvet Brown, the inventiveness of the Swiss Family Robinson, the travels of James and his giant peach, or even the romance of Cinderella if our first introduction to each of them had been on the veranda of a retirement home? In these examples, the linear journey provided a way not only to apply our problem-solving abilities to the story but to apply the lessons of the story's outcome to our own lives.

When writers opt to depart from the linear route, the challenge shifts from the question of, "Will the hero get his wish?" to "How did that wish transform him?" Plots in which fictitious characters interact with historical figures are especially good candidates for the bookend method, as are stories in which the protagonist's present-day circumstances are not made entirely clear to us. For instance, a child helping her grandmother clean out the attic discovers a letter. Whose is it? The flashback is full of clues for us to guess about its authorship but we won't know the answer until the reward of the final chapter.

Example: Titanic. In James Cameron's 1997 epic, we know that Rose didn't perish in her collision with destiny. What we don't know is how that provocative picture of her ended up in the vault.

Happily Ever After (Not)

Once upon a time, we were taught that every story had to have a happy ending. What wasn't taught, of course, is the difference between *happy* and *satisfying*. If the conditions you've set forth have already closed the door on a cheerful resolution, the use of a miracle reversal will come off as fake with your readers.

That's especially true if they're as discerning as 10-year-old Katie Dimond, who offers this assessment of Rodman Philbrick's *Freak*

the Mighty: "The ending was sad and I knew it was going to happen. Freak (the main character's best friend) dies but it was normal for that to happen, and I was glad the author didn't just make a happy ending where everything was going to be okay."

Hollywood film agent Cynthia Brohas-Gulacsy defines such satisfaction further in saying, "I need to come away feeling emotionally charged in some way—whether it is angry, happy, relieved, or exhausted—for me to feel we have a solid contender for today's demanding market. Whether you like the ending or not, you should still be able to walk away satisfied and saying, 'Yes, I get it. I don't agree with it, but I get it.'"

Example: Shakespeare in Love. Who among us didn't want Will and his muse to ditch their significant others? The Queen, of course, would not have been amused.

The Never-Ending Story

If you're like most writers, you hate leaving the characters with whom you've bonded. The good news is that sometimes you don't have to. Sequels and prequels have proven themselves to be hot commodities in publishing and film, especially since repeat performances are guaranteed to attract a majority of the fans who loved the original.

The bad news, however, is that it's harder than it sounds. Unless your heroes are in a job or environment that generates a regular stream of external stimuli, you'll run out of adventures for them fairly fast. Consider the longevity of the Nancy Drew series. Setting aside the irony that her hairstyle, clothing, and car have transitioned with the times while Nancy herself has remained ageless since 1930, today's headlines are replete with enough material to keep this plucky girl detective going until the next millennium.

While your own protagonist may not have a comparable shelf life, there's always the option of passing the baton to a secondary character. "Let's do this again sometime" as a closing line to a pleasing plot leaves the door open either to continue the existing relationship or send the speaker into partnership with someone new.

Example: Harry Potter, et al. As if the curriculum at Hogwarts isn't enough fodder, the trio's propensity for courting danger will keep this series cooking for the foreseeable future.

Never Underestimate Your Readers

Too often in my reading, writing, and professional consulting, I encounter superficial endings that reflect a writer's belief that a younger readership has low expectations. The following quote by Nick Morgan of Peru, Vermont, is included in postscript as a wake-up call to anyone who thinks the next generation isn't paying close attention:

"I recently read Virginia Woolf's *Mrs. Dalloway*, which had a fabulous ending. It was very low-key, featuring two of the minor characters discussing Mrs. Dalloway herself. Mrs. Dalloway's absence from this final scene reflected my own opinion of her, that she was not the vital character; those she surrounded herself with were the really exciting ones. The novel ended where she is spotted by Peter Walsh, the man who has loved her for too many years. It was a yearning, angst-ridden moment but tastefully done with few words. That ending left me breathless, partly because it ended so quickly and with such tortured feelings, and partly because of the gorgeous prose involved. It was a satisfying book, and the ending was subtle enough to please me even as I wanted more."

Nick just turned 15.

Editors & Writers

Where Do I Go from Here?

By Leslie Davis Guccione

Most writers will tell you their top professional priority is developing rapport with that all-important editor. She's bought your manuscript; his revision suggestions are clear; you've signed your first multiple book contract.

Nearly 20 years have sailed by since my agent's "Leslie, I've sold your manuscript" danced through the phone lines. Armed with my IBM Selectric typewriter and a lifetime supply of White Out, I set sail. To belabor the metaphor, with calm seas and a steady breeze I left port heading toward long-term relationships with supportive, enthusiastic editors; increasingly lucrative multiple book contracts; and sterling reviews. Fan mail! Classroom visits! Book signings! Royalty checks!

Here's where the musical score from *Jaws* begins to play. During the years since I proofed that first set of galleys, unexpected industry obstacles have burst to the surface of my charted waters like the shark under Quint's boat.

Despite a solid working relationship and the best intentions on both sides of the editor's desk, it can take no more than a phone call to disrupt, delay, or even derail a career.

House Orphan: The Sun'll Come Out Tomorrow

Writers are *orphaned* so often we could keep *Annie* in continual production. I came face-to-face with the publishing term when Editor A wrote to say she was leaving her Midwestern publishing house for one in Manhattan. Within months, Editor B at the major New York house where I had 10 titles published left under a cloud that still hasn't lifted.

Chances are strong that you'll be orphaned at least once during your career. In today's market, where editors house-hop and publishers swallow each other like trout after flies, it happens with alarming frequency. As in my case, the blanket term *orphaned* applies to several situations, and the how and why of an editor's departure can drastically

179

affect the careers of the writers in the editors' *stable*.

Was your editor fired or did he jump to another house? Will she take you with her or has she left you with a capable replacement? Is he leaving the industry? Might she be switching to a related field—literary agent or freelance copy editor?

As soon as you are notified, ask questions. Do not abandon the rapport the two of you, ideally, have established. Equally important, begin to create that bond with the editor's replacement.

Middle-grade author Barbara O'Connor learned the hard way: "When you work with one editor for a long time, it becomes clear what is expected of each of you—so you begin to make assumptions that may not always be accurate with a new editor. When my editor left and I was orphaned, I wish I had taken the time to find out exactly who would be responsible for the various things I had, in the past, gone to my editor for. Who'd be responsible for sending me copies of reviews? Who'd be responsible for marketing questions? Who would I call if I needed a complimentary copy of a book sent somewhere?

"For all of this I had gone to my editor and she filtered it out to whomever. With her departure I was left floating around trying to find out whom to ask for what. When I began working with a new editor, a more delicate problem arose: Expectations weren't always clear. Would she run every single no-matter-how-minor change by me or would she just do it? (That became a big problem.) Was she flexible with deadlines or not? Would she keep me posted of schedule changes?"

O'Connor's experience illustrates how covering essentials in an initial contact saves time and cuts down on frustration for both of you. Establish *rules of conduct* early on, including the most basic: Does your editor's replacement prefer email or voice mail? Will you deal directly with him or her or with an assistant for marketing or publicity issues?

Karen Lynn Williams made the best of an unsettling situation. "In the midst of plans for my third book, my editorial team moved to a new publishing house and two of my best-selling books, *Galimoto* and *Baseball and Butterflies,* became orphans. The team told me they would have taken the proposal we were working on, *First Grade King,* with them, but it was too far along for them to begin work with it at the new house. Even though there was no one to advocate for them, my two books with publisher number one continued to sell steadily. I now had editors at a new company who had made it clear they liked my work, so I looked at this as a chance to branch out. I was able to submit to both these publishers with a guarantee that someone would read my work. I went on to publish two more books at each."

When possible, ask your departing editor what you can expect from the change. Request the name of the replacement. Will your departing editor continue to look at your work at the new publishing house? You should expect clear answers, whether you stay behind, are invited along or, as in Williams' case, wind up with feet—literally—in both doors.

Sour Notes and Cool Heads

"You're so easy to work with," I heard regularly as my career took hold. Editors meant that when requested, I revise, polish, and cut-and-paste to their liking. Eighty percent of the time editors' suggestions and our working relationships breeze along smoothly. The remaining 20 percent requires a cool head and clear thinking. When dealing with a brand-new boss, however, most writers are back to giving 100 percent of the effort to get the relationship —and the project—up and running to everyone's satisfaction.

Freelancer and middle-grade novelist Lori Pollard-Johnson always gives the new editor "a chance to appreciate my hard work. Once I chose not to work with a particular editor after several rude and sarcastic interactions, and once I became 'too busy with my fiction work' to accept assignments from an editor I found very rough around the edges.

"This doesn't happen very often, though, because my attitude (even stated orally at times) to revision requests has always been, 'No problem. You know the audience better than I do, and I want the article to fit your publication, because I want to help you build your reader base.'"

Nancy Alberts fought frustration with her first editor and project "for a picture book manuscript called *Fried Mittens*. The release date was set for two years later. I signed the contract, made some requested revisions, received my advance, and then waited—and waited. The two years came and went. I had trouble reaching my editor and when I did, she assured me that the book was forthcoming. In the meantime, a new editorial director had come on board, and my book, among others, fell through the cracks. It was never published.

"Naturally, I kept my advance and asked for my rights back. It was a disappointing setback to deal with so early in my career. Nevertheless, I determined not to give up, and as a result, I eventually sold two more books to that publisher before moving on. While I still think *Fried Mittens* has merit, the experience taught me the value of perseverance and not to take publishing decisions personally."

Whether the topic of difficult editor situations is raised at conferences, via Internet chatboards, or within a hometown critique group, patterns emerge among successful writers. Whenever possible:

▨ They make a deliberate effort to establish a solid, pleasant, and productive relationship with the replacement editor.

▨ They stay in touch with the departing editor and look for potential within his or her new publishing house.

Protocol Counts

Despite today's informality and mind-boggling electronic time-savers, author Lori Pollard-Johnson offers advice on time-honored protocol:

"My approach to new editors stems from my experience in the business world. My family owned an importing business, and I learned very early on that when dealing with people from other countries, I had to learn as much about their culture as I could, and keep communications very simple and very clear. It made me use concise, but basic vocabulary and a positive, very professional voice in written and oral correspondence. The same holds true for editors. I do research on them and their publication, and write straightforward, formal letters, addressing them by surname. I try to keep the letters *glance-able*, meaning they can read the first sentence and a few words in the paragraph and know what I mean.

"Once I know an editor well (two or more articles or an invitation to correspond by e-mail):

– I use their first name, but only if they use my first name first.
– I try very hard not to ask questions I can get answered myself.
– I always respect their time, thanking them for prompt replies.
– I always, always, always promise satisfaction, but deliver excellence.

"Sometimes that means negotiating an extra two weeks for an article and then delivering it a week early in a highly polished condition. All the client remembers is that they got it early and it looked great. Other times, such as last fall, I offered to retype an entire short story (around 20 pages) because I didn't know if I could find it on diskette (it had been sitting in the slush pile for over four years!). The editor was tickled by my willingness to go the extra mile.

"In a nutshell, I want my editor to say, 'I can always count on Lori, and I barely have to touch her work!'"

Philippa Greene Mulford was left an orphan, she says, "when my editor at Macmillan was fired. Simon & Schuster bought the house shortly thereafter and I never heard from anyone until [the book in production] was about to be published. Someone called and asked for a photo for the catalogue. It was not a particularly happy experience but the book did well, received good reviews, and was named to numerous advanced reading lists for that age group.

"Eventually my ex-editor landed at another house and bought my middle-grade novel, *The Holly Sisters on Their Own*. Again, it did well and was well reviewed, this time all over the country so I was pleased. I liked that editor very much and was sorry when she retired. You just have to hang in there and stay in touch with the individual, which I did through my agent, who was very fond of this particular editor."

I Like It, But...

You followed your editor to his new publisher or you've been assigned to the new person replacing him. Perhaps your work has been welcomed at both houses. No matter the scenario—e-zine to magazine, novel to nonfiction—the ultimate goal never varies: giving your editor your best effort. When that work still needs polish, remember who's requesting revisions.

When polled for this article, the editors repeatedly list flexibility as a top asset in their writers. Consider revisions to be a professional's opin-ion on what will make your work even more appealing—to the publisher as well as to their readers.

Children's author and science educator Carolyn DeCristofano says, "When writing and revising, I view any and all feedback as valuable, free advice. I try to look for patterns, like that I don't develop the content enough and stay at arm's length from sufficient detail. I try to see if they are articulating something I knew on an emotional level anyway. I try to phone only for complex concerns and I e-mail ahead of time to give a heads-up."

Pollard-Johnson says, "I let them know I'm a team player. I've also frequently said, 'I have little to no writer's ego,' so editors will feel comfortable offering me assignments that need some extra care."

Questions or disagreements? Keep the interaction flowing.

Author and children's book reviewer Sue Corbett says, "The key to a good working relationship is just simple communication. I have worked with editors for 20 years because I am a career newspaper reporter. Though I have had good relationships with many, I am not in awe of them. They are human, too. I'm not sure where this hesitation to contact editors comes from among writers. I guess it stems from the perception that there is an imbalance in power."

"Even if I don't like an editor's suggestions," DeCristofano says, "I will try them. Sometimes, I have to sit at the computer and unfreeze my reluctant fingers by reminding myself that my original version is saved, and that I can hit delete after I try making the changes as suggested. I sometimes have to speak out loud to convince myself just to try suggestions. But I believe that I, personally, would not have a chance of blossoming into any kind of writer without this kind of commitment to trying to implement someone's advice."

"I've heard writers counsel other writers to stick to their stories and be wary of editors suggesting changes," novelist Coleen Paratore says. "Having enjoyed the exciting experience of selling my first four children's books to three different publishers in one year, this is what I have to say about editors: I love them. They are goddesses. Listen to them. They absolutely do know best. As I told a young reader, 'The author-editor relationship is a partnership. Each brings something of value to the process of creating good books.' We need each other."

Take heart; buck up; stay the course. Truth lies in every cliché. No matter how rough the waters, never forget that editors want to establish long-term professional relationships, to publish the best version of the best book from the best writer, to make your work shine.

The Literary Contract & You

By Robert Brown and Sharene Martin

A literary contract is a beautiful thing. It spells out in its pages—sometimes many and sometimes few—what is expected of both parties in a book deal. If written well, a literary contract protects the writer and the publisher in case of circumstances foreseen and unforeseen. This is its purpose. While agents negotiate with publishers and advise their clients, the final decision is yours, the writer's, whether to sign or not to sign any agreement binding you to a publishing entity. Therefore, it is essential to understand some important contract concepts before signing on the dotted line.

Books have been written on contracts and contract negotiation. There are lawyers who specialize in nothing but intellectual property law. The best teacher is experience, since that is how you begin to understand the nuances of the contract and how each item connects to another. Many times, if even one sentence is changed, others will have to be updated to match that change.

What follows is by no means a complete analysis of literary contracts or negotiations, but rather a review of some of the most important concepts involved in publication agreements. We always suggest—even to our own clients—that you, the signatory of the contract, should know some contract basics. An informed writer is a successful, confident, and professional writer.

Before You Submit Your Work

The very idea of getting published can be so overwhelmingly appealing that writers sometimes forget other considerations, and there are many. These business-related items should be considered, whether you have an agent or not.

For example, what have you written and what is its realistic potential? If you have created a 10-word baby book about greetings in different languages, then should dramatic subsidiary rights be a deal-breaker? If you have written an edgy, contemporary young adult novel, retaining dramatic rights might be a consideration.

You need to think about these issues before you get the contract, not after. To do this, you must stay abreast of your book's potential markets and popular culture, no matter what you write. Who your agent is has little bearing on this.

Writing commercially is a business. As a professional writer, you must have the ability to assess where your book fits into the literary scheme of things. Having this knowledge ultimately affects career decisions. Fighting a publisher, or insisting your agent do it, over unimportant, non-negotiable items is a waste of valuable time and energy that might cause you to lose a good deal or sign on for a bad one.

Take a few moments to sit down and write out your goals. What do you want your book to do? Whom do you want to read it? What kind of publisher do you think would profit most from taking it on? If you have an agent, this should be one of the first matters you discuss, and if you don't have an agent, knowing the answers to these questions will help you avoid signing anything that will work against your best interests.

Copyright

You own the copyright to your work, as the writer, and a good publishing contract will state that you are not being asked to sell your copyright. A publisher should merely be granted permission to copy and distribute your book and to license other entities to print, or otherwise utilize, some or all of the many subsidiary rights connected

with your copyright in the work. Remembering this will alleviate the shock when you initially read the language in this section, which can include phrases like:

> The Author grants to the Publisher the exclusive right to publish and to assign or license others to publish any and all rights listed herein for the life of this copyright. The rights granted to the Publisher are granted exclusively to the Publisher throughout the world.

Publishers should register the copyright and pay for this registration. They must, according to law, print the appropriate notice in all editions of your book in accordance with the copyright laws of the United States and the provisions of the Universal Copyright Convention.

Advance

For the right to copy your work, a publisher must compensate you. Depending on the publishing house, this includes a royalty package and, most times, an advance. The advance amount and how it will be distributed to you should be detailed in your contract. If not, make sure that it is before signing.

The first question authors usually ask is, "How much of an advance do I get and when?" An advance is actually a loan from the publisher to you, the author, no matter what the amount, and it will have to be paid back through royalties before you receive another penny from the publisher. The question usually never asked is whether it makes a difference if an advance is offered or not. Originally, the idea behind advances was to give a starving artist something to live on until the book was finished, or, if finished, until the royalties came rolling in.

Today, when most writers have day jobs (and should keep them—even Leonardo da Vinci had a day job!), the large advance has become more of a bragging right or measure of prestige than a necessity. Agents, of course, love to have the money come in upfront, instead of waiting for royalty checks. For most, being an agent *is* their day job. The amount of advance you are willing to accept depends on the goals you set for yourself as a writer.

Royalty

Royalty percentages vary and can be based on the retail value of your book or on the actual monies from sales received by the publisher. All of this is negotiable by you or your agent and is based on where you stand in the writing profession. Beginners have little to bargain with, so accepting standard fare is sometimes considered a rite of passage. It is up to the individual writer what he or she deems acceptable. What is important is that there is a royalty package included that at least meets the industry standard for your project.

Standard royalty package numbers are usually available from writers' organizations. In our opinion,

the best arrangement is a sliding scale wherein the author earns a higher percentage of royalties after certain benchmarks are met, based on the number of books sold. Remember also that a certain amount of money is held back in the event of possible returns. When bookstores return books to the publisher's distributor, money for these returns must be refunded to the distributor, and royalties are not paid on this money.

A contract must also detail when you are to receive your royalty payments. Most publishers pay royalties twice a year, but some pay only once a year. For obvious reasons, especially if you haven't been offered an advance, this needs to be negotiated. Twelve months is a long time to wait; it is not necessary for this amount of time to pass without some kind of compensation.

Primary & Subsidiary Rights

Most standard contracts, in addition to stating the advance and royalty package, are very broad in nature and deal with the following:

- the primary rights the publisher will exploit (which can include, but are not limited to, hardcover, trade paperback, mass market, etc., depending on the publisher's focus and needs);
- the amount of time the publisher wants these rights (usually the life of the copyright);
- which subsidiary rights they want to retain to license to others (i.e. dramatic, electronic, audio,

foreign, and a variety of others);
■ the right to distribute and sell what they print.

Primary rights are those the publisher is contracting to exercise itself. Subsidiary rights, or sub-rights, are those rights that the contracting publisher might license to others for an agreed upon sum of money that is to be shared (usually on a 50-50 basis) with the author. These can include rights licensed to English-speaking nations like Britain, Australia, or New Zealand; translations; large print; book club; and voice recordings. Most agents try to include language that says any rights not exploited within a given time period will revert back to the author.

Reversion

Although you should know when your publisher plans to publish your book, it is also important that every contract you consider signing has a reversion clause. Your real purpose for entering into this contract is to get your book published, but if this is not realized, there should be an easy way to force publication or have the contract become void.

In most standard book contracts, an example of a reversion clause would be that if your book is not published within a specified time from the date of the contract signing, then all rights revert back to you. This time period is usually 18 to 24 months. Also contained in this clause is a statement that the author may keep any advances paid

up to this point, since the fault for non-publication lies with the publisher, not the author. If this clause is not in your contract, negotiate one into it.

Out of Print

Every contract should include an out-of-print clause. This clause states that if a book becomes unavailable from the publisher or its distributors, then the book is declared out of print. If the publisher has no intention of publishing a new edition, then all rights should revert back to the author.

There must also be some procedure in the event a book is declared out-of-print. Language to watch for in an out-of-print clause is that which includes licensees. Those with licenses to produce the book may be given permission to continue to produce it, but a book should not be deemed in print just because there is one copy in a warehouse in a remote location across the globe.

Characters

Writers should always beware of language that allows a publisher to control their characters. This might seem innocent and unimportant on the surface, but rights to characters should always remain with the author. With control of your characters, a publisher would no longer need you to produce books containing those characters and could hire others to create sequels, paying them a work-for-hire rate, with no compensation to you.

Your Next Book

Most publishers want to control the author's output and will include an option clause stating that the author agrees to let the publisher see his or her next book before shopping it around to any other publishers. This clause defines how much time the publisher has to accept or reject the project. It also states that if the publisher makes an offer on the author's next project and the author refuses that offer, he or she cannot accept a lower offer from a different publisher.

In itself, this is not bad, as the author still has right of refusal. What happens in some cases, however, is that publishers try to insert language to control the sale of the author's next book. This language states that the author's next book might interfere with the sales of the present book if released within a certain time period.

We see the option clause as unnecessary as long as the author is treated well by the publisher, and it can be downright restrictive depending on the language. Vigilance is the watchword when it comes to these clauses.

Editorial

A contract should never allow a publisher to change an author's work without his or her approval. Never agree to the hiring of a professional editor if you cannot or will not make the revisions necessary for publication. Any language like this should be stricken in its entirety from the contract.

A publisher has no right to hire someone to edit your work if you refuse to do so or cannot make the changes requested; however, the publisher always has the right of refusal and should also contractually have the right to have monies paid to the author refunded promptly upon rejection of the author's work. Your book belongs to you, its author, and a literary contract allowing the publisher to refuse the final manuscript is enough.

General

Contracts are filled with general provisions, such as the author guaranteeing that the work is original and that the publisher has the right to take to court anyone who steals (infringes upon) all or part of the work.

Contracts say who pays the lawyer fees if infringement occurs, and how damages are to be split up if the case is won. Literary contracts detail:

- who is responsible for getting permissions when another writer's work is incorporated into your book;
- what date your completed book must be delivered to the publisher;
- what happens in a case of bankruptcy;
- what kind of a discount the author can expect when buying copies of the book from the publisher;
- the number of author copies; and

■ if there is a restriction on sale of your author copies.

These provisions comprise most of the contract, are general in nature, and almost never need to be negotiated.

Picture Books

Picture book authors, in particular, must understand that royalties, subrights splits, and some other items in your contracts will be slightly different. The reason is simply because you are splitting your compensation package with the illustrator. The very nature of a picture book is that it uses a combination of pictures and text to convey a story, and without the writer and the artist, there is no product.

There is much to contracts that we do not have time or space to discuss here. Our advice to any author who is in doubt is to not sign on the dotted line until he/she feels comfortable with the contract. Talk with your agent, or, if you don't have one, do more research or contact an attorney who specializes in intellectual property. Always remember that, ultimately, the decision whether or not to sign a publishing agreement is yours, and yours alone.

Break with Tradition & Self-Publish

By Katherine Swarts

Many a children's book author, despairing of ever finding a publisher, has thought: "Why go to all this trouble? Why not just publish the book myself?" After all, some bestsellers famously have started out as self-published. Think of *Eragon*, first in the Inheritance Trilogy being published by Random House (the second book, *Eldest,* appeared in summer 2005); or G.P. Taylor's *Shadowmancer*, both blockbusters originally financed and promoted by the authors.

It may very well be worth a try, but in this article we'll also confront the uphill battle that self-publishing can be. Don't be put off. Publishing your own work, especially in this age of Print-on-Demand (POD) technology, is an excellent opportunity for many, as are other self-publishing avenues. Authors nonetheless should know the downsides before they throw their resources into the exciting possibilities.

Unfortunately, the eager self-publisher typically overlooks hard facts: For every self-published book that has become a bestseller, hundreds stopped selling after the writer ran out of family and friends. Moreover, self-publishing a book is not less work than finding a traditional publisher, at least not if the book is going to be a commercial success. Self-published books are likely to be more work, since the full duty of marketing the books and running the business falls on the writer.

While even traditionally published authors have to do their share of promotional work (few major publishers have the resources to launch extensive campaigns for every title or to keep a slow seller in print for long), such authors at least have the advantage of being backed by a proven name. Authors who self-publish books because of impatience waiting for a traditional publisher to see their writing's merit often wind up waiting at least as long for the public to see that merit.

Quality control in self-publishing is subjective at best, usually minor, and sometimes nonexistent. It's like the Wild West—every author for him or herself. The writer has to handle all the editing, evaluate the printer for reputation and skill, and supervise the printing. Lack of quality control also makes it difficult to sell a self-published book to libraries, schools, or bookstores, which have reputations to uphold and are careful about what they endorse. Since these major markets rarely have time to review every book and make sure that each one is worth offering to their customers, they rely on proven authors and publishers. Very few self-publishers qualify as proven and so they must engage in considerable work either marketing to individuals or finding sufficient reviewers and testimonials to convince large buyers that a book is worth the risk.

Self-publishers often have to buy large print runs for the sake of economy; the smaller a print run, the higher the unit cost (cost per book). This means that authors have to find storage space for large quantities of printed books and then may be left with hundreds more books than they can sell.

Some of the problems of the last point can be avoided through modern technology. The ease of today's electronic storage allows an author to opt for e-books or print-on-demand (POD) books. POD is a high-speed printing technology that can economically run off a very limited number of books from an electronic file. Saving storage space and printing expense, however, doesn't mean that the text will be any higher in

quality or that the book will be any easier to sell. POD hard copies tend to be lower-quality than traditionally printed books—not enough to bother the average individual buyer, but a potential handicap when selling to libraries and bookstores, which favor top-quality printing. POD technology also is limited to black-and-white printing, so forget about using it for a picture book.

The worst-case scenario is a writer desperate enough to try anything that produces a result resembling a book, and who is willing to pay any price for that momentary satisfaction.

Never Trust Vanity

Virtually everyone who has made a serious study of publishing has heard some version of this horror story: A writer produces what he's convinced is a masterpiece, but the first three or four attempts to market to major publishers come back with impersonal rejection letters. Frustrated with continuing failure and embittered with the idea that "only the famous get published anymore," the writer one day sees an advertisement for a so-called publishing service. "Many famous writers started off this way," the ad reads. "We provide full editing, printing, and marketing services at reasonable rates. Don't wait to find the right publisher. Send in your manuscript today!"

"Maybe this is my opportunity," thinks the writer, who mails off a manuscript to the publisher. Back comes a reply singing the praises of

Marketing Hints

If you're your own publisher, you're also your own marketer. Few small businesses can expect to sell to the biggest buyers—at least not immediately—so don't expect to see your books in the big chains right away. Here are a few reasonable steps you can take to market your book:

■ Most bookstores and libraries have "local author" days. Find out when the next one is, and pitch your book directly to the person in charge. Once you've secured a spot, bring promotional materials—bookmarks are a good bet—and refreshments to hand out to visitors. You'll get some free publicity from the event, and if you sell several copies, your host may be sufficiently impressed to buy books for the stock.

■ Ask nontraditional markets such as toy stores, sporting-goods stores, children's clothing stores, museum shops—or wherever your potential buyers gather—about stocking your books. If the book is of good quality in text and appearance and related to the store's main product, they'll likely oblige you in exchange for a share of the proceeds.

■ Most libraries accept title requests when considering future purchases. Have some of your friends and relatives request your book. Make sure they provide information on how to buy it, and that the source doesn't look like a fly-by-night operation. Having someone make a special request for your book can also be effective with bookstores. Ask interested friends to buy from the stores instead of directly from you.

■ Send the local newspaper a press release on your book. Include ordering information, but make the release sound like news, not like an advertisement.

■ Send copies of your book to book reviewers. Include minor, local reviewers as well as major ones; the former are more likely to be interested anyway.

■ Buy a mailing list and create a good direct mail packet to send to the names on the list. Choose your lists carefully; they should be made up of parents and others likely to be interested in your specific book.

■ Advertise in trade magazines for teachers and/or your most likely buyers. Advertise in local parenting magazines as well.

■ Create a website for yourself as a writer, which is better than creating one for an individual book. Link to all the relevant sites you can.

A Starting Point

If you're looking for a generally reputable and reliable publishing source, here are a few best bets recommended by disinterested sources who know the field. There are no guarantees, however. As with anyone you hire, carefully check out businesses to learn exactly what they offer and how reliable they are.

- **BookMasters:** www.BookMasters.com
- **Data Reproductions:** www.datarepro.com
- **Hignell Printing:** www.hignell.mb.ca
- **IUniverse:** www.iuniverse.com
- **Printing Industry Exchange:** www.printindustry.com
- **Xlibris Publishing:** www2.xlibris.com

If money is a serious issue, you might want to follow the outsourcing trend and look for an overseas printer. Many offer high-quality work for a fraction of what it would cost in the United States.

his work, telling him he is nothing short of the next J.K. Rowling and that they are honored to have the privilege of publishing his future classic. Enclosed is an invoice for the first print run, complete with proofreading and marketing services. The cost is higher than expected, but the writer figures that if they're doing all that work to get his career off the ground, it should be worth it. He sends in a check for the full amount.

After a while, a half-dozen or so author's copies arrive, along with a special offer to buy more at a lower price. The author thumbs through the copies and is disappointed that neither the binding nor the printing quality are particularly high. Worse, he notices several typos that he overlooked in his

eagerness to get the manuscript in, and that the publisher's editors apparently missed as well. Still, a really good story shouldn't need a fancy cover to sell, right? He sits back and waits for the orders to roll in.

They don't. Months pass and all he sells are a few copies to family and friends. No major magazines run any reviews or ads for his book; no bookstores or libraries stock any copies. The author asks his publisher about their promised advertising services and gets either no reply, or a note that says "these things take time, so be patient" (combined with an offer to sell him a few more books). If he pushes his inquiry, the company may insist indignantly that it did market his work. Which means that it listed the book in an annual (and little-distributed) catalogue. In small print. Without picture, annotation, or review.

A couple of years later, his book is still unknown to the world, and he's out several thousand dollars for expenses and purchased copies, not to mention months of time and a good chunk of pride. The vanity publishers, as their victims call them, have struck again.

How Not to Be Victimized by Your Ego

Most legitimate publishers and writing experts regard subsidy publishers (the "respectable" name for vanity publishers) as little more than con artists who sell empty hopes and will publish anything for a price, who take all the money they can from aspiring authors and return only shoddily printed books at best. As with any con artists, these supposed publishers get away with giving nothing for something because their victims want something for nothing. Most writers who buy vanity publishing services want all the services of an established publisher and then some—with the writer's share of the work stopping after the first draft. If you want to be recognized as a genius with no effort on your own part, you are setting yourself up for a particularly bitter disappointment.

Granted, there are a few legitimate publishers who share costs with the author. Most of these have rejected the terms subsidy or vanity publisher and call themselves

"co-operative publishers." More important than any name they use, of course, is what they give you. Here's how to spot an honest co-op publisher:

▨ An honest publisher won't promise you the world. They won't tell you your work is perfect; nothing ever is. They'll be concerned about their own reputations and won't publish everything that comes their way. They should provide full editorial services, or at least suggestions for improvement.

▨ An honest publisher tells you exactly what you're paying for: not only the number of books to be printed, but what specific marketing services are included, if any. They will never lead you to expect more than you get.

▨ An honest publisher gives you some control over the process. Look for someone who allows you a say in the binding or typeface, and who lets you see the page proofs and cover illustration before the book goes to print.

▨ An honest publisher is willing to provide references from satisfied customers. An honest publisher also provides information on what, and how, other books have been sold. If the only way you can buy this publisher's other books is directly from the publisher, and if it's "against policy" to distribute the contact information of other authors—run, don't walk, to the door!

Know What You're Getting Into

Even with a well-proven, highly recommended publisher, the non-traditional route may not be the best for you. Even if it is, rushing forward without a map can be a shortcut to disaster. Ask yourself a few hard questions before you even think about using a nontraditional publishing method:

▓ Why do you want to do it this way? If your answer is "to save myself work" or "to establish my reputation faster," you are deluding yourself and should return to the traditional approach. If the answer is "because my work will have a potentially profitable but limited market that few traditional publishers will be interested in," you are cleared to proceed to the next question.

▓ Do you prefer self-publishing or co-op publishing? If the former, you will be completely responsible for editing and marketing your book and for finding the right printer. Choose one that specializes in books and has a good reputation.

▓ Are you prepared to edit the work thoroughly on your own, or with the assistance of a competent critique group? Even traditional publishers resent being expected to clean up slipshod writing; few nontraditional publishers will even bother trying.

▓ Are you prepared to handle most of the marketing work: finding reviewers, setting up book signings, contacting potential customers, making arrangements with stores to sell your book? Again, you'd be

doing a good deal of this even with a traditional publisher; but if you self-publish, you'll have to do nearly all of it. A good co-op publisher will likely provide some promotional services. If you go co-op, choose a publisher with a proven marketing program.

▓ Are you free from delusions of instant success? Unless you're a celebrity, a self-published book is even harder to sell than a traditionally published book. Instead of making your sales pitch a dozen times to different publishers, you'll have to make it a hundred times to potential buyers. Those buyers are unlikely to be the most obvious or lucrative ones since most libraries and bookstores buy only from well-

---

Resources

▓ *Complete Guide to Self-Publishing: Everything You Need to Know to Write, Publish, Promote, and Sell Your Own Book,* 4th Edition. Tom and Marilyn Ross (Writer's Digest Books, 2002).

▓ *Do You Really Want to Self-Publish Your Book?* H.L. Nigro (Strong Tower Publishing, 2002).

▓ *The Self-Publishing Manual: How to Write, Print, and Sell Your Own Book,* 14th Edition. Dan Poynter (Para Publishing, 2003).

▓ **Writing World**: http://www.writing-world.com. The archives have several good articles on the topic.

established publishers. Patience and tact are the highest virtues in any kind of publishing, and this is where they come into full play.

▇ In what genre are you writing? How-to or other practical nonfiction for preteens and teens is the most suitable for self-publishing. It is less expensive to print because it needs little illustration and it is fairly easy to sell in nontraditional settings such as game stores or local shops. Fiction is much harder to sell without a publisher's brand name. Heavily illustrated books such as early readers and informational nonfiction are very expensive to produce.

▇ Do you know exactly how you want your finished book to look? Hard-copy or e-book? Paperback or hardcover? Comb or perfect binding? Times or Courier typeface? Photos, diagrams, or no illustrations? If you express no preferences, your publisher will give you a default version, which may not be best for your particular work or your preferred marketing methods.

▇ How big a print run do you want to start with? Be realistic about how many copies you can sell. Have a marketing plan ready before you go to the printer.

▇ Do you have space to store printed books until they are sold? A co-op publisher may provide storage for your books, and POD or e-books can easily be stored electronically. If you choose straight self-publishing, however, you'll likely have full responsibility for several hundred or more hard copies. Do you have a place to keep your books where

they'll be safe from mildew, paper-eating insects, and family members who may be tempted to throw the "clutter" out?

▇ Do you prefer traditional printing or print-on-demand? There are advantages and disadvantages to both. If you value efficiency and economy, if your book is all text, and if you plan to start your sales program with a focus on individuals and small retailers, POD may be a good idea. If your book turns out to be a bestseller, you can always find another printer to do a larger, higher-quality run. If you're signing a POD contract, look it over for any restrictions on your ability to change printers.

Conclusion: No Easy Way

If your nontraditionally published book sells especially well, you may even attract the interest of a traditional publisher. That's another reason not to sign a contract that limits your future options to use of the original printer. If a traditional publisher does make you an offer—perhaps including an option on future books—you may be glad by then to have someone take a good bit of the marketing effort off your hands and throw a respected name behind yours.

Whatever route you take, never expect others to do your work for you. Even if you become famous, try not to dream too much of the day people will buy your work solely on the power of your name. Do you really want to become one of the many writers who leave people shaking their heads sadly at the twenty-fifth book, saying, "His work just isn't what it used to be"?

Writing is work, even with the best of talent and opportunities. Selling your writing is work, too. Whatever your choice of publishing, it's going to be a hard and some-times heartbreaking path to success.

The true secret to success is not in finding the right publisher. It's in being the right writer, at the right place, at the right time. And it usu-ally takes plenty of hard work to get there. No publishing method can do that work for you.

Time Management

How to Get Your Writing Done Without Driving Yourself Crazy

By Suzanne Lieurance

If you're like most writers, there just don't seem to be enough hours in the day to write all you want to write and still have time for any kind of a life. Whether you're trying to carve out a full-time career as a freelance writer, or you're just wanting to schedule a little regular writing time each day, sometimes you fear you'll drive yourself (or your family) crazy in the process.

You start each day with good intentions. But by bedtime, you don't have as much to show for those intentions as you would like. Too much else got in the way of your writing, or you sat down at the computer and felt blocked, and the words wouldn't flow. More often than not, you're left feeling stressed and disappointed in yourself, especially when you hear about other, more prolific writers who crank out a novel or two every year or an impressive array of short stories and magazine articles.

How do they manage to write so much and still have a life? Did they learn something about time management you never learned? Maybe. But consider another possibility: What you learned about time management may be wrong.

Different Time, Different Needs

While researching this article, I ran across the website for Management Issues, an independent online resource based in London, in the U.K. In addition to many other interesting ideas, the site reprinted an article by Jurgen Wolff, a writer and teacher with a particular interest in creativity. Wolff wrote: "Most of what you've probably learned about time management is wrong . . . [I]t's based on research and development that was done back in the first half of the twentieth century." At that time, the emphasis was on helping people do repetitive tasks quickly and efficiently. "That's great if you're working on an assembly line or filling in forms. Not so great if you're in a creative profession in the year 2005." ("The Time Revolution: Time Management for Writers and Other Creative People." www.management-issues.com, March 2005.)

This got me to thinking. Writers and other creative people do have unique problems managing their time. A factory worker can instantly get to work producing a product. A sales clerk can always stock merchandise or ring up a customer's purchases. In both cases, these workers quickly experience a sense of accomplishment and completion of a task, which gives them more incentive to keep working.

A writer isn't always so lucky. Usually it's not so easy to crank out the work. For most of us, writing is not something that can be done quickly and efficiently. Much of the time a writer stares at a blank page, trying to figure out how to get started with the next chapter or paragraph, or even the lead sentence to a new article. This becomes frustrating and frustration leads to procrastination. Procrastination means time wasted, when a writer could be writing. Then, the phone rings, a child needs attention, or the laundry is suddenly piling up everywhere, and the writer's focus is lost. That all-important writing project is postponed once again, which means that the frustrated feeling of not writing at all or not writing enough becomes a regular occurrence.

Is it any wonder, then, that writing (or trying to write) can make a person feel a little crazy and frazzled? Must writers completely change their lives and their personalities to get their writing done? Maybe they just have to learn to think a little differently.

Life as a Horse Race

I found a time management expert who offers some hope for those of us who don't feel we can completely overhaul our lives to accommodate our writing careers.

Dr. Donald Wetmore is a full-time professional speaker who specializes in the topic of time management and offers seminars through the Productivity Institute in Stratford, Connecticut. He says that effective time management is not necessarily working harder, but it is working smarter. Wetmore compares life to a horse race. "The first horse may earn a $50,000 purse and the second horse may earn a $25,000 purse. The first horse gets twice as much money as the second horse, not because it ran twice as far or twice as fast. It was only a 'nose ahead' of the competition," says Wetmore.

That's good news for writers. It means that even a little extra effort can create significant results. We don't need to completely redo our lives. We just need to learn to think a little differently to get "a nose ahead." In fact, Dr. Wetmore offers just five time management suggestions that can help each of us win the writing race.

■ *Start each day with a plan of action.* "Without a plan, you will

Time Tips from Two Popular Authors

Here are a few time management tips from two well-known children's authors.

Cynthia Leitich Smith is the author of *Jingle Dancer, Indian Shoes,* and *Rain Is Not My Indian Name,* as well as short stories published in several recent anthologies. Her upcoming titles include a picture book, *Santa Knows,* co-authored by Greg Leitich Smith, and a young adult novel, *Tantalize.* Here's how she manages her time.

"Because it's so difficult to focus on novel writing while on the road speaking all the time, I have developed a months on/months off plan. From December to March, I stay home and write. In April and May, I tour and speak. In June and July, I teach. In August and September, I stay home and write again until October/November when I hit the road." But Smith says this schedule is not too rigid. "I may book a local event in January or August. I certainly will write in hotel rooms in the late fall and spring. But, globally, I know that there are certain months set aside where one or the other has dominance."

This time management system seems to be working for Smith. She reports, "In the past couple of years that I've been doing this, my productivity has soared and I've sold two books in what for me are new genres."

Linda Sue Park was awarded the Newbery Medal for her book, *A Single Shard,* and has written four other novels, including *Project Mulberry, The Kite Fighters,* and *When My Name Was Keoko,* as well as four picture books. She follows simple writing advice she learned from writer Katherine Paterson, author of *Bridge to Terabithia, The Great Gilly Hopkins, Jacob Have I Loved, Lyddie,* and many others: Every day write two pages of the novel that is your current work-in-progress. Think about it. Two pages doesn't sound like a lot. But write just two pages every single day for a while and it won't take long to complete your own novel.

begin your day by responding to other people's and events' demands," says Wetmore.

Most writers probably do start their day with a plan. But that plan probably doesn't make writing a priority. Many writers, especially beginners, make writing the lowest item on their to-do list, so it isn't surprising that they rarely get around to doing it.

If your plan is to get some writing done each day, then make it one of the top tasks on your daily to-do list. Also schedule time for phone calls, interviews or research, and e-mail. If you know you have these tasks on your schedule, you won't be as tempted to check your e-mail every five minutes or answer the phone every time it rings (let your answering machine do that) when the writing isn't going smoothly.

Balance your life. Our lives are made up of the following seven vital areas: health, family, financial, intellectual, social, professional, and spiritual. "You don't need to spend time every day in each area or equal amounts of time in each area," says Wetmore. "But, if in the long run, you spend a sufficient quantity and quality of time in each area, your life will be in balance."

On the other hand, if you neglect any one area, it will put your life out of balance, which will eventually sabotage your success. Knowing this should make you feel less guilty for scheduling a little fun in your daily work routine. But, if you do decide to include lunch with friends in your schedule now and then, just make sure you only allow an hour or two for this activity each time. Then get right back to work.

Get organized. Why spend precious hours of the day searching for something in a messy work area or on a messy desk? Even a few minutes here and there add up by the end of the day. "Studies have shown that the person who works with a messy desk spends, on average, one-and-a-half hours a day looking for things or being distracted by things. That's seven-and-a-half hours a week," says Wetmore. "And, it's not a solid block of an hour and a half, but a minute here and a minute there, and like a leaky hot water faucet, drip, drip, drip, it doesn't seem like a major loss, but at the end of the day, we're dumping gallons of hot water down the drain that we are paying to heat."

Keep your desk and work area neat, so you can focus on more important things (like writing) during the day. File papers as they come in.

Here's a simple, extremely helpful tip. Keep a spiral notebook handy and jot down notes and reminders there instead of on scraps of paper that either get lost or clutter up your workspace. When you need to find that important phone number or note from an editor, all you have to do is look in your notebook.

Get enough quality sleep. If you've run yourself ragged during the day, chances are you won't get enough quality sleep, even if you manage to get enough hours. When you finally do go to bed you'll toss and turn, worrying about current projects, the bills, how to pay for your child's college education— anything and everything. By planning your day, then following your plan, you'll be less stressed all day and therefore able to enjoy a more restful night's sleep.

▇ *Take a break during the day.* Sometimes just taking a short break can make you more productive since we all tend to slow down when we've been working consistently at something for a few hours. Take a short break (maybe that lunch date with friends you've included in your schedule). You'll end up getting more done in the long run.

It's also helpful to know that you probably don't need to spend all day writing to become successful. Many accomplished writers write for only a few hours each day. The key here is they work for those few hours each and every day, no matter what. So, again, make writing one of your top priorities and stick with it, even if it's for only an hour or two every day.

Think of Time as Tangible

Wetmore's suggestions are simple, but most writers need help following through on them. Julie Morgenstern, founder of Task Masters, a professional organizing company that provides consulting services to individuals and businesses, offers additional tips that might help you with Wetmore's first three suggestions.

In her book, *Time Management from the Inside Out,* Morgenstern says to think of time in tangible terms. She compares time to a closet. A closet is a limited space that will hold only a certain number of items. Similarly, a schedule is a limited number of hours "into which you must fit a certain number of tasks," says Morgenstern. "If an overstuffed closet and overstuffed schedule are similar, then you can apply the same organizing strategy to each." An organized closet has similar items grouped together. There is no guesswork as to where to put things. An orderly arrangement makes the most of the space available. It's easy to see what's there at a glance and easy to see when you've reached capacity. Order can be maintained by following a "one in/one out rule."

This same organizing method can be applied to a daily schedule. Using some sort of daily planner, similar tasks should be grouped together. Then, there is no guesswork as to when to do things, and an orderly arrangement makes the most of the day. It's easy to see at a glance what needs to be done each day, and easy to see when you've reached capacity. Order can easily be maintained with the same "one in/one out rule."

When you think of a daily schedule in terms of a closet, you begin to realize how many activities you can comfortably schedule into your workday. You'll probably also begin to realize that you need to start eliminating at least a few other activities from your daily schedule if you want to have time to write without feeling frazzled.

Time Management Titles

▓ *101 Ways to Make Every Second Count.* Robert W. Bly (Career Press, 1999). Much of this information is plain common sense, but it's always good to be reminded of it if you're having trouble managing your time.

▓ *A Complete Waste of Time: Tales and Tips about Getting More Done.* Mark Ellwood (Pace Productivity, 2000). This title just sounds fun, and the book is. Ellwood includes time trivia and poetry to make this an enjoyable yet informative read that will help you profit from more efficient use of your time.

▓ *Getting Things Done: The Art of Stress-Free Productivity.* David Allen (Penguin, 2003). This book is great if you need to learn how to de-clutter your workspace and your life. You'll learn to follow Allen's two-minute rule to free your mind and your time for other things (like writing).

▓ *Get Organized, Get Published! 225 Ways to Make Time for Success.* Don Aslett, Carol Cartaino (Writer's Digest Books, 2003). If you spend too many hours of the day checking e-mail, watching TV, or playing computer games, this book is for you. Aslett and Cartaino will help you develop a "getting published action plan."

▓ *First Things First: To Live, to Love, to Learn, to Leave a Legacy.* Stephen R. Covey (Free Press, 1996). The author of *The 7 Habits of Highly Effective People* helps you develop principle-based life goals. Once you have those in place, it is easier to plan daily goals because you'll begin to see how you can eliminate any tasks that aren't in alignment with your life goals.

Gauge Your Writing Time

Chip Scanlan is a former newspaper reporter, now a faculty member of the Poynter Institute in St. Petersburg, Florida. He produces a writing advice column, "Chip on Your Shoulder," for Poynter Online. Some of Scanlan's tips might help you follow through with Wetmore's five suggestions, too.

"Break down your next story into components. Then keep track of the actual time for those steps," Scanlan says. Steps include idea development, research, character development, rewriting drafts, final polishing, and so on. "It will take you time and experience to be able to estimate accurately. Invariably, the jobs that we think take a long time can be accomplished more quickly, while the tasks that we think are a snap take more time than we thought. Develop a more accurate gauge of your time."

Learning to track exactly how much time you need for specific writing tasks will help you schedule

beyond the basics becomes a matter of choice. Explore the world of
books, share titles with writing
friends, and find the works that
"speak" to you and your needs.
Then clear some space on the shelf
to make room for a book you'll read
over and over again.

adequate time. Scanlan warns against procrastinating for hours and then writing in binges to meet a deadline. Writers who do this, says Scanlan, tend to build up "a steam of guilt, anger, and rage that ultimately leads to indifference: 'I don't care how bad it is, I've only got 15 minutes left.' Then, once they're writing, they are afraid to stop. They write in a fury until deadline. Unfortunately, they've robbed their readers of a fresh eye that might notice a confusing sentence or important information buried deep in the story. And when it's all done, they're exhausted, stressed out, and ready for a drink."

Your Prime Time

One tip that might help you avoid procrastinating is to learn to identify, and make the most of, your prime time—the hours of the day when you tend to have the most creative energy. If you know you are the most creative in the morning, for example, schedule your writing time then. Leave phone calls, interviews, and other less creative tasks for the afternoon when your creative energy wanes.

Perhaps the best writing advice came from Ernest Hemingway, who developed a trick that helped him avoid writer's procrastination. I've tried this and it has become one of the most helpful devices I've found. Hemingway said to always stop writing when the writing is going well and you know what's going to happen next in your story. That way, when you sit down to write

the next day you won't find yourself staring at a blank page, wondering what to write. You'll know what needs to come next. Try it. The man knew what he was talking about.

Most writers don't need to be told they shouldn't fritter away their time watching television, playing endless games of computer solitaire, or constantly checking their e-mail. They know these things are all big time wasters. Still, the tendency is to turn to any, or all, of these activities when the writing isn't going well. But stick to Wetmore's five suggestions, think of time as something tangible, and you might find yourself engaging in these little time-wasters less and less often. Best of all, you'll get more and more writing done without driving yourself (or your family) crazy in the process.

A Writer's Library

By Joanne Mattern

Library time is essential to a writer. Poring over books, reading, researching, using the databases or special collections, conferring with the librarians, or just enjoying the blending of words and pictures on the page are the essence of a writing career. Writers also need a home library made up of books to reach for again and again—for inspiration, markets, or just the right word or phrase to make their writing the best it can be. Let's take a look at some of the books successful writers recommend.

The Basics

A writer's business is all about words. Guides that help writers spell, punctuate, create the correct grammar and phrasing, or just find the right words are essential for developing style.

Most writers have a copy of *Webster's Collegiate Dictionary* at their fingertips. This dictionary is the publishing industry's bible when it comes to how to spell a word. It's also a fun place to look up etymologies, or word histories. It even provides the year a word first came into the language, which can be a handy tool for writers creating historical fiction and who want their characters to speak appropriately for a time period.

Having a children's dictionary on hand is also helpful, especially when preparing a glossary or defining difficult words in your text. *Scholastic Children's Dictionary* might have an important place on a bookshelf.

A thesaurus is another important writer's tool. A thesaurus lists synonyms for many words in the English language. Are you trying to avoid repeating the same word three times? Do you want your characters to say something in a fresh and different way? *Roget's Thesaurus* has been the industry standard for generations, but other excellent thesauruses are available, too. Mel Boring is the author of 10 children's books, including *Guinea Pig Scientists: Bold Self-Experimenters in Science and Medicine,* written with Leslie Dendy and published by

Henry Holt. Boring recommends *The Synonym Finder,* by J.I. Rodale. He prefers this book because "it seems not so *wooden* as Roget's, and gives more usable-with-children synonyms. I wouldn't be without it."

Alejandra Mojilner's *The Children's Writer's Word Book* is a tremendous help in finding grade-appropriate language. This handy guide lists words by grade level, along with synonyms also labeled by grade. It's an essential book to have if you want to keep your writing on target for specific grade levels.

Writers need to focus on the nuts and bolts of writing—punctuation, grammar, correct phrasing, and just plain good writing. Two of the best style guides are *The Elements of Style,* the classic by William Strunk and E.B. White, and *Essentials of English,* by Vincent F. Hopper, et al. Both of these books can put writers on the right track when it comes to basic grammar and punctuation.

Finally, writers often have style questions that go beyond punctuation and grammar. *The Chicago Manual of Style* is a vital resource that should be on every writer's bookshelf. It can tell you everything from how to cite a newspaper article in a bibliography to proper ways to use numbers in text.

For Reference

An author's bookshelf should also contain topical reference materials. Encyclopedias are useful starting points for nonfiction authors, but can also come in handy for fiction writers looking for background in-

formation on aspects of their story's setting, time period, or other elements: Think of the science in a mystery, or topical references to people or news events in contemporary fiction.

Because my office does not have room for a complete set of encyclopedias, I often check the *World Book* at my local library. One-volume works like the *Random House Encyclopedia* or the *Columbia Encyclopedia* are alternatives. Another space-saving choice is to use online encyclopedias, such as Britannica.com, or texts on CD-ROM, such as Microsoft's *Encarta.* Online encyclopedias are also frequently updated, giving writers a better chance of finding the most current information. (Do remember, however, that research should never be limited to encyclopedias.)

Nonfiction writers often have a library filled with books pertaining to their particular subject matter. Lyn Sirota specializes in magazine articles about animals and nature topics, so it's no surprise that she lists "all the Audubon books about birds, insects, etc." as an important part of her library. Another good source of basic information about a variety of animals is *Zoo Animals: A Smithsonian Guide.*

Tell Me How

Everyone needs a helping hand, someone who can guide them along the path and make the journey easier. Most writers could not work without style guides, and industry or career books that navigate

---

Writers Recommend

Here are more book recommendations from published authors:

- *The ABCs of Writing for Children.* Elizabeth Koehler-Pentacoff. Ellen Jackson calls this a "wonderful book that gives advice from 114 children's authors."
- *Self-Editing for Fiction Writers: How to Edit Yourself into Print.* Renni Browne and Dave King. "All the editing tips are wonderful. You need to read this slim book over and over to get all the good meat," says Gail Martini-Peterson.
- *Ten Steps to Publishing Children's Books: How to Develop, Revise, and Sell All Kinds of Books for Children.* Berthe Amoss and Eric Suben. This book "offers some fascinating glimpses into the success stories of an eclectic bunch of authors and illustrators," says Nancy Furstinger.
- *35,000 Baby Names.* Bruce Lansky. "Why? I like to name my characters, taking the name's translation into consideration," says Lyn Sirota.
- *The Writer's Journey.* Christopher Vogler. Vijaya Bodach turns to this book "to make sure I have a worthy enough story," and to "*Plot and Structure,* by James Scott Bell to keep my story organized."
- *Writing with Pictures: How to Write and Illustrate Children's Books.* Uri Shulevitz. Mel Boring classifies this writing book as "a bible on its topic, heavier on the illustration than the writing, but this master of the art is also a master teacher."

---

the often tricky roads of children's writing and publishing.

Vijaya Bodach has written more than 50 articles and books for children. Her top three style guides are *Writing for Children and Teenagers,* by Lee Wyndham; *Writer's Guide to Crafting Stories for Children,* by Nancy Lamb; and *How to Write a Children's Book and Get It Published,* by Barbara Seuling.

Ellen Jackson, who has published more than 50 fiction and nonfiction books, says, "If you want to know more about structure, including how to craft a scene, how to create dyna-mite characters, and how to choose a point of view, Lamb's *Writer's Guide to Crafting Stories for Children* is the book for you."

Once you've written your story, how can you increase its chances of getting published? A good writer's library can help. *The Complete Idiot's Guide to Publishing Children's Books,* by Harold D. Underdown, is a hands-down favorite of many writers in the field. Boring raves, "I don't know of any single volume with such a wealth of information about absolutely every aspect of publishing children's books." Jackson agrees, saying, "I keep a copy by my desk and refer to it often. Harold Underdown knows the children's book business from the editor's perspective. His book covers many topics not usually covered in general how-to books. He gives a short overview of publishing and discusses the various components of a book, the different kinds of publishers, how to get your manuscript read, and how to promote your book once it's been published."

Negotiating contracts is another important part of the writer's life. To understand this aspect of publishing, Jackson recommends *How to Be Your Own Literary Agent,* by Richard Curtis. Along with giving an overview of what agents do, the book has a section on contracts, which proved especially helpful to her. "This book helped me negotiate a contract the first time I was forced to face the publishing world without an agent by my side. I must have sounded like I knew what I was talking about because I was able to retain more rights, even though at the time I wasn't sure exactly why I was retaining them!"

If you're looking to publish in the educational market, author Rita Milios highly recommends *How to Get Your Teaching Ideas Published: A Writer's Guide to Educational Publishing,* by Jean Stangl. "This book is the best source of information I've found for writers interested in educational publishers and curriculum materials," Milios says. "It covers every type of educational market, from book and textbook publishers

to publishers of activity sheets, workbooks, posters, and other non-book curriculum tie-ins. One of the most helpful things about the book is the numerous specific examples." It includes listings of publishers, sample cover letters, and even advice on doing school visits and other promotional appearances.

When you're ready to find a publisher, the Writer's Institute publishes its annual *Book Markets for Children's Writers* and *Magazine Markets for Children's Writers.* Both books include new and updated listings for hundreds of publishers, as well as a submissions guide, sample cover letters and queries, listings for contests and awards, and articles filled with tips and advice from leading editors and authors.

Writer's Digest Books publishes a one-volume market directory, *Children's Writer's and Illustrator's Market,* which includes the names and addresses of children's book and magazine publishers, their manuscript requirements, and other information.

Finding Inspiration

Along with the nuts and bolts of how to write, authors often need inspiration to put pen to paper, or fingers to keyboard. Once again, many books on the market help writers to sit down and write.

Nancy Furstinger, author of 33 nonfiction books, as well as many educational texts and newspaper and magazine articles, highly recommends *Dear Genius: The Letters of Ursula Nordstrom,* collected and edited by Leonard S. Marcus. "What a remarkable editor—her nurturing genius shines through in each letter!"

Yvonne Ventresca is the author of *Publishing* (part of Lucent Books' Careers for the Twenty-First Century series) and more than 30 articles. She names *I'd Rather Be Writing,* by Marcia Golub, as one of her essential books. "It's a great book on how to get back to writing when other things get in the way," she says. "Golub approaches the topic with humor, inspiration, and practicality. She includes exercises and interesting quotes, along with excellent advice. This book has gotten me unstuck many times."

Diverse author Jane Yolen has written several books of practical and inspiring advice for writers. Mel Boring's favorite among them is *Take Joy: A Book for Writers.* "Her positive sense of you-can-do-it seems to shine brightly in this very uplifting book for writers," he enthuses.

Jackson names another renowned author's work on writing: "For general inspiration, nothing can beat *The Wave in the Mind: Talks and Essays on the Writer, the Reader, and the Imagination,* by Ursula K. LeGuin. Some of the articles in this book will make you think. Others will speak to your heart. These are intriguing essays from a very thoughtful author."

Many authors list *Bird by Bird: Some Instructions on Writing and Life,* by Anne Lamott, as a wonderful source of inspiration. Furstinger calls this book "a generous slice of writing life." Bodach agrees, saying "I need this book to inspire me to keep going when the going is tough."

Widening Horizons

Books are an essential part of any writer's library, of course, but the World Wide Web is a virtual library available to anyone with Internet access. Writers can also use the Web to find information on just about every topic under the sun. A Google search is a good place to start, but major libraries, museums, and news and media outlets also contain an amazing amount of information on topics far and wide and can lead you to books you want on your own shelf. The Web can also provide access to local libraries from home.

Wendie Old, an award-winning author of 44 books, talks about how valuable her local library is. "I consider the whole public library essential for writers. Nowadays, you can look at the catalogues of every library in Maryland and borrow books from wherever you find them, for free. Plus, libraries subscribe to full-text magazine article databases where you can find any article on any subject in just a few minutes. I couldn't survive without the public library!"

Bodach agrees. "My library has a huge database and I can access it from home with my library card. I am able to do my background research for science-related articles by reading original papers and review articles without leaving home."

Building your own writer's library

A Writing Bibliography

Amoss, Berthe and Eric Suten. *Ten Steps to Publishing Children's Books: How to Develop, Revise, and Sell All Kinds of Books for Children.* Cincinnati: Writer's Digest Books, 1997.

Bell, James Scott. *Plot and Structure.* Cincinnati: Writer's Digest Books, 2004.

Book Markets for Children's Writers. West Redding, Connecticut: Institute of Children's Literature, 2005.

Browne, Renni, Dave King. *Self-Editing for Fiction Writers.* New York: HarperResource, 2004.

The Chicago Manual of Style. Chicago: University of Chicago Press, 2003.

Curtis, Richard. *How to Be Your Own Literary Agent: An Insider's Guide to Getting Your Book Published.* Boston: Houghton Mifflin, 2003.

Golub, Marcia. *I'd Rather Be Writing.* Cincinnati: Writer's Digest Books, 2001.

Hopper, Vincent F. *Essentials of English.* Hauppage, New York: Barron's Educational Series, 2000.

Kipfer, Barbara Ann. *Roget's 21st-Century Thesaurus.* New York: Dell, 1999.

Koehler-Pentacoff, Elizabeth. *The ABCs of Writing for Children.* New York: Quill Driver Books, 2002.

Lamb, Nancy. *Writer's Guide to Crafting Stories for Children.* Cincinnati: Writer's Digest Books, 2001.

Lamott, Anne. *Bird by Bird: Some Instructions on Writing and Life.* New York: Anchor Books, 1995.

Lansky, Bruce. *35,000 Baby Names.* Minnetonka, Minnesota: Meadow-brook Press, 1995.

LeGuin, Ursula K. *The Wave in the Mind: Talks and Essays on the Writer, the Reader, and the Imagination.* Boston: Shambhala, 2004.

Magazine Markets for Children's Writers. West Redding, Connecticut: Institute of Children's Literature, 2005.

Marcus, Leonard S. *Dear Genius: The Letters of Ursula Nordstrom.* New York: HarperTrophy, 2000.

Merriam-Webster's Collegiate Dictionary, 11th Edition. Springfield, Massachusetts: Merriam-Webster, 2003.

A Writing Bibliography

Microsoft Encarta Deluxe 2005.

Mogilner, Alijandra. *The Children's Writer's Word Book.* Cincinnati: Writer's Digest Books, 1992.

Pope, Alice, editor. *Children's Writer's and Illustrator's Market.* Cincinnati: Writer's Digest Books, 2004.

Robinson, Michael and David Challinor. *Zoo Animals: A Smithsonian Guide.* New York: Macmillan, 1995.

Rodale, J.I. *The Synonym Finder.* New York: Warner Books, 1986.

Scholastic Children's Dictionary. New York: Scholastic Reference, 2002.

Seuling, Barbara. *How to Write a Children's Book and Get It Published.* New York: John Wiley, 1991.

Shulevitz, Uri. *Writing with Pictures: How to Write and Illustrate Children's Books.* New York: Watson-Guptill Publications, 1997.

Stangl, Jean. *How to Get Your Teaching Ideas Published: A Writer's Guide to Educational Publishing.* New York: Walker and Company, 1994.

Strunk, William, Jr., E.B. White, Roger Angell. *The Elements of Style.* Boston: Allyn and Bacon, 1999.

Underdown, Harold D. *The Complete Idiot's Guide to Publishing Children's Books.* New York: Alpha, 2004.

Vogler, Christopher. *The Writer's Journey: Mythic Structure for Writers.* Studio City, California: Michael Wiese Productions, 1998.

World Book Encyclopedia. Chicago: World Book, 1997.

Wyndham, Lee and Arnold Madison. *Writing for Children and Teenagers.* Cincinnati: Writer's Digest Books, 1989.

Yolen, Jane. *Take Joy: A Book for Writers.* Writer, Inc., 2003.

Publicity

Blog Day Afternoon: Promoting Your Work

By Mark Haverstock

Authors' websites used to be on the leading edge of Internet communication with readers and editors. Now *blogs* (a contraction of *Web* and *logs* that rhymes with *dogs*) are the next big thing in on-line information. Blogs don't require much technical savvy and most are free or cheap to maintain. They're the perfect medium for authors to get the word out about their new projects, communicate with fans, share their personal thoughts, and perhaps land a few jobs.

According to the folks at blog-ger.com, "A blog is a personal diary. A daily pulpit. A collaborative space. A political soapbox. A breaking-news outlet. A collection of links. Your own private thoughts. Memos to the world." Millions of them, all shapes and sizes, are scattered across the Internet. They have no real rules, as long as First Amend-ment activists can keep them free of government regulation.

In concrete terms, a blog is a kind of website where someone writes material or makes comments on an ongoing basis, much like a public journal. New information shows up at the top, so your visitors can start with the most current posting. Then they comment on it, link to it, or e-mail you, or—not.

For writing professionals, one bankable purpose for blogging is to impress potential clients who may consider you for a writing project, consulting job, or speaking engage-ment. "I've gotten many queries from people who want to work with me through my blog and my site," says Web expert David Meerman Scott. "Much of my work is consult-ing on website content and I've got-ten several corporate gigs as a result of the blog. I've also been invited to speak at conferences."

Blogs are also a way to gain a few brownie points among fellow writers and readers who surf the Web. "The key issue here is that I'm supplying information that people want and I'm not charging them a damn thing for it," says author Crawford Kilian. "That builds some goodwill, which leads to explorations of your site

Tips for Bloggers

Penny C. Sansevieri of Author Marketing Experts offers this advice:

▦ Blog regularly and on topics that would be of interest to your readers.

▦ Much like book writing, don't switch topics in your blog: Stay in your genre/topic or you'll confuse or lose your audience.

▦ If you're stuck on what to blog, consider using your blog as a character diary (The Adventures of . . .) or you can do a round robin, engaging your blog visitors to help write the story.

and inquiries about your services." Results won't necessarily be instantly or directly measurable, since readers don't pay for access to your blog. Think of it as an investment, with a payoff later down the road as you increase your exposure.

The Art & Science of the Blog

Penny C. Sansevieri of Author Marketing Experts has done a considerable amount of work with authors teaching them to blog for the purpose of marketing their published books and introducing future work. "I've found that the biggest challenge for authors is figuring out what to blog, how often to blog, and how to blog to gather momentum

and engage their readers," she explains. "We've also done a lot with virtual book tours and connecting authors with marketing opportunities as well as with their audience."

Need ideas? Would you like to share the trials and tribulations of being a writer? Techniques on finding good sources? If you're a published writer, you might give previews or some inside information about your next project. Make your blog an extension of your published writings. "Grant visitors an opportunity to experience more of their favorite author. Give them insight into your thoughts. Provide a glimpse of what makes you the kind of person you are," says Brent Skinner, communications consultant and President of STETrevisions. "They will appreciate how your published writing stems from your personality and you will develop a loyal fan base over time."

Author Lara M. Zeises uses a unique approach—blogging in her young adult author persona and also blogging as the protagonist of her YA novel, *Contents Under Pressure*. "The latter has been trickier because it's hard to maintain. The characters take on a life of their own, and readers who follow the journal get really ticked off with me if I don't update it regularly," Zeises says. "They start sending harassing messages and everything. I'm glad they enjoy it, but they have no idea how hard it is to slip back into the voice of a character I finished writing about three years ago. Not only that, but the character is about a year and a half older than she was

Author Blogs

Want to see some author blogs in action? Here are just a few, from children's authors to syndicated columnists representing a wide variety of styles and genres. Note that all have entries made at regular intervals.

Dave Barry: http://weblog.herald.com/column/davebarry/
Meg Cabot: Meg's Diary, www.megcabot.com/blog/blogger.html
Neil Gaiman: www.neilgaiman.com/journal/journal.asp
Linda Hall: http://writerhall.com.hosting.domaindirect.com/blog.html
E. Lockhart: www.theboyfriendlist.com/e_lockhart_blog
M. J. Rose: Buzz, Balls, and Hype, http://mjroseblog.typepad.com/buzz_balls_hype
Anastasia Suen: Create/Relate, News from the Children's Book Biz, http://create-relate.blogspot.com
Penny C. Sansevieri: www.amarketingexpert.com/blog.html
Lara Zeises: Girl Uninterrupted, www.livejournal.com/users/zeisgeist
For a large assortment of blogs from published and unpublished authors, try this site: www.authorsblogs.com

in the book, so I also have to take that into account."

Chris Anderson, Editor in Chief of *Wired*, uses his blog to post ideas connected to a nonfiction book in progress and to solicit reactions. Author John Battelle has also made the blog a part of his writing process. He was surprised by the number of people who read his journal, offering feedback and suggestions for interviews or articles to read that eventually find their way into his forthcoming book. "It has provided such a wealth of sources," Battelle says. "The readers pointed me to things I might not have paid much attention to."

Success Stories

Some writing professionals say that their blogs have helped them get noticed and build valuable contacts that later turn into paying assignments. "Actually, my blog has been really successful. It's driven quite a bit of business to my site," says Sansevieri. Author Marketing Experts, she says, was "doing a virtual tour for a book we were working on called *Cookin' for Love*. One day, because of several blog features, it soared to number 23,130 on Amazon. We also got a feature on this book in *More* in July, but it never even spiked at Amazon . . . ah, the power of blogs!"

When Zeises was getting ready to

Blog Subscriptions—Simple

Want more traffic on your website? An easy way to distribute your news? Then you need an RSS news feed.

RSS stands for Really Simple Syndication, a service that alerts readers when new posts appear on their favorite blogs. Think of it as a distributable "what's new" for your site. Visitors to your site can subscribe to your blog by clicking on the orange RSS feed button (sometimes labeled XML) when they visit. Just about all blogging sites mentioned in the sidebar include the RSS links as a standard feature and require no additional setup.

To keep up with writers in the blogosphere, readers need an RSS reader. It's a kind of clipping service that organizes chosen blog subscriptions into a manageable digest. These RSS readers come in the form of downloadable programs for a single computer, or they can be Web-based, which allows you to read your subscription list from any computer or Internet-capable mobile device.

Free and easy-to-use RSS readers include:

- **Awasu:** www.awasu.com
- **Rocket RSS Reader:** http://reader.rocketinfo.com/desktop
- **Bloglines:** www.bloglines.com
- **Pluck:** www.pluck.com. Registering, downloading, and setup of a few author blogs in Pluck took a little less than 15 minutes.

launch *Contents Under Pressure* in the spring of 2004, she put together a brochure, and included her experience in blogging to get speaking engagements. "I wanted to add a new program, so I tried to think of something I could offer some expertise in," she says. "Blogging was just starting to become more mainstream, so I added two programs. One was for teens—'Get Your Blog On! Finding Your Voice Through the Safety of the Screen'—and one for adults, adaptable for other authors, librarians, teachers, school media specialists, etc. Then I applied to speak at conferences catering to those individuals, and that's how I get the teen gigs."

Author Brian Carroll credits his blog with helping to land a book contract with McGraw-Hill. Screenwriter James Hess used his blog to mention work on a screenplay. "A producer who knows of my blog contacted me and wanted to know: 'Did I have a deal for said script?'" Hess already did. The producer then asked Hess if he was interested in talking about a deal for another screenplay. "The odds are good, before year's end, I will be writing a new screenplay," he says.

Your mileage may vary. It doesn't mean that if you have a blog you'll get these kinds of results. But if you write well and the blog is read by the right person, who knows?

Complement to a Website

Blogs can add to the traditional website by telling more about the real you. They're a more authentic way to showcase who you are as an expert.

"Websites tend to be more formal than a blog and that formality makes it more difficult to show who you really are as an author—your true personality," says Scott. "Blogs also allow you to take content in different directions that will appeal to specific target demographics, without negatively impacting the strategy and content of your primary website. As a way to experiment, to test new ideas, or to reach narrow niche markets, smart marketers use highly focused blogs." If the experiment fails, you can shut down or start a new blog topic with little or no negative effect on your main site.

Another approach is to have the blog double as a person's main site. "The latest blog entry always serves as the main page of the website, and traditional website content is available via links in some sort of intuitive layout," says Skinner. "I think traditional website models that fully embrace and incorporate the blog concept reflect the future of the Internet." He sees the blog format morphing with traditional site layouts and concepts more and more. That will, Skinner says, "catapult interactivity."

Zeises suggests that blogs may even have more pulling power than the traditional website. "It's immediate in a way that a website isn't. I have a pretty expansive website that I put a lot of time, money, and effort into which gets about 700 to 800 unique visitors a month," she says. "My blog, which I update almost daily, gets about 1,500 to 2,000 unique visitors every day. Why? Because it comes up in search engines more, since I blog about every pop culture-y thing imaginable."

Making the Rounds

Once you're established, you won't necessarily need to rely on search engines to generate traffic. Sometimes word-of-blog referrals will be passed on to other readers. "Before too long I found that quite a few other bloggers were linking to my site and mentioning this or that item on it," says Kilian.

The people on LiveJournal who have "friended" Zeises also have their own list of friends. "So, say John Doe lists me as a friend, and 10 of his friends decide to read the people on John Doe's friend list. Five of them link to a post I wrote. Then 10 people on their individual friends lists read my post—it becomes exponential," she explains. "This happens more when I write about targeted issues, such as one about cruelty between young girls. It got a lot of responses, and I know that link was passed around. Eventually, people who read my posts will check out my bio or my website."

Scott says many links to his blog are a result of his writing. "I list my site and blog in my byline and people will link from there. I get perhaps a dozen links per day through my various bylines on the Web," he says. "I also get another dozen links a day through the search engines."

Becoming Part of the Blogeoisie

Your blog posts will start and perpetuate the blog, but it's the comments that give a blog life. "Life is interactivity—a blog visitor expects one-on-one interaction with the blogger (in this case, the author) through the use of a comment tool," says Skinner. "Blog posts should inspire blog visitors to engage the author, and the author should be prepared to interact. It is a time commitment, but one that is worthwhile."

To attract and keep those visitors coming, add to your blog entries at least once a week, and preferably more often. Give your blog the appearance of being up-to-date and active. If you procrastinate and skip posts, people will begin to drop you from the list of blogs they read regularly. This will reduce your readership, the one thing you are trying to cultivate. Remember, you want to get your ideas read by as wide an audience as possible.

Keep it short and sweet. Posts should be no longer than a few paragraphs at most. Longer pieces may be better handled in the form of articles or e-books. Some bloggers start with a few introductory sentences or teasers and allow readers to click to a link with the full-length piece if they're interested in more information. In this way, the page looks less cluttered and readers can move easily to other posts on the page with minimal scrolling.

Don't skimp on your writing quality, either. Your blog writing should be on par with your articles, essays, or books. If you're really serious about using your blog as a marketing tool, don't follow the tendency of some bloggers to write stream-of-consciousness ramblings. Think of your blogs like the published clips you use to impress editors and other potential clients.

Blog Sites

These are a sampling of blog sites that are available to the public. All offer at least a free trial, and many do not charge for your blog space, at least for the time being. Be sure to read the terms of service and privacy statements before you sign up.

- **www.altablogs.com** Free blogs with easy sign-up.
- **www.blogalley.com** Free blogging with basic account. Pro account fee with full features at $22 a year.
- **www.blogbud.com** For writers who want to publish blogs on their own website and maintain a site free of editorial control.
- **www.blogger.com** Easy to set up, free, and easy to modify. Part of the Google empire. Also offers on-the-go blogging from mobile devices.
- **www.blog-city.com** Basic is free, $2.50 a month gives you the advanced version, with lots of extras, such as the ability to add to your blog by email, allow public contribution to your blogs, and post photos.
- **bloggercrab.com** Free, easy to use, and new features are added all the time.
- **www.blogigo.co.uk** Free blogs with built-in directory and help forums.
- **www.blogsource.com** A free yet powerful blogging service built by bloggers for bloggers.
- **www.blosxom.com** Free to use, with donations accepted.
- **www.cafelog.com** News and a weblog tool are under ongoing construction.
- **ebloga.com** Free, fast, reliable, full-featured blog.
- **www.livejournal.com** Basic service is free, $25 upgrades to advanced version.
- **spaces.msn.com** MSN lets you create your own blog space, integrating Hotmail and MSN messenger into the package.
- **typepad.com** Free trial. Different features are available at $5, $10, or $15 a month.

Got Ideas? Authors on the Idea Hunt

By Mark Haverstock

Where do you get ideas? That's the question every author is asked at one time or another, whether at a school visit or a writers' conference. It's also the same question authors ask themselves when they want to pitch an editor, write next week's column, or have to face dreaded writers' block.

In an age of instant solutions, wouldn't it be great to subscribe to a daily Ideas 'R' Us email service? Or maybe you could visit www.awesomeideas.com 24/7 for the latest list of quick prompts or character dossiers to jumpstart your next YA novel. Perhaps the pharmaceutical industry will come up with a new blue pill that will cure idea dysfunction and help you rise to the task of writing for up to 36 hours.

Unfortunately, the means to materializing a phantom idea aren't quite that simple. As personal growth guru Earl Nightingale once said, "Ideas are elusive, slippery things. Best to keep a pad of paper and a pencil at your bedside, so you can stab them during the night before they get away."

The article that follows gathers remarks of various authors, revealing their perspectives on the idea generating process. Use these for your next article, story, or book, or take a stab at some ideas of your own before you go to bed tonight.

In the News

Where do writing professionals go for ideas? One of the most frequently mentioned sources is the news media. Television, newspapers, tabloids, magazines, and weblogs are rich sources of human interest items, statistics, and trends for writers who take the time to peruse them on a regular basis.

"I find ideas everywhere. The idea for the dead body in *The Trouble with Lemons* came from a tabloid news article about a boy's body being found floating in a quarry in the Midwest. *Eye of the Beholder* was based on a true story of phony Modigliani sculptures turning up in Modigliani's hometown during a centennial celebration. The idea for my fourth book, *Flyers*, came from a newspaper article on a pair of local student filmmakers who regularly enlisted their friends and relatives to star in and help out with their film projects.

"I've also been known to stop teaching to jot down something funny a kid in class has said. When I'm in the middle of a book, you have to be careful about what you say around me because it just might end up in print."

Daniel Hayes

"Since my books are mostly realistic fiction, I get my ideas from the things that happen to me, to my kids, to my dogs and cats, to my friends' dogs and cats, and from things I see on TV and read about in the newspaper. I sometimes think my books are like scrapbooks of my life because almost every incident brings back a memory."

Betsy Byars

"I read the newspaper every day. I watch TV. I listen to the radio. I go to the movies. I visit a lot of schools, where I have lunch with a small group of kids and they give me ideas. I have two children of my own, and they give me ideas. I'm constantly keeping my eyes and ears open for things I can make into an interesting story."

Dan Gutman

"Simple extrapolation is so effective, I marvel that more science fiction writers don't use it. The U.S.

Census, for example, tells us that by mid-century something like 40 million Americans will be women over the age of 80, with perhaps 25 million men of that age. No society has ever had to deal with such a large population of super-seniors, so it's a natural idea for *Henderson's Tenants*, set in 2030 Vancouver."

Crawford Kilian

Personal Experiences

As some of the preceding quotes reveal, another valuable source is your own life and experience. Remember the advice given at almost every writer's workshop: Write about what you know. Tap your journals and memory banks for material you can use in your next article or story.

"Ideas come from ordinary, everyday life. And from imagination. And from feelings. And from memories. Memories of dust in my sneakers and humming whitewalls down a hill called Monkey. I still have my Ranger Joe mug."

Jerry Spinelli

"Both *Bridge to Terabithia* and *The Great Gilly Hopkins* grew out of real life experiences. I wrote *Bridge* because our son David's best friend, an eight-year-old named Lisa Hill, was struck and killed by lightning. I wrote the book to try to make sense out of a tragedy that seemed senseless. I wrote *Gilly* after I'd been a foster mother for a couple of months and didn't feel as though I'd been such a great one, so I tried

to imagine how it might be to be a foster child. How would I feel if I thought the rest of the world thought of me as disposable?"
Katherine Paterson

"Where do you get your ideas? I used to be afraid to answer that question. I thought if I ever figured it out I'd never have another one! But now I know that ideas come from everywhere—memories of my own life, incidents in my children's lives, what I see and hear and read—and most of all, from my imagination."
Judy Blume

"The idea for the book *Julie and the Wolves* struck me when I was in Barrow, Alaska, on an assignment for a national magazine. Barrow is the land of the midnight sun, of sea ice and Eskimos, of caribou and polar bears—and of wolves.

"When I arrived, the scientists at the Barrow Arctic Research Lab were studying wolves and breaking their communication code. A few men were talking to them in their own language with posturing, whimpers, and various actions. I was fascinated and eventually was able to learn how to talk 'wolf' and communicate with a beautiful female in her own *language*. When she answered back, I knew that I wanted to write a book about a little girl who is lost on the tundra and saves her life by communicating with the wolves. So I did."
Jean Craighead George

"Sometimes column ideas are thrown in your path—you just have to pick them up and run with them. Perhaps someone sitting next to you on a plane will be enough to get your juices going. That's what happened to me a few years ago. I was flying home from Cincinnati, and a young boy plopped down next to me. I wasn't too thrilled, since I try to avoid children on planes. But he started talking and, the next thing I knew, I had my notebook out, taking down every word.

"He asked me why I was doing that. I told him everyone has a story to tell and that I liked his spirit. He paused for a moment to ponder that thought, then started right in again about everything from his favorite bird to the death of his father. 'Jeff' became one of my most popular columns [in *USA Today*]."
Craig Wilson

"I have an exercise book and each day set myself the task of writing down one memory or thought or observation or dream or line from a book I'm reading. Whenever I need an idea, I read the book, pick out the ones I like, and play with them."
Andy Griffiths

Friends, Family, & Strangers

People are great sources of ideas, so be attuned to the world around you. Be an eavesdropper, listen to stories from friends, and don't be afraid to pose *what-if* questions to any captive audience you can find.

"Where do the ideas come from? My ideas come from everywhere. I'm constantly tripping on them. The ghost story idea in *Lily's Ghosts* came to mind because a friend had a house that supposedly was haunted. She had a bunch of weird things happen there and I thought her stories were too perfect and creepy to go to waste. I used it for the setting.

"Other books grow out of what-if questions. For example, my next book is a fantasy called *The Wall and the Wing*. My stepdaughter was having a sleepover with some friends, and I asked them, 'If you could have any superpower, what kind would you have?' Three of the girls said they wanted to fly, one said she wanted to be invisible. I thought, what if there was this one girl in a city full of people that could fly, and she was really jealous of them until she learned she could be invisible? The whole book grew out of answers to this one weird question.

"Listen to snippets of conversation you hear on the bus and the grocery store—ideas are everywhere. I think what happens for me is that I unconsciously gather all these little snippets and one day they organize themselves into something. I never know which snippet is going to blossom in my head."

Laura Ruby

"Everybody has ideas. The vital question is, what do you do with them? My rock musician sons shape their ideas into music. My sister

Recurring Themes

Will your past creep into your writing someday? For these famous writers it did.

Arachnophobia? It wasn't a problem for E. B. White, who once let hundreds of spiders hatch and build webs on his dresser. Pigs also fascinated him, and he soon began to wonder why he took such good care of the pigs he raised, despite the fact they would later end up on his dinner table. Combine these two ideas and you come up with *Charlotte's Web,* featuring the most famous pig and spider in children's literature.

Shock value. As a boy, Edgar Allan Poe used to scare people by putting a sheet over his head and pretending to be a ghost. Later, his creepy side reappeared in stories such as "The Telltale Heart," "The Pit and the Pendulum," and "The Black Cat."

Ugly duckling. Hans Christian Andersen knew he was an ugly duckling and described himself this way: "His nose as mighty as a cannon . . . . His eyes are tiny, like green peas." All his life he felt awkward and longed to be accepted. "The Ugly Duckling" became one of his most well-known tales.

takes her ideas and fashions them into poems. My brother uses his ideas to help him understand science. I take my ideas and turn them into stories. Now, what do you think you'll do with your ideas?"

Avi

"Some of my ideas come from my editors. The basic idea of Sweep [a series] wasn't mine, but almost everything else about it was. However, with my new series coming out later this year, Balefire, from Penguin, all the ideas are mine. Everything influences me, things occur to me all the time, ideas I had years ago suddenly find a home. It's sort of a constant creative process of thinking and thinking.

"A good story is a good story, no matter what genre. Just be imaginative and have it come from you—who you are as a person."

Cate Tiernan

Out of the Blue

Often ideas seem to come from nowhere and everywhere. Other times, authors take random and disconnected bits of information, play with them, and eventually they take shape in written form. The idea comes once this jigsaw puzzle is assembled, or at least at the point of becoming recognizable.

"I get mine from a lot of different places. Sometimes I'll come up with a title. I wrote *I Was a Teenage Mermaid* just based on the title. With *Vampire Kisses*, I wanted to write something with an unusual

and feisty character. I'd done stand-up and my dad suggested that I write a book about stand-up, which became *Comedy Girl*. Other times, ideas just pop into my head like, 'Oh that seems like a neat idea for a character or a plot or setting.' I always like to tell people I can get ideas from just about anything."

Ellen Schrieber

"Each story I've written starts out as a vague idea that seems to be going nowhere, then suddenly materializes as a completed concept. It almost seems like a discovery, as if the story was always there. The few elements I start out with are actually clues. If I figure out what they mean, I can discover the story that's waiting."

Chris Van Allsburg

"I never try to think up a story; stories just come to me. I live a very simple life, and often spend several hours each day just daydreaming. It is usually during these times that my ideas come to me."

Dav Pilkey

Exercising Your Creative Side

Keeping your body in shape requires

The Highly Quirky Habits
of Effective Writers

Some writers go to great lengths to keep the flow of ideas and words coming. Here are a few examples from authors past and present.

On a good day, Charles Dickens worked hard, often completing two to four pages a day. He started his morning with a cold bath and wrote until lunch using a goose quill pen on blue-gray paper. On a bad day, he often doodled or picked fights with his wife, kids, or servants.

Even after the invention of the typewriter, some writers still preferred pencil pushing. Thomas Wolfe preferred pencil stubs he kept in a coffee can. Ernest Hemingway began his writing with the ritual of sharpening dozens of pencils. Contemporary authors Stephen King and Norman Mailer still choose to write their works in longhand instead of using computers.

Zora Neale Hurston would travel to the ends of the earth to gather material. As a single woman traveling solo, she braved bedbugs, zombies, and hurricanes, as well as other incidents that forced her to carry a revolver. To gain the trust of a Creole conjurer, she once spent 69 hours lying face down on a couch without food or water.

Langston Hughes started his day at noon, chain-smoking Camels. After a large breakfast, he'd dress in a striped sailor's jersey, write letters, and entertain visitors. After club hopping in the evening, he finally got down to the business of writing while everyone else slept.

When George M. Cohan needed a script, he'd buy a train ticket and spend the entire time on the train writing. On a trip from New York to Chicago, he could routinely complete 140 pages.

Too bad Emily Dickinson never took to diaries or journals. The vast body of her poetry was found scrawled on the backs of envelopes, in the margins of newspapers, or on odd scraps of paper.

some exercise on a regular basis. The same is true for your brain. Other than reading and using some of the author tips mentioned, you can use writing exercises to generate ideas or break through writer's block. These writer-tested suggestions can help you get those words flowing.

How can you *not* get ideas? Writer Gene B. Williams suggests that ideas are all around you, flooding you from the moment you wake up to when you fall asleep, and again through your dreams. When he was teaching creative writing, the question of ideas came up often enough that he developed a simple exercise to generate them. "I'd have the students close their eyes, swing an arm all around, then point at random. Whatever they pointed to when they opened their eyes was the subject," he says. "The exercise was to start working up ideas about that subject." For example, your finger is pointing to the clock on the wall. Now you have the endless topic of time, plus the mechanism of the clock, or the history of the clock, and so on.

Other authors have other favorite idea generators. As a teacher and a writer, one of mine arrived years ago as a freebie sent along with my sixth-grade class's Scholastic Book Club order—mix-and-match cards labeled *plot, setting*, and *character*. On the reverse side were events, places, and character descriptions, respectively. The idea was to pick one or more cards from each category at random and compose a story or story synopsis based on them. Sure, you could come up with some crazy combinations—a pirate sings opera at a hockey arena—but your choices can be less off-the-wall. Write them on index cards using a different color for each story element.

Author Apryl Duncan suggests that you can generate new ideas or break writer's block using one of your favorite magazines. Cut out pictures, headlines, even certain blocks of text. Now write a short story based on your clippings. "For example, you might cut out a picture of a man riding a bicycle on page 14 . . . . On page 22 you cut out a quote that says, 'Anyone caught doing this will be prosecuted to the fullest extent of the law,'" she says. "Your story could turn into one man's crusade. Perhaps this man is riding his bicycle across country because he's outraged by automobile pollution levels."

For those who embrace computer technology, several writers' software packages promise to get those creative juices flowing. WriteSparks (www.writesparks.com) claims to generate more than 10 million story sparks, such as character profiles, quick plots, metaphors, and random paragraphs to jump-start your writing. Idea Fisher (www.ideafisher.com), Writer's Edge (www.writersedgeservice.com), eXpertSystem (www.richcontent.com), and ParaMind (www.paramind.net) use concepts and word associations to help brainstorm.

Sorting and Applying
Sometimes the problem really isn't

Web Idea Generators

If you're looking for free idea generators on the Web, try these sites. They range from comical to seriously useful.

- **Calihoo Writing Generators:** 37 dramatic situations. www.sff.net/people/julia.west/CALLIHOO/ideagen2.htm
- **Hatch's Plot Bank:** Features 2,000 story scenarios. www.angelfire.com/nc/tcrpress/plots1.html
- **Feath's Bookcase:** Random quote generator, character generator. www.feath.com/idea/quote.htm, or www.feath.com/idea/char.htm
- **Seventh Sanctum:** Various generators for games, sci-fi, and fantasy. www.seventhsanctum.com/index-writ.php
- **Tails Pro Productions:** Dozens of miscellaneous generators. www.geocities.com/tailspropro/gens.html

having an idea, but sorting out which ideas are good ones. There is no universal rule for determining whether an idea is worth writing about, but it should at least meet the following criteria:

- It must be interesting.
- It must appeal to a large readership.
- It should deal with a specific aspect of a subject. If you can't express the main idea or purpose in 10 words or less, it's time to go back and rethink your idea.

Another consideration for the professional writer should be the idea's saleability: Is there a market that will buy the article or story? This is when checking guidelines and editorial calendars is important.

But ideas are just the beginning. "I can't believe that everyone isn't having ideas all the time. I think they are, actually, and they just don't recognize them as potential stories," says author Philip Pullman. "Because the important thing is not just having the idea; it's writing the book. That's the difficult thing, the thing that takes the time and the energy and the discipline. The initial idea is much less important, actually, than what you do with it."

Recycle Research to Rethink & Resell Ideas

By Lizann Flatt

Recycling household waste was a new concept for North Americans not so long ago. Most of us are now accustomed to it as part of our daily routines to reduce landfills. It's a great concept: reuse or reform materials already manufactured instead of starting the process from raw material. Is recycling your writing research a new concept for you? Let's look at how several authors have done it, then see if you can make recycling research part of a writing routine.

Intense Interest

To have research to recycle, of course, you have to do the research the first time. When you start, you usually have a purpose in mind. You're going to write a novel perhaps, or a nonfiction article on a particular topic. Do you willingly while away hours chasing facts, sources, or quotes and confirmations, or is every step an effort? If the thought of going back to a research topic you've already delved into has you groaning instead of gearing up

for excitement, maybe it's just not a good subject for you to recycle.

Writers who recycle research feel a deep connection with the topics they reuse. This seems to be the first requirement for sustaining a prolonged involvement with a topic. Award-winning author Jane Yolen describes this connection as *resonance*. She says, "I cannot do a book unless, at the deepest levels, it resonates for me. I have two huge file drawers—and lots of computer folders—of stuff I started and never connected to emotionally."

The topics you don't ever revisit are likely not good candidates for recycling. Yolen knows that other factors are involved in manuscripts becoming books, but she is definitive on the writer's primary role: "Of course, none of what I write becomes a book unless it further connects with an editor and the publishing committee. But that deep connection must begin with me."

That deep connection is similar to what Fiona Bayrock found when she began researching a scientist's "discovery that spiny lobsters make sound using the same mechanism as a violin bow across a string—something never seen in any other animal," says Bayrock. "I was hooked. I thought the way the scientific process worked in this story was very cool. Usually when I'm excited about a topic, it comes through in my writing." That exciting writing translates into sales.

Joanna Emery's excitement about her topic resulted in her joining a group doing ongoing research. "It all started when I did research for a middle-grade nonfiction book I wanted to write featuring crop circles," says Emery. "I became so involved that I even joined a Canadian Crop Circle research group!" That's dedication to your craft.

Time Investment

Besides being involved in a subject you love, why bother recycling when you could move on to more topics that fascinate you? Recycling research makes sense in terms of receiving more returns for the time invested. If you can research once and then use the labor to write several pieces, you're doubling your investment. More sales with less work is always a plus, but recycling research can also be a way to break into a market you might not otherwise be willing to put time into cracking.

Bayrock used research recycling as a way to cut down her time investment when a sale might not have materialized. "Like many children's writers, one of my goals was

to see my work in *Highlights for Children*," she explains. "However, they only wanted completed articles submitted—something I rarely do. Most of my articles are written on assignment, usually in response to a query letter. I sell the idea to a particular magazine first, then research and write the article."

That's what many established nonfiction writers do. But Bayrock came up with a solution. "I was reluctant to invest a lot of time researching an article for which I didn't already have a publisher, so I decided to write my *Highlights* submission using the research and interview I'd done for an article that had already sold. That way my time investment would only be in the writing, not in the time-consuming research." She made the sale.

Change the Age

To make sales with whatever subject resonates, you still have to rethink that topic to make it new. There are several ways to do this. One is to think about what other audiences might find your topic interesting.

Although the time Emery invested in crop circle research for her middle-grade project hasn't yet resulted in a sale, she has made that research work for her by rethinking the subject's appeal. "I've written and sold two nonfiction articles on the subject, but okay, both articles are for adults," she admits. "One is a 2,000-word feature for *UFO Magazine*—'Crop Circles: The Canadian Connection.' I also sold another article, 'Crop Circles,' a 500-word special interest piece, to *Daytripping,* a Southern Ontario tourism newsletter."

You can target your topic to appeal to kids of different ages as well. Remember that spiny lobster? The differences in target age group made a difference in how Bayrock presented her research in the two articles she sold on the subject. She explains some of the differences this way: "A *YES Mag* article was for older readers so the writing style was a little more sophisticated—more complex sentence structure, more scientific jargon introduced, deeper into the science and the scientific process. I was able to use abstract metaphors in the older article, but stuck to concrete similes in the younger piece."

Bayrock also explains that word count is different. "Surprisingly, the *Highlights* article for younger readers is about 150 words longer than the *YES Mag* article for older readers. This is because of the different styles of the two pieces. The *YES Mag* article was a news item, with all of the details packed densely into a low word count; the *Highlights* meet-the-scientist article had more room to explain concepts thoroughly and to introduce things more gradually, which the younger age group required in a way the older one did not."

Look at the Lead

One key to making sales to different magazines is to change your lead to appeal to each magazine's style. For Bayrock's two sales, the difference in target age and in approach is quite obvious. Take a look at the lead for the *YES Mag* article:

> What do spiny lobsters play—violin or guitar? Until recently, most scientists thought spiny lobsters made their raspy warning sounds the same way crickets do— by rubbing two hard surfaces together, like a pick across guitar strings . . .
>
> "Symphonic Spiny Lobsters," *YES Mag,* March/April 2002

Compare that to the lead for the *Highlights* article:

> Dr. Sheila Patek is a scientist who studies how animals talk to each other. She is curious about spiny lobsters. These lobsters make a noise to scare away predators. One day, Dr. Patek watched a lobster . . .
>
> "How Lobsters Make 'Music,'" *Highlights,* May 2005

From just those snippets you can see how the same material was recycled into completely different end products. The topic takes on a whole new look when targeted for two different magazines.

Jumping Genres

Another way to reuse your research is to expand on short manuscripts you've already had published. Perhaps you've already sold several articles on one topic. Could you compile your research and package it into a book? Or what if you found so much information doing research for an article that you had to leave out considerable interesting information? Could you make a book from it?

That's what smart recycler Bayrock did. "My book *Shark Sunglasses* grew from a magazine article I did about animals with suckers for *WILD*. There was just too much cool stuff I had to leave out of the article due to space constraints, so I wanted to write a book on the subject, but it ended up morphing into a book with a much broader scope."

Of course that broader scope meant more research, but Bayrock didn't have to start from scratch. "Chunks of the sucker article research will be reused on one of the spreads in *Shark Sunglasses*." Also recycled in articles for *YES Mag* is "research I did about a Namibian beetle standing on its head to drink, and about shark anatomy." Bayrock reveals, "In fact, the shark article is where the book's title, *Shark Sunglasses,* comes from."

Just as you could go from a short piece to a book, you can also write different books about a single topic if the market interest is high. Yolen has had success writing about women pirates. Her very first book, published in 1963, *Pirates in Petticoats,* was a nonfiction chapter book for ages 9 to 12. Thirty years later she wrote *The Ballad of the Pirate Queens,* a picture book about two of those pirates, Anne Bonney and Mary Read. Was this part of her plan all along? Surprisingly, it wasn't. Yolen says, "I was so green when I wrote that first nonfiction book, it never would have occurred to me that there was any place for a lady pirate picture book. Probably at that time, the early '60s, there wasn't." So how did it come about?

The opportunity arose and Yolen stepped forward, using her previous pirate research as the basis for volunteering herself for the job. "I began the picture book when one of my editors mused that David Shannon, with whom I'd just done *Encounter*, wanted to do a pirate book and did I know anyone who might be interested in writing, say, about women pirates? She hadn't known about my other book," says Yolen. "I offered myself and the editor said, why not a ballad that every child will want to recite?" That's what she wrote. This time Yolen went from a long book to a short book.

To write the picture book, Yolen did do more research specifically on the two women pirates but didn't find much new on these characters.

Recycle or Re-Research?

Should you simply recycle your research or do more research? Consider your topic. Is it feasible that there have been new discoveries since you last looked into your topic? Could once widely held scientific truths now be debunked? What new information might have come to light? Would you be making assumptions? It's worth your while to check with new sources.

Based on her experiences with historical assumptions, Carol Matas cautions writers about recycling. "I did think I could use research from my book *Greater Than Angels,* set in France during World War II, for a new book, *Turned Away,* since the new book would have the prospective refugees living in France," Matas says. "This, however, got me into the biggest trouble I had when writing the book."

That trouble was a tiny yet critical detail. Matas explains: "My old research had shown that letters went from refugee camps in France to Paris and also from refugee camps to the U.S. during the war. I extrapolated from this that mail was also possible from Paris to the U.S. and Canada during those same years and based my outline and first draft on letters going back and forth. However, my editor wanted this double-checked and when I did I discovered, much to my horror and after three weeks of searching (my editor and I both going crazy since no one seemed to know this) that mail did not go from Paris to North America at that time. I then had to find a different route for the mail in order to keep my basic story."

Matas has also found it's not possible to recycle much historical research if the city setting and characters change, as in *Turned Away* and another of her books, *The Whirlwind,* which both take place in the same year. "I am finding little I can use from one book to the next, even though they are set at exactly the same time, 1941," Matas muses. "This is because the characters are so different and are interested in totally different things. Devorah, in Winnipeg, loves movies and keeps track of everything to do with the war because she has two brothers overseas. Ben, in Seattle, is a recluse and a refugee and is not integrated into his society yet. Even the slang Devorah uses is useless for Ben as he's a German refugee and doesn't speak the way she does."

So how do you know if you can recycle? It depends on your subject, how much time has elapsed between first research and recycling, and the end product you want to produce. But even a check to see what's new, or to fill in some missing details, is a savings over starting again.

Crossing genres this way wasn't so much a research challenge as a writing one: "The difference between writing a ballad and writing a chapter in a nonfiction book is condensing. The ballad is such a condensed form that much is implied, but not spelled out," Yolen says.

The story of Yolen and women pirates doesn't end there. She has authored another book about women pirates, *Sea Queens,* for 8- to 12-year-olds, coming out in 2007 from Charlesbridge Publishing. Yolen explains the difference between this nonfiction book and her first nonfiction book as "a number of additional things that the first book didn't have: pirates like Grania O'Malley, who was someone I'd never discovered for the first book. My bibliography is longer, with a lot of books new since my first book came out. It will also have marginalia, which covers many other aspects of sea-going and pirating. But it is more an illustrated book, not a chapter book." With updates and a change in format to appeal to today's market, Yolen has made her topic new again.

Find a Narrow Focus

Three different types of books on one topic is optimal recycling. Another way to reuse research is to delve into the details of a large topic and use it as the setting and plot premise for several novels.

This was Karleen Bradford's tack in using research on the Crusades. Bradford has written a trilogy set in the Crusades by narrowing the time frame of each book. Her books do not follow the same characters because they are too far apart in time, but each book is focused on one particular part of the Crusades, allowing her to use more of the information she found.

"I researched the Crusades for the four years I was in Germany," says Bradford. "By the time I actually wrote the book *There Will Be Wolves,* I had far, far too much material for one book, and I was hooked on the subject." That book is about the People's Crusade. But she didn't shelve her sources there. "I used a lot of my extra research for the second book, *Shadows on a Sword,* which told the story of the First Crusade, the one that was successful in recapturing Jerusalem. Totally obsessed by now, I added to the research by going to Israel and writing the third book in the series, *Lionheart's Scribe.*" Each of these books focuses on different events within the overall subject, and each carries the theme of what happens to innocents during war.

But for Bradford, the writing didn't end there. Her research led her on— on in time and on to more novels. "I was going to finish there, but got intrigued with the Children's Crusade after I learned that many of these unfortunate kids ended up in Egypt as slaves, but managed to make good lives for themselves. The Muslims treated slaves well and those kids who were literate were used as teachers and tutors in the western languages. For that book, I went to Egypt to do the research. It turned into two books, actually: *Angeline* and *The Scarlet Cross.*"

Whether it's for a magazine article or a book, recycling research does mean some more work. But working from a base of knowledge is better than starting anew. Yolen sums up recycling research with this apt metaphor: "It is standing on the shoulders of the giant you were, but not relying on its footing."

It's not that you that don't have to lift a finger to make more sales from the same basic information, but with a little creative thinking to retarget the age, refocus the lead, expand or condense the story, update to the current market needs, or hone in on a time period, you can make use of material again. Isn't that a more efficient use of your own precious writerly resources?

Idea Generators

A Compendium of the Unusual

By Louanne Lang

To spur the imagination, begin the brainstorming, open the floodgates, get the juices running— or any of those other metaphors for creativity—here is a list of miscellaneous fun facts and records.

Living Things

Mammals

- Dogs cannot perspire. They pant in hot weather to evaporate water through their tongue.
- A woodchuck breathes only 10 times an hour while hibernating, but 2,100 times when active.
- The elephant is the only animal that can't jump.
- A cow can be led upstairs but not downstairs.
- Squirrels' eyes are positioned so they can see behind them.
- The hearts of many mammals, including humans, beat about three billion times during a lifetime.
- A chimpanzee can learn to recognize itself in a mirror, but monkeys can't.
- No two Holsteins have the same pattern of spots.
- A single cow produces nearly 200,000 glasses of milk in its life.
- A horse has 16 muscles in each ear, which allows it to rotate its ears a full 180 degrees.
- An elephant is able to smell water three miles away.
- The cheetah is the only member of the cat family with non-retractable claws, designed for traction instead of tearing. Much lighter than most other cats, it can also outrun them at speeds of up to 70 miles per hour.
- The heart of a giraffe weighs 25 pounds, is 2 feet long, and has walls 3 inches thick.
- At birth a panda bear weighs only about four ounces, less than a mouse.
- Emus and kangaroos can't walk backward.
- A squirrel never returns to a nut storage site it has abandoned.
- A key gauge for the overall health of ecosystems is amphibian health. Amphibians' highly permeable skin makes them more immediately

sensitive to environmental changes and pollutants than other creatures.

▨ Only two pigment colors—black (eumelanin) and yellow (phaeomelanin)—combine to produce virtually every color found in mammals, humans included.

▨ Kangaroos measure only about an inch at birth.

▨ Cheetahs' chirping sounds, similar to a bird's chirp or dog's yelp, can be heard up to a mile away.

▨ Cats cannot survive on a vegetarian diet.

▨ All pet hamsters are descendants of a wild golden hamster found in Syria in 1930 that had a litter of 12 young.

▨ An adult lion's roar is used to gather pride members or to discourage intruders. It can be heard as far as five miles away.

▨ The calls of Howler monkeys can be heard two miles away.

▨ Beaver teeth are so sharp that Native Americans once used them as knife blades.

▨ Camel milk does not curdle.

▨ At birth, an elephant may weigh 200 pounds or more. While both male and female African elephants have tusks, only male Asian elephants have them.

▨ Elephants can communicate using sounds between 14 and 35 hertz, below the range of human hearing ability.

▨ Tunneling moles can move through 300 feet of earth in a day.

▨ Only about 10 percent of all known animal life forms are still in existence.

▨ Pigs, walruses, and light-colored horses can sunburn.

▨ Camel eyes are shielded against blowing desert sand by three eyelids.

▨ Some baby giraffes are more than six feet tall at birth.

▨ The bloodhound is the only animal whose evidence is admissible in an American court.

▨ Carnivorous animals will not eat another animal that has been hit by a lightning strike.

▨ Shakespeare's *The Two Gentlemen of Verona* is his only play to include a dog.

▨ The cat is the only domestic animal not mentioned in the Bible.

▨ Snails are able to sleep for up to three years. The protective discharge that snails produce is so effective they can even crawl along a razor's edge without getting cut. The fastest-moving land snail, the common garden snail, has a speed of 0.0313 miles per hour.

Fish and Sea Creatures

▨ Whales are mammals that spend their entire lives in water. The blue whale is the world's largest mammal, weighing 50 tons at birth and as much as 150 tons when fully mature. Certain whales can inhale more than 500 gallons of air in two seconds when they surface.

▨ Herring, the world's most eaten fish, has as much nutritional fuel value as beef steak.

▨ The Pacific Giant octopus is the largest octopus in the world. In its two-year lifespan, it grows from the size of a pea to 150 pounds and 30 feet across.

Sharks are the only animals that never get sick. They appear to be immune to every known disease, including cancer. Tiger shark embryos fight each other until only one survives to be born. Epaulet sharks, which live in the shallows around coral reefs, can survive without oxygen, and even without water, for extended periods of time. Sharks have a special gel in their noses that generates an electrical current to stimulate sensitive nerve endings and send information to their brains when water temperatures change even slightly. It is thought that this unique ability helps them to locate prey.

The giant squid is the largest creature without a backbone. It weighs up to 2.5 tons and grows up to 55 feet long. Each eye is a foot or more in diameter.

The African lungfish can live out of water for up to four years.

All clams start out as males. It is uncertain at what point some become females.

An electric eel can produce charges up to 650 volts.

The unusual Australian walking fish not only can survive without water, it can also climb trees to feed on insects.

At night, dolphins sleep just beneath the water's surface. Dolphins can hear underwater sounds from up to 15 miles away. Before dolphins initiate any group action, the pod floats together just below the surface of the water and each animal vocalizes.

The male seahorse is the only male in the world that becomes pregnant, carries the eggs, and after they hatch, expels them live. Male catfish carry the eggs of their young in their mouths until they are ready to hatch. They do not eat for the entire time, which may be weeks.

Minnows are a subcategory of the carp family. The largest in North America is the Colorado River squawfish, which can reach lengths of more than 6 feet and weights of greater than 100 pounds. A species of the mahaseer minnow found in India can grow to 9 feet and more than 100 pounds.

A female mackerel lays approximately half a million eggs each time she spawns.

Lizards, Snakes, & Reptiles

Every continent except Antarctica is home to some of the approximately 2,600 different species of frogs. Certain varieties continue to live even after being frozen solid and thawed. A poison-arrow frog has enough poison to kill about 2,200 people.

Be wary if you smell fresh-cut cucumbers in the wild: It is the aroma of poisonous copperhead snakes.

Chameleons are more than just color-changers. They can move their eyes in two directions at the same time, and their tongues are twice as long as their bodies.

Squirting blood from the eyelids is one technique the horned lizard uses to discourage enemies.

Gecko eyes operate independently so they can simultaneously

look in two directions. The lizards can also climb on very smooth surfaces due to millions of sticky hairs on the bottoms of their feet.

The green anole and several other types of lizards use their lungs as hearing aids, detecting vibrations through their air-filled lungs.

Australia's estuarine crocodiles excrete salt through their tongues, allowing them to exist in salt water, unlike alligators and other crocodiles. It's impossible for a crocodile to stick out its tongue. Although a large crocodile can close its jaws with a force of more than 3,000 pounds, the same jaws can be held shut by someone of average strength.

Cobras cannot move their neck muscles to bite something over their heads, so they can be patted on the head without danger. They also follow the head of a person playing an instrument, making it appear as if they are dancing.

Birds

An ostrich's eye is bigger than its brain.

A duck's quack doesn't echo, and no one knows why.

The European cuckoo and the American cowbird, classic parasitic birds, lay their eggs in other species' nests to avoid having to bring up their own chicks. These foreign chick eggs are the first to hatch, and then the cuckoo chicks kick out their competitor's eggs, making the adoptive parents feed chicks that aren't even theirs. The cowbird chicks allow the indigenous chicks to hatch, but the cowbirds'

larger and more colorful mouths attract the majority of the food.

Cassowaries are flightless birds in Papua New Guinea that use extra low frequency sound waves to communicate. Because these sound waves are below the range of human hearing, people near the birds feel rather than hear the sounds. Weighing up to 125 pounds, cassowaries are among the world's most dangerous birds. Not only do they kick when fighting, they are also equipped with a spike on their feet that can rip open their opponents, often with fatal results.

Researcher and physiological ecologist Scott McWilliams at the University of Rhode Island discovered how migratory birds maintain energy for their long flights. Their guts expand enormously a few days before the journey, enabling them to eat many times the normal amount of food. To save energy in flight, they reabsorb gut tissue. When they stop, they have to re-grow their gut before they can eat again.

When cormorant offspring are ready to go off on their own, the mother makes sure they do by destroying the nest.

Penguins often build nests out of many small stones. The current record is held by a gentoo penguin whose Antarctic nest was constructed from over 1,700 little rocks. A father Emperor penguin withstands the Antarctic cold for 60 days or more to protect his eggs, which he keeps on his feet, covered with a feathered flap. During this entire time he doesn't eat a thing.

Most father penguins lose about 25 pounds while they wait for their babies to hatch. Afterward, they use a special liquid from their throats to feed the chicks. When the mother penguins return to care for the young, the fathers go to sea to eat and rest.

Survival in harsh desert conditions has led to many creative solutions among animals. The male desert grouse of Africa's Nabib desert makes use of a sponge-like mat of fluffy breast feathers to soak up water for its chicks. When the male grouse gets to the nest, the chicks lick the water off him.

A diving peregrine falcon can reach a speed of more than 200 miles per hour.

The eggs of the South American tinamou reflect mirror-like images from their highly polished surfaces.

An eagle's beak can close with a force of 350 pounds per square inch.

The arctic tern is an intrepid traveler, breeding in the Arctic in late spring, then flying 10,625 miles to the Antarctic to spend its winters.

Although only nine inches tall, the roadrunner can run as fast as a human sprinter.

Bird eggs come in a wide variety of sizes. The largest egg from a living bird comes from the ostrich. It is more than 2,000 times larger than a hummingbird's egg. Ostrich eggs usually weigh 2.7 pounds. Hummingbird eggs weigh less than a fifth of an ounce. One ostrich egg can hold more than 5,000 hummingbird eggs. It takes 40 minutes to hard boil an ostrich egg.

Herons have been observed dropping insects on the water and catching the fish that surface for the bugs.

An albatross can sleep while it flies. It apparently dozes while cruising at 25 mph.

Pigeon bones weigh less than the bird's feathers.

The hummingbird, the loon, the swift, the kingfisher, and the grebe are all birds that cannot walk.

The Kiwi, New Zealand's national bird, can't fly. Nearly blind, it lives in a hole in the ground and lays only one egg a year. Yet, the species has survived for more than 70 million years.

Mockingbirds can imitate sounds as wide-ranging as a squeaky door and a cat meow.

Owls can't move their eyes because of their tubular shape.

Domesticated parrots usually acquire a vocabulary of no more than about 20 words. The exceptions are Tymhoney Greys and African Greys, whose vocabularies can exceed 100 words. Pet parrots can eat almost every kind of human food except avocados and chocolate, which are highly toxic to them.

Insects

The average bed is home to more than six billion dust mites.

Butterflies taste with their feet.

An average acre of fertile land hosts about 50,000 spiders. Female wolf spiders will eat strange-looking males that try to mate with them, but let familiar-looking males live or mate with them. One ounce of spider's silk can stretch 2,000 miles. Spider silk, by weight, is stronger than steel.

▨ During a queen bee's epic mating flight, she flies higher than all the male bees except one. That is the male bee she chooses to fertilize all of her eggs at one time, enough to last a lifetime. It takes the nectar from 2,000 flowers to make one tablespoonful of honey. In its entire lifetime, the average worker bee produces one-twelfth of a teaspoon of honey.

▨ The English spittlebug can jump 27.5 inches straight into the air. Since the bug measures only a quarter of an inch, that would be equivalent to a man jumping as high as a 70-story building.

▨ A mosquito has 47 teeth that enable it to drill through human skin in a half second.

▨ The total weight of all insects on Earth is 12 times greater than the weight of all people.

▨ Dragonflies may have as many as 20,000 lenses in each eye. They can fly up to 50 to 60 miles per hour, making them the fastest insect.

▨ Caterpillars have more than 4,000 muscles, compared to 639 muscles in a human.

Plants

▨ Tomatoes were first cultivated in 700 AD by Aztecs and Incans, but for a long time were thought to be poisonous by Europeans. Today, more than 10,000 varieties make tomatoes the world's most popular fruit, with 60 million tons produced annually. Bananas are second with 44 million tons, apples third with 36 million tons, and oranges, 34 million tons.

▨ The seeds of the candlenut contain about 50 percent unsaturated oil and burn like a candle for about 45 minutes.

▨ One ragweed plant can release as many as a billion grains of pollen a year.

▨ Carrots were black, green, red, and purple until the sixteenth century, when a Dutch horticulturist discovered mutant yellow seeds that produced the orange color we know today.

▨ The leaves of the water lily Victoria Regia grow as large as eight feet across.

▨ One coffee tree yields one pound of ground coffee annually.

▨ The roots of an oat plant can reach down as much as 100 feet to find water. One plant's roots can total as much as a mile in length.

▨ An oak tree can give off 28,000 gallons of moisture during one growing season.

▨ Scientists claim that the creosote bush, which grows in the Mojave, Sonoran, and Chihuahuan deserts, may live for up to ten thousand years. Radiocarbon dating has shown some plants to have been around since the birth of Christ.

Extremes

▨ Arica, Chile, is the driest spot on Earth, with only 0.03 inches of rain a year. At that rate, it would take a century to fill a coffee cup.

Arica is situated in the Atacama Desert, parts of which have had no recorded rainfall.

▩ Antarctica has the lowest humidity, with an absolute humidity lower than that of the Gobi desert.

▩ South America has one of the two wettest spots on earth—Lloro, Columbia, with more than 40 feet of rainfall annually. The other is Mount Waialeale on the island of Kauai; it records nearly 500 inches of rainfall a year.

▩ Lightning is 30,000°F, three times hotter than the surface temperature of the sun.

▩ With temperatures reaching 860°F, hot enough to melt lead, Venus is the hottest planet in the solar system

▩ Wal-Mart, the world's largest corporation, is comparable to the nineteenth-largest economy in the world. The company has a total income larger than the gross domestic product (GDP) of Sweden, Austria, or Norway.

▩ Human lungs contain the largest surface area in the body. If stretched out, they would cover the area of a tennis court.

▩ About 800 million gallons of gas are used annually for lawn mowing in the U.S.

▩ The Siloam Tunnel, built around 700 BC by King Hezekiah of Israel, is one of the oldest structures still in use today. It brought water into Jerusalem and was vital in the city's siege by Assyrians in 701 BC. In 2003 it became the first structure mentioned in the Bible to have its age confirmed by archaeologists through carbon dating.

▩ Every square inch of human skin contains 19,000 sensory cells, 19 feet of blood vessels, 90 oil glands, 60 hairs, 625 sweat glands, and between 10,000 and 1,000,000 bacteria.

▩ Humans have more hair follicles per square inch than most mammals, even though they appear much less hairy.

▩ The most options for eating are in Singapore, with more than 6,500 restaurants and 11,500 streetside food stands within city limits.

▩ The body's largest organ is the skin, covering about 6,241 square inches and containing around 120 billion cells.

▩ A tiny bacteria-like creature of the domain Archaea (from the Greek for *ancient*), which many biologists believe are the most primitive forms of life on earth, holds the record for living in the hottest temperature—121°F. Many species of Archaea live in extreme conditions of cold, pressure, salinity, alkalinity, and acidity.

▩ Cold water inhabitants have the longest life spans, including the ocean quahog Arctica islandica, which can live 220 years in subarctic waters. The cold temperature slows down their metabolisms.

▩ The coldest areas of intergalactic space have temperatures of about 4.5°F above absolute zero, warmer than would be expected. Scientists attribute this to leftover warmth from the Big Bang, the theoretical birth of the universe.

▩ About 400 quadrillion (4 and

17 zeros) British thermal units (BTU) of energy were used in 2002 by the world's 6 billion people. That is equivalent to the amount of energy produced by about 54 billion horses working 8- hour shifts each day for a year.

A child in the U.S. or U.K. spends an average of 1,000 hours a year in front of the TV (not including computer games), compared to just 900 hours in school.

The most energy-dependent country in the world is Japan, importing 99.8 percent of its oil, and 80 percent of its overall energy supplies.

The cheapest seashells in the world today are two species of cowries (Cypraea moneta and Cypraea annulata), which were once used as currency. It is thought that the most expensive is a strange black and white shell (Chimaeria incomparabilis Briano) found in deep water off the coast of Ethiopia, which can fetch as much as $40,000 in prime condition.

Fast-paced Americans annually spend more than 4.5 billion hours stuck in traffic.

The country with the most donut shops in the world is Canada.

Saffron, a delicate spice, is the most expensive item in most grocery stores, selling for more than $2,700 a pound, about half the price of pure gold.

The longest recorded flight of a domestic chicken is 13 seconds.

Yonge Street in Toronto, Canada is the world's longest street, running 1,190 miles from Lake Ontario past Lake Superior.

Antarctica, the world's fifth largest continent, was not sighted by Europeans until 1820. It is so cold at the South Pole that the temperature never rises above 3°F.

Tornadoes produce the most intense winds on Earth. The highest recorded wind was more than 318 miles per hour, on May 3, 1999, in Oklahoma City. The fastest-moving tornado on record was the Tri-State Tornado of March 18, 1925, which sped along at 73 miles per hour.

Neptune's winds can rage to 900 miles per hour.

The game of Yahtzee has 1,279,054,096,320 different possible sequences of play.

The Middle East's Stegodyphus pacificus spider spins the thinnest natural thread known. It is almost 1,000 times thinner than a human hair. This same spider also has the most silk spigots, about 40,000.

An estimated 500 million people died from smallpox in the twentieth century alone, making it possibly the most deadly disease ever to ravish humans.

The most expensive stamp in the world is the Sweden 1855 Three Skilling Yellow, last selling at auction for $2.27 million.

The hottest recorded temperature, 136°F, occurred in El Azizia, Libya, on September 13, 1922. The runner-up was 134°F in California's Death Valley on July 10, 1913. Scalding water measures 125°F.

The world's fastest land animal is the cheetah. Its aerodynamic tail helps it turn in high-speed chases.

The Great Wall of China is the world's largest *rammed earth* structure, made by packing earth solidly between two harder surfaces. The second largest is an Australian office building.

In our solar system, the most volcanically active heavenly body is Io, Jupiter's second largest moon. It can have magma eruptions up to three miles high and covering thousands of square miles. These are the result of tidal stresses caused by Jupiter's huge gravitational force, which heats up Io's interior.

The largest deep water species of shrimp ever caught is on display at the Old Spanish Fort Museum in Pascagoula, Mississippi. Caught in the Gulf of Mexico, the shrimp measures 14 inches.

A form of slime mold found on the northwest coast of Australia may be the most ancient life form on earth. It forms structures called *stromatolites* that have been found in rocks estimated to be nearly three billion years old.

Spearfish, South Dakota, holds the record for the fastest temperature change. The temperature rose from -4°F to 45°F in two minutes.

Dwarf willows, the world's smallest trees at two inches, grow on Greenland's tundra.

Mars claims the largest known volcano. It is Olympus Mons, measuring 370 miles wide and 79,000 feet high, nearly three times higher than Mount Everest.

Alaska is the northernmost, westernmost, and easternmost state in the U.S. The Aleutian Islands extend past the 180 degree line of longitude, putting them in the Eastern Hemisphere.

The southernmost point of the U.S. is the southern tip of the island of Hawaii.

The largest iceberg ever seen was 208 miles long and 60 miles wide.

An extinct bird native to Madagascar laid the largest bird egg ever, with a volume of more than two gallons.

The world's smallest known primate is the hairy-eared dwarf lemur of Madagascar. It weighs three and a half ounces, about the size of a mouse.

The sperm whale has the largest brain on the planet, at 20 pounds. A human brain weighs about 3 pounds.

The fastest moon in our solar system travels at 70,400 miles per hour, circling Jupiter every seven hours.

The Caspian Sea, located between southeast Europe and west Asia, is actually the largest lake in the world. The largest freshwater lake on Earth is Lake Baikal, in Siberia. It contains roughly 20 percent of the world's total surface fresh water, as much fresh water as the Great Lakes of North America combined. At a mile deep it is also the deepest lake in the world, and at 25 million years old, probably the oldest.

The world's largest metal coins, in size and standard value, were copper plates used in Alaska about 150 years ago. They were about 3 feet long, 2 feet wide, weighed 90 pounds, and were worth $2,500.

The Mid-Atlantic Ridge is the longest mountain chain on Earth. It splits nearly the entire Atlantic Ocean north to south, rising above the sea surface at Iceland.

Talc is the softest mineral and is commonly used to make talcum powder. A diamond is the hardest mineral.

The highest tides occur in Minas Basin in the Bay of Fundy, Nova Scotia. Tides reach 38.4 feet.

The Sahara Desert is more than 23 times the size of southern California's Mojave Desert. The largest desert in the world, the Sahara was fertile land until about 5000 BC. The world's highest measured sand dunes are those in the Saharan sand sea of Isaouane-n-Tifernine in east-central Algeria. They have a wavelength of 3 miles and attain a height of 1,526 feet.

Yosemite Falls in California is the highest waterfall in the U.S., at 2,425 feet. Angel Falls in Venezuela drops 3,212 feet, making it the world's highest waterfall. Of all the waterfalls in the world, the most water flows over Niagara Falls on an annual basis.

Hells Canyon, dug by the Snake River, is 8,000 feet deep, more than 2,000 feet deeper than the Grand Canyon. It is located along the Oregon-Idaho border.

The most earthquake-prone state in the U.S. is Alaska, which experiences a magnitude 7 earthquake almost every year, and a magnitude 8 or greater earthquake on average every 14 years. The states with the fewest earthquakes are Florida and North Dakota. A 1960 Chilean earthquake, which occurred off the coast, had a record magnitude of 9.6 and broke open a fault more than 1,000 miles long. The world's deadliest recorded earthquake occurred in 1557 in central China, where most of the residents lived in soft rock caves. It is estimated that 830,000 people died when the dwellings collapsed. More recently in Tangshan, China, more than 250,000 people died in an earthquake in 1976.

The Indian Ocean tsunami in December 2004 was the deadliest tsunami ever recorded. Caused by an underwater earthquake lasting several minutes, the tidal wave resulted in casualties numbering between 165,000 and 235,000.

By far the coldest temperature ever measured on Earth was -129°F at Vostok, Antarctica, on July 21, 1983. The Boomerang Nebula is the coldest known place in the universe, with a temperature of -521.6°F. The chilliness is caused by the gas and dust cloud being thrown off by a dying star, a white dwarf, as the center of the Nebula is forced to expand further and faster.

Mexico City is the oldest capital city in the Americas.

The Arctic Ocean is the smallest and shallowest ocean in the world, and is covered by solid ice, ice floes, and icebergs.

The border between Canada and the U.S. is the world's longest frontier between two countries, stretching for 3,987 miles.

▩ The Pantheon is the largest building from ancient Rome still intact.

▩ The San Diego Zoo in California has the largest collection of animals in the world.

▩ The smallest island country is Pitcairn in Polynesia, 1.75 square miles.

▩ The Vatican City is the smallest independent state. It has a population of about 1,000 and a zero birthrate.

▩ The tallest monument in the U.S. is the 630-foot Gateway Arch, in St. Louis, Missouri.

▩ The world's highest railway is the Central Railway in Peru, which climbs to 15,694 feet in the Galera tunnel, 108 miles from Lima. The train takes tourists to the ruins of Machu Picchu. The longest railway in the world is the Trans-Siberian. Built between 1891 and 1916, it is 5,787 miles long and extends through 8 time zones.

▩ Japan's Akashi Kaikyo Bridge is the world's longest suspension bridge, measuring 12,831 feet long. It opened to traffic on April 5, 1998.

▩ Hummingbirds are so tiny that one of their enemies is an insect, the praying mantis. The Cuban bee hummingbird is the world's smallest bird, about 2 inches long. Its heart beats about 300 times a minute and its wings flutter 200 times a second.

▩ The pygmy shrew is the smallest mammal in North America. A relative of the mole, it weighs one-fourteenth of an ounce, less than a dime.

▩ The fastest bird in the world is the Spine-tailed swift, clocked at speeds of up to 220 miles per hour.

▩ The largest animal ever seen alive was a 113.5-foot, 170-ton female blue whale.

▩ The 2,552-pound Big Bill was the largest pig ever recorded. He was a Poland China hog. Kotetsu, a pot-bellied pig on the Mokumoku Tedsukuri Farm, in Mie, Japan, holds the world's record for the highest jump by a pig. Kotetsu soared to 27.5 inches on August 22, 2004.

▩ The world's largest rodent is the capybara, an Amazon water hog that looks like a guinea pig. It can weigh more than 100 pounds.

▩ Thailand claims the world's smallest mammal: Its bumblebee bat weighs less than a penny.

▩ The Cullinan Diamond is the largest gem-quality diamond ever discovered. Found in 1905, the original 3,100 carats were cut for the British Crown Jewels.

▩ The largest gold nugget ever found was 172 pounds, 13 ounces.

▩ The largest hailstone ever recorded was 17.5 inches in diameter, bigger than a basketball.

▩ The most abundant metal in the Earth's crust is aluminum.

▩ The only rock that floats in water is pumice.

▩ The largest living organism ever found is a honey mushroom, Armillaria ostoyae. It covers 3.4 square miles of land in the Blue Mountains of eastern Oregon, and it's still growing.

The bloodiest one-day conflict during the American Civil War was the Battle of Antietam, September 17, 1862. More than 20,000 men were killed, wounded, or missing.

The longest reigning monarch in history was Pepi II, who ruled Egypt for 90 years, from 2566 to 2476 BC. The second longest was France's Louis XIV, who ruled for 72 years, 1643 to 1715 AD.

The people of Iceland read more books per capita than any other people in the world.

There are more statues of Sacagawea, Lewis and Clark's female Indian guide, in the United States than of any other person.

The heaviest living snake is Baby, a 21-year-old Burmese python residing at the Serpent Safari Park in Gurnee, Illinois. It weighs 403 pounds, is 27 feet long, and has a girth of 28 inches.

The largest measured wingspan of any bird of a living species is that of a male wandering albatross, with a span of 11 feet, 11 inches.

The koala eats only six of the 500 species of eucalyptus leaves, searching through 20 pounds of leaves daily to end up with just 1.3 pounds to eat. The most voracious creature is the larva of the polyphemus moth of North America, which consumes 86,000 times its own birth weight in the first 56 days of life. In human terms, this would be equivalent to a 7-pound baby eating 273 tons of food.

A Ruppell's vulture collided with a commercial aircraft over the Ivory Coast at 37,000 feet on November 29, 1973. The incident earned the bird the record for the highest flight by a bird.

Alaska's Columbia glacier is the fastest-moving major glacier in the world. In 1999 it was measured to be flowing at an average rate of 115 feet a day. When a flowing glacier meets the sea, chunks of it can break off to form icebergs.

The Amazon Basin holds two-thirds of all the flowing water in the world. Flowing through the largest and wettest rain forest on the planet, it is fed by more than 1,000 tributary rivers—many of them more than 1,000 miles long—and runs to the Amazon River. The Amazon Basin covers the entire northern half of South America.

The Amazon rainforest is the home of 250 species of mammals, 3,000 freshwater fish, 1,800 birds, 10,000 trees, and 70,000 other plant species.

The cliffs on the north coast of Molokai, Hawaii, near Umilehi Point, are the highest sea cliffs in the world, dropping 3,300 feet to the sea.

For several months a year, the 3,442-mile-long Yellow River in China dries up. This is due to below-average rainfall, increased irrigation, and industry.

A 15-second echo, the longest on record in a building, was heard at the closing of the door of the Chapel of the Mausoleum in Hamilton, South Lanarkshire, Scotland.

The world's largest swamp is Brazil's Pantanal. Its area is about 42,000 square miles.

The rarest element in the Earth's crust is astatine, discovered in 1931. Only about 0.9 ounces exist naturally. Astatine is a member of the halogen group of elements, which includes chlorine, fluorine, and iodine.

The largest fish is the whale shark. The record holder is a 59-foot specimen caught in Thailand in 1919. The largest great white shark ever caught measured 37 feet and weighed 12 tons.

The loudest sound made by a living creature is the low frequency call of the humpback whale, which can be heard up to 500 miles away.

Science

Oceans/Waterways

The Pacific Ocean has three times as much surface area as Asia, the earth's largest continent, and 46 percent of the world's water (about six sextillion gallons of water). The Atlantic Ocean has 23.9 percent of the world's water; the Indian Ocean has 20.3 percent; and the Arctic has 3.7 percent. The oceans make up about two-thirds of the Earth's surface. The mineral salts in sea water cause it to weigh about half as much as the same volume of fresh water. The Atlantic Ocean is saltier than the Pacific, and Utah's Great Salt Lake is more than four times as salty as any ocean.

Only 3 percent of the Earth's water is fresh. Of this, about 79 percent is in ice and glaciers (70 to 76 percent is in the ice caps of Antarctica and Greenland); 20 percent is in ground water; and 1 percent is in lakes, rivers, air, soil, and living creatures.

The Amazon River moves 23 percent of the Earth's fresh water with a daily flow that is three times that of all the rivers in the U.S. combined. Each hour, enough water flows from the mouth of the Amazon to fill Lake Erie. It pushes so much water into the Atlantic Ocean that fresh water is available 100 miles away from the riverhead.

The world's oceans contain about 200 times more gold than the entire amount that has been mined throughout history.

Epaulet sharks, which live in the shallows around coral reefs, can survive without oxygen, and even without water, for extended periods of time. Researchers believe that understanding this phenomenon may have positive medical implications for humans.

Space

One square inch of the sun's surface shines with the intensity of 300,000 candles.

The sun converts more than four million tons of matter into energy every second.

Scientists estimate that there are at least 15 million stars for every man, woman, and child on Earth.

The sun had two north magnetic poles for a short time in 2000 during its solar maximum, an event that occurs every 11 years. The magnetic south pole simply shifted to the sun's equator for the duration.

The atmosphere on Mars is about one percent as dense as Earth's at sea level. It supports only the finest dust grains, as thin as cigarette smoke. Winds on Mars can approach the speed of sound, making for spectacular storms that are sometimes visible from Earth with a small telescope.

Modern astronomers have determined that, in addition to the traditional 12 zodiac constellations, the sun cuts through a thirteenth called Ophiuchus, or Serpent Bearer. That would make people born between November 30 and December 17 Ophiuchi, not Sagittarians.

Information from observations made available from the Hubble space telescope has increased estimations of the number of galaxies in the known universe from 5 billion to nearly 500 billion.

The moons of Uranus are named after Shakespearean characters. All the rest of our solar system's moons are named after Greek and Roman mythological figures.

On February 7, 1969, a meteorite weighing over one ton fell in Chihuahua, Mexico.

Only 55 percent of Americans know that the sun is a star.

Uranus is the only planet that rotates on its side.

The sky as we know it is merely the limit of our vision into the atmosphere. It changes with our position in space and is always as far away as one can see.

The sky is blue because of a process called Rayleigh scattering, in which shorter wavelengths of light—like blue—are absorbed by gas molecules in the atmosphere and reflected back. If light coming directly from the sun went through a pure atmosphere with no gas, water, dust, and other particles, the light of the sky would be white, which contains all the colors of the spectrum.

Earth

Intense heat is the only thing that can destroy a diamond.

Absolutely pure gold is so soft that it can be molded with the hands. An ounce of pure gold can be made into a 50-mile-long wire, and a lump of pure gold can be flattened into a tennis court-sized sheet.

The moon is moving away from the Earth at about 4 centimeters a year, and at the same time the Earth's rotation is slowing. A billion years ago, the moon rotated around the Earth in a much closer orbit and a month was only 20 days.

Alaska contains more than half of the U.S. coastline.

A typical lightning bolt is two miles long, and only two to four inches wide.

Most lightning flashes are multiple events. A flash can contain as many as 42 strokes, each precipitated by a leader stroke from the ground. Intervals between strokes account for most of the duration time of the flash. Therefore, each flash of lightning is mostly empty time, much like solid matter is mostly empty space.

Mud avalanches can move at speeds in excess of 100 miles per hour. The molten material in and around the core of the earth moves in vortices, similar to the way tornadoes and hurricanes rotate.

Rain forests receive nearly half of all the rain that falls on land, yet cover less than 7 percent of the surface of the Earth.

Scientists theorize that Earth began as one big, extremely dry supercontinent, which they call Pangaea (Greek for *all earth*). It began to break up 225 million years ago and form separate continents.

A controversial theory among scientists is that water was originally brought to Earth via comets, rather than being indigenous.

Rain contains vitamin B-12.

The blood of mammals is red, the blood of insects is yellow, and the blood of lobsters is blue.

The heaviest known meteorite to fall to Earth weighed about 60 tons. Every year up to 150 tons of meteorite fragments slam into the planet.

The Earth is struck by lightning approximately 200 times a second, or about 17 million times a day.

Rainfall worldwide averages 960 million tons of water a minute.

The number of species on Earth is conservatively estimated at between 10 and 30 million. Of these, about 2 million have been formally named. Science has a working knowledge of only about one-tenth of those named.

An estimated 95 percent of all life forms on Earth are now extinct. Of the eight major extinctions that have occurred, at least five are linked to sudden climatic changes. It is believed that sudden temperature warmings of between 9 and 14 degrees causes release of trapped methane gas. This release of methane, which is 25 times more potent than CO_2, probably contributed to the vast extinction at the end of the Permian period, about 250 million years ago.

Ancient obsidian knives are often sharper than today's sharpest scalpels. Incisions made with the obsidian tools heal quickly and cause very little scarring.

Earth's only equatorial glacier is on Mount Cotopaxi in Ecuador.

Ice is a mineral, as described in Dana's System of Mineralogy.

Science estimates that three-fourths of Earth's surface is of volcanic origin. Most volcanic rocks are found on the sea floor.

It takes an estimated 98 tons of prehistoric, buried plant material to produce each gallon of gasoline. In the U.S. the amount of fossil fuel people use daily is equivalent to all of the plant matter, including ocean plant life, that grows in a year.

Everyday Life

More than 1,000 chemicals make up a cup of coffee, and 3,000-plus chemicals for cigarette smoke.

Most mosquito repellents don't repel. They hide the wearer from the mosquitoes by blocking the insect's sensors.

▓ Toilet seats are usually one of the cleanest surfaces around the home or office, probably because they are frequently cleaned. Phones, computer keyboards, desktops, sink faucets, and doorknobs are commonly inhabited by 10,000 to 100,000 bacteria per square inch.

▓ The average office worker uses about 10,000 sheets of paper each year. In the U.S., annual copy paper use consumes as much wood as it would take to build nearly one million average homes, and releases as much pollution as two million cars.

▓ All proteins, which number in the tens of thousands, are made from 20 amino acids and all of them are left-handed amino acids. Bacteria use right-handed amino acids to coat themselves, and escape being digested.

▓ A single drop of liquid can contain as many as 50 million bacteria, the smallest free-living cells.

▓ The average automobile in North America produces about five tons of pollutants each year.

▓ U.S. paper currency must have about 4,000 back-and-forth folds before it will tear easily.

▓ One pound of beef requires about 3,500 gallons of water to produce.

▓ More than 10 percent of all the salt produced annually in the world is used to de-ice American roads.

▓ Across the globe, people use about 400 billion gallons of water a day.

▓ Most landfilled trash retains its original weight, volume, and form for 40 years.

▓ When honey is swallowed, it enters the blood stream within a period of 20 minutes.

▓ According to recent studies, about half of the food produced in the U.S. is discarded, spoiled, or otherwise wasted. On average, up to 15 percent of all food that enters an American household is thrown out, about 500 pounds a year.

Cultures

▓ In ancient Egypt, priests plucked every hair from their bodies, including eyebrows and eyelashes.

▓ It was a custom in ancient Egypt to mummify certain baboons when they died.

▓ The umbrella originated in ancient Egypt, where it was used by the royal family and nobility as a symbol of rank.

▓ Twenty percent of all road accidents in Sweden involve a moose.

▓ Russia's 2002 census revealed more than 13,000 uninhabited Russian villages, and nearly 35,000 with 10 or fewer people living in them. Factors include a declining birth rate and urbanization.

▓ One in five accidents in Britain occurs in the garden, making gardening the nation's most hazardous activity.

▓ Lotteries have been used to raise money for thousands of years, by Roman emperors and European royalty. In America, colonial legislatures held lotteries to raise money for paving streets and building churches and wharves. In 1750 and 1772, lotteries financed buildings for Yale and Harvard; and a 1777 lottery by the Continental Congress raised money for revolution.

Women's rights in ancient Sparta were hard to come by: dying in childbirth was the only way a woman could have her name inscribed on a tombstone.

Dreams were very important in the life of the Seno, who lived in the Malaysia mountains and had a society free of crime and mental illness. Every morning the entire family discussed their dreams, and by the time children became teenagers, they had no more nightmares.

The Romany, or gypsies, originated as part of Northern India's Dom tribal group. Displaced circa 1500 BC, they migrated through Syria and Byzantium and eventually arrived in Europe between the thirteenth and fifteenth centuries.

Sunglasses were invented in thirteenth-century China.

It was widely believed in the Middle Ages that the heart was the center of human intelligence and that the brain's purpose was to cool the blood.

Pepper was used for bartering in the Middle Ages, and it was often more valuable than gold.

Prior to the Middle Ages, golden strands from the pen shell were used to make very fine gloves for women. Divers collected the shells on the Mediterranean coast.

Traffic congestion in ancient Rome was so bad that a ban was placed on wheeled vehicles during the day.

Until the sixteenth century, many Europeans considered it effete and even scandalous to dine with a fork.

The caduceus, the medical symbol, comes from an ancient Greek legend in which snakes revealed the practice of medicine to human beings.

Three dog night is an Eskimo expression that graphically describes cold: Some nights were so bitter that people would go to sleep with three dogs to stay warm.

One theory for the derivation of the phrase *raining cats and dogs* is that in seventeenth-century England so many cats and dogs drowned during heavy rains in poorly drained towns that their bodies would float down the streets. Other possibilities are that it sounded like an ancient Greek expression meaning *an unlikely event*, or that it comes from a rare French word for waterfall, *catadoupe*.

Aluminum was used by the Chinese as early as 300 AD, but the West didn't rediscover it until 1827.

Mayonnaise is said to be the invention of the French chef of the Duc de Richelieu in 1756. While the duke defeated the British at Port Mahon, his chef created a victory feast that included a sauce made of cream and eggs. When the chef realized there was no cream in the kitchen, he improvised, substituting olive oil for the cream. A new culinary masterpiece was born, and the chef named it *Mahonnaise* in honor of the victory.

Colored eggs were first used by the Persians to celebrate spring in 3000 BC. The custom was brought to Europe from the Middle East by the Crusaders and was soon converted for use at Easter and other spring holidays.

▓ Respecting the fact that Hindus don't eat beef, the New Delhi McDonald's serves mutton burgers.

▓ The English word "soup" comes from the Middle Ages word "sop," which means a slice of bread over which roast drippings were poured. The first archaeological evidence of soup being consumed dates back to 6000 BC. The main ingredient was hippopotamus bones.

▓ Guests must come hungry to Bedouin wedding feasts. The banquet sometimes includes roast camel stuffed with a sheep's carcass, which in turn is stuffed with chickens, stuffed with fish, stuffed with eggs.

▓ The Chinese emperor Shen Nung first used acupuncture in 2700 BC.

▓ Fourteenth-century physicians didn't know what caused the plague, but they knew it was contagious. As a result, they wore an early kind of bioprotective suit that included a large, beaked headpiece. The beak was filled with vinegar, sweet oils, and other strong smelling compounds to counteract the stench of the dead and dying plague victims.

▓ For several hundred years, barbers performed a variety of medical procedures, including dentistry, blood letting, and minor surgeries. The striped barber's pole started off in the Middle Ages as a pole for patients to hold onto while being bled.

▓ The Ku Klux Klan began in 1865 as a private social club formed by veterans of the Confederacy.

▓ The minimum age for marriage for girls in Italy was raised to 12 years old in 1892.

▓ The ancient Egyptians slept on pillows made of stone. They also had the first known contraceptive—crocodile dung—first used in 2000 BC.

▓ Until 1965, Swedes drove on the left-hand side of the road. The conversion to right-hand driving took place on a weekday at 5 PM. All traffic stopped as people switched sides. This time and day were chosen to prevent accidents where drivers would have gotten up in the morning and been too sleepy to realize *this* was the day of the changeover.

Language & Communication

▓ No English words rhyme with *month, silver, purple,* or *orange.*

▓ The shortest sentence in English is *Go* or *Be.*

▓ The language of the Basques, in northeastern Spain and southwestern France, is not related to any known language. Since its word for *ax* is closely related to the word for *stone,* however, many linguists think Basque may have its origins in Neolithic Europe.

▓ Of the world's identified languages, 4.5 percent have disappeared in the past 500 years.

▓ Approximately 90 percent of

the estimated 6,809 languages in the world are spoken by fewer than 100,000 people. A total of 46 languages have just a single speaker remaining.

▓ The most widely spoken language in the world is Mandarin Chinese—by 885,000,000 people.

▓ More than 100 language families endure today, ranging from Indo-European (English, Bengali, Urdu, German, French, Danish, and many more) to Sino-Tibetian, Dravidian (southern India and Sri Lanka), and the 35 or so language families in the Americas. In pre-Columbian times, people in what is now California spoke in about 20 linguistic families, far greater linguistic diversity than Europe.

▓ Studies show that people who speak Mandarin Chinese use both the left temporal lobe, associated with organizing sounds into words, and the right temporal lobe, associated with processing melody and intonation. English speakers use only the left lobe.

▓ People who gesticulate while talking are twice as likely to be understood. Hand movements can convey both solid and psychological images.

▓ For more than 600 years, French was the official language of England.

▓ The ancient Greeks, Romans, and Hebrews liked anagrams, which were also fashionable at times in the Middle Ages.

▓ French chemist René Maurice Gattefossé used the word *aromatherapy* in the 1920s to describe the extraction of essential oils from plants, flowers, roots, and seeds for healing purposes.

▓ *Kemo sabe* is Navajo for *soggy shrub*.

▓ The saying *long in the tooth* to denote old age came from the fact that horses' gums recede as they age, making their teeth appear to grow. The longer the teeth, the older the horse.

▓ In the Middle Ages, archers carried a second string for their bows, in case of breakage. *Second string* came to mean a backup or replacement.

▓ The prefix *O'* in Irish surnames means *son of*. In Irish names such as Fitzgerald, the *Fitz* derived from the French *fils,* for *son*. That formulation dates to the twelfth and thirteenth centuries, when Norman French settled in Ireland, invited by the King of Leinster.

▓ The *y* in *ye olde* is pronounced *th*, not *y,* and is a remnant of an Anglo-Saxon letter known as *thorn*. The *th* sound does not exist in Latin, so when the ancient Romans occupied Britain they used thorn to represent *th* sounds. When the printing press came to be used centuries later, the letter in the Roman alphabet that most resembled thorn was *y*.

▓ With 74 letters, the Cambodian alphabet is the world's largest.

▓ *Les Miserables* contains a sentence 823 words long.

▓ To protect their necks from swords, the first U.S. Marines wore high leather collars. They became known as *leathernecks*.

When a consonant is pronounced, the sound waves are more than 600 times more powerful than when a vowel is pronounced.

People

Ninety percent of New York City taxi drivers are recent immigrants.

One person in two billion will live to be 116 or older.

Our eyes are full-grown at birth. Our nose and ears never stop growing.

Americans eat 18 acres of pizza every day.

Neanderthal brains were on average larger than those of modern humans. It is theorized that Neanderthals died out because they were unable to adapt to changing environments and challenges from other human species.

Taken together, the assets of the three richest people in the world are greater than the gross domestic products of the world's poorest 48 countries combined.

A typical 4-year-old asks more than 400 questions daily.

Men and mice share 99 percent of their genes, including the one that produces a tail, not active in humans. They also share 90 percent of the same diseases. The similarity makes mice ideal for medical research. Mice have more genes for smelling and for producing large, frequent litters.

European diseases such as smallpox decimated the pre-Columbian population of Native Americans, who once numbered 100,000,000 and now number just a few million.

Creative people are apparently more open to stimuli from their environments than other people, who filter out stimuli if it isn't important to their everyday needs. This can be a two-edged sword, as people unable to filter out stimuli can have psychotic disorders. Madness and extraordinary creativity may result from the same source.

At birth, we have 300 bones in our bodies. As adults, we have 206.

The human brain is capable of 10 quadrilllion calculations a second, far faster than any computer.

A normal person's height is higher in the morning than at night due to the compression caused by gravity during the day. The daily variation can be as much as an inch.

The male tendency to be larger than females begins in the womb.

Left-handed people are six times more likely to die in accidents. Twice as many men as women are left-handed.

The combined length of arteries, veins, and capillaries in the body is more than 60,000 miles, an average of 20 feet of blood vessels in every square inch of skin. Each square inch also has 72 feet of nerves.

Nerve impulses can travel as fast as 170 miles per hour. The speed of pain is 350 feet per second.

The human brain consists of about 1,000,000,000,000 nerve cells. The brain in a developing fetus grows by about 250,000 cells a minute.

The human liver can function and regenerate even if up to 80 percent of it is removed.

The human body has about 60 trillion cells, and each cell has about 10,000 times as many molecules as stars in the Milky Way.

The cornea is the only part of the human body that takes in oxygen directly from the air, therefore requiring no blood supply.

Historical People

Anne Boleyn had an extra fingernail on one hand. She covered it with long sleeves.

In addition to his influential scientific work, Sir Isaac Newton also published works on philosophy (*Principia*), and the Bible, including interpretations of the prophecies of Daniel and Revelation.

The only U.S. president to be granted a patent was Abraham Lincoln, for a device to lift boats over shoals.

Theodore Roosevelt was the only U.S. president to deliver an inaugural address without using the word *I*. Abraham Lincoln, Franklin D. Roosevelt and Dwight D. Eisenhower tied for second place, using the word only once.

Catherine de Medici introduced the French to forks, spinach, and several other native Italian foods when she married France's Henry II.

In 1917, Britain's royal family changed its name to Windsor from Saxe-Coburg and Gotha. In the aftermath of World War I, they wanted distance from German association.

Martha Washington is the only woman whose image has appeared on a U.S. currency note, and Sacagawea and Susan B. Anthony are the only women on coins.

Only John Hancock and Charles Thomason signed the Declaration of Independence on July 4. Most of the rest signed it on August 2, with the last name added five years later.

Law

In Atlanta, Georgia, it is illegal to tie a giraffe to a telephone pole or street lamp.

Kentucky has a law that every citizen must bathe once a year.

In Toronto, Canada, it used to be illegal to ride a streetcar on Sundays after eating garlic.

The Byzantium Emperor Justinian ordered all laws governing life and commerce to be recorded. This codification, called the Institutes of Justinian, formed the basis of law for many European countries, including England.

The Institutes of Justinian included a civil law granting public use of tidelands, water, and ocean access. This law exists today in the U.S., with the exception of Maine and Massachusetts. Because of the costs of building long wharves to provide access to the ocean at all times of day, those states gave property owners rights to the shoreline so they would assume the cost of building the wharves. Even so, the public has shore access for the purpose of fishing, fowling, and navigation.

It is common for bears to tear the bark off of trees in the spring for the sap, which gives them quick energy after their winter hibernation. In Oregon, it is unlawful for bears to do this on trees that are part of tree plantations owned by lumber companies. The penalty for bears caught ripping bark is death. Hundreds of bears have been killed as a result of this law.

A seventeenth-century Massachusetts law required smokers to be five miles out of town before lighting up.

In Belgium, it is legal for children to throw bananas at police cars on Christmas Eve, and for police officers to throw bananas at children on Christmas Day.

To duel legally in Paraguay, both people have to be registered as blood donors.

Napoleon simplified 14,000 French decrees into a set of 7 laws, making it the first time in history that a nation's laws applied equally to all citizens. By 1960, more than 70 governments worldwide had used the *Code Napoleon* as a model for their own laws.

Superstition

Fear of Friday the thirteenth is demonstrated in many ways: More than 80 percent of high-rise buildings lack a thirteenth floor. Many airports skip the thirteenth gate.

Airplanes have no thirteenth aisle.

Hospitals and hotels regularly have no room number 13.

Italians omit the number 13 from their national lottery. On streets in Florence, Italy, houses between numbers 12 and 14 are designated as 12 1/2. Many cities do not have a Thirteenth Street or a Thirteenth Avenue. Those who fear the unlucky integer are known as triskaidekaphobes. Many people today wear old shoes on Friday the thirteenth for good luck.

Initially, Europeans thought that potatoes were disgusting and responsible for diseases such as leprosy and syphilis. In colonial America, they were believed to shorten a person's life.

If you honk at a crow on the road you will have good luck all day if it doesn't move.

Many Asians believe that crickets bring good luck to their owners.

An itchy left hand means that money is coming your way.

Rain is caused by intentionally stepping on a caterpillar or spider, seeing a blue-jay, cows laying down, or a potato pot boiling dry.

Storms are portended by cows huddling together or a flock of seagulls on land.

Wishes are granted when you see a rainbow, touch blue, see the first robin in spring, enter a church for the first time, see a shooting star, toss a coin into a well, or blow the white seeds off a dandelion.

When you see a one-eyed cat, spit on your thumb, stamp it in the palm of your hand, and make a wish. The wish will come true.

Bad luck follows sticking a knife in butter, looking at a new moon through a window, breaking a sewing needle while sewing a trousseau, planting corn in the dark of the moon, or wearing gray mittens on a fishing boat.

Throwing spilled salt over your left shoulder temporarily blinds the devil that is present there.

Whistling on a ship incurs the ocean's wrath.

Company is coming if a rooster crows; special company is coming if you drop a potato.

Hungry company is coming if you take seconds while there is still food on your plate.

Dropping silverware causes company. Drop a spoon and the company will be female, drop a fork and the company will be male. Dropping a knife will break the spell.

Put money in a wallet that is a gift so that person will have money for the rest of his or her life.

Old shoes were good luck charms. They would be placed in the roofs of old houses to fend off evil spirits.

Shoes were dropped outside the front door before beginning a journey, and were thrown after someone starting on a journey to bring good luck.

Scottish Highlanders used to throw a shoe over the house. The way the toe points when it reaches the ground is the direction you are destined to travel before long.

Putting ferns in your shoes will bring treasure.

Superstitious actors think good luck accompanies squeaky shoes or putting the right shoe on first. Bad luck comes by putting shoes on a chair.

Bad luck is brought on by shoes placed on a table or under the bed, and giving shoes on Christmas Day. It's bad luck to put your left foot down first when getting out of bed.

A child born with an extra toe or finger will be lucky throughout their life.

If the bottom of your right foot itches, you are going to take a trip.

It is bad luck to meet someone with flat feet or bare feet, especially in the morning.

A bird call from the north means tragedy; from the south brings good crops; from the west is good luck; from the east, good love.

An important message is coming if a bird flies into your house.

It's considered excellent luck to hear the first cuckoo on April 28.

Your condition on hearing the first cuckoo will remain all year.

Eagles are symbols of strength, divinity, resurrection, and immortality.

Peace follows several eagles flying together.

Hearing the cry of an eagle is an omen of death.

Jaybirds go down to the devil's house on Fridays to tell all the bad things that have happened during the week. Jaybirds that remain on Friday are checking up on what people are doing.

Eating three lark eggs will improve your voice.

Greeting a magpie is said to

remove the bad omens it brings.

■ A building won't fall down if there is a single magpie on the roof.

■ When you hear an owl, take off your clothes, turn them inside out, and put them back on to prevent bad luck.

■ If an owl nests in an abandoned house, then the dwelling must be haunted. An owl is the only creature that can abide a ghost.

■ A raven on a chimney is good luck to those within. If a raven is seen flying toward the sun, good weather will follow.

■ Money will follow if a bee lands on your hand. A bee settling on your head means you will rise to greatness.

■ Expect rain if a cat sneezes once.

■ If a cat sneezes three times, everyone in the family will catch a cold.

■ In the Netherlands, cats were not allowed to be around to hear family discussions. The Dutch believed that cats would spread gossip around town.

■ In France it is considered bad luck to carry a cat while crossing a stream.

■ Scots believe that a strange black cat on your porch brings prosperity.

■ In England, a cat sleeping with all four paws tucked under means cold weather ahead.

■ When moving to a new home, a cat won't leave if you put it through a window first instead of the door.

■ The cure for whooping cough or measles was to place three hairs from a donkey's shoulders in a muslin bag and wear it around the neck. Sitting backwards on a donkey would cure snakebites and toothaches.

■ If a pregnant woman saw a donkey, her child would be wise and well-behaved.

■ Catch a dragonfly and be married within the year.

■ Look for treasure hidden if you meet a black goat on a bridle path.

■ More people say they are afraid of spiders than afraid of death.

■ You'll take a trip if you see a spider run down a web in the afternoon.

■ If you run into a spider's web you'll meet a new friend.

■ Wearing a spider in a walnut shell around your neck was believed to prevent catching the plague.

■ You'll have new clothes soon if you see a spider running over clothing.

■ A marriage will be prosperous and happy if a spider crosses the bride's path on her way to church.

■ The folk etymology of loophole was that it came from French *loup*, for *wolf*. In the woods, stone shelters with a spy hole were built to protect people from wolf attacks—thus *loophole*. It is more likely the word came from the narrow windows in castles, and that the word *loup* is related to the Dutch *lupen*, to watch.

■ Good luck comes from sneezing three times before breakfast, meeting three sheep, spilling wine

while proposing a toast, nine peas
in a pea pod, putting on a dress inside out, sleeping on sheets that
haven't been ironed, itching on the
top of your head, dolphins swimming near a ship, seeing a white
butterfly before any other kind in
the year.

If you cut a loaf of bread irreg-
ularly, you have been telling lies.

Women have luck on Tues-
days and Fridays. Men have luck on
Mondays and Thursdays.

Dropping matches is good
luck. A girl who spills a box of
matches will marry soon. Crossing
matches by chance means joy to
come.

You must give a poor person a
new pair of shoes in this life, or you
will be barefoot in the next.

A shoelace repeatedly coming
untied is a sign of coming good
news or good fortune.

To prevent an unwelcome
guest from returning, immediately
sweep out the room they stayed in.

Count the number of Xs in the
palm of your right hand to know
how many children you will have.

A cook whose soup is salty is
in love.

Prevent winter colds by catching a falling leaf on the first day of
autumn.

Build a Well-Rounded Bibliography

By Leslie Wyatt

The mailbox held an SASE. Inside was what every author dreads: the form rejection. But unlike others I had received, this one did not indicate "does not meet our current needs." The check mark singled out a different category: insufficient bibliography.

Reviewing my article, I had to agree. It had three sources, one a children's book—definitely a pitifully small list, especially given that the magazine I had targeted was *Highlights for Children*. Yes, I blush to admit this major error of my early days in writing for children, but I include it to show that such missteps can be remedied. I did more research, resubmitted the revised manuscript with a much more solid bibliography, and sold the article to *Highlights*.

A Friend Indeed

Bibliographies. These time-honored lists of sources enable an editor to know where you have obtained your information and whether those sources are authoritative. This requirement forms the basis of fact-checking and is not a lack of confidence in you as a writer. It is an essential part of any publisher's job to confirm accuracy, since their reputation would be on the line if they were to publish erroneous or slanted information.

But a bibliography is not just an editor's ally. It is a writer's as well. According to Adam Oldaker, Associate Editor of *Cricket* and *Cicada*, a bibliography enables authors "to inform editors how extensively a manuscript has been researched." When reviewing nonfiction or historical fiction, Oldaker routinely turns to the bibliography before reading the manuscript.

A bibliography also gives credit where credit is due. If writers go around borrowing other people's research, words, and statements without giving some kind of credit, they could end up in embarrassing and expensive legal wrangling.

More than being our legal friend, a solid, well-rounded bibliography works to a writer's advantage in another important way. Heather Delabre, Editor of *Spider,* says, "An author becomes well known by presenting solid bibliographies time and time again."

Carolyn Yoder, History Editor at *Highlights for Children* and Editor of the company's U.S. history imprint, Calkins Creek Books, says: "The bibliography is *always* essential. It is *my* guide to see if the manuscript is original. Extensive research means originality. It's as simple as that." (See Yoder's "At the Source: Field Research," page 273.)

Truth is sometimes harder to believe than fiction, which is another reason your nonfiction needs the support of a well-rounded bibliography. Fiction often has the same needs—historical fiction in particular, though think of the accuracy needed in science or current events or even sports stories.

Lest we forget our readership in the midst of the editorial swirl, a bibliography also offers opportunities for interested readers to dig deeper into a subject. Not every publication takes the step of publishing a bibliography with the article, but many do and can adapt your more extensive list of sources to the audience. Certain sources you use for your research may not be suitable for children, but the details of which sources remain in your published bibliography can be worked out with the publisher.

With the oceans of research opportunities waiting to be explored, where should a writer start? Oldaker advises, "Unique research methods

are needed for every project. For instance, someone writing about a Civil War battle should review primarily history books, while an author writing on current medical research should review mostly science journals and, if possible, interview the scientists conducting the research."

The Structure: Primary & Secondary

Want to make your research stand out like a skyscraper among ground-hugging structures? Building always goes better with some sort of plan, and bibliographies are no exception. Start with a strong foundation: *primary sources.*

Joanne Mattern, author of more than 130 children's books, gives her definition of this sometimes misunderstood term: "A primary source is a firsthand account. For example, if you were writing about the Great Chicago Fire and found an eyewitness account, that would be a primary source. A secondary source is *secondhand*—written by someone who wasn't there, but gathered information or spoke to people with firsthand knowledge. So, a newspaper account or a book about the Great Chicago Fire would be a secondary source (unless the author was describing his or her own experience). Diaries, letters, and oral histories are all examples of primary sources."

Paula Morrow, Editor of *Ladybug* and *Babybug*, reiterates: "*Primary* is as in *original*: If you're writing a historical piece, a secondary source is a book about the period, and a primary source is a journal or newspaper published during the period. If it's a science piece—or the same thing in a different field—a secondary source is a book or article about someone else's research, and a primary source is a book or article written by the researcher personally. Primary just means going back to the first source."

Museums and libraries are the most obvious places to uncover primary sources, from firsthand accounts to artifacts. They facilitate research by sharing displays, microfilm records, diaries, letters, government publications, and so on. Don't overlook audio or visual recordings. Documentaries can furnish quotes from biography subjects or experts in the field you are researching. Be very careful when documenting these sources, and include information not only about the people or experts, but about the documentaries or recordings themselves.

Stretch your imagination. Regina Griffin, Editor at Holiday House Publishers, wants to see writers make more use of primary sources such as "timetables of stage coach lines, letters, naval reports—whatever fits the subject." Consider everything from almanacs, maps, and atlases to bills of lading to how-to books from earlier times as possible sources for your bibliography. Databases can provide exhaustive lists of sources to explore. (See the articles, "Digging into Local History," page 285, and "Online Databases," page 291.)

Bibliographies of books you use for research can lead you to other great primary sources. If you're writing about a medical topic, you might be able to find a teaching hospital. If you're working on a historical piece, historical sites can yield great information.

Interviews and experts are primary source categories all their own. Whether you interview an expert or ask one to review your work, people who are skilled in a certain field are an important part of a well-built bibliography. Most experts are more than willing to share their passions. This can be done via e-mail, phone conversation, or even over coffee at the local café. If you are asking them to review your manuscript for accuracy, and then write a letter of endorsement, do them the favor of providing a SASE to facilitate the process. Though most experts are willing to share their knowledge free of charge, a SASE is common courtesy and a little postage can buy enormous goodwill. (See "Cook up a Great Interview," page 279.)

The next stages of your building are the levels of secondary sources: books, official Internet sites, magazines, newspaper articles, government pamphlets. The list is huge and your imagination is key. With the wealth of facts available on virtually every subject, the challenge is not usually finding material but limiting it to pertinent information. Make sure the sources in your bibliography are of the best caliber.

Documenting & Citing Your Research

It may seem at the time that you could never forget which source you're quoting, but just in case, take the precaution of always recording this information ASAP. It saves time if you list it as you would for your bibliography. While you're at it, take the time to note page number as well as source. This can save you a lot of backtracking if the publisher asks for this information at a later date, as some have been known to do.

With so many types of resources available, is there a correct way to list the different varieties in your bibliography? Yes, and if you have a question, *The Chicago Manual of Style* explains how to cite virtually any source you can find, as well as how to footnote correctly, and other tidbits.

Use headings in your bibliography—books, magazines, periodicals, interviews, etc. Under these headings, list entries alphabetically by author's last name, then first name. If the author is unknown, alphabetize the entry by title. After the author comes the title, the place of publication if available, the publisher, and the date. An example would be, Rajtar, Steve. *Indian War Sites: A Guidebook to Battlefields.* Jefferson, NC: McFarland & Co., 1999.

To cite a magazine, list author, article title, magazine title, date, volume number, issue number, and page numbers: Roberts, David. "A Social Divide Written in Stone." *Smithsonian,* February 1999. Volume 29, Issue 11, pages 40–51.

Internet sources don't always have consistent information, but if available, list the author's name, the title of the article, website title, and URL. An example of this would be: Smith, Harry. "Riding with Crazy Horse." University of Nebraska. http://www.crazyhorse.lecture.uon.edu.

Phone interview? Start with the interviewee's name and title. State that it was a phone interview, and give the time and date the interview was conducted: Morris, William R., Chief of Interpretation and Visitor Services, Public Affairs Officer, Mesa Verde National Park, CO, Telephone interview, 2:30 P.M. - 3:30 P.M., July 10, 2000.

To list museums and other sources, you might have to be a little creative. For example, you might say, "Notes from Exhibit on Sandals and Pottery of the Cliffdwellers." Mesa Verde Museum, Colorado, July 11, 2005. Just be sure to include all relevant information to enable fact-checking and proper attribution.

A Solid Build

Technology has advanced communication and the number of resources available to Everyman to a staggering level. It is exciting and fascinating—and for the researching writer seeking accuracy, a little dangerous.

"Editors have noticed that many authors are plugging key words into search engines, reading the first sites that come up, and then using them as main sources for their manuscripts," Oldaker says. "This is bad research. Authors should be looking for the best sources for their projects, which are seldom found by doing a simple Internet search."

Delabre advises against having a bibliography made up entirely of Internet sources. "A bibliography consisting of all Internet sources or a bibliography containing encyclopedia sources (Web-based or otherwise) would be highly suspect to me. Internet sources are okay to have in a bibliography, as long as they're *official* sites." Such bibliographies send the message that the author "didn't want to exert the effort to go to a library or historical society, or pick up the phone to interview an expert."

Reliance on encyclopedias is the same. They are too easy and too broad for a good writer to rely on. Encyclopedias are great as an entry point, but they can't cover a subject in the depth needed to support an article or some fiction. Timeliness is also a concern. Delabre says, "Kids use encyclopedias for research to get a general overview of their topics. As adults, we have to be extremely specific with and careful about the information we present to the world, especially to children, who are likely to take any book or article's word as fact."

The current trend toward relying more on Internet sources and less on traditional research—books, journals, interviews, museums, historical sites—results in misinformation leaking into submissions. Consequently, editors are more careful than ever about what they accept. Irresponsible research backfires and affects the entire writing community. So be kind to yourself and fellow authors by only submitting stellar research.

"Books are longer and allow the author to go into more depth about a subject, so they are a better source of information," says Mattern. She cautions, "Anyone can put up a website and say whatever they want—there's no filter, as there is with book or magazine publishers—so every piece of information should be carefully checked. Some websites are just unusable for research altogether."

Writers must look for proof that the website author is qualified to write about a topic before including the information, says Oldaker. "The page may be a professor's lifework, but it may also be the labor of a still-in-training graduate student, or even an undergraduate paper dashed off the night before." He also mentions the difficulty with knowing when a Web article was published, since "even a source written by an expert may contain out-of-date information."

Morrow notes, "Even an *official* website can throw you a curve. I once had someone cite a statistic from a university site, ending in .edu, which should be reliable. But when I checked it out, I discovered the university had sponsored a science fair, and the statistic was taken from an 11-year-old child's project. It was *not* accurate. The author should have caught that! Do check your sources carefully."

Timeliness is also an issue with books and magazines as sources, however. Can you use older books and articles? Yes and no. If you're writing about something in science, you're going to want cutting-edge information. This is not important in the same way for historical research, but bear in mind that details can vary from source to source, and new research may have changed earlier perspectives on any subject. The best choice is to read widely among old and new sources to uncover accurate information.

When new nonfiction acknowledges previously published works as integral, read those older sources, no matter how long ago they were first printed. A case in point: In the late 1800s, Crow Indian chiefs told stories to a dentist, who published them in a 1932 compilation. Later books mention this source. Going back to that 1932 book is examining primary research. More than 70 years old, the compilation would be a very valuable addition to a bibliography on the subject of the Crow Indians.

Yoder says, "A bibliography has to be detailed. It has to be diverse—made up of the most up to date and classic resources, adult *and* children, primary *and* secondary. I also like to see if the author includes other sources of information—interviews, magazine articles, places to visit, for example. I also request annotated bibliographies to see how the author has *interpreted* the research."

An annotated bibliography is the list of source citations with your brief paragraph after each explaining the core nature of the source, what it offers, and why it is relevant to your subject. It can be an impressive addition to any submission.

Employ the Tools

Believe it or not, more than one writer has been guilty of amassing a great bibliography but using only one of the sources to write their article or story. Besides not being honest, this is not wise. Use a quality bibliography not only to make a sale, but to put together your work.

"It's frustrating to accept a manuscript on the basis of a good bibliography, only to learn in fact-checking that the author had read only one or two of the sources carefully," says Oldaker. "This is poor etiquette and, in a sense, false advertising." It is not something you want editors to remember you by.

In addition, some sources contain information that contradicts or cancels out the information in other sources. It's important to read each and every source you list in order to compare the data. According to

Mattern, "A good writer will verify any fact or story in at least two or three sources. Usually, if a story is verified by several sources, it is generally accepted as truth."

If you cannot corroborate with two or three sources, Mattern says that writers can sidestep by using the fact but indicating that it is a *rumor*, or by saying, "Some sources report that . . . ." Don't overdo this device, however. It will undermine your credibility.

Is there a minimum number of sources editors like to see in a biblio? Griffin says that for her, quality matters, rather than quantity. She goes on to say that while she evaluates a nonfiction or historical fiction manuscript on the quality of writing, "Even for a short picture book, there should be more than five [sources]." Other editors may look for more sources.

It is a good idea to mention your research in your cover letter. Oldaker says writers may want to "explain what their main sources were and how long they've been looking into the topic, as well as address any questions that may arise during the reviewing process (such as why the bibliography is full of websites or lacks books)." Be sure to sculpt the information, of course, to fit your target market and your proposed project.

A well-built bibliography may take extra work, but if you've done a thorough, responsible job of research and correctly notated it in your biblio, you can smile when you slip your manuscript into the mail. It's articles and stories like yours that get the good attention from editors. With some additional time and effort, you'll increase the chances that the envelope you receive in return will contain the magic phrase, "We are pleased to inform you . . . ."

At the Source: Field Research

By Carolyn Yoder

Today authors and editors must break away from their computers and local libraries and stretch their legs. They can't limit their research to printed and electronic material only. It is a must for authors and editors to get out in the field and search for the tiny nuggets of truth. Field research means visits to museums, historic sites, cities, and people—to name only a few of the possibilities—and getting to know subjects up close and personal. Who wouldn't want to break away from *deadly* books and magazine articles? Field research is alive— exciting and enlightening, although at times excruciating.

Most editors and authors do not take field research lightly. It requires plenty of planning and a solid understanding of the subject. Getting out in the field tends to happen once the printed and electronic research is well underway. Author Susan Campbell Bartoletti visited the anthracite coal region of Pennsylvania for *Growing Up in Coal Country;* Ireland for *Black Potatoes:*

The Story of the Great Irish Famine, 1845-1850; and Germany for *Hitler Youth: Growing up in Hitler's Shadow.* She offers this bit of advice: "Prepare, prepare, prepare. Learn all you can about your subject before you go out in the field."

Getting Close

For Bartoletti, field preparation can save time and money. She says, "For instance, before I traveled to Germany, I conducted as much research here in the States as I could. I didn't want to waste time and money on research in a foreign country that could be accomplished at home."

Meg Chorlian, Editor of *Cobblestone,* an American history children's magazine with monthly themes, travels to museums, historic sites, and to meetings with people on a fairly regular basis. For her, field research is "getting out of the office and as close to the topic I am focusing on as possible." When she edited an issue on Deerfield, Massachusetts, she "worked very closely with the staff at the historic town and made several trips there to meet with people, organize the issue, and take and research photographs in their collections." For Chorlian, "the personal visits and tours through the houses helped me understand Deerfield's 300-year history in many other ways than if I had just read their website."

Author James Cross Giblin is also a big fan of on-site research, calling it the icing on the cake and using it for most of his book projects. He has journeyed to the Cloisters at the Metropolitan Museum of Art for *The Truth about Unicorns;* to Philadelphia for *The Amazing Life of Benjamin Franklin;* to Ford's Theater in Washington, DC, for *Good Brother, Bad Brother: The Story of Edwin Booth and John Wilkes Booth;* and to Mount Vernon and Monticello for his books on George Washington and Thomas Jefferson, respectively.

Sometimes these personal visits work their way into the actual text. Giblin points out, "Years ago for *Fireworks, Picnics, and Flags: The Story of the Fourth of July Symbols,* I went to Philadelphia, toured Independence Hall, visited the Liberty Bell with a third-grade class (one of whom climbed under the bell and said it was 'like a tent' after he was hauled out; I used that anecdote in the book), and paid a special visit to the house where Thomas Jefferson drafted the Declaration of Independence."

Even when trips to sites are well planned and researched ahead of time, most authors and editors are often surprised when they get there. Giblin has experienced serendipity many times, mostly when researching the images for his books. For his book on Lindbergh, Giblin traveled to the Minnesota Historical Society in St. Paul because the famous aviator grew up in Minnesota. Little did Giblin know how much he would discover there, including "Lindbergh's photo albums containing family snapshots taken during the summers he spent as a boy on the Upper Mississippi, and later pictures of Lindbergh as a flight student in Texas."

Years later, Giblin journeyed to Washington, DC's National Archives and had a similar experience. "I was able to look through, and order prints from, the photo albums that Hitler's mistress Eva Braun assembled from the 1920s through the early 1940s. A U.S. Army colonel unearthed the albums after the war at Braun's apartment in Munich and gave them to the Archives. I used a selection of photos from these albums in *The Life and Death of Adolf Hitler,* and they helped to flesh out my portrayal of the dictator's strangely bourgeois lifestyle."

Sometimes serendipity leads authors and even editors onto entirely different paths and toward entirely different subjects. Author and *Highlights for Children* Coordinating Editor Kim Griswell finds that travel can be helpful for writing both fiction and nonfiction. She's gone to places where her stories are set to write down details about what she observes—street names, shops, what people wear, what the weather is like. But it was on one trip to a local aquarium that something special happened. Griswell discovered an idea for a new story.

"I saw an article on the wall about a gigantic lobster that had once lived there," Griswell reveals. "One day, someone stole the lobster and fled with him. I thought that would make a great story to tell kids, so I arranged an interview with the manager who'd been there when it happened. I also got copies of everything that had been written about the lobster-napping at the time it happened. I guess that was research that found me, rather than the other way around."

These research trips can also offer deep personal connections to the subject, something that looking through pages of books or magazines and even talking to people cannot. For an issue on the USS *Constitution*, Chorlian spent much time in Boston working closely with the ship's education department and touring the museum there. Later she was invited to ride on the ship. "I think it was the first time the ship had been mobile (not towed) in more than 100 years. It was one of those moments I still can't believe I was part of. It was such a celebratory event, and I switched from an editor doing her job to a person with a deeper enthusiasm and interest in this remarkable ship's history."

Search for Primary Sources

Author Lois Miner Huey, an archeol-ogist and historian, follows the traditional definition of field research: gathering data from the ground. "The artifacts and features found in the ground are evidence of past behavior," Huey says. She connects this evidence with documentary finds. For that documentation through field research, she goes back to what the actual people said, either through interviews or reading primary sources.

The search for primary source or original material—diaries, journals, newspapers, artifacts, photographs—is a large and important part of field research. In evaluating primary source material, Huey recommends thinking about why the person wrote the document. What underlying reason might there be for some of the statements? How self-serving are they?

Because copies or transcripts are sometimes wrong due to the transcriber's misreading of the originals, a researcher should read the original documents personally.

"Talk" Research

For issues on topics that would take her too far away from the magazine's base in Peterborough, New Hampshire, Chorlian turns to another kind of field research—talking directly to experts. Like most editors and authors, Chorlian relies on experts for two main reasons. Experts can be sources of information just like books or articles, offering insights that become part of the text. In addition, Chorlian sometimes asks their help in writing for the magazine.

"Interviewing people is a great way to learn something that might not be obvious in a straight narrative," Chorlian says. "In the course of conversation, who knows what morsels of information or memories might be revealed?"

Rosalie Baker, Editor of *Calliope* and *Dig*, two theme-related nonfiction magazines, sees field research as really *talk research*—"conversations and discussions with those who are considered experts in a particular topic." She tends to take to the field after putting together an outline for a magazine issue, with solid research behind her. "I use the Rockefeller Library at Brown University and research each theme. Then I check the Internet for current updates, information, and the like on the theme. I use reference books and the Web to find the names of those considered scholars in the field and, after drafting a tentative outline, contact various scholars for more input and consulting/writing help with the issue."

For Baker, both book and field research are critical. "To understand a topic, I believe you need to read about it first for some background information and be able to set the topic in its proper historical place, and in its place with regard to current and past research. I also think you need to talk with people directly involved in the topic. So much is changing day to day, and books take so long to come to print that they are really out of date when they are published."

Andy Boyles, Science Editor at *Highlights*, relies on experts for almost every article, interviewing them for research and for quotations to use. Like Baker, he also worries about the timeliness of research and accuracy and tends to work with scientists who are noted authorities and up-to-date on the latest studies.

Boyles learned the hard way about being fully prepared before contacting experts. "When I was working as a science writer for the University of Pittsburgh, I was assigned to write a story about a scientist who studied frogs. I don't remember the details, but it had something to do with the reflexes of the leg muscles. I walked into the interview cold, without having read anything about the research at all. Whatever the point was to the scientist's research, I had missed it entirely. I was a university employee, so the scientists had quite a lot of influence over what we published. He basically had to rewrite the whole thing. It was a huge embarrassment, and represents the moment when I learned the hard way that I could not fly by the seat of my pants and hope to land right-side up—not in science writing, at least."

Many people are nervous about contacting experts. Griswell reassures authors and editors, "Don't be afraid of interviewing. Even if you're an introvert like me, people love to talk about what they do or what they know. Most people will be more than happy to talk with you. Be sure that you are well prepared, that you've done all the reading you need to do and have formulated questions to ask."

Remember in this kind of field research to be armed with the right tools. (See more on interview techniques in "Cook up a Great Interview," page 279.) Huey recommends taking two tape recorders in case one fails or runs out. "You don't want to stop the whole flow of words to change a tape! And take notes, too. Often what I write down turns out to be the main idea hidden in the many sentences being recorded. That's helpful later on."

During the interview, Bartoletti suggests "listening for the gaps in their stories, places you think they have more to say. Jot them down. Circle around and come back to those gaps. If a person doesn't want to answer a question, circle around, come back to the question, but use different words. Sometimes it's the wording that shuts them down. And always have them sign an interview release before you begin."

Fortunate Mistakes

Author Ellen Levine interviews people for most of her books—veterinarians for *If You Were an Animal Doctor*, and Jewish survivors who were rescued by Danes during World War II for *Darkness over Denmark*.

For *Freedom's Children*, Levine wanted to tell the stories of young African Americans in the South, who didn't just live through the Civil Rights movement but were actively involved in it. Finding people to interview who were young in the 1950s and 1960s was difficult. She wasn't looking for famous names, rather ordinary people who had been part of something extraordinary. They weren't names in history books or encyclopedias. For one chapter of the book, Levine planned to cover the Montgomery bus boycott of 1955-56.

"I didn't want Rosa Parks. She was an adult. But I also knew she had worked with young people; perhaps she remembered some names. This was in 1989. So from the safety of my apartment in New York City, I called Montgomery, Alabama, phone information and asked for the listing for Rosa Parks. And I got it. Excited and nervous, I dialed. And she answered! I couldn't believe I was talking to Rosa Parks. But I gained confidence as I described what I was doing and what I was interested in. There was a long, sweet silence when I finished. Then she said, 'I'm not that Rosa Parks.'

"Absolutely humiliated, I remembered of course that Rosa Parks had moved to Detroit. I began to apologize profusely, but she cut me off. 'That sounds fascinating and important,' she said. 'On Sunday when I go to church I'll ask who was a young person at the time of the boycott. Call me on Monday and I'm sure I'll have some names for you.' And she did! And when I went South and interviewed people in Montgomery and others in Birmingham and Selma, I found out about Claudette Colvin, the teenager who 'did it' before Rosa Parks. And all this from a mistaken phone call!"

Author Laurence Pringle offers the following very human story: "Working on the book *Bearman: Exploring the World of Black Bears,* I used my own funds to fly to Minnesota to interview biologist Lynn Rogers. I rented a car and drove way up north to be with him. The highlight of the trip was to be a weekend excursion, using snowmobiles, to visit a mother bear and her cubs in their winter den. I was ready to take many photos, and interview Lynn for many hours."

Instead, says Pringle, "I came down with the flu and spent the weekend in a motel. I didn't see much of Lynn Rogers and never got near a bear, just managed to drive to the airport and fly home, for more recuperation at home. However, this expensive and fever-ridden journey wasn't a total loss. On the first afternoon, before the full flu hit, I saw for the first time the wealth of photographs that Lynn Rogers had available, and knew that the book could be well illustrated even if I took no photos myself."

Whether it's talking to people or visiting places, field research is full of possibilities. Bartoletti believes that the type of field research varies with each book. That's the beauty of field research or going directly to the source. With every new project comes new adventures and fresh approaches. The energized and enlightened author or editor who has spent many hours in the field is sure to offer something new.

Cook up a Great Interview

By Leslie Wyatt

We're used to interviews in modern culture. We watch television journalists and talk show hosts conduct them, usually with celebrities. We read them in glossy magazines. We listen to them on the radio. But in the writing world, interviews have an importance that extends from basic research to article format. Like a certain ingredient that gives a dish distinction—from a little salt in the soup to the very identity of a meal like a curry—an interview flavors your writing.

Interview Purpose

Writers interview because they need information. But information can be gathered by other means—books, journals, websites, personal experience, and so on. So how do you know when you should do an interview? One of the big indicators is the need for expert or personal commentary on a subject.

Sue Bradford Edwards is a writer, book reviewer for the *St. Louis Post-Dispatch,* and regional advisor for the Society of Children's Book Writers and Illustrators (SCBWI) in Missouri. She speaks of a recent assignment in which an educational editor who knew her work asked her to do a piece on geology. With characteristic humor, Edwards says, "I'm not being modest here; my background in geology is nonexistent. I know what it is, and I know a rock when I see one, but that's it." Not only was her knowledge limited, but her research turned up some contradictory information. That's when she turned to an expert in the field. The geologist informed, clarified, and as a bonus, offered to review her article when completed.

Laura Backes, Editor of *Children's Book Insider* and the author of *Best Books for Kids Who (Think They) Hate to Read,* points out that interviews give a human face to a subject. It also gives writing weight: "In the context of a larger article, the interview gives the writer quotes from experts in the field, as well as information that may not be easily obtained from other sources," Backes says.

Timeliness is another advantage. "An interview is especially needed when necessary information is too current to have been covered by books, perhaps even to have been covered by magazine articles," says Mel Boring, author of many books, stories, and articles. Information can become old. It takes a certain amount of time to make it to print, so research sometimes has a *use by* date. New facts or theories come to light, other works affecting ideas are written. Consulting an expert allows you to access the latest possible information, at the same time giving you a primary source to list in your bibliography.

Interviews can be a great tool in many ways. Limited time or deadline? An interview can be the core of an entire piece, take a relatively brief time, and add *heart* to your writing. You've got a great, edgy subject, but are having a hard time finding quality research sources? The perfect interview can pull it all together.

More typically, interviews provide you with quotations for articles, whether the project takes an educational approach, a journalistic tack, or uses a real life, personal voice. Analyze the bulk of nonfiction articles and you'll find them liberally peppered with quotes. Including statements from interviewees prevents a manuscript from being predominantly an exposition of facts. It adds color and life.

Edwards offers this additional tip: "By breaking up an article with quotes, you provide much needed white space. Otherwise people might look at your super dense article and pass. And the first person to do this might be your potential editor."

Backes makes the point that "sometimes the interviewee is the subject himself." Rather than just doing research about someone, interview that person to give your work extra punch.

Making Contact

If you're trying out a new recipe, you might assemble your ingredients only to discover that the finished product is doomed without a certain spice that neither you nor your local grocer happens to have on hand. Needing to conduct an interview can be a similar experience if you don't know where to look or how to make contact.

Let creativity kick in as you begin to search, and you'll soon have a plethora of potential interviewees. Experts are frequently within your circle of acquaintances, and are usually happy to share their knowledge. If no one comes to mind right away, one easy way to uncover authorities in a field is to conduct an Internet search on your topic. When researching for an article on Alaskan bush pilots, a Google search led me to a museum of bush pilot history and a very gracious curator who had been a young bush pilot himself during the pioneering of Alaskan aviation.

When you have your list of potential interviewees, the golden rule comes into play: "Do as you would be done by." Courtesy will carry you a long way.

When making initial contact, here are some do's and don'ts:

◾ Be considerate of the interviewee's time. Don't just call (or e-mail) and start asking questions. Edwards says, "Even if I am only asking if they want to do an interview and if I could e-mail them the questions, I ask if they have time for a quick question before I begin. If I am contacting an editor or someone with staff, I often ask to speak to someone 'in their office,' so that I don't intrude needlessly. If their policy is to take such calls, the staff person will put me through."

◾ Tell the interviewee the article's focus and what publication the interview is slated for. Indicate the subject; the kinds of questions you expect to ask and how long you think it will take; what kind of project you're working on (article, book, background for fiction); the place of publication and deadline, or if the piece is being written on speculation; and a little about your background.

◾ Set up a convenient time and method of interviewing. Boring suggests, "Rather than just trying to talk to them on that spur of the moment, I would explain why I wanted to interview them, and ask when would be a convenient time for them to have me phone and interview them."

◾ Respect the interviewee's right to deny the interview. Don't press if they seem reluctant. Just thank them and look elsewhere.

◾ Don't wait until there is an urgency in doing the interview because your deadline is very close.

◾ Foot the bill. If an interviewee has to return your call, offer to call right back so he or she won't incur any charges.

In Person, Phone, or Print

Should you interview via phone, person-to-person, or e-mail? Just like finding a certain veggie for your recipe, it depends on what is available. The expert you want to interview may prefer a certain method, and of course, you go with that.

If you have a choice, here are a few considerations. Telephone or in-person interviews lend themselves to spontaneity and the possibility of unexpected and interesting tangents on a subject. In addition, Backes says, "I find I build more lasting connections with phone interviews."

If you're a people person and do well with conversations, personal interviews may be right up your alley. The downside is that you must take notes, or record the conversation to type up later, to be sure to quote correctly.

Although it precludes spontaneity, an e-mail interview also has much going for it. You will have the answers already typed up, which helps accuracy. A written response gives the interviewee time to consider your questions and craft their

Separating the Good Quotes from the So-So

"Not every phrase that drops from even the best interviewee's lips is worth repeating verbatim in an article . . . . In general, use direct quotes for emotion and personality. Paraphrase for explication, efficiency, and clarity," writes David Fryxell, author of *Write Faster, Write Better,* and publisher of the magazine *Desert Exposure,* so aptly put it in his article "Quota on Quotes" (*Writer's Digest,* March 2005).

So how do you decide when to use direct quotes or not? Go direct if:

▨ The subject said it better than you could. Try it in your article and then try a paraphrase. Which works best?
▨ The quote reveals something about your interviewee's personality.
▨ The quote packs an emotional punch. (Indirect quotes dilute the intensity.)

questions are well-informed and professionally written, no one need know you agonized over them ahead of time. The downside of e-mail interviews is that if you don't get a satisfactory answer to a question, you may have to e-mail again. This process can get tedious for both you and the interviewee.

"I've found that most people are flattered to be interviewed and happy to do it if I approach the interview professionally and don't waste their time," says Backes.

Crafting Questions

At the risk of stating the obvious, the questions you ask during an interview are vital—sort of like using the highest quality ingredients for your recipe. Generic input gives generic results. As journalist Penelope McMillan once said, "Questions are the heart of an interview. If they're good, they're triggers; if they're bad, they're silencers."

Information and insight are what you're looking to gain from an interview. Generally speaking, your questions should be based on what a reader might expect to learn from the article. So take the time necessary to research and craft good questions. Find out as much about the person as you can before the interview. Do they have a website? Have you read something they've written? As Edwards says, if you bring this extra awareness into the interview, not only will your questions be more suitable, but you will compliment the individual with your knowledge. That makes for a

answers more carefully, and you may end up with more usable quotes. For the more timid, e-mail doesn't let on that you may be nervous, so you don't have to worry about saying something dumb during the interview process. If your much better interview.

Eliminate any questions that invite a *yes* or *no* answer in favor of ones that ask *when, how, where,* and *why*. Play with the wording and polish your phrasing. Determine how many questions you should ask—enough to get the information you need, but not so many that you become a nuisance.

Even if you're conducting a person-to-person interview, it still works best to write out your questions so you can guide the conversation. That way, though you may not take them out of your pocket, they'll be in your mind and come across naturally as opposed to canned. Have a list of topics—keywords, if you will—so you don't forget anything important.

John Brady, publishing consultant, teacher at Ohio University's E.W. Scripps School of Journalism, and author of *The Interviewer's Handbook: A Guerrilla Guide,* says the following in his article "Just Asking" (*The Writer,* November 2004): "My advice: Do not write out 'tough' questions in advance. Jot down key words or phrases as a reminder, but do not walk into an interview with hard-edged questions written out as though you are prejudging the interviewee. Instead, try to make the tough ones seem like spontaneous, natural inquiries that come up as a result of the give-and-take of conversation."

Keep in mind that many questions can be recycled to fit new topics. Note which ones work well and adapt them to your next interview.

Life reporter Richard Meryman once said, "I keep telling myself that the perfect interview is a perfect set of questions."

Here are some pointers for your perfect set:

▨ Think conversational, not scripted.

▨ Arrange questions in ascending order of interest to enable conversation to grow as you add ideas and opinions. Save any potentially tense topics for later in the interview, using quick and easy ones to get started.

▨ If you already know the answer, don't ask the question, unless you're looking for a quote. In that case, be straightforward about it and inform the interviewee of your need.

▨ Never debate a subject's answer. If you disagree with it, point out the reason courteously, or compose a question that presents the opposing side, listen to the answer, and move on.

▨ To get more depth in an answer, put a spin on your question. Don't ask, "How long have you lived in Missouri?" Instead, ask: "How has the community changed over the years you've lived here?" Flat facts don't usually spark lively conversation.

Now for the Interview

For e-mail interviews, you're almost home free. Having obtained a go-ahead and crafted your questions, just hit the send button and wait for the answers to come back to you.

With personal or phone interviews however, you've entered the critical stage, like folding egg whites into your soufflé. Do a good job here and the end product has a much better chance of turning out like the picture in the cookbook.

Before starting a personal interview, be sure to ask permission if you want to record the session. Even if your recorder is running, take notes. Jot down names, dates, and contact information, and have the expert review them for accuracy. Edwards offers this bit of advice as well: "Use fresh batteries. Do not plug into an outlet. If you do this and you are in a historic building, you may be the victim of inconsistent levels of electricity and your tape will speed up and slow down at irregular intervals."

Try to put the interviewee at ease. Chat about the weather, family, and so on. Boring advocates promoting laughter, "because, with Victor Borge, I believe that laughter is the universal language."

If you get off on the wrong foot (heaven forbid!) or the interviewee doesn't open up, don't agonize. Switch gears. Brady suggests asking non-questions like "take me through the process" or "tell me what is important to you."

A series of several interconnected questions are best delivered one at a time so that you get a complete answer for each. Sometimes a subject may stumble over a question. If this happens, you can suggest a possible answer, then quote him if he borrows your phrasing.

Just be careful not to fill in so many blanks that you have only yourself to quote.

Putting It on the Table

When you've gone off and written your piece, it is a good idea to let the interviewee preview your finished manuscript to verify facts and quotes. Follow up by letting him or her know when and where the piece will be published. If the publication you're writing for doesn't automatically send interviewees a complimentary copy when the issue appears, take a moment to send a copy of the publication or a tear sheet of the published article. In the meantime, a thank-you note or e-mail is definitely in order.

Once you've made your contacts, formed your questions, and conducted your interviews, all you need to do is combine the results into a harmonious whole. You're ready to serve up your literary meal.

Digging into Local History

By Mary Northrup

I f you write biography, history, or historical fiction, among your best research sources may be the places of local history. A rather broad term, *local history* comprises physical locations, organizations, buildings, people, publications, artifacts, and more—anywhere and anyone and anything that helps make your nonfiction writing accurate and true, or your setting and characters as close to the reality of a time period as possible.

Clues to long-ago events in your town or nearby can lead to writing that will make children understand, but also enjoy, history.

When researching history locally, it is very important to document resources as you go along. There is nothing more frustrating than returning to notes you've taken or copies you've made and not knowing where they came from. Because your source may be small and out-of-the-way, it may be hard to track again. Write down any information you can. For print resources, note the title, author, place, publisher,

date of publication, and pages; indicate title, author, and URL for websites. This will save you work down the road, especially if your publisher requires a bibliography.

As with all research, check any facts against other sources, especially since local resources may not have the same broader substantiation found with materials from larger resources: A local event reported in a single hometown paper won't have the same possibilities for confirming that a national event would have, for instance. It is a good idea to establish a rule that you will not accept as fact anything that cannot be proven in at least two or preferably even three sources.

Enjoy your search as you dig into local history. The facts of long-ago lives and events can be fascinating, and this can translate into history that comes alive as you write.

Sources of Information

■ **Newspapers:** For accounts of events as they happen, you can't beat newspapers. In the United

Primary Sources

What is better for research: to read the diary of a person who lived through the Civil War or to read an account of the Civil War written in 2005? No matter how well-written the modern book is (and you should certainly consider using it for your research, too), the diary will give you information that you cannot get in a source written years later.

Primary sources, sometimes referred to as *primary documents,* are a researcher's treasure. They enable you to get up close and personal to a person or event, even if it happened ages ago. Journals and diaries, letters, eyewitness accounts, memoirs, autobiographies, speeches, and public records provide a look at the person or event you are researching in a very immediate way.

If at all possible, use primary sources to research topics in your writing, whether it is fiction or nonfiction. This is especially important in writing history or historical fiction. The sources will provide those details of time, place, and even emotions that you just will not find in a secondary source.

States, newspapers have been around for hundreds of years. Even the smallest towns had (and may still have) them to spread the news. Various ethnic groups and associations have also published newspapers. Just as you do with all sources, read with a critical eye; not every newspaper subscribes to the "journalism as objective" principle.

For initial access to local newspapers in areas not close to home, take a look at NewsVoyager (www.newspaperlinks.com), the website of the Newspaper Association of America.

Research tip: While you are searching local papers, don't forget to look at the advertisements; they can be very revealing about a time period's economic conditions and culture.

Interviews and Oral Histories: These sources can provide a you-are-there immediacy. The wonderful thing about interviews is that they can reveal an individual's point of view, feelings, or everyday experiences that do not show up in books and other accounts. Keep in mind that people's memories are not always accurate, so be sure to check facts with print sources afterward.

Research tip: Look for published interviews or histories in your library's online book catalogue or in a magazine or history database. Local historians, librarians, and archivists can help you locate them as well.

Diaries, Letters, Papers, and Scrapbooks: The next best thing to interviewing a person is going through his or her personal papers. Although this can be time-consuming, it can also be an enlightening experience. Where can these sources be found? Try special collections in libraries, museums, or even people's homes.

Research tip: Publicize your effort. If people know you are working on a project, you may be put in touch with some relatives or caretakers who have the sources.

Photographs: You can read all you want about fashion, hair styles, and home furnishings for a particular period, but until you see them, they are often hard to imagine. For those details in your writing where you describe how a person or a place appeared, look to pictures. Old photos will also give you a clue as to the social standing of people, their customs, architecture, and the geographical setting of their town.

Research tip: Many libraries and museums have digitized photo collections on their websites.

Maps: Very early maps were drawn by explorers. In the U.S., after the Civil War, county atlases began to be published. The United States Geological Survey, established in 1879, issued many maps, focusing on map accuracy. By the twentieth century, aerial photography was used to map places. Historic maps can provide clues to geographic settings and help track name changes.

Research tip: Old maps can be found in historical atlases at libraries or local museums.

Official Records: Those pieces of paper that record impor-

tant events in our lives are a great way of tracking down local history. Birth and death certificates, marriage and divorce papers, draft records, passenger lists, and military records can all provide information about people. Deeds and probate records can give information on property. To find these records, consult county and city government offices, churches, businesses, and associations.

Research tip: Census records can provide information on population; they are published in books and on the Web (www.census.gov). The National Archives and Records Administration is the federal government body in charge of records (www.archives.gov/index.html).

Places and Artifacts: Objects offer a rich source of historical information. Buildings, monuments, cemetery headstones, furniture, clothes and jewelry, tools and machines all provide a look into a time past. How people lived in their homes, how they cooked their food, how they transported goods, how they communicated: All of these can be learned through looking at preserved historical sites and objects.

Research tip: The Web is a good place to find historic sites, but don't forget Chambers of Commerce and tourist guide books.

Places to Find Information

Local history is one of those fields where it is good to consult an expert. The following are places where you can find resources and, almost as important, you can find people to help you. Let them know about your project and you may get a behind-the-scenes tour and more information.

■ **Libraries:** Many public libraries have local history collections, and your state historical library may also be a source of help. The types of resources that can be found in libraries are almost endless: books, old phone directories, census information, county and city histories from all time periods, historical atlases, maps, old newspapers (these are usually on microfilm), photographs, and city directories.

Some libraries keep a vertical file, which may have a city or state subject file with pamphlets and other sources of information too small to be put on regular shelves. Your library may also have any variety of special collections of historic interest. The most important source in a library is the reference librarian, a trained professional who can help you find what you need at the library and suggest sources outside of the library. Some libraries even have a genealogical or special collections librarian who is uniquely qualified to help with local history questions.

■ **Museums:** A good historical museum can be a treasure trove for the history researcher. This is the place to find relevant objects— clothes, tools, and other clues to everyday living; old photographs; books; and maps. Some museums may put on demonstrations conducted by staff or volunteers who have studied the time period and can answer questions. You may want to talk to the curator or director of the museum to help guide you to what you need.

■ **Historical Societies:** Many cities and towns support a local historical society, as do many states. Like museums, they may collect artifacts, old letters and diaries, maps, photographs, and old newspapers.

■ **State Archives:** These governmental bodies hold documents and records, some extending back to colonial or territorial times. The records are either governmental or historical in nature, although some may also be reports, minutes, or old photos. Check the archive's website for online collections and other information.

■ **Organizations:** Some local or national organizations may have museums with exhibits or produce publications about their activities. They may also be a source of experts for a particular time period.

■ **Churches:** Places of worship that have existed for many years may be a good source of historical information, especially records of births, deaths, and marriages.

■ **Cemeteries:** Graveyards connected to churches or cities provide a unique source of information: gravestones, on which you can find birth and death dates.

■ **Historic Places:** The actual place where an event occurred or a person lived can be a primary source of information, especially if the place has been preserved. Many landmark buildings feature museums.

Books on Local History

At your public library, browse through the shelves in the 970s section (General History of North America), or search the online catalogue using *local history* as a subject, or using your state or city with *local history* as a subheading (for example, *Connecticut - local history).*

Here are some books that may be of particular interest:

Genealogical and Local History Books in Print, 5th ed. Baltimore, MD: Genealogical Publishing, 1997. A four-volume set of books currently in print, covering United States sources (arranged by state, then county), family histories, general references, and world resources (arranged by country). Provides the title of the book, author, publication year, cost, number of pages, and vendor.

Nearby History: Exploring the Past Around You, 2nd ed., by David E. Kyvig and Myron A. Marty. Walnut Creek, CA: AltaMira, 2000. Everything that the local or family history writer needs, from questions to ask as one researches to the actual sources to use, with description and usefulness explained: published documents, unpublished documents, oral histories, photos, artifacts, landscapes, and buildings.

Virtual Roots 2.0: A Guide to Genealogy and Local History on the World Wide Web, revised ed., by Thomas Jay Kemp. Wilmington, DE: Scholarly Resources, 2003. A list of websites by general subject (historical societies, church records, newspapers, etc.), state, and country. Gives title and URL. Some are designated "Extraordinary Site." State listings include archives, state libraries, state genealogical societies, state historical societies, and other state sites such as digital collections.

Writer's Guide to Places, by Don Prues and Jack Heffron. Cincinnati: Writer's Digest, 2003. Billed as a source for writers to use to get the setting right. Arranged by state and Canadian province; includes big cities, too. Includes state basics, significant historical events, food and drink, myths/misperceptions, interesting places for a scene. Includes list "For Further Research," which contains books and websites. Fun to browse, too!

You may be able to view old maps and artifacts there, too.

■ **County Offices:** The office of the county clerk may offer historical sources in the form of records. Check the government pages in your local phone book to find your county clerk's office.

■ **Experts:** Researchers in any area can always benefit by the expertise of a person. Obviously, someone who has witnessed a historic event would be a prime candidate for an interview. If this is not possible or the history is so old that no survivors remain, it might be helpful to find a history professor who specializes in that area. Call the history department of your local college or university; even if a professor there cannot help you, he or she may be able to recommend some names in the field.

Internet Sources

The Internet may guide you to some local history sources in your area. Since many libraries, museums, and other local history collectors may have special collections unique to your area, you may also want to do an online search using the terms *special collections* and *history*, with your state or city; for example, *special collections Missouri history* or *special collections Boston history.*

■ **American Local History Network:** www.alhn.org. This is a gateway to many independent genealogy and history websites. Go to the state pages, then the individual county you are researching.

■ **U.S. State Historical Societies & State Archives Directory:** http://web.syr.edu/~jryan/infopro/hs.html. Here you can find websites for the historical societies and archives in each state, plus other official sites that have to do with state history.

■ **American Association for State and Local History:** www.aaslh.org. This national organization is dedicated to state and local history.

In this day when many people believe that everything is on the Internet, know that much is *not* online. References to sources may appear on a website, but you might have to search for the book or text itself somewhere else. Or, no clues at all may be online. Much local history information is in museums, county offices, attics, basements, and other places, and someone has not had the time or inclination to put it on a website. So, do not limit yourself to what you find on the Web. Look for all sources.

Online Databases

By Mary Northrup

You need information about a famous person for a nonfiction profile. You are seeking the latest published research on health topics. You want to capture a certain historical time and are searching for old newspaper articles to help. Right now you can find these and so much more. All you need to do is check with your local library, where you have access to a wealth of information through online databases.

Most public libraries subscribe to online databases for the use of their patrons (and college libraries, for students, faculty, and alumni). In many cases you can access these databases at home, too, if you cannot make it to the library or want the comfort of researching at home.

The following represent just a few of the resources available. Ask at your local library—or visit their website—to see which resources it offers. Then log on the next time you need to do research for your writing.

Arts

Need some facts about the fine arts? Check here first.

Grove Art (Oxford University Press). Search or browse through 45,000 entries from the 34 volumes of *The Dictionary of Art* and *The Oxford Companion to Western Art*. View images in the text or link to 40,000 images from museum and gallery websites. Includes artists, styles, movements, geographical locations—anything to do with the art world.

Grove Music (Oxford University Press). Here you have access to the full text of *The New Grove Dictionary of Music and Musicians, The New Grove Dictionary of Opera,* and *The New Grove Dictionary of Jazz.* Search or browse entries on people, places, instruments, and styles. Includes links for listening, too.

Biography

Just as libraries have many shelves of books with biographical information, these databases contain thousands of biographies.

American National Biography (Oxford University Press). Biographies on 17,400 men and women. Most also provide a list of additional sources, illustrations, and cross references. Special feature is "Biography of the Day."

Biography and Genealogy Master Index (Thomson Gale). Provides 13.6 million citations to biographical reference sources. A good place to start looking for information on people. Updated twice a year.

Biography Reference Bank (H.W. Wilson). Contains biographies and obituaries on 500,000 people excerpted from standard reference books. May include lists of articles and books about the person, plus images, if they exist. Daily updates.

Biography Resource Center (Thomson Gale). Consists of 414,000 biographies on 320,000 people from reference sources (including *Who's Who*) and magazine articles. Special features include "Spotlight on . . ." and "People in the News." Updated daily.

World Biographical Information System Online (Thomson Gale). Compiled from print reference sources from the sixteenth through the twenty-first centuries. Includes 3.85 million digitized articles. A good place to find some obscure biographies.

Books

These databases can be extremely helpful in tracking down a title or even finding out where a little-known book is.

Books in Print (R.R. Bowker). Browse by broad subject or search this database of five million titles by keyword, author, title, or ISBN. Information that appears includes title, author, release date, publisher, format, price, language, audience, active or out of print, and more. Some titles include reviews.

WorldCat (OCLC). Find book information in this catalogue of libraries. Search by keyword, author, title, ISBN, or year. Information includes title, author, publisher, date, place, language, reading level, how many and which libraries have it, and more.

Careers

Research a career for nonfiction articles or books, or if you need more information about the profession of one of your fiction characters.

CIS - Career Information Systems (intoCareers, University of Oregon). Search or browse through career listings and find a job overview, working conditions, physical demands, skills and knowledge needed, wages, employment outlook, and a "Real World Interview" with a person in the field. Also includes information on self-employment, the military, how to job search, education, and training.

Ferguson's Career Guidance Center (Facts on File). Search careers or industries. Each entry gives a description of duties, salary range, education, skills, work environment, best geographic location, and unions and trade associations connected

Online Databases: What Are They & Why Are They so Great?

The researcher has one job: to get his or her facts right. Accuracy is all-important and the finding and double-checking of all sources is what makes research a true search.

Online databases are sometimes referred to as *subscription databases* because libraries subscribe to them, paying their license fees every year just as they subscribe to magazines and newspapers. So, even though databases appear to be similar to websites—and they are indeed Web-based—they are not the same as free websites that anyone can access. The information contained in online databases has been checked by editors, fact-checkers, perhaps even experts in the field, before it is published, just the same as print books, magazines, and newspapers. By contrast, free websites have no quality control. Anyone can put anything on the Web; the person finding it must look at it critically to determine the credentials of the author, the accuracy of the facts, the objectivity of the information, and its currency.

Starting research with online databases improves the chances of finding legitimate, authoritative information. With the variety of sources and types of information now being loaded into databases, most any subject can be found.

The thorough researcher will want to be aware of print and online sources. As more information becomes available in online databases, writers who research have much to gain.

with the profession. Additional information is provided on how to find a job, employability skills, and Web resources.

Geography

The whole world is at your fingertips in this category, where you can find information on places.

■ **The Columbia Gazetteer of the World** (Columbia University Press). Search three ways in this geographical encyclopedia: (1) type of place search, as in ancient city, fort, mountain, refuge, zone; (2) place name search; or (3) word search, which searches the full text of the Gazetteer. Includes information on political boundaries, physical geography, and special places such as theme parks, airports, mythic places, or monuments. Entries include locations and relative importance of the sites.

■ **World Atlas** (Facts on File). Provides maps, pictures of flags, and statistical charts for more than 200 countries, all the states, and 13 Canadian provinces and territories in the areas of geography, politics, and culture.

Health

Medicine is one of those areas where the importance of authoritative information cannot be overstated. Consult these databases for basic information or current research on medical topics for your fiction or nonfiction.

■ **Alt HealthWatch** (EBSCOhost).

Find full-text articles in publications dealing with alternative and complementary medicine, such as acupuncture, herbs, homeopathy, nutrition, aromatherapy, yoga, and more.

■ **Health & Wellness Resource Center** (Thomson Gale). Search medical dictionaries, encyclopedias, alternative health encyclopedias, drug and herb finders, health organizations directories, magazine and journal articles, health assessments, and websites in this comprehensive center.

■ **Health Reference Center** (Facts on File). Search or browse through thousands of entries on diseases, health and wellness, body systems, mental health, and medical tests. Includes links to good websites.

■ **Health Reference Center, Academic** (Thomson Gale). More than two million articles from medical, nursing, and consumer journals (many full-text), and from reference books, pamphlets, and newsletters appear in this database.

■ **Health Source, Consumer Edition** (EBSCOhost). Magazine articles on topics in health, medicine, nutrition, childcare, and sports medicine. Geared toward the layperson rather than the health professional.

History

Whether you are searching for American or world history sources, ancient or recent, history is well represented in the database world.

■ **African-American History & Culture; American History Online;**

and **American Women's History** (Facts on File). All of these databases contain biographies, subject entries, primary sources, timelines, images, and maps and charts. Covers 500 years. Includes links to good websites.

American Indian History & Culture (Facts on File). Same as above, except covers 1,500 years in the history of 500 North American Indian tribes.

American Journey Online (Thomson Gale). Find primary sources here: diaries, letters, documents, pictures, and archival audio and video with commentary. Covers historical periods from the American Revolution to modern times. Also includes information on multicultural groups.

American Slave Narratives (Greenwood). One of the WPA's Federal Writers' Projects during the Depression, this collection of almost 4,000 interviews with former slaves offers valuable oral histories. Search by the narrator's name, subjects discussed, master's name, interviewer, or narrator's county.

Ancient History Online (Facts on File). Search in six areas: ancient Africa, Egypt, Greece, Rome, Mesoamerica, and Mesopotamia. Find biographies, subject entries, primary sources, timelines, and maps.

Greenwood Daily Life Online (Greenwood). Search by keyword or browse by time, region, or broad subject. Find material from reference works, books, and primary documents; includes images, maps, timelines, and Web links. The subtitle, "Exploring Everyday Life Past and Present," gives a clue as to the focus of the information.

Historical *New York Times* (ProQuest). Find articles from the most famous United States newspaper. Provides coverage from 1851 to 2001. Search by topic or browse a specific date or date range.

History Resource Center, Modern World (Thomson Gale) and the **History Resource Center, U.S.** (Thomson Gale). These databases include reference materials, primary documents, magazine and journal articles, images, and maps. Includes a guide that instructs the user in how to research, explains the difference between primary and secondary documents, and tells how to evaluate sources.

NewspaperARCHIVE Elite (EBSCOhost). More than 22 million newspaper pages, covering the year 1753 to present. Includes United States, Canada, United Kingdom, and more.

Magazine & Newspaper Articles

Find articles on just about any subject you can think of through these databases, which index a wide variety of publications.

InfoTrac OneFile (Thomson Gale). Coverage goes back about 25 years in this general magazine database. Many of the indexed articles link to the full text of the article. Updated daily.

LexisNexis (Reed Elsevier). Search magazines and journals, newspapers, transcripts, newsletters, wire services, and government documents. All articles are full text. Also includes business, legal, and medical information.

▨ **MasterFILE Elite** (EBSCOhost). Find about 20 years of coverage in this database of citations, many of which link to the full text. Also contains an Image Collection, comprising 107,000 images: people, places, natural science, historical, maps, and flags.

▨ **ProQuest Research Library** (ProQuest). Search generally in this magazine database or in subject modules: arts, business, children's, education, health, humanities, international, law, military, multicultural, psychology, science, social sciences, or women's. Many of the citations link to full-text articles.

Reference

Need some quick facts? A subject overview? There's a little bit of everything here.

▨ **Associations Unlimited** (Thomson Gale). Find information on 460,000 organizations in the U.S. and around the world, including description, publications, websites, contact information, and more. A good place to find experts in specialized fields.

▨ **Corbis Images for Education** (Thomson Gale). Search or browse through more than 400,000 images in history, art, biography, science, culture, or entertainment. Read "Terms and Conditions" for permissions, use, and restrictions.

▨ **Encyclopaedia Britannica Online** (Encyclopaedia Britannica, Inc.) Search several of Britannica's encyclopedias and the Merriam-Webster dictionary and thesaurus, or browse through topics. Includes a world atlas, "Year in Review," timelines, websites, "Biography of the Day," and "This Day in History."

▨ **Encyclopedia Americana** (Grolier). Browse through topics, search by keyword, browse profiles (biographies), or search articles; includes Web links and cross-references. Includes dictionaries, thesaurus, and atlas.

▨ **Facts.com** (Facts on File). Read the top news stories for each decade back to 1940. Search by keyword through the *World News Digest*. Includes "Today's Science," "Issues & Controversies," country profiles, historical documents, profiles of newsmakers, and more.

▨ **Gale Virtual Reference Library** (Thomson Gale). Search through particular titles or through all reference books in this collection of e-books covering a variety of areas. Different titles in different libraries.

▨ **HeritageQuest** (ProQuest). Provides access to more than 25,000 family and local histories (search through full texts), the United States Census from 1790 to 1930, an index to general and local history periodicals, and other records.

▨ **Opposing Viewpoints Resource Center** (Thomson Gale). A good source for information on controversial issues. Contains articles, excerpts from books, reference sources, statistics, images, primary documents, and websites.

■ **Oxford English Dictionary** (Oxford University Press). Search a word and get its definition, year of first use, part of speech, examples, language, and a timeline. Or search a word in full text and find that word anywhere in the full text of the *OED*. New entries are added each year; users can look at a new entries list. A word lover's delight: includes half a million words and 2.5 million quotations.

■ **Oxford Reference Online** (Oxford University Press). A collection of reference tools, including dictionaries, thesauruses, other language reference books, and subject reference sources. Search through all the books or a specific subject. Also includes timelines for various topics and countries, and links to good websites.

■ **Ulrichsweb** (R.R. Bowker). Find information on magazines: publisher, starting year, frequency, price, title history, description, e-mail address, and website. A quarter million publications; international in scope. Updated weekly.

■ **World Book Online** (World Book, Inc.). More than 25,000 encyclopedia articles, 10,000 illustrations, audio and video clips, atlas, historic articles from past World Book Yearbooks, a dictionary, special reports, "Today in History," links to good websites, and "Behind the Headlines."

Science

We can all increase our science literacy and these databases will help.

■ **AccessScience** (McGraw-Hill). Includes McGraw-Hill's *Encyclopedia of Science & Technology Online*; *Dictionary of Scientific & Technical Terms*; yearbooks; biographies; and *Science News* articles. Search or browse through the information, view an image gallery, check out related websites, or read headline news. Includes more than 8,000 articles and 13,000 illustrations.

■ **Science Online** (Facts on File). Biographies of scientists from antiquity to present, essays on current issues, definitions of terms, diagrams, experiments, and timelines. Organized by National Science Education Standards.

■ **Science Resource Center** (Thomson Gale). Search by keyword or topic. Includes dictionary, timeline, biographies, information on science magazines and journals, and science standards for grades 9 to 12 (both national and state). Includes content from magazines, journals, reference books, newspapers, images, and websites. Coverage includes all sciences, plus the history of science.

Play Ball! Researching Sports

By Lisa Harkrader

You've just gotten an incredible idea for a story that revolves around basketball. Or your editor has just assigned you an article on cycling or kayaking. You can't wait to get started . . . but you don't know the first thing about the sport. How can you possibly pull it off?

The answer, as every writer knows, is research.

Hit the Books

Dori Hillestad Butler, whose books include *Sliding into Home,* never considered herself athletic. "But I have managed to publish a couple of novels where sports are part of the main story line," says Butler. "So you bet I've had to research!"

When Butler first began writing a novel centered on gymnastics, her first step took her to the library. "I checked out all the books I could find on gymnastics—fiction and nonfiction," she says, "and immersed myself in the subject."

A quick glance at the sports section of your library or bookstore will show that there's no lack of books on sports, from basketball and soccer to curling, fly fishing, and Tae Kwon Do. If you're unfamiliar with your sport, or need a refresher, it's best to start with the basics. Series such as the Dummies books and Complete Idiot's guides, as well as many single-title books, offer broad overviews of individual sports, including history, rules, and tips on how to play. Many libraries also carry instructional videos on various sports.

Books on coaching youth sports can be valuable resources, too. Coaching books usually cover the rules and play of the game, as well as strategies, drills, and mistakes young players make—information that could round out your knowledge for a nonfiction piece or round out your characters for fiction.

Fish for the Facts

When writing about sports, it's usually not enough simply to know the rules or the dimensions of the playing field. A writer also needs to understand the mental aspects of the sport and the culture that surrounds the game.

A. M. Jenkins, author of *Out of Order* and *Beating Heart: A Ghost Story,* says that when first researching football for *Damage,* she "read anything I could find at the library which looked non-excruciating, about basic rules of the game." But she didn't stop there. Jenkins also read high school football memoirs, such as *Friday Night Lights.*

Jenkins advises writers to pay close attention to the types of books they choose as research sources. "There's a lot more information about professional football in books," she says, "so you have to be careful, because of course there are differences between pro, college, and high school games."

Sue Corbett knew quite a bit about minor league baseball before she wrote *Free Baseball,* a novel about a Cuban-American refugee who becomes the batboy for a minor league baseball team. Still, she says, "I did not know enough about Cuba or Cuban baseball." Corbett turned to memoirs to round out her knowledge. "I read Carlos Eire's Pulitzer Prize-winning memoir *Waiting for Snow in Havana,* and *Pitching Around Fidel,* by S.L. Price, a *Sports Illustrated* reporter. The Price book, in particular, made me feel knowledgeable about a situation I will never know firsthand— the plight of Cuba's star athletes."

Get the Scoop

Books aren't the only printed material you can turn to for sports research. Libraries and newsstands are filled with magazines ranging from general interest sports publications, such as *Sports Illustrated,* to publications devoted to specific sports, such as golfing, bodybuilding, or snowboarding.

Readers' Guide to Periodical Literature, an index of articles published in more than 240 magazines and available in almost any library, can help you track down stories on your particular sport. Large libraries carry many magazines in loose or bound form, or on microfiche or microfilm. If the library doesn't have the magazine you need, you can request it through interlibrary loan.

Many libraries also have periodical databases online. If you have a library card, you can usually access the databases from your home computer. The databases contain full texts of many articles, so you can often retrieve the information you need without leaving your desk.

Newspaper sports sections are another good source of information. The articles can give you a better understanding of the world of athletics, while sports columns offer an insider's view—and often strong opinions—of various sports. Both use colorful sports lingo, which you can adopt to make your own sports story sound more authentic.

Corbett based her fictional minor league team, the Miracle, on a team she'd written about for the *Miami Herald.* "I had been wanting to write about baseball and this wonderfully wacky team for years," says Corbett, "so I had a thick file of articles

I had saved that I could rely on when I got stuck for a detail. I read widely about baseball. Every time I find something funny or interesting, I clip it out and stick it in my file."

Go Surfing

Flip on the TV on any given Sunday, and you'll find nothing to watch but sports. Which is bad news if you're looking for nonathletic entertainment, but great news when you're researching your own sports story.

Jenkins watched a lot of football while writing *Damage.* "I listened to the announcers closely—John Madden was especially helpful—to find out about strategy and why coaches and players chose to do certain things, and what errors were specifically made."

Televised sports often center on college or professional athletics, but sometimes you can tune into sports featuring younger athletes, such as the Little League World Series or junior motocross races.

While researching her novel *Making Weight*, Jan Czech, author of *Grace Happens,* used an Internet search engine to find high school wrestling websites, "which brought a gazillion hits," says Czech. "To narrow it down a bit, I specified a couple of successful programs I knew of in New York State."

Besides websites, authors can use other Internet resources to help find sports information. "I have a Google news alert for high school wrestling that sends to my inbox each day anything in the news having to do with the sport," says

Czech. "It has given me specific news stories about matches that have helped me write scenes of actual matches." To sign up for Google e-mail news alerts, go to the Google website: www.google.com. Other search engines, such as Yahoo (news.yahoo. com), also offer news alerts.

Czech also read Internet message boards devoted to wrestling. Message boards are virtual bulletin boards on which subscribers can post messages about specific topics. "The message boards have been very helpful in giving me almost a firsthand peek into the mentality of wrestlers and wrestling," says Czech.

Linda Joy Singleton, author of *Last Dance* and *Don't Die, Dragonfly,* joined a cheerleading listserv—an e-mail discussion group—while researching for her Cheer Squad series. "I honestly posted about being a writer and having questions for experts," says Singleton.

You can often find links to message boards or listservs on Web pages devoted to your topic. You can also find them through search engines by typing in specifically what you're looking for, such as *high school wrestling message board*

Confessions of an Athletic Fraud

I have a confession to make. I wrote a basketball novel, and I know nothing about basketball. Sure, I love watching the game, and yes, I did the required research. But outside of ninth-grade P.E. class, I've never played basketball in my life. From the moment I conceived the idea for *Airball: My Life in Briefs,* I've lived in fear that I'll be exposed for what I am: an athletic fraud. So I employed a few tricks to keep my cover from being blown:

▪ I turned my main character into a klutz. I'll never know the exhilaration of slamming a basketball through the hoop in an above-the-rim tomahawk dunk, but I can accurately describe what it feels like to dribble the ball off my foot. By infusing my own ineptitude into my protagonist, Kirby Nickel, I hoped to also infuse a bit of credibility into my basketball scenes.

I'm not the first author to use athletic incompetence to her advantage. "I am not an athlete," says Dori Hillestad Butler. "My middle-grade novel, *Trading Places with Tank Talbott,* is about an 11-year-old who can't pass beginning swimming lessons because he can't put his face in the water—that was me!"

▪ I injected my own passion into the story. While it's true that I've never played competitive basketball, I am a rabid fan of the University of Kansas Jayhawks. So guess what? Kirby loves Jayhawk basketball, too. I used some of my knowledge of the team—such as former Jayhawk Wilt Chamberlain's NBA scoring record and another former player's penchant for changing shoes at halftime—to, again, make the story more believable.

or *cheerleading listserv.* Yahoogroups (www.yahoogroups.com) hosts thousands of listservs, which you can search by subject matter.

Go Pro

While reading about athletics can give you a solid grounding, most sports authors agree that to understand a sport well, you must go to the experts: athletes and coaches.

Kristin Wolden Nitz, author of sports nonfiction such as *Play-By-Play Track* and *Fundamental Softball,* as well as sports fiction such as *Defending Irene,* says her best resource was attending practices, games, and meets. "I took pages and pages of notes as I watched the officials, coaches, and athletes in action," says Nitz. "But I made the most out of those occasions by arriving with knowledge—rules, jargon, and techniques."

To research her gymnastics novel, Butler "practically moved into

Confessions of an Athletic Fraud

I turned to an expert. I asked my stepbrother, who coaches his daughter's high school team, to read my manuscript, searching for basketball faux pas. Once he'd given the basketball scenes his stamp of approval, I felt more confident sending the book to my editor.

Lara Zeises also called in the pros—a professional female skater and a writer for skate magazines—to vet her novel about a girl skateboarder. These experts helped her fix small mistakes. "I called her helmut and pads her *tricking gear,*" says Zeises, "and was told it was just gear, plain and simple." One expert double-checked the kind of wheels on the skateboard her protagonist, Sea, builds, and another suggested she change the kind of wood Sea's board was made out of, so it would have more *pop* for her tricks. "All great fixes that will make it feel and sound more authentic," Zeises says.

If these tricks don't keep you from feeling like an imposter, take comfort in the advice one editor gave author Julie Swanson. Swanson, a former highly driven basketball player, was writing a series about—surprise—a highly driven basketball player. "But [the editor] advised me to try writing about a sport other than my own," says Swanson. "The theory is that you can disconnect from the truth of your past more easily and write true fiction if you are not holding to things that really happened and basing it on your exact self."

So keeping some distance between you and your subject matter can actually help your story. What a relief. Being an athletic fraud may not be such a bad thing after all!

the gymnastics studio for a week and observed classes nonstop. I continued to go to the elite classes while I was working on the book because little things kept cropping up that I needed to know. The girls answered all my questions, told me what it felt like to do some of these moves, talked me through various scenes. The coach helped me write routines for the book."

Attending games and interacting with athletes can give you a more intrinsic understanding of a sport. It can also help you pick up details you might not otherwise notice.

"Soccer people have terms that are a little bit different," says Julie Swanson, author of *Going for the Record.* "For instance, in basketball you would say two players were going *one-on-one,* but in soccer they say *1 v 1,* as in *one versus one.* Due to the influx of coaches from countries where soccer is even more popular, the slang is a little more

European sounding, a little more British—'Well done!'—not as American as in other sports."

Do It Yourself

Sometimes the only way to truly understand a sport is to put yourself in the game. As research for her novel *Anyone But You,* which features a skateboarding protagonist, author Lara Zeises learned to build her own skateboard. Singleton took fencing lessons for her book *Sword Play.*

When she was writing her *Cheer Squad* books, a cheerleading coach invited Singleton to pose as a coach at a cheerleading camp. "She explained we should keep it a secret so as not to distract the girls," says Singleton. "I had a great time pretending to be starting a new team. I took spotting lessons and got a certificate."

For her softball book, Nitz started with a basic knowledge of the sport. "While I could hit, catch, and throw a softball, I had no idea of how to pitch," she says. "My softball book dedicated an entire chapter to pitching, so I had a lot to learn. After studying the basics of pitching, I started going through the motions in my study. I learned how to hold the ball, how to shift my weight, and when to release the ball. When I started going to practices and games, I studied the pitcher's footwork and listened to the coach shout advice. Then I went home and worked on my technique. I was finally ready to put the process into my own words."

Jump Back in Time

Although modern sports seem to permeate every aspect of our lives, information on sports from the past can be harder to find.

Sally Wilkins, author of *Sports and Games of Medieval Cultures,* found two extremely valuable sources of historical information: "One was the academic world—journals, museums, and collections dedicated to the study of historic games. The other was the fantasy world of recreators—the Society for Creative Anachronism being the most well-known. Now some of the recreators are also serious scholars—Regia Anglorum—but most of the recreators are more concerned with having a good time than with being historically precise. So while the academic sources gave me lots of solid material, documented and reliable, the recreators helped me figure out what it was really like to play these games."

"Fascinating articles can be found by requesting tapes from old newspapers and magazines," says Suzanne Hilton, author of historical books including *Miners, Merchants, and Maids (Settling the West).* To find information on early sports uniforms and the public's attitude toward games, Hilton has used articles from nineteenth- and early twentieth-century magazines such as *The Ball Players' Chronicle* and *Collier's Weekly.*

Historical articles are usually archived on microfilm. "Ask your local librarian for the years that you want to see a newspaper with sports pages," says Hilton. "If that library is not able to get certain years, then the largest library near you can have them sent to you. You'll have to go to the library to do the reading on their microfilm machine, but you are usually allowed to keep them—at the library—for your own use at least a month."

Researching sports takes time and creativity, but the results can be worth it. As Nitz says, "Sports offer a natural setting for action and conflict. There's something at stake."

SCBWI Conference Report

Add Light to Your Junk

By Judy Bradbury

"Feel," said author Sue Alexander. "Spark," said author Steven Swinburne. For marketing agent Susan Salzman Raab, it was "inspiration" and for irascible author Bruce Coville, "fartboogernakedunderwear." Knowing the word-loving audience, Brenda Bowen, Vice President, Associate Publisher, and Editor in Chief of Disney Children's Books offered the word "ineluctable."

These were among the faculty who paraded across the stage at the 34th Annual Summer Conference of the Society of Children's Book Writers and Illustrators (SCBWI), the largest international organization devoted solely to "offering a variety of services to people who write, illustrate, or share a vital interest in children's literature."

Lin Oliver, Executive Director and co-founder of SCBWI, had opened the four-day event in her usual warm and endearing style by welcoming and introducing the faculty. Each paused at the microphone to offer their one word of advice to the audience.

More than 750 attendees had gathered at the Century Plaza Hotel in Los Angeles, in addition to the more than 50 faculty members who spoke at general sessions, participated in panel discussions, conducted breakout sessions on specific topics, or reviewed manuscripts and art in private one-on-one sessions.

In addition to the annual and much anticipated juried art show, new this year was a VIP reception honoring all published authors and illustrators in attendance. With their books on display, they were able to meet and discuss their work with bookstore owners, agents, publishers, and their peers.

The Rose Window

The first on the roster of impressive speakers to address the audience was Rosemary Wells, author and/or illustrator of over 125 books for children. In addition to reflecting on her career, Wells spoke about the Read to Your Bunny campaign she spearheads to bring books, young children, and parents together by encouraging adults to read to their children every day, "All it takes is a library card and will," believes Wells. She also offered encouragement and advice to today's aspiring authors. "The news from the publishing world," she reported, "is that it is very difficult to break in. But if you are good, if you have talent, you will be published. Someone will find you."

Wells shared a photograph of a box of junk from her kitchen drawer that symbolizes where she gets her ideas—a question she is often asked by children. Although everyone has such items, "It is what you do with junk that makes the difference," believes Wells. She recommends "adding light" to your junk. The result will be like "a rose window" seen in the medium of a kaleidoscope. "What is junk is different for everyone, and so is the view through the kaleidoscope."

Graham Salisbury, the award-winning author of books for young adults that include *Under the Blood-Red Sun, Lord of the Deep,* and *Island Boyz,* thinks of his emotional reactions to events and people as diamonds. He mines the precious gems as as he forms ideas for his books.

Salisbury revealed to the audience that he met his long-time editor Wendy Lamb by the pool while attending an SCBWI conference as an unpublished author. As they sat side by side, he told her about his story, unaware of who she was. In-

trigued, Lamb asked Salisbury to send her the manuscript. He did and she has been publishing his work ever since.

Another of Lamb's authors, Christopher Paul Curtis, was also on the faculty and gave a talk titled "The Journey: A Flintstone's Love Affair with Writing." Curtis regaled the audience with amusing and touching anecdotes about his family, their appearance in his three novels (look for his then preschool-aged daughter's copyrighted lyrics in *Bud, Not Buddy*), his relationship with Lamb (and her book-length editorial letters), and his work ethic.

Curtis acknowledged a five-year hiatus between the publishing of his second novel, the Newbery and Coretta Scott King Award winner, *Bud, Not Buddy*, and his next, *Bucking the Sarge,* winner of the SCBWI's Golden Kite Award for fiction. *Bud, Not Buddy* had quickly followed his first novel, the Newbery Honor and Coretta Scott King Honor winner, *The Watsons Go to Birmingham—1963.* Although Curtis humorously blamed the lengthy break on the purchase of a satellite dish, he was serious when he cautioned the audience to "work at your craft; write daily" to keep their writing muscles toned and in peak condition.

When It's a Good Day

In a breakout session entitled "Building a Novel: Brick by Brick," Kathleen Duey, author of more than 60 books for young readers, including fantasy, horse stories, and a magic series, implored those who want to succeed to write regularly. "Pay attention to your process. Do whatever works best," said Duey. "If you have a good writing day, ask yourself why it was such a good day. Then set up all your writing days that way."

Duey believes that if you write best in the early morning, for example, then you must find a way to write at that time every morning. In discussing the critique process, she outlined a procedure she has found successful, even with youngsters enlisted to review a manuscript. The B-C-D method, as she calls it, is simple. Ask readers to mark a B in the margin when they are bored, a C in the margin with they are confused, and a D in the margin when they don't believe it.

Finally, in answer to a question on writer's block, Duey suggested, "If you can't write about something, it is because you are *not* writing about something," an observation she attributed to songwriter Paul Simon. She also suggested interviewing your characters. "Be conversational with them." Other advice this prolific author offered: Don't shoot the whole wad in the first chapter. Don't summarize the backstory. Don't avalanche the reader with details. Show, with dialogue and scene description. Don't let the puppet strings show, (i.e., don't manipulate the characters). If you admire a phrase, take it out of your story. If you remind the reader he is reading, that's a flaw in your writing.

YA Do's & Don'ts

Each YA panel member—Carolyn Mackler, Sonya Sones, Julia DeVillers, and Megan McCafferty—listed things she felt authors should *never* do and things authors should *always* do when writing for teens.

Never:
- Call parents Mr. and Mrs.
- Shoehorn overt messages.
- Linger on parents and their backstory.
- Fake it.
- Dumb down.
- Preach or be didactic.
- Let an adult solve the problem.
- Be afraid.

Always:
- Get to the point.
- Recognize when something is not working and move on.
- Put something "sexy" on the first few pages.
- Remember teens have hormones.
- Care about your reader.
- Think back on your own childhood.
- Delve into your memories: even if the details aren't there, the feelings will remain.
- Be an advocate.
- Write responsibly.
- Face challenges.
- Be honest.
- Use humor (with angst).
- Let there be hope.

Conference Bons Mots

▓ "If you can get yourself out of the way, art will happen." *Kathleen Duey, author*

▓ "Dreams do come true." *Christopher Paul Curtis, author*

▓ "If there's a hole in your story and you can't plug it up, point to it." *Sid Fleischman, author*

▓ "Form follows function." *Kevin Lewis, editor (quote originated with architect Louis Sullivan, teacher of Frank Lloyd Wright)*

▓ "Make the world worthy of its children." *Lee Bennett Hopkins, poet*

▓ "Storytelling is risk. Storytelling is truth telling. Tell your story." *Bruce Hale, author*

▓ Voice is the "choices you make" in your writing, what is particular about you. It comes from looking over and evaluating your work. "It's the feeling you remember from a book." *Hudson Talbott, author and illustrator*

▓ Voice is "something no one else could write; it's everything that contributes to your make-up." *Brenda Bowen, editor*

Four editors, Bonnie Bader of Grosset & Dunlap; Krista Marino, Associate Editor at Delacorte Press; Julie Strauss-Gabel, Senior Editor at Dutton Children's Books; and Timothy Travaglini, Senior Editor at G. P. Putnam's Sons, gathered to discuss today's market. Marino encouraged those hoping to break into today's tough market to enter contests such as the Delacorte Dell Yearling Contest for a First Middle-Grade Novel (formerly the Marguerite de Angeli Contest) or the Delacorte Press Contest for a First Young Adult Novel (www.randomhouse.com/kids/writingcontests). Marino profiled herself as an editor in search of middle-grade and YA fiction. She is not currently looking for picture books, and only edits a limited amount of nonfiction. She likes funny as well as scary.

Travaglini reported that he signed up 10 projects in two months' time when he recently left Walker Books for Putnam's. He enjoys funny "laugh out loud" stories that are unusual and unique. He avoids those that are "overly familiar."

Bader likened Grosset & Dunlap, where 99.9 percent of the books are paperback, to "the Old Navy of publishing—cool, but cheap." The current list includes a number of licensed properties, such as Strawberry Shortcake; series, such as the Hank Zipzer books co-written by Lin Oliver and Henry Winkler; and novelty and holiday books.

Strauss-Gabel at Dutton is not interested in quiet, sweet, gentle, or historical fiction stories at this time, but she is very interested in fiction for older readers.

In discussing current challenges publishers face, Bader pointed to overcrowding of the market with series; Travaglini cited nonfiction. There was general agreement that buyers for big booksellers dramatically impact sales. Said Strauss-Gabel: "One person's opinion will keep a book out [of these stores]." The panel also agreed that the federal No Child Left Behind Act and Accelerated Reader programs have significantly impacted sales of trade books in the school market.

Steven Chudney of the Chudney Agency advised authors on a long list of agenting issues. He encouraged attendees to find an agent by "word of mouth, through networking with other writers, both in person and in online groups, and by visiting agents' websites." Chudney said to keep queries to agents brief and to the point.

Once an agent shows interest, "interview the agent, but don't interrogate him or her." He encourages authors and illustrators to ask a prospective agent about his or her background. Ask:

How do you work (more as an editor or more as one who simply markets work)?

How long have you been an agent?

Do you specialize in one genre or are you a generalist?

How long can I expect to wait for a response to submitted work?

How do you communicate with clients (by e-mail, phone, regular mail, or a combination of these)?

Chudney also suggests writers find out whether the agent deals in foreign rights, what fees are assessed, and the commission rate. Most of all, Chudney implores writers to gauge the chemistry between themselves and the agent they are considering hiring.

In terms of general advice, Chudney urges authors to read widely in the genre in which they hope to publish, join or form a critique group, and read reviews of recently published children's books in such publications as *School Library Journal, Publishers Weekly, Horn Book,* and *Kirkus*, which can be found at the reference desks in most public libraries. Chudney's website is www.thechudneyagency.com.

Zing

The first author chosen to occupy the Paula Danziger Chair, established in memory of the popular and effervescent author of dozens of books for preteens and teens, was Carolyn Mackler, who has written three popular young adult novels, including *The Earth, My Butt, and Other Big Round Things*.

In a talk entitled "Revenge of the Wallflower: Getting Published and Making a Career Out of Your Teen Years," Mackler advised those new to the YA genre to read recently released novels and reread old favorites. Make certain your first paragraph "zings." It is crucial to "yank the reader in." Mackler stays in touch with teens and listens to the way they talk, and claims to have a vivid memory of her high school experiences and emotions. She writes from these memories: "not memoirs, but using bits and pieces." She told the audience to "handwrite thank-you notes to anyone in the business who shows a personal kindness or responds personally to your work." When submitting to either an agent or editor, says Mackler, a great query is essential. She also suggests calling an agent's office before submitting and talking to the receptionist for details on the kinds of materials that the agent requests.

Mackler was also a member of a panel on teen literature, still a hot genre in children's publishing. Sonya Sones, Julia DeVillers, and Megan McCafferty were also on the panel. Ranging in age from the late-20s to the 50s, the panelists agreed that listening to their fans helps them to write authentically for teens.

McCafferty, who once worked at *YM* magazine and is the author of *Sloppy Firsts* and *Second Helpings,* says, "All teens have innate BS detectors." She believes "humor goes a long way" in getting the message across.

Sones said she writes about "first experiences." Author of *Stop Pretending: What Happened When My Big Sister Went Crazy,* which is semi-autobiographical, Sones "writes honestly" even if it is "humiliating."

She believes that "what people are ashamed of makes for a great story," and that "even if what you write is not autobiographical, teens think that it is."

In a session on writing for the middle grades, Travaglini said there is a "solid, steady demand" for fiction and nonfiction. She characterized middle-grade readers as "underserved." The key word for middle grade is "immediacy," which he explained as drawing the reader into the scene and setting, and allowing the reader to care about the character right away. The protagonist must be "in motion" and "engaged" in the story. Avoid a story that is "too quiet," or one in which the introduction is "slow." Shun flashback and too much description. Voice, a likeable protagonist, narrative tension, and originality are tantamount. "Readers want to recognize themselves," said Travaglini, who urged authors to read piles of middle-grade books.

Former editor and the author of *The Complete Idiot's Guide to Publishing Children's Books* Harold Underdown terms this the "golden age of picture books," even though many see the picture book market as struggling. Though static, there is still some demand for this genre, but picture book texts must be very strong and well-written.

Barbara Seuling conducted a three-session series on picture books. The author of more than 60 books for children, she has also penned *How to Write a Children's Book and Get It Published,* now in its

Golden Kite & Sid Fleischman Humor Award Recipients

Each year at the Society of Children's Book Writers and Illustrators' summer conference, the Golden Kite Awards and the Sid Fleischman Award for Humor are presented at a luncheon given in honor of the recipients. The Golden Kite Award is the only major children's book award presented by peers and is one of the most prized honors in the field. The Sid Fleischman Humor Award is presented to an author whose work exemplifies excellence in the genre of humor. Winners in 2005 were:

- **Fiction:** Christopher Paul Curtis, *Bucking the Sarge* (Wendy Lamb Books). Honor book: Steve Lyon, *The Gift Moves* (Houghton Mifflin).
- **Nonfiction:** Michael L. Cooper, *Dust to Eat: Drought and Depression in the 1930s* (Clarion Books). Honor book: Judith Bloom Fradin and Dennis Fradin, *The Power of One: Daisy Bates and the Little Rock Nine* (Clarion Books).
- **Picture book text:** Deborah Hopkinson, *Apples to Oregon: Being the (Slightly) True Narrative of How a Brave Pioneer Father Brought Apples, Peaches, Pears, Plums, Grapes, and Cherries (and Children) Across the Plains* (Atheneum/Schwartz & Wade; illustrated by Nancy Carpenter). Honor book: Pamela S. Turner, *Hachiko: The True Story of a Loyal Dog* (Putnam; illustrated by Yan Nascimbene).
- **Picture book illustration:** Jean Cassels, *The Mysterious Collection of Dr. David Harleyson* (Walker Books). Honor book: Loren Long, *When I Heard the Learn'd Astronomer* (Simon & Schuster; written by Walt Whitman).
- **Sid Fleischman Humor Award:** Gennifer Choldenko, *Al Capone Does My Shirts* (Putnam).

third edition. Her sessions delved into developing an idea, writing the text, and revising the picture book manuscript.

Hudson Talbott, author and illustrator of over a dozen books, also discussed the process of writing. "Don't get attached to your words," he advised, especially when writing picture books, which don't afford the "luxury of space" a novel does. "Think visually about the whole" when working on the first draft. "Don't get bogged down in details" but instead, "get the structure down first." Talbott believes there is "opportunity for discovery" with every pass or draft. He likened revision to "filigree" and termed it the "fun stuff" of the writing process.

The jam-packed four-day conference ended with a stirring speech by the beloved Lee Bennett Hopkins, called the "national spokesperson for Children's Poetry." He encouraged those in attendance to "go home and get to work. Write, write, write good books, good times."

The Call, the Award, the Writing Life

By Joan Broerman

Two phone calls came on a January morning a few years ago. The first startled Linda Sue Park: She had won the Newbery Medal for *A Single Shard*. When the second call came, she thought it was to tell her there had been a mistake. But no, the speakerphone on the award committee's side of the conversation hadn't been working and the committee members wanted to hear her reaction.

"For most of us who write novels for young people, to win a Newbery is manifestly the summit of achievement," said winner Avi in his acceptance speech. He won three years ago for *Crispin: The Cross of Lead.*

Achievement also leads to other forms of success. "Awards are important for sales. A major award like a Newbery Medal or honor can change the life of the book: It can result in massive printings, and the life of the author can be changed as well. The book will have a longtime place in the industry and will always be alluded to," says Susan Salzman Raab, a marketing and public rela-tions consultant who heads her own firm, Raab Associates.

Yet the Newbery is only one of more than 300 awards listed in the database of the Children's Book Council (CBC). Many ages, stages, and types of work for children are categorized and acknowledged, and the judges are many and varied— librarians, teachers, parents, peers. Even the child reader has a chance to honor best books. The signifi-cance of awards to the recipients also varies. For some they repre-sent status, and in the case of the Newbery or Caldecott, skyrocketing sales. For other writers of every level of accomplishment, awards are a welcome confidence booster.

Driving Interest

"The people most cognizant of the meaning of these awards are indus-try people like booksellers, librari-ans, and teachers," says Raab. "Then there are awards developed by organizations that have their own constituencies. These awards have different impacts, depending

315

on what those reached know about the awards and what the awards mean to those groups. The goal of a writer should be to succeed in a mix of consumer, library, and school markets. In all of these areas, an award enhances a book's appeal."

Raab explains the difference among markets in book publishing, and the place awards have in them. "The business at one time was school- and library-oriented, and driven by starred reviews that helped librarians and teachers make informed choices. The consumer market is different. It is not undergirded by a backlist of classics. Awards add weight to consumer choices, but they are not the guiding force. The consumer market is driven by trends." These, she explains, "could be format trends, as seen in graphic novels; in trends such as the ongoing interest in fantasy fueled by Harry Potter; or certain topical trends." Awards are distinct from best-seller lists, Raab notes, which reflect what is happening, not what is recommended reading. Both can help drive market interest.

Most awards recognize excellence, and reveal something about a book that should be singled out, says Raab. She believes it is an important service to educate the reading public about what those awards mean.

Independents

If there is any population that is most knowledgeable about the crop of awards, it's independent book-sellers. They have long been known for hand-selling books they love to read. Marie Peerson, co-owner of Crosshaven Books in Vestavia Hills, Alabama, is not only well-read but highly aware of her customers' tastes. She is also a published children's author. "Our store is unique in that I make all book selections. If an author is an award winner, I want to see other books that he has written or illustrated, but my selections are based on content and style, not whether it is a winner. There was a time that I read every book I ordered, but that is not true today. I listen to suggestions from parents and teachers, and I read reviews. Some of our favorites have come from customer suggestions."

Peerson says publishers' sales representatives make a point of calling attention to awards, but "I don't think many actually read the books." She adds, "A book that wins *any* award should make booksellers, educators, and parents take a closer look, but that doesn't always happen." Peerson has tracked sales on several titles before and after winners were announced and found that "the Coretta Scott King award winners have sold well in our store, but part of the reason is that so many of our schools were lagging behind in having well-rounded libraries with plenty of multicultural titles."

Quality usually wins out. "In our store, some Newbery winners were selling well even before the awards were announced. Interest picked up after the awards," says Peerson, who notes that these books were equally popular with parents and educators.

In Clinton, New Jersey, Harvey Finkel of the Clinton Book Shop observed similar trends among buyers. "I've noticed the awards are very meaningful to teachers, educators, and parents. I especially think when a seal is placed on the cover, it lets the customer know that this book is a standout from all the other great books out there. When we do book fairs at the schools, some of the top requested books are the award winners. The Caldecott and Newbery are the most requested." Finkel has customers who come into his shop looking for honored books for school reports, but "more often than not they don't ask [for an award book] unless they need it for a specific purpose."

Like Peerson, Finkel reads widely and says that official recognition gets his attention, but "there are so many great books out there that I like to look at many others, award winners or not."

The Village

"It takes a village to write my books," said Richard Peck, crediting colleagues in his acceptance speech for the 2001 Newbery for *A Year Down Yonder*. Awards are themselves a much discussed topic in the village of agents, editors, publicists, publishers, and writers. Drop the topic into a gathering at a writers' conference and schedules are put on hold so everyone can comment.

Liza Pulitzer Voges, a literary agent for children's writers with Kirchoff/Wohlberg, says, "When you win a Caldecott or Newbery, everybody knows your name. This increases marketability." Voges understands name recognition. Her great-great-grandfather endowed the Pulitzer Prize, and although she is not part of the Pulitzer awards process, she is pleased that children's authors have been recognized. Pulitzers have been awarded to E.B. White and Theodor Seuss Geisel.

Publishers also value state awards, usually determined by a two-step process, says Voges. Teachers nominate a selection of books and children then vote for the winners. "I think state awards are the key to an author's long-term success," Voges explains. "When an author's book is nominated for a state award, all teachers and students in that state have to read it. This awareness can lead to inclusion in the curriculum or on a reading list. Ideally, awards could elevate an author to another level in terms of demand—such as being invited to speak at a national conference."

Front Street Editor Joy Neaves decisively says the same: "Awards sell books. Publishers are in business to sell books." She thinks that awards help establish in the public eye who is publishing what types of books. Authors should take note that if they track award winners in their marketing research, they will have one more aid in determining whether their own manuscripts might fit a given house.

Writers must match manuscripts to publishers, and publishers match books to awards. Neaves says, "We follow the award guidelines and criteria. If a book doesn't fit within the guidelines, we don't send it. Many award committees don't review books in translation, for instance. Or, we wouldn't send a middle-grade novel to the Printz Award committee," which recognizes young adult literature.

Susan Campbell Bartoletti recognizes that "each award has its own significance." Her *Black Potatoes: The Story of the Great Irish Famine, 1845-1850* won the 2002 Robert F. Sibert Medal for nonfiction. Her *Growing up in Coal Country* won the 1997 Jane Addams Children's Book Award, which annually honors the book "that most effectively promotes the cause of peace, social justice and world community."

Author Sue Alexander says that awards make her feel good and they signal that "I've touched somebody's heart. The Newbery and Caldecott awards can make you a fortune, but that is not what really matters. It's touching hearts, reaching the audience for whom it is intended." Alexander has won awards for her fiction titles, *Lila on the Landing* and *Nadia the Willful*, and her nonfiction book, *Behold the Trees*.

Open Doors?

As a marketing consultant, Raab recommends that authors use the CBC list of awards when they are submitting, to see if their books might tie to any groups or organizations. She believes an author educated in this way has added strength in working with a publisher. (See also the award listings in this book, pages 347 to 387.)

Authors might note to their publishers that they have researched awards, and indicate why a proposed book fits criteria for a certain society's awards. The publisher might already have considered this possibility, but if not, the author could ask if the publisher would pursue it, or offer to contact the society him or herself. The point is to be politely proactive and participate in building a network of contacts that support the book—and as Raab says, the author is also building long-term contacts for future work. (The CBC website is www.cbcbooks.org. The database is available for $9.95 for one-day use, or $150 annually.)

Etta Wilson of March Media says editors focus on the following, in this order: (1) quality of the writing in that manuscript; (2) the fit of the manuscript with the publisher's line and with current book market tastes; and (3) the author's previous publishing record, including any awards. Following publication, she thinks, publishers expect authors to contribute to publicity, and says, "So, it's a good thing when an author can talk about an award on a previous book in order to promote a current or coming book."

For the un-agented especially, when submitting a manuscript to a publisher, "Writers should be encouraged to list awards that are relevant to their work in a cover letter," says Neaves.

Patricia Curtis Pfitsch, whose novel *Riding the Flume* was nominated for a young adult Edgar Award from the Mystery Writers of America, agrees. She thinks editors approached her early work with a different attitude when she was able to mention placing fourth in a *Writer's Digest* contest. "I think winning the *Highlights for Children* fiction contest and two of their Pewter Plates Author of the Month awards had the same effect. Think about the editors: They read the cover letter before they even look at the manuscript. If the cover letter lists an award, especially if it's an award they've heard of, they are in a slightly more open frame of mind when they begin reading your submission. They're expecting it to be better than most they've read. I think that helps."

Winning the *Pockets* fiction contest gave Pamela Greenwood a greater level of confidence at the start of her writing career. "It led me to try more stories for *Pockets*, and I sold them three other stories, one of which has been reprinted several times." Later she joined with Elizabeth Macalaster to co-author nonfiction books under the pen name of Ryan Ann Hunter. Their *Dig a Tunnel* won the 2002 Austin Young Engineers Award for kindergarten to grade two, demonstrating how specific awards criteria can be.

Among Elaine Marie Alphin's first awards were Magazine Merit Awards (MMAs) from the Society of Children's Book Writers and Illustrators (SCBWI). She won the fiction award during her first year as an active member. She also won the SCBWI Work-in-Progress Grant for her middle-grade novel *Ghost Cadet*. "This was incredible validation that yes, I might still be paying my dues, but it was worth it because I might be getting somewhere." Five years later, winning the MMA gave her the lift she needed to continue struggling with *Confederate Son*. The novel rewarded her persistence when it won an Edgar for best young adult mystery.

Newbery winner Paul Fleischman sees a major award as broadening his opportunities to publish books off the beaten track. Alphin agrees that an award equals a stamp of fame, "but it raises the rail." The Edgar gave her name recognition but, "An award becomes a hard task master. With greater name recognition, people will read you more carefully." Always one to see both sides, she says, "but this gives you the opportunity to take risks." This is her chance to push the envelope and challenge the readers as well as herself.

Bartoletti also wants to "risk more, go deeper, travel farther." When she does that, recognition with an award is a strong affirmation that her efforts worked.

Selections

Not only did Alphin win both fiction and nonfiction MMA awards, but

A Fleischman Family Affair

Sid Fleischman won the Newbery Medal in 1987 from the American Library Association (ALA) for *The Whipping Boy*. Paul Fleischman won the Newbery Medal in 1989 for *Joyful Noise: Poems for Two Voices* and a Newbery Honor for *Graven Images* in 1983.

"The Newbery has a tremendous impact," says father Sid. "The phone doesn't stop ringing for a year. You are asked to speak everywhere but the neighborhood grocery store. Your quiet writing schedule is blown. But who cares when you are awarded that pot at the end of the literary rainbow, the Newbery?"

The pluses are apparent. "Quite naturally there is a huge jump in book sales and royalties. Your lines at book signings are longer. A librarian told me as she reached my table and handed me a pen that she'd read the entire *Whipping Boy* while waiting in line. Foreign interest for translation rights is intensified. Film interest, too. And it all has a drag-along effect on your earlier titles."

But some downsides are possible. "A problem for me after I was able to settle down to my next book was what I call the Newbery Freeze," says Sid. "You feel that the Newbery committee is looking over your shoulder at every word and sentence you write. It took me a while to loosen up and get going again. Despite this worried start, I think the next book I wrote, *The Scarebird,* is one of my best works."

The author also has some humor about the award: "The greatest burden: getting your friends to spell Newbery correctly." He also has humility: "It needn't be said that the Newbery trumps all other awards. The secondary awards are wonderful and we all are grateful for them, but their effect is often local and brief. Let me quickly add that I give these honors top placement; they sit on a Steinway grand in my living room."

Paul's experience followed soon after. "My father hadn't won his awards when I was young. This was beneficial to me, if not for him, sparing me growing up under the shadow of the Newbery. It also taught me that his books that I adored—*By the Great Horn Spoon!, Chancy and the Grand Rascal*—were no less wonderful for being passed over by award committees. The unspoken moral was that you continue to write the best books you can, that awards are unimportant for writers and readers alike."

A Fleischman Family Affair

Paul is perhaps objective about such honors. "Indeed, I was shocked after my own Newbery to see how award-tilted the population is. Signing books at ALA, it was rare to see one of my other books presented to me; people only wanted the one with the gold seal, the very same book that had sold poorly before the announcement. I think we give far too much importance to awards, especially given how necessarily chancy the selection process is in such a subjective realm."

At the same time, Paul admits, "Awards are wonderfully affirming for authors, who labor in solitude and often feel underappreciated." He notes, too, that awards can give an author needed momentum, "sometimes for years, helping to carry you over dry spells and through difficult projects. To be a writer is to be haunted by doubt. An award can send doubt packing for a while. . . . Major awards can indeed open doors. In a way, the Newbery Honor awarded to *Graven Images* was more important than the Newbery itself. It put me on the map early in my career—it was just my third book and meant that I would likely publish books that were fairly far off the beaten track—such as *I Am Phoenix,* the precursor to *Joyful Noise,* which had been turned down by several publishers, including Harper, until the Newbery Honor award.

"The real award that writers get is that feeling of doing good work, day after day, of being so excited about what you're working on that you wake up at 3 AM to get back to it, that feeling—which only comes around once in a while—that the book you're writing could be written by you and only you, that you were put on earth to write it, that joyous, scary, enthralling sensation of riding the book's wave, improvising, feeling that magnetism drawing the different parts together, that incredible satisfaction at the end that you did what you set out to do. It's a feeling that no award committee can give you, and one that no one and nothing—not fire, flood, or earthquake—can take away."

she later served on the selection committee. The MMA committee members study photocopies of stories and articles taken from magazines. Members of the SCBWI's Golden Kite selection committees need extra bookshelves and an understanding mail carrier to handle all the books to be read. In 2004, the judges reviewed 1,130 books published in the preceding year by members of the organization.

SCBWI members who are well-known, well-published, and can spare the time to read are chosen to sit on the selection committees, a one-time appointment. One of the founding members of SCBWI, Alexander coordinated the award for 25 years. During that time, she says, "Many of the judges told me that, though it was a lot of work, it was a very illuminating experience for them and they were glad they'd done it."

Alexander discriminates between awards given by writers and those from other groups of professionals. "Teachers and librarians have the power to put books in kids' hands. Their awards thus result in big sales. The Golden Kite doesn't command sales and the resulting sales of Golden Kite winners may not be enormous, but the prestige is big."

Susan Faust served as Chair of the 2005 Newbery Committee, which consists of 15 members drawn from the membership of the Association for Library Service to Children (ALSC). Members are most often librarians, but teachers, booksellers, publishers, reviewers, and

academics also belong to the organization. The term of service is one year and members attend two mandatory meetings. (See the sidebar on pages 324–325).

From the Kids & Librarians

For many authors, awards straight from the young readers themselves are among the most important of all.

Kathi Appelt was touched when *Bubba and Beau: Best Friends* won the Irma and Simon Black Award for Excellence in Children's Literature. "That book was indeed selected by children. That was very gratifying. When I first embarked upon this journey of writing for children, I believed the ultimate goal was simply to get the darned story published. Publishing the book is just the beginning. Then the work of getting the book into the hands of young readers becomes the goal. When an adult sits down with a child and reads to him or her, the possibility of magic appears and the rest of the world slips away. But that can't happen if the book doesn't find its way out of the publisher's catalogue, onto the bookseller's or library's shelves, and into the hands of a real, live child. An award often provides that small boost, so I'm grateful for any award my books receive, but the ones chosen by children, those are the ones that matter most."

Aileen Kilgore Henderson was surprised to find her first book on children's choice lists. When *The Summer of the Bonepile Monster* first came out, one reviewer was less than enthusiastic. "I thought the book's future was impaled on the reviewer's words." Instead, the book won the Milkweed Prize and the Alabama Library Association Award and was on the short list for Connecticut's Nutmeg Award, Florida's Sunshine State Award, and others. These awards gave Henderson, at the age of 75, self-esteem as a writer and the motivation and impetus to plow ahead and write more books and enjoy other nominations.

Those who want to know what children's librarians consider important can benefit from this tip from Lisa Von Drasek, a librarian at Bank Street School who has served on the Newbery Committee and the Notable Children's Books Committee. "My favorite book with criteria for excellence is called *Cover to Cover,* by Kathleen T. Horning. This book is about book reviewing and gives insights into what librarians are looking for in good children's books."

Becoming Award-Worthy?
Would Bartoletti keep writing if her books didn't win awards? "Absolutely! Work is passion-driven."

Raab thinks authors can no more write with the objective of receiving an award than they can make marketing the primary reason for their writing. The work must come first; the rest may follow. Don't copycat something that succeeded. "It could do an injustice to the work by trying to find a pattern and map to the success of another book, almost becoming a copy of that book. Some

might say, however, that if you have found the recipe for success, why not use it?"

When he accepted the Newbery for *Bud, Not Buddy,* Christopher Paul Curtis recalled winning the Newbery Honor four years earlier for *The Watsons Go to Birmingham—1963.* "I remembered the fun I had writing *The Watsons* and decided that writing *Bud* would be no different. I decided I had a story to tell, that I was going to tell it the best way I could, and that I'd give no consideration whatsoever to how it would be received. I figured Wendy Lamb [his editor] could worry about that."

Paul Fleischman says, "You can't make awards happen. They're a matter of luck. My advice here is the same I give for writing in general: Avoid thinking about the marketplace and award committees and write the book you're most committed to, from within, not without. I certainly wasn't aiming for the Newbery with a book of two-voiced poems about insects."

Wise writers will understand awards' twofold importance, to literature and to career. But the best writers always write from within.

Inside the Newbery

Susan Faust was the Chair of the 2005 Newbery Committee for the American Library Association (ALA) and also served on the 2000 Newbery Committee, as Chair of the 1998 Notable Books for Children Committee, and Chair of the 2001 Sibert Informational Book Award. She gives an inside look at the workings of the Newbery selection process.

The committee comprises 15 members drawn from the membership of the ALA's Association for Library Service to Children (ALSC). Members serve for one year and must attend two meetings. In considering books for the Newbery, Faust says the committee is responsible for surveying, reading, and evaluating all eligible books. In addition to mainstream books submitted by publishers by the deadline of December 31, self-published books, original paperbacks, and even e-books are eligible for consideration as long as they are original work written by a U.S. citizen or resident and published in the U.S. in the year under consideration. Committee members do extensive research on the publishing output of a given year and must obtain copies of books not sent by publishers. Libraries are often a source.

"The criteria on our website, www.ala.org, provide guidance as to what elements contribute to distinguished writing . . . and that contribution can be found in picture books, fiction, poetry, nonfiction and so on," says Faust. A note at the end of the Newbery Terms and Criteria states clearly that the award is not for didactic intent or for popularity.

The committee works for a year surveying the field of eligible titles, reading and taking notes. In addition, the Chair calls for monthly suggestions from members—titles that are deemed strong enough contenders to merit the attention of all. In October and then again in December, each committee member must suggest three titles. Along with a nomination must come a written justification that explains how a book meets the Newbery criteria. The suggestion and nomination process keep the committee focused throughout the year.

When the committee meets for final selection, all books that have been suggested or nominated are under consideration. The committee meets in midwinter for in-depth discussions of those books, revolving around the Newbery criteria and allowing for comparisons of the books under consideration. Next, a balloting procedure takes place. A numerical formula helps

Inside the Newbery

determine when consensus has been reached, the debate is over, and the committee stands behind its decision. To allow for an openness and security in the discussion, specifics about the year's work remain forever confidential.

The committee chair has all the same responsibilities as the other 14 members in surveying the field of eligible titles, reading, taking notes, making suggestions and nominations, taking part in discussion, and balloting. In addition, the chair organizes the work of the committee—preparing the committee for its charge in myriad ways, seeing that deadlines are set and met, maintaining a database of suggested and nominated titles, checking books for eligibility, communicating with committee members on individual and group matters, checking to see that committee members have access to books, soliciting participation from the ALSC membership, planning and running the meetings, and so on.

As one would imagine, spots on the Newbery, Caldecott, and Sibert Award Committees are coveted, as are spots on other ALSC book and media committees. ALSC members may submit volunteer forms to let the nominating committee know that they would like to be considered. ALSC members, well-known for their evaluative skills, may be asked to run or to serve even without having filled out a volunteer form. Service on one of these committees is often the high point of a career.

Faust concludes, "Chairing the Newbery is a once-in-a-lifetime privilege. I loved every minute."

Writers' Conferences

Conferences Devoted to Writing for Children— General Conferences

BYU Writing for Young Readers Workshop

230 Harman Continuing Education Building
Brigham Young University
Provo, UT 84602
http://ce.byu.edu/cw/

Designed for people who want to write for children or young adults, this five-day workshop features daily four-hour sessions where participants focus on a single market: picture books, book-length fiction, fantasy/science fiction, general writing, beginning writing, and illustration.
Date: June.
Subjects: Sample workshops include "The Picture Book Fantasy," "Acquisition to Publication: Picture Book and Novel," and "What I've Learned So Far."
Speakers: Previous conference speakers included Dean Hughes, Laura Torres, and Rick Walton.
Location: Provo, Utah.
Costs: Full workshop registration is $399. Afternoon-only registration is $200. University credit is available for an additional fee.

Celebration of Children's Literature

Children's Book Guild
7513 Shadywood Road
Bethesda, MD 20817
www.childrensbookguild.org

Open to all writers and book lovers, this one-day conference includes morning and afternoon speakers, workshops, and autograph sessions. It features inspiration and information for writers at all levels. Visit the website for the 2006 workshop schedule.
Date: April.
Subjects: Past workshops have covered point of view, and marketing your work.
Speakers: Previous conference speakers included Patricia Lee Gauch, Jerry Pinkney, Joseph Lekuton, and Elizabeth Levy.
Location: Montgomery College in Rockville, Maryland.
Costs: $90.

Central Ohio Writers of Literature for Children

Jim Mengel, Developmental Director
Saint Joseph Montessori School
933 Hamlet Street
Columbus, OH 43201
www.sjms.net/conf/contact.html

Open to writers of all levels, this one-day conference provides quality educational programs for children's writing. It features workshops, lectures, and manuscript evaluations by nationally acclaimed, published professionals. Conference proceeds benefit the local community.
Date: TBA.
Subjects: Topics include poetry, easy readers, picture books, illustrating, and workshops on how to pitch ideas.
Speakers: 2005 keynote speakers included Margaret Peterson Haddix, Anna Grossnickle Hines, Robert Pottle, and Christopher Canyon.
Location: Columbus, Ohio.
Costs: $110; $95 for early registration; $120 for late registration.

Highlights Foundation Writers' Workshop at Chautauqua

814 Court Street
Honesdale, PA 18431
www.highlightsfoundation.org

This well-known not-for-profit organization hosts a week-long conference that includes seminars, small-group workshops, and one-on-one sessions with prominent children's authors, illustrators, editors, critics, and publishers. It is open to all writers interested in children's literature.
Date: July.
Subjects: 2006 workshops include "Wordplay: Writing Poetry for Children," "Room to Create," "More than Just the Facts," and "Mixing Research with Imagination."
Speakers: 2006 keynote speakers include Patricia Lee Gauch, Rich Wallace, Jerry Spinelli, Eileen Spinelli, and Juanita Havill.
Location: Chautauqua, New York.
Costs: $2,200 (includes meals).

The Loft Festival of Children's Literature

Suite 200, Open Book
1011 Washington Avenue South
Minneapolis, MN 55415
www.loft.org

Morning and afternoon sessions are offered at this two-day writing festival. Keynote speeches, lectures, and workshops are offered by well-known authors, editors, and publishers in the field.
Date: TBA.
Subjects: Past workshops included "Writing Your Humor," "Process and Progress," and "The Art of Metaphor."
Speakers: Speakers from past workshops include Anna Meek, Betsy Amster, and Mary Jo Pehl.
Location: Minneapolis, Minnesota.
Costs: Costs range between $120 and $135 for the two-day event.

Oregon Coast Children's Book Writers Workshop

PMB 623
7327 SW Barnes Road
Portland, OR 97225
www.occbww.com

This intensive workshop targets individuals who dream of becoming published children's book authors. The workshop is designed for beginning through advanced writers and offers presentations by writing instructors, group manuscript sharing, and intensive consults with children's book authors and editors.
Date: July 17–21, 2006.
Subjects: Workshops for the 2006 conference include young adult and middle-grade novels, picture books, children's poetry, and children's nonfiction.
Speakers: Speakers this year include David Greenberg, Patricia Hermes, and Marsha Diane Arnold.
Location: Oceanside, Oregon.
Costs: $595.

Pacific Northwest Children's Book Conference

Portland State University Haystack
    Summer Program
P.O. Box 1491
Portland, OR 97201-1491
www.haystack.pdx.edu

This conference offers morning lectures, afternoon workshops, and small group critique sessions with faculty, focusing on the craft of writing and illustrating for children. An outstanding faculty of acclaimed editors, authors, and illustrators provide guidance and instruction to writers of all levels.
Date: July–August.
Subjects: 2005 topics included fantasy, poetry, humor, dialogue, picture books, nonfiction, and writing for young adults.
Speakers: 2005 faculty included Susan Fletcher, Maria Frazee, Ann Whiteford Paul, and Elsa Warnick.
Location: Portland, Oregon.
Costs: $590–$1,220.

Perspectives in Children's Literature Annual Conference

University of Massachusetts
    School of Education
226 Furcolo Hall
813 North Pleasant Street
Amherst, MA 01003-9308
www.umass.edu/childlit

This one-day conference provides an opportunity to learn more about the world of children's literature though interaction with the creators themselves. University credit is available. Check the website or send an SASE for updated conference details.
Date: April.
Subjects: 2005 conference workshops included "Elements of Picture Book Illustration," "Authors in Wonder-Land," and "Editing for the Very Young."
Speakers: 2005 conference speakers included Wendy Watson, Jane Yolen, and Grace Maccarone.
Location: Amherst, Massachusetts.
Costs: TBA.

Conferences Devoted to Writing for Children— Society of Children's Book Writers & Illustrators

Alabama
Alabama Writing and Illustrating for Kids
Jo Kittinger, Co-Regional Advisor
P.O. Box 26282
Birmingham, AL 35260
www.southern-breeze.org

Celebrating its 15th year, this two-day conference brings authors, editors, agents, and illustrators together for activities geared toward the production and support of quality children's literature. Writers of all levels and abilities are welcome.
Date: June.
Subjects: Sample workshops include "Picture Book Dummy," "Who Shrunk My Book?" and "Partners in Rhyme."
Speakers: Past conference speakers included Kim Siegelson, Han Nolan, Arianne Lewin, and Patrick Collins.
Location: Hoover, Alabama.
Costs: Conference fees range from $95–$120 and include lunch.

Arizona
SCBWI Arizona Conference
Michelle Parker-Rock, Regional
   Advisor
www.scbwi-az.org

Subtitled "Children's Books Make the World a Better Place," this annual conference offers lectures and presentations from prominent children's book editors and art directors.
Date: November.
Subjects: Past lectures included "Why Do We Do This?" "Books that Stand Out," "Is It Time to Get an Agent?" and "Nonfiction."
Speakers: 2005 keynote speakers included Tim Travaglini, Carolyn P. Yoder, Tim Gillner, Janette Rallison, and Laura Jacobson.
Location: Scottsdale, Arizona.
Costs: TBA.

California
Asilomar Conference and Retreat
Shirley Klock
#219
2625 Middlefield Road
Palo Alto, CA 94306-2516
www.scbwinorca.org

In its 23rd year, this annual retreat features focus sessions, workshops, and portfolio evaluations. Presenters include prominent publishers, editors, authors, and illustrators of children's literature. Manuscript critiques are available for an additional fee.
Date: February.
Subjects: Past workshops have included "Giving Engaging and Professional Talks," "Games to Explore Voice," "Writing Lively Nonfiction for Kids," "Writing for Magazines," and an illustration workshop.
Speakers: Past main speakers included Gerald McDermott, Jane

Kurtz, Patricia Lee Gauch, Nicole Geiger, and Jeannette Larson.
Location: Pacific Grove, California.
Costs: Conference fees range from $325–$440.

Los Angeles Annual Retreat

P.O. Box 1728
Pacific Palisades, CA 90272
www.scbwisocal.org

This annual three-day retreat promises to give new life to your "droopy, fluttering, or ready-to-fly manuscripts." Groups are organized by genre track and allow participants to stay with the same people throughout the weekend.
Date: October.
Subjects: Topics include marketing, networking, crafting an opening line, and writing for magazines.
Speakers: 2005 conference speakers included Gretchen Hirsch, Sherry Shahan, and Julie Williams.
Location: Encino, California.
Costs: Conference fees range from $320–$435.

Canada
SCBWI Canada Conference

Noreen Kruzich Violetta, Regional
    Advisor
www.scbwicanada.org

Open to established or aspiring writers and illustrators, this three-day retreat features guided activities, an opportunity to display your work, assigned group critiques, social gatherings, and lectures and discussions from award-winning authors.

Date: September.
Subjects: Workshops from the 2005 retreat included "Inviting the Reader In," and "Creative Energies at Work."
Speakers: The keynote speaker from the 2005 retreat was Ted Staunton.
Location: Mattawa, Ontario.
Costs: $175.

Hawaii
SCBWI Hawaii Conference

4224 Waialae Ave., #493
Honolulu, HI 96816
www.geocities.com/scbwihawaii/

This annual one-day conference presented by the Hawaii chapter of SCBWI provides wonderful opportunities for those interested in writing and illustrating for children. In addition to networking, you can meet professional authors, illustrators, and editors, and learn inside secrets of successful writing for children. Panel discussions, question and answer sessions, and critiques are also offered.
Date: March.
Subjects: 2005 sample workshops included "The Character Makes the Book: How to Make Irresistable Characters," "What Books Are Children Looking For?" and "Children's Book Agents: Who Needs 'Em?"
Speakers: 2005 keynote speakers included Caitlyn Dlouhy, Maile Davis, and Scott Treimel.
Costs: $75 for members; $90 for non-members.
Location: Honolulu, Hawaii.

Colorado/Wyoming
SCBWI Rocky Mountain
Chapter Spring Conference
www.rmcscbwi.org

Titled "Sharpening the Tools of Your Trade," this three-day conference offered by the Rocky Mountain Chapter of SCBWI brings authors, editors, and agents together to give writers an opportunity to network and improve their writing and marketing skills. Visit the website for further information on the 2006 conference.
Date: April 9, 2006.
Subjects: Workshops from the 2005 conference included "Nonfiction Is Not for Nerds," "Three Exercises to Help You Get and Hold Your Reader," "The Narrative Voice," and "Character Development."
Speakers: Past speakers included Michele Burke and Cheryl Klein.
Location: Golden, Colorado.
Costs: $95 (member early registration); $110 (member late registration); $115 (non-member early registration); $130 (non-member late registration).

Maryland/Delaware/
West Virginia
SCBWI MD/DE/WV Region
Annual Summer
Conference
3377 Littlestown Pike
Westminster, MD 21158
www.boo.net/%7Ebecka/scbwi.htm

This one-day conference is packed with presentations, panel discussions, and workshops by award-winning and prominent authors, illustrators, and editors. Lectures are intended to provide fresh ideas. Participants may also take part in question & answer sessions with the experts.
Subjects: TBA.
Speakers: Keynote speakers from the 2005 conference included Mary Downing Hahn, Lisa Jahn-Clough, Sarah Ketchersid, and Tara Weikum.
Date: TBA.
Location: TBA.
Costs: Check website for 2006 conference fees.

New England
SCBWI New England Annual
Conference
Sally Riley, Regional Advisor
www.nescbwi.org

This annual conference of the New England chapter of SCBWI offers workshops, writing intensives, one-on-one critiques, and breakout sessions led by authors, editors, and illustrators of children's literature. The three-day event welcomes writers of all levels—from novice to seasoned. Number of participants is limited, so early registration is recommended.
Date: May.
Subjects: 2005 workshops included "Writing from Your Core," "Nuts and Bolts of Writing," and "A New Way of Seeing."
Speakers: Speakers from the 2005 event included M.T. Anderson,

Kirsten Cappy, and Toni Buzzeo.
Location: Nashua, New Hampshire.
Costs: TBA.

Oregon
SCBWI Spring Conference
Judith Gardiner
4921 SE 76th Street
Portland, OR 97206
www.scbwior.com

This one-day conference offers a wide array of keynote speakers, lectures, and workshops aimed at advanced to novice writers. Topics range from the nuts and bolts of the writing business to ways to increase creative flow. Manuscript evaluations are available for an additional fee.
Date: May.
Subjects: 2005 workshops included "Write Funny for Money," "I Think I Can, I Think I Can," "Everything You Shouldn't Be Afraid to Ask about Contracts," and "Kids Writing 101."
Speakers: Keynote speakers from the 2005 conference included Judy Cox, Melissa Hart, Rebecca Hickox, Joy Peskin, and Margaret Bechard.
Location: Wilsonville, Oregon.
Costs: $85 for members; $95 for non-members (early registration).

Texas
Austin Fall Conference
Julie Lake, Regional Advisor
5310 Musket Ridge
Austin, TX 78759
www.austinscbwi.com

This one-day conference for writers and illustrators includes keynote speakers and round table discussions aimed at helping novice to advanced children's writers hone their skills and sharpen their craft. Manuscript and portfolio evaluations are available for an additional fee. Participation is limited, so early registration is recommended.
Date: October.
Subjects: TBA.
Speakers: Past speakers included Melanie Cecka, Mark W. McVeigh, Stephen Fraser, David Caplan, and Pun Nio.
Location: Austin, Texas.
Costs: $105 for 1-day conference (includes meals); $25 manuscript critique.

Brazos Valley Winter Workshop
Janet Fox
5692 Polo Road
College Station, TX 77845
www.scbwi-brazosvalley.org

Each winter, this one-day conference promises an inspiring and rejuvenating mix of lectures, workshops, and activities presented by successful professionals. Topics such as negotiating a contract, building a website, and managing a writing career are addressed. Visit the website for 2006 workshops.
Date: November.
Subjects: Lectures for the 2005 conference included "What Editors Really Want," "Fresh Ideas in Marketing," and "Sizzling School Visits."
Speakers: 2005 speakers included Kathi Appelt, Kate Farrell, Sherry Garland, and Anne Perry.

Location: College Station, TX.
Costs: Conference fees range
from $80–$100.

Washington
Annual Writing and
Illustrating for Children
Conference

P.O. Box 799
Woodinville, WA 98072-0799
www.scbwi-washington.org

The Western Washington
chapter of SCBWI offers this
one-day conference that includes manuscript consultations,
portfolio reviews, workshops,
lectures, and an art show for
writers and illustrators of children's literature.
Date: April.
Subjects: Past subjects have included picture books, writing
nonfiction for early readers, and
magazine stories and articles.
Speakers: 2005 faculty included
Marion Dane Bauer, Heather
Delabre, Dianne Hess, Wendy
McClure, and Scott Piehl.
Location: Seattle, Washington.
Costs: Check website for 2006
conference fees.

Conferences with Sessions on Writing for Children—University or Regional Conferences

Aspen Summer Words

Aspen Writers' Foundation
Suite 116
110 E. Hallam Street
Aspen, CO 81611
www.aspenwriters.org

An intensive writing retreat and stimulating literary festival, this five-day conference offers workshops, readings, discussions, and social gatherings along with galas with best-selling authors. It offers private consultations for an additional fee.
Date: June.
Subjects: Past workshops included the topics of fiction, screenwriting, poetry, memoir, and essay.
Speakers: Past speakers have included Edna O'Brien, Malachy McCourt, and Polly Devlin.
Location: Aspen, Colorado.
Costs: Vary; visit website.

Harriette Austin Writers Conference

Georgia Center for Continuing
    Education
University of Georgia
Athens, GA 30602-3603

Open to novice writers and published professionals alike, this two-day conference features workshops, book signings, manuscript evaluations, social events, professional critiques, and panel discussions with notable professionals in the field.

It seeks to provide opportunities for attendants to explore, enhance, exchange, and market their work.
Date: July.
Subjects: Past workshops have included "Beyond the Basics," "Ask the Book Doctor," "Publishing 101," "The Internet and Writers," and "Vital Book Publicity."
Speakers: Past speakers have included Beverly Connor, Emily Craig, Elizabeth Hailey, and Don Keith.
Location: Athens, Georgia.
Costs: $175–$310.

Bear River Writers' Conference

Department of English Language &
    Literature
3187 Angell Hall
University of Michigan
Ann Arbor, MI 48109
www.lsa.umich.edu/bearriver

This four-day conference offers workshops on the topics of fiction, poetry, essay, memoir, and creative nonfiction. It combines informative lectures with inspirational outdoor pursuits and is open to writers of all levels and genres. In the past it has welcomed both local and international writers and boasts a highly varied crowd of participants and professionals. Participation is limited so early registration is recommended. Check the website for complete conference details and registration materials.

Date: June.
Subjects: Past workshops have included "Reading, Writing, and Rummaging for Your Own Voice," "Writing and Remembering," "The Short-short As Medium for Creative Nonfiction," and "A Sense of Place."
Speakers: Past speakers have included Jerry Dennis, Elizabeth Cox, Keith Taylor, and Thomas Lynch.
Location: Walloon Lake, Michigan.
Costs: $550–$750 (includes meals and lodging).

Canadian Authors Association Annual Conference

Box 419
Campelford, Ontario K0L 1L0
Canada
www.canauthors.org

In its 85th year, this annual conference provides an educational forum for professional and emerging writers throughout Canada. Perfect for meeting people with like interests, it features lectures, workshops, and panel discussions about all aspects of writing.
Date: June.
Subjects: 2005 workshops and events included writing for children, travel writing, political writing, writing for the Internet, and getting published.
Speakers: 2005 speakers included Chris Banks, Veronica Ross, Kelley Armstrong, and Erin Noteboom.
Location: Peterborough, Canada.
Costs: Member fees range from $150 to $175; fees for non-

members range from $190–$225.

Cape Cod Writers' Conference

P.O. Box 408
Osterville, MA 02655
www.capecodwriterscenter.com

In its 43rd year, this annual week-long summer conference brings published and aspiring authors together for lectures, workshops, and courses by authors, editors, and agents. Manuscript evaluations and personal conferences with the faculty are available for an additional fee. Continuing education credits are also available.
Date: August.
Subjects: Subjects from the 2005 conference include "Story Structure for Fiction and Screenwriters," "Creative Nonfiction: Did That Really Happen?" "Fiction: Theory and Practice," "The Heart of Creativity," and "Writing the First Novel."
Speakers: 2005 speakers included Nancy Geary, Kevin Griffin, Melvin Donalson, and Peter Tolan.
Location: Craigville Beach, Massachusetts.
Costs: Visit the website for 2006 conference fees.

Columbus Writers Conference

Angela Palazzolo, Producer/Director
P.O. Box 20548
Columbus, OH 43220
www.creativevista.com

This annual conference brings together literary agents, authors, and editors for workshops and lectures on the nuts-and-bolts of fiction and non-fiction writing and the business of writing. Both aspiring writers and published professionals will find something of interest here.

Date: August.

Subjects: Subjects from the 2005 conference included "And Your Genre Is . . .," "From Writer to Reader," and "Nonfiction Books for Children."

Speakers: 2005 conference speakers included Rachel Vater, John Becker, and David Weissman.

Location: Columbus, Ohio.

Costs: Visit the website for updated 2006 conference fees.

Coveside Writing Workshop

Coveside Studio
503 Main Street
Old Wethersfield, CT 06109

This two-day intensive workshop is open to writers of all levels who seek hands-on activities designed to help them "discover their well-spring of ideas." It features presentations from well-known writers and editors, and critique and networking sessions. The number of participants is limited, so early registration is recommended.

Date: October.

Subjects: Past topics included "Selection and Revision," "Making the Journey from Here to There," and guided meditation.

Speakers: Conference is led by author Anita Riggio.

Location: Old Wethersfield, Connecticut.

Costs: $375 (includes meals).

Flathead River Writers Conference

P.O. Box 7711
Kalispell, MT 59904

Open to writers of all levels, this annual conference is affordable and packed with quality lectures and workshops. For those who submit proof of writing ability, one-on-one meetings with editors and agents are available. Fiction and nonfiction writing intensives preceding the general conference are also offered.

Date: October.

Subjects: Topics include writing for children, horror, humor, marketing, mystery, nonfiction, playwriting, publishing, and writing for young adults.

Speakers: Past speakers included Richard Wheeler, Linda Segar, Wayne White, and Alice Stanton.

Location: Whitefish, Montana.

Costs: $180 for weekend conference; $150 for early registration; $460 for 3-day workshop and weekend conference.

Gig Harbor Writers' Conference

Kathleen O'Brien, Director
P.O. Box 826
Gig Harbor, Washington 98335
www.peninsulawritersassociation.org

This annual three-day conference provides workshops and lectures on fiction, autobiography, romance, screenwriting, horror, journalism, publishing, science fiction/fantasy,

travel, and writing for children and young adults. Space is limited to 75 participants, so early registration is strongly recommended.
Date: March.
Subjects: Past workshops included "Write a Good Synopsis," "The Story Machine," "Find Your Voice," "Welcome to Plotting," and "The Trustworthy Narrator."
Speakers: 2005 keynote speakers and presenters included Tad Bartimus, Gail Tsukiyama, Jill Barnett, Pete Fromm, and Randall Platt.
Location: Gig Harbor, Washington.
Costs: $175 not including Friday workshop; $100 Friday workshop.

Indiana University Writers' Conference

464 Ballantine Hall
Bloomington, IN 47405
www.indiana.edu/~writecon

Now in its 66th year, this six-day conference attracts nationally prominent authors and aspiring writers alike. There are workshops in fiction, poetry, and creative non-fiction; readings and one-on-one consultations by faculty are offered. Submission of a manuscript is required prior to the conference. Applications are available at the website with an SASE. University credit is available.
Date: June 11–16, 2006.
Subjects: 2005 conference workshops included "Risk Taking in Compact Fiction," "The Essay and the Memoir," "Introduction to Screenwriting," and "The Emotional Arc of Poetry."

Speakers: 2005 speakers included Carol Bly, Mark Axelrod, Ruth Ellen Kocher, and David Leavitt.
Location: Bloomington, Indiana.
Costs: Check website for 2006 conference fees.

Iowa Summer Writing Festival

University of Iowa
C215 Seashore Hall
Iowa City, IA 52242-5000
www.uiowa.edu/~iswfest

Open to writers of all levels over the age of 18, this week-long literary festival offers lectures, workshops, keynote speeches, and critiques on writing fiction, nonfiction, poetry, and more. Weekend-long workshops are also available, either separately or in addition to the week's events, for an additional fee. There is no prerequisite for attendance beyond the desire to write. Visit the website or send an SASE for complete conference description.
Date: June/July.
Subjects: Topics for the 2006 conference include "Creating Picture Book Characters from Head to Toe," "The Novel Process," and "Fiction Basics."
Speakers: This year's speakers include Stephen Bloom, Janet Desaulniers, Jacqueline Briggs-Martin and Jane Mead.
Location: Iowa City, Iowa.
Costs: $475–$500 per week; $200–$250 per weekend.

Kentucky Women Writers Spring Conference

251 West Second Street
Lexington, KY 40507
www.uky.edu/WWK/kywwc

Established in 1979 by the University of Kentucky and the longest-running of its kind, this four-day conference focuses on women's literature and writing. Workshops include children's literature, fiction, journalism, memoirs, poetry, and playwriting. Panel discussions, scheduled readings, manuscript critiques, writing sessions, and social events are also offered. Limited to 100–200 participants, early registration is recommended.
Date: April.
Subjects: Topics have included women teaching writing to women, publishing, and reading women's literature.
Speakers: 2005 keynote speakers included Carrie Mae Weems, Candace Bushnell, and Louise Glück.
Location: Lexington, Kentucky.
Costs: TBA.

Manhattanville Summer Writers' Week

Manhattanville College
School of Graduate and Professional Studies
2900 Purchase Street
Purchase, NY 10577
www.mville.edu/graduate/writers-week.htm

Open to writers of all levels, this week-long event offers lectures, workshops, and writing intensives presented by established authors and teachers of writing. Keynote speakers and sessions with editors and agents are also offered. Participants may attend readings by distinguished faculty or network with others in the field. Visit the website for complete information.
Subjects: 2005 workshops included "Blueprint for Creating," "Getting to Know the Journals," and "Character-based Fiction."
Speakers: 2005 speakers included Alice Elliott Dark, Patricia Lee Gauch, and Phyllis Shalant.
Date: June/July.
Location: Purchase, New York.
Costs: $1040 (for graduate credit); $675 (for non-graduate credit).

Maui Writers Conference

P.O. Box 968
Kihei, HI 96753
www.mauiwriters.com

This five-day conference strives to be an inspirational and learning resource for novice and experienced writers alike. Each year, best-selling authors, award-winning journalists, and top agents, editors, and publishers gather here and provide the opportunity for meeting prominent professionals in the field. Professional consultations are available for an additional fee.
Date: August/September.
Subjects: 2005 topics included children's fiction, mystery, poetry, narrative nonfiction, science fiction, thrillers, and screenwriting.
Speakers: 2005 keynote speakers

included Tess Gerritsen, Jennifer Crusie, Jacquelyn Mitchard, Erik Larson, and Linda Sue Park.
Location: Wailea, Hawaii.
Costs: Check website for 2006 conference fees.

New England Writers' Conference
P.O. Box 5
Windsor, VT 05089
www.newenglandwriters.org

This affordable one-day event provides lectures, workshops, readings, panel discussions, book signings, and open microphone sessions. It is open to writers of all levels, but participation is limited to ensure small groups, so early registration is recommended. Visit the website or send an SASE for complete details.
Date: July.
Subjects: Past conferences have covered writing for children, fiction, nonfiction, and marketing.
Speakers: 2005 featured speakers included Matthew Zapruder and Dave King.
Location: Windsor, Vermont.
Costs: $20.

Northeast Texas Writers' Organization Writers' Roundup
P.O. Box 411
Winfield, TX 75493
www.netwo.org

Marking its 20th year, the Northeast Texas Writers' Organization

sponsors this annual conference to support the endeavor of creative writing. It includes critique sessions, book signings, and workshops on writing, publishing, and marketing your work.
Date: April 21–22, 2006.
Subjects: Workshops from the 2005 conference were "Publishing from the Agent's Perspective," "The Creativity Box," "Creating Pins-N-Needles Suspense," and "Publishing Your Children's Book."
Speakers: 2005 conference speakers included Bill Crider, Victoria Chancellor, H. J. Ralles, and Ginnie Siena Bivona.
Location: Winnsboro, Texas.
Costs: TBA.

Oklahoma Writers' Federation Conference
P.O. Box 2654
Stillwater, OK 74076
www.owfi.org

Titled "Writers' Inspiration," this conference presents lectures, workshops, autograph parties, scheduled appointments with editors and agents, and social events. It aims to be an affordable and informative retreat where writers may enjoy networking and learning more about their craft.
Date: May 5–6, 2006.
Subjects: 2005 conference workshops included "Writing for Young Readers," "The Heart of Nonfiction," "Understanding Publicity," and "Creating the Perfect Hero."
Speakers: 2005 presenters included Dian Curtis Regan, Milton Kahn,

Hannibal Johnson, and Sharon Sala.
Location: Oklahoma City, Oklahoma.
Costs: $100–$125.

Philadelphia Writers' Conference

Rhonda Hoffman, PWC Registrar
121 Almatt Terrace
Philadelphia, PA 19115-2745
www.pwcwriters.org

Since its founding in 1949, this three-day annual conference has presented workshops and lectures about all aspects of the craft of writing. Open to writers of all genres, many satisfied participants return year after year. Attendance is limited to 180 attendees, so early registration is recommended.
Date: June.
Subjects: 2005 conference workshops included "The Writer Within Us," "Writing for Children," "The Nuts and Bolts," and "Magazine Writing."
Speakers: 2005 presenters included Penny Pollock, Fran Pelham, Debbie Lee, and Richard S. Bank.
Location: Philadelphia, Pennsylvania.
Costs: Visit the website for 2006 conference fees or mail inquiry and SASE.

Seven Hills Writers' Conference

Tallahassee Writers' Association
2636 West Mission Road #16
Tallahassee, FL 32304
www.tallahasseewriters.net

This annual two-day conference provides fourteen varied workshops on topics such as the business of writing, advertising, and public relations. One-on-one meetings to pitch your work to noted agents and editors are available. Interested writers should visit the website or send an e-mail to conference@tallahasseewriters.net.
Date: April.
Subjects: Workshops from the 2005 conference included "Creating Memorable Characters," "Inspirational Writing," and "How to Write a Query Letter."
Speakers: The 2005 keynote speaker was Leonard Pitts, Jr.
Location: Tallahassee, Florida.
Costs: Conference costs range from $75–$85.

Skyline Writers Conference

P.O. Box 33343
North Royalton, OH 44133
www.skylinewriters.com

This annual one-day conference offers workshops, lectures, manuscript critiques, readings, and keynote speeches from a wide range of writing professionals. It offers programs specifically aimed at helping children's writers hone their skills.

Participation is limited to 75 participants. Early registration is recommended.
Date: October.
Subjects: Workshops from the 2005 conference included "Inside the World of Publishing," "Writing with a Job to Do," "Songwriting," and "Humorous Grammar Review."

Speakers: Speakers from the 2005 conference included Clinton Friedley, John Ettorre, and Anne E. Dechant.
Location: North Royalton, Ohio.
Costs: $55 for members; $70 for non-members; $40 for students; and $55 for half day.

Southern California Writers' Conference

SCWC
#54
1010 University Avenue
San Diego, CA 92103
www.writersconference.com

This two-day conference focuses on sharpening your writing skills as well as the exploring of ideas, technology, and the future of creative writing. Held at two locations in California, it addresses the challenges of being a writer in today's world. Visit the website for updated conference information.
Date: February 17–20, 2006.
Subjects: 2006 workshop topics include fiction, nonfiction, business and alternative, film, and television writing.
Speakers: 2005 speakers included Tod Goldberg, Michael Steven Gregory, and Nicholas Berry.
Location: San Diego and Los Angeles, California.
Costs: $365.

Steamboat Writers Group

P.O. Box 774284
Steamboat Springs, CO 80477
www.steamboatwriters.com

Celebrating its twenty-fourth year, this one-day conference aims to provide writers with a sharp focus and productive activities within a limited time frame. The conference format emphasizes active participation within a relaxed and friendly atmosphere that is conducive to networking. The number of participants is limited to ensure personal interaction, so early registration is recommended. Visit the website or send an SASE for complete 2006 workshop itinerary and conference information.
Date: TBA.
Subjects: 2005 workshops included "Anatomy of an Article," "Nature and Fiction," and "Elements of the Short Story."
Speakers: 2005 keynote speakers included Sally Stich, Kent Nelson, and Susan deWardt.
Location: Steamboat, Colorado.
Costs: Visit the website for 2006 conference fees.

Willamette Writers Conference

9045 SW Barbur Boulevard #5A
Portland, OR 97219
www.willamettewriters.com

Sponsored by a non-profit writing group, this three-day event promises a diverse and inspirational conference led by accomplished authors and well-known professionals in the field. It offers keynote speakers and professional guidance, as well as networking and opportunities to pitch your ideas to editors and agents.
Date: August 4–6, 2006.

Subjects: 2005 workshops included "Crafting the Mystery," "Unblocked, Uninhibited, Unleashed," and "Plot Points."
Speakers: 2005 faculty included Lee Lofland, Kathi Macias, D. P. Lyle, and Chris Baty.
Location: Portland, Oregon.
Costs: Check website for 2006 conference fees.

Write on the Sound Writers' Conference

Frances Chapin, Coordinator
700 Main Street
Edmonds, WA 98020
www.ci.edmonds.wa.us/artscommission/wots.stm

This annual two-day conference is sponsored by the Edmonds Arts Commission and attracts regional, national, and international participants. It features over 30 presenters, numerous book signings, one-on-one manuscript critiques, and a variety of evening activities. Participation is limited to 200 and fills quickly, so early registration is recommended.
Date: October.
Subjects: 2005 workshops included "Adding Sensory Detail," "Creating Suspense," "Getting out of the Slush Pile," and "Non-Published? Try Children's Nonfiction."
Speakers: 2005 conference speakers included Greg Bear, Marcia Woodard, Holly Hughes, and Diana Abu-Jaber.
Location: Edmonds, Washington.
Costs: Check website for 2006 conference fees.

The Writers' Institute Annual Conference

Room 621
610 Langdon Street
Madison, WI 53703
www.dcs.wisc.edu/lsa/writing/awi

Offering an opportunity for fiction and nonfiction writers to gather in a relaxed and comfortable atmosphere, this annual conference provides inspiration and informative lectures on the latest techniques of writing and marketing. It also features book sales, take-home materials, and appointments with a copyright attorney.
Date: July.
Subjects: 2005 conference workshops included "First Children's Book," "So You Want to Freelance?" "Sell to Parenting Magazines," and "Creating a Fiction Niche."
Speakers: 2005 keynote speakers included Margaret George.
Location: Madison, Wisconsin.
Costs: $205 for early registration; $225 for late registration.

Conferences with Sessions on Writing for Children— Religious Writing Conferences

East Texas Christian Writers Conference

East Texas Baptist University
1209 North Grove Street
Marshall, TX 75670
www.etbu.edu

This one-day conference promotes Christian writing for children through lectures and workshops that develop the skills and stimulate the ideas of novice and established writers. Through networking, it offers potential publishing and writing opportunities.
Date: June.
Subjects: Workshops from the 2005 conference included "Writing for Children," "Writing and Directing Plays," "Inspirational Writing," and "What Editors Want."
Speakers: Past speakers included Carolyn Pedison, Marv Knox, Faye Field, and Marcia Preston.
Location: Marshall, Texas.
Costs: Conference fees range from $40–$50.

Florida Christian Writers Conference

2344 Armour Court
Titusville, FL 32780
www.flwriters.org

Bringing together Christian writers, editors, and agents from around the country, this annual conference offers workshops, classes, networking opportunities, and one-on-one manuscript evaluations. It also provides an opportunity to sell your books in the bookstore on consignment and "after hours" special interest group meetings.
Date: Match 2–5, 2006.
Subjects: 2005 topics included young adult short stories, children's books, devotional novels, articles, fiction, and nonfiction.
Speakers: Past speakers included Stephen Bly, Jack Taylor, Jamie Buckingham, Len LeSourd, Gloria Gaither, and Dr. Calvin Miller.
Location: Bradenton, Florida.
Costs: Check website for 2006 conference costs.

Glorieta Christian Writers Conference

P.O. Box 66810
Albuquerque, NM 87193
www.classservices.com

In its eighth year, this inspirational conference for Christian writers features devotionals, music, and panel discussions on a wide range of writing topics. Morning and evening activities and workshops are featured, along with lectures targeting writing for children and young adults.
Date: October.
Subjects: 2005 conference workshops included "Get Published

Now," "How to Write for Kids When You Don't Have Any," "Ten Tidbits to Get You Started in Children's Writing," and "Picture Books Cover."

Speakers: Speakers from the 2005 conference included Janet Bly, Sharon Elliot, Gwen Ellis, Judy Gann, and Diane Gardner.
Location: Glorieta, New Mexico.
Costs: $130–$390.

Jewish Children's Book Writers' Conference

92nd Street Y
1395 Lexington Avenue
New York, NY 10128
www.92y.org

This all-day conference is sponsored by the 92nd Street Buttenwieser Library and the Jewish Book Council and features presentations from children's authors, illustrators, and editors. Its mission is to provide valuable information and an opportunity to network with experts in the field of Jewish children's literature.
Date: November.
Subjects: Sample lectures from the 2005 conference included "Finding Ideas in Chicken Coops and Other Places," "Publishing Jewish Children's Books," and "Taking Your Books to the Market."
Speakers: Past speakers included Michelle Edwards, Regina Griffin, Jodi Kreitzman, Michael J. Miller, and Rebecca Sherman.
Location: New York, New York.
Costs: Early registration, $80; late

registration, $95 (includes meals).

Mount Hermon Christian Writers' Conference

P.O. Box 413
Mount Hermon, CA 95041
www.mounthermon.org

An intensive four-day event, this annual Christian writing conference is celebrating its 37th year. Faculty and participants from around the world gather for classes, intensives, and workshops on all aspects of writing and to share their message alongside Jesus' teachings. It seeks to provide opportunities for inspiration, education, and spiritual renewal.
Date: April 7–11, 2006.
Subjects: 2005 workshops included "Kid's Stuff," "From the Ground Up," "Self Publishing and Marketing," "Spiritual Writer," and "Teen Track."
Speakers: Speakers from the 2005 event included Liz Curtis Higgs, Dave Talbott, and Mary Rice Hopkins.
Location: Mount Hermon, California.
Costs: Check website for 2006 conference costs.

Oregon Christian Writers Conference

1075 Willow Lake Road North
Salem, OR 97303
www.oregonchristianwriters.org

Designed to help participants learn and improve the craft of writing, this annual conference offers a time of learning and fellowship. Workshops, critique groups, and

lectures are part of its program.
Date: TBA.
Subjects: Past conference topics included creating fictional characters, writing for children and young adults, self publishing, and submitting book proposals.
Speakers: Past speakers have included Karen Kingsbury and Anne Shorey.
Location: TBA.
Costs: TBA.

St. Davids Christian Writers' Conference

87 Pines Road East
Hadley, PA 16130
www.stdavidswriters.com

This annual conference has been held since 1957 and offers one-day to five-day sessions. Participants will find separate programming tracks for beginners and professionals along with one-time workshops, five-day continuing workshops, one-on-one meetings with editors, tutorials, and critiques.
Date: April, June, October.
Subjects: 2005 workshops included "Insider Help to Getting Published," "The Writer As an Artist," "No Grown-ups Allowed," and "The Nitty Gritty of Getting Published."
Speakers: 2005 faculty included Melanie Rigney, Lin Johnson, Ethel Herr, Virelle Kidder, Paul Raymond Martin, and Evelyn Minshull.
Location: Beaver Falls, Pennsylvania.
Costs: $50–$300.

Book Publishing

Writers' Contests & Awards

Jane Addams Children's Book Award

Donna Barkman, Chairperson
Jane Addams Peace Association
777 United Nations Plaza
New York, NY 10017
www.janeaddamspeace.org

Solving problems non-violently, overcoming prejudice, and accepting responsibility for the future of humanity are some of the topics promoted by this contest. For nearly 50 years, the Jane Addams Children's Book Award has recognized outstanding picture books and longer books that promote peace, social justice, world community, and equality of the sexes.

Books targeting children ages preschool through fourteen are eligible. Send an SASE or visit the website for further information.

Deadline: December 31.

Representative winners: *Harvesting Hope: The Story of Caesar Chavez,* Kathleen Krull; *Out of Bounds: Seven Stories of Conflict and Hope,* Beverley Naidoo.

Announcements: Winner is announced in April.

Award: Winner receives an honorary certificate and cash award at a dinner in New York City.

Amazing Kids! Annual Essay Contest

PMB 485, 1158 26th Street
Santa Monica, CA 90403
www.amazing-kids.org

Following a specific theme, this annual essay contest is sponsored by the Internet publication, *Amazing Kids!* It is open to entries from children and young adults between the ages of 5 and 17.

Submissions should include author's name, address, and a parent or guardian's permission to enter. Prefers e-mail submissions to essays@amazing-kids.org. Accepts photocopies and computer printouts. Visit the website or send an SASE for theme list.

Deadline: August 15.

Representative winners: Sabahat Fatima, Jessica Kim, Pace Tyson, and Terrenique Kilgore.

Announcements: Winners are announced on the website 60 days after the deadline.

Award: Winners receive publication of their essays in the September issue of *Amazing Kids!*

American Book Cooperative Children's Picture Book Competition

11010 Hanning Lane
Houston, TX 77041-5006
www.americanbookcooperative.org

This contest, sponsored by the American Book Cooperative, recognizes books that represent the true voice of America and celebrate "Freedom of Speech." Finalists are chosen by judges and posted on the website where the winners are determined by a vote. It is particularly interested in hearing from novice authors. Visit the website for complete information.

Deadline: November.

Representative Winners: *The 12 Dog Days of Christmas in New York*, *No Pig's Brain Soup Please*, *Sunny the Star*, and *The Rainbow Kangaroo*.

Announcements: September.

Award: Winner receives a publishing contract, inclusion at the Author SchoolGigs website, and a national marketing campaign.

Arizona Author's Association Literary Contests

Toby Heathcotte, Chair
P.O. Box 87857
Phoenix, AZ 85080-7857
www.azauthors.com/contest.html

These annual contests are sponsored by the Arizona Author's Association and award both previously published and non-published work. Unpublished categories include short story, essay, article, true story, and novel. Previously published categories include children's literature, novels, nonfiction, and short story anthologies.

Entry fees range from $15 to $30 depending on category. Submit first 25 pages for novel entries. Accepts photocopies and computer printouts. Visit the website or call Toby Heathcotte at 623-847-9343 for complete details.

Deadline: July 1.

Representative winners: *The Ice Floe*, J. Tracksler; *Will Work for Food or $*, Bruce Moody; *More Than Petticoats*, Wynne Brown; and *Blaze of the Great Cliff*, Mark Fidler.

Announcements: Winners are announced at an awards banquet in November.

Award: First-place winners in each category receive a cash prize of $100 and publication in *Arizona Literary Magazine*.

ASPCA Henry Bergh Young Adult Book Award

ASPCA Education Department
424 East 92nd Street
New York, NY 10128-6804
www.aspca.org/bookaward

This annual award recognizes an author of young adult literature who contributes to the ethics of respect and compassion for all creatures through empathic and responsible behavior. It is sponsored by the American Society for the Prevention of Cruelty to Animals.

Books should be written for young adults between the ages of 13 and 17 and include fiction, nonfiction, and collections of short stories, essays, or poetry by one author. Eligible entries must be books written in English that were published in the U.S. or Canada the year preceding the announcement of the award. Check the website or send an SASE for complete details.
Deadline: October 31.
Announcements: Winner is announced in December.
Award: Winners receive the Henry Bergh Young Adult award.

AuthorMania.com Writing Contests

Cindy Thomas
c/o AuthorMania.com Contest
1210 County Road 707
Buna, TX 77612
www.authormania.com

AuthorMania.com awards an outstanding poem and work of fiction each year written by authors residing in the U.S. Entries must be written in English and be previously unpublished. There are no word limits for poems and all topics are considered with the exception of violence, hate, racism, and adult themes. Fictional works must not exceed 5,000 words. Multiple entries are accepted. Visit the website for complete guidelines.

Deadline: March 31.
Representative winners: "I Am the Mountain," Shiila Safer; "Time Heals all Wounds," Tara Wiltz.
Announcements: Winners are announced May 31.
Award: Winners of the poetry contest receive a cash prize of $400; winners of the fiction contest receive a cash award of $1,000.

AWA Contests

Appalachian Writers Association
Attn. Kim Holloway
Department of English
Bristol, TN 37620
www.king.edu/awa/awa_contests.htm

This annual contest is open to members of the Appalachian Writers Association and presents awards in several categories including poetry, essay, short story, and playwriting. Only previously unpublished material will be considered.

No entry fee. Word lengths vary for each category. Submit 2 copies of each entry. Fiction and prose entries must be typed double-spaced. Manuscripts will not be returned. Accepts photocopies and computer printouts. Visit website or send an SASE for complete category list and further guidelines.
Deadline: June 8.
Representative winners:
"Knoxville: Summer, 2003," Judy Loest; "Story Suite," David Lee Kirkland; "Red, White, and Jesus," Janice Willis Barnett; "A Long Summer," Dan Leonard.
Announcements: Winners are announced in the fall.

Award: First-place winners in each category receive a cash prize of $100. Second- and third-place winners receive cash awards of $50 and $25, respectively.

Baker's Plays High School Playwriting Contest

Baker's Plays
P.O. Box 699222
Quincy, MA 02269-9222
www.bakersplays.com

This contest recognizes outstanding plays by high school students for high school students and looks to promote playwriting in young people.

It maintains an open submission policy and accepts full-length plays, one-act plays, theater texts, musicals, and collections of scenes and monologues. Plays that have been production tested are preferred. All entries must be accompanied by the signature of a sponsoring English or drama teacher. It is recommended that all entries have a public reading or production prior to submission. Accepts photocopies and computer printouts. Include an SASE for return of manuscript. Visit the website or send an SASE for complete guidelines.

Deadline: January 30.
Announcements: Winners are announced in May.
Award: First-place winner's play is produced. Cash prizes ranging from $100 to $500 are awarded.

John and Patricia Beatty Award

California Library Association
Suite 200
717 20th Street
Sacramento, CA 95814
www.cla-net.org

Sponsored by the California Library Association, this annual award honors a book for children or young adults that fosters awareness of California and its people. The winner is selected by a group of librarians during the year preceding the contest.

Include a cover letter with author's name, address, telephone number, and e-mail address with each entry.
Deadline: February 10.
Representative winner: *Al Capone Does My Shirts*, Gennifer Choldenko.
Announcements: Winners are announced at the California Library Association's annual conference in November.
Award: Winner receives a cash award of $500 and an engraved plaque.

Geoffrey Bilson Award for Historical Fiction

Canadian Children's Book Centre
Suite 101, Lower Level
40 Orchard View Boulevard
Toronto, Ontario M4R 1B9
Canada
www.bookcentre.ca

In memory of Geoffrey Bilson, a respected historian and author, this annual award recognizes excellence in historical fiction for young adults. Entries must be published the year preceding the contest and be written by a Canadian author.

Authors must submit 6 copies of each entry and winners will be chosen by a jury appointed by the Canadian Children's Book Centre.
Deadline: January 9.
Representative winner: *Boy O' Boy*, Brian Doyle.
Announcements: Winner is notified in June.
Award: Winner receives a cash award of $1,000 and a certificate.

The Irma Simonton Black and James H. Black Award for Excellence in Children's Literature

Linda Greengrass
610 West 112th Street
New York, NY 10025
http://streetcat.bankstreet.edu

This award goes to an outstanding children's book, where illustrations and text enhance and compliment each other.

A panel of authors, librarians, and educators choose 20 to 25 books that they consider candidates for the award. Copies are then sent to the Bank Street School for Children where students examine them for four weeks before choosing the winner.
Deadline: December 15.
Representative winner: *Knuffle Bunny, A Cautionary Tale*, Mo Willems.

Announcements: Winners are announced in May at a breakfast ceremony in New York City.
Award: A scroll with the recipient's name and a gold seal designed by Maurice Sendak will be given to the winning author and illustrator.

Waldo M. and Grace C. Bonderman Youth Theatre Playwriting Competition

Dorothy Webb, Contest Chair
1114 Red Oak Drive
Avon, IN 46123
www.indianarep.com/Bonderman

The purpose of this contest is to encourage the creation of theatrical productions for young people. It is open to all writers who are able to be involved in the developmental process beginning in April.

Only uncommissioned plays are eligible. Musicals are not accepted. Plays for grades 1 through 3 should not exceed 30 minutes; grades 3 and up must be at least 45 minutes in length. Submit 3 copies of entry along with a synopsis and cast list. The author's name should not appear on the manuscript. Enclose an SASE for returned manuscripts.
Deadline: October 6.
Representative winners: "La Ofrenda," José Cassas; "The Realm," Sarah Meyers; "Pennies in My Hand," Deni Krueger; "Can't Believe It," R. N. Sandberg.
Announcements: Winners are notified in January.
Award: The top four winners receive a cash award of $1,000 and a

staged reading of their play.

The Boston Globe-Horn Book Awards

Suite 200
56 Roland Street
Boston, MA 02129
www.hbook.com

Since 1967, these prestigious awards have recognized excellence in children's and young adult literature. Books published in the U.S. and submitted by publishers are eligible.

Awards are chosen in the genres of fiction, nonfiction, picture book, and poetry by a panel of judges who are appointed by the editor of *Horn Book*. One copy should be sent to each of the three judges. Visit the website or send an SASE for further information.

Deadline: May 6.
Representative winners: *Traction Man Is Here!*, Mini Grey; *The Schwa Was Here*, Neal Shusterman; *The Race to Save the Lord God Bird*, Phillip Hoose.
Announcements: Winners are announced in May.
Award: Winners in each category receive a cash award of $500 and an engraved bowl. Honor recipients receive an engraved plaque.

Ann Connor Brimer Award

P.O. Box 36036
Halifax, Nova Scotia B3J 3S9
Canada
www.nsla.ns.ca/

Presented by the Nova Scotia Library Association, this annual award honors authors who have made an outstanding contribution to children's literature.

Authors who have published a book for young readers up to the age of 15 and reside in Atlantic Canada are eligible. Works of fiction and nonfiction that have been published during the year preceding the contest are considered.

Deadline: April 30.
Representative winners: *Pomiuk, Prince of the North*, Alice Walsh; *There You Are*, Joanne Taylor; *Rainy Days with Bear*, Maureen Hull.
Announcements: Winner is announced in May at an awards ceremony.
Award: Winner receives a cash award of $1,000.

Marilyn Brown Novel Award

Association for Mormon Letters
125 Hobble Creek Canyon
Springville, UT 84663
www.aml-online.org/awards/mbna.html

This award is sponsored by the Association for Mormon Letters and honors the author of the best unpublished novel. The contest is held every two years.

No entry fee. Accepts photocopies and computer printouts. Author's name should not appear on manuscript. Include cover letter with author's name, address, and telephone number. Limit one entry per competition. Send an SASE or check the website for complete competition guidelines.

Deadline: July 1.
Representative winners: *My Mom's a Mortician*, Patricia Wiles; *Hunchback*, Randall Wright; *Enna Burning*, Shannon Hale.
Announcements: Winners are notified by mail.
Award: Winner receives a cash award of $1,000.

ByLine Magazine Contests
ByLine Magazine
P.O. Box 5240
Edmond, OK 73083-5240
www.bylinemag.com/contests.asp

These contests are sponsored by *ByLine Magazine* and are open to all writers. By providing a forum for competition, *ByLine* hopes to motivate writers to produce their best work.

Awards are presented in multiple categories including fiction, poetry, nonfiction, creative nonfiction, humor, memoir, and journalism. Entry fees and word lengths vary. Check website for complete category list and guidelines.
Deadline: Deadlines vary by category.
Announcements: Winners are announced in *ByLine Magazine*.
Award: Winners receive cash awards ranging from $10–$70.

Randolph Caldecott Medal
American Library Association
50 East Huron
Chicago, IL 60611
www.ala.org/alsc/caldecott.html

Presented by the Association for Library Service to Children, this prestigious medal is awarded annually to the artist of the most distinguished American children's book.

Open to citizens of the U.S., all illustrations must be original work that has been published during the year preceding the award. Several honor books are also recognized.
Deadline: December 31.
Representative winner: *Kitten's First Full Moon*, Kevin Henkes.
Announcements: Winner is announced at the ALA Midwinter Meeting.
Award: The winner is presented with the Caldecott Medal at an awards banquet.

California Book Awards
The Commonwealth Club of
 California
595 Market Street
San Francisco, CA 94105
http://commonwealthclub.org

Honoring the exceptional literary merit of California authors, these awards are presented annually. Authors must have been legal residents of California at the time the manuscript was accepted for publication. Awards are presented in several categories including fiction or nonfiction for children up to the age of 10; fiction or nonfiction for children ages 11 to 16; and poetry. Submit 5 copies of entry.
Deadline: December 31.
Representative winners: *Evidence of Things Unseen*, Marianne Wiggins; *River of Shadows: Eadweard*

Muybridge and the Technological Wild West, Rebecca Solnit.
Announcements: Winners are announced in May.
Award: One gold medal winner receives a cash award of $2,000; two silver medal winners receive a cash award of $300.

Canadian Library Association's Book of the Year for Children Award

Coordinator of Children's and Young
  Adult Services
North Vancouver District Public
  Library
North Vancouver, BC V7J 1S1
Canada
www.cla.ca

This annual award is sponsored by the National Book Service and honors the most outstanding children's book published in the year preceding the contest.

The Canadian Library Association seeks nominations of works of creative writing for children, written by a Canadian author and published in Canada. Eligible categories are fiction, poetry, and re-tellings of traditional literature regardless of publication format.
Deadline: December 31.
Representative winners: *Last Chance Bay,* Anne Laurel Carter; *Boy O' Boy*, Brian Doyle.
Announcements: Winner is announced in June.
Award: Winner is presented with a leather-bound copy of the book and a cash award of $750.

Canadian Writer's Journal Short Fiction Contest

Box 1178
New Liskeard, Ontario P0J 1P0
Canada
www.cwj.ca

Sponsored by *Canadian Writer's Journal*, this annual contest accepts original, unpublished short stories in any genre. Stories should not exceed 1,200 words.

Entry fee, $5. Multiple entries are accepted. Accepts photocopies and computer printouts. Author's name should not appear on manuscript. Include a cover sheet with author's name, address, and title of entry. Manuscripts will not be returned. Send an SASE or visit the website for further information.
Deadline: March and September.
Representative winners: "Too Much to Say," Deb Mowat; "Whatever You Want," Jim Spicer; and "Colour Copy," Florence McKie.
Award: First-place winners receive a cash award of $100. Second- and third-place winners receive cash prizes of $50 and $25, respectively. All winning entries are published in *Canadian Writer's Journal*.

CAPA Competition

Connecticut Authors and Publishers
  Association
223 Buckingham Street
Oakville, CT 06779
www.aboutcapa.com

This annual competition is open to Connecticut residents and accepts entries of children's short story (to 2,000 words), adult short story (to 2,000 words), personal essay (to 1,500 words), and poetry (to 30 lines).

Include an SASE for written confirmation that your entry was received. Multiple entries are accepted. Submit 4 copies of each entry. Manuscripts are not returned. **Deadline:** May 31.
Representative winners: *In a Pickle*, Maureen Annette Morris; *The Falcon*, Alvin Laster; *Dreaming and Spider Webs*, Windy McGlinsky; *Paper Necklace*, Kristine L. Girardin.
Announcements: Winners are announced at the October CAPA meeting.
Award: Winners receive a cash award of $100; second-place winners receive a cash prize of $50. Winning entries will be published in a special issue of *The Authority*.

Rebecca Caudill Young Readers' Book Award

P.O. Box 6536
Naperville, IL 60526
www.rebeccacaudill.org

Developed to encourage children and young adults to appreciate reading for personal satisfaction, the Rebecca Caudill Award honors outstanding literature for young people. It is sponsored by the Illinois School Library Media Association.

Books are nominated by children in grades four through eight. A list of 20 titles is sent to participating schools, where elementary and middle-school students read the books and vote in February.
Deadline: Tallied votes must be received by February 28.
Representative winners: *Hoot*, Carl Hiaasen; *Ruby Holler*, Sharon Creech; *House of the Scorpion*, Nancy Farmer.
Announcements: Winner is announced in March.
Award: First-place winner receives a cash prize of $500 and a plaque.

Children's Writer Contests

Children's Writer
93 Long Ridge Road
West Redding, CT 06896-1124
www.childrenswriter.com

Open to all writers, *Children's Writer* sponsors two contests each year in the areas of YA fiction, profile, pre-K nonfiction, humor, early reader mystery, YA personal experience, and middle-grade adventure. Only previously unpublished material is accepted.

No entry fee for subscribers; $10 for non-subscribers (includes an 8-month subscription) and multiple entries are accepted.
Deadline: February and October of each year.
Announcements: Winners are announced in the *Children's Writer* monthly newsletter.
Award: First-place winners receive publication in *Children's Writer* newsletter and a cash award of $500. Second place, $250; third-, fourth-, and fifth-place winners each receive a cash prize of $100.

Christopher Awards
The Christophers
12 East 48th Street
New York, NY 10017
www.christophers.org

These annual awards are presented in multiple categories including books for children and adults and feature films. They look to honor artistic vision that "affirms the highest values of the human spirit."

No entry fee. Only original titles published in the year preceding the contest are accepted. Send 4 copies of entry with press kit, press release, or catalogue copy.

Submissions are reviewed year round. Send an SASE or visit the website for further guidelines.
Deadline: November.
Representative winners: *Never Ever Shout in a Zoo*, Karma Wilson; *The Hungry Coat: A Tale from Turkey*, Demi; *Shredderman: Secret Identity*, Wendelin Van Draanen; *Thura's Diary: My Life in Wartime Iraq*, Thura Al-Windawi.
Announcements: Winners are announced in February.
Award: Winners are presented with bronze medallions.

CIPA National Writing Contest
Joan La Grone, Chairman
101 Crabapple Drive
Windsor, CO 80550
www.cipabooks.com

This annual contest is geared to mostly works of nonfiction and seeks to help writers gain experience in manuscript submission techniques, working to a deadline, and focusing on sales and marketability. It accepts entries in the categories of children's books, business, self-help, health, and cookbooks.

Entry fee, $35. Length of entry should not exceed 20 pages. Only original, unpublished material is accepted. Send 3 copies of each entry. All entries must include a cover letter that lists the title, category, author's name, and contact information. Visit website or send an SASE for complete submission guidelines.
Deadline: January 25.
Representative winners: *Palmistry 101*, Myrna Lou Goldbaum; *Oh Dear! What's in Your Ear?*, Elizabeth A. Rider; *The Monster Solution,* Sara Zimet.
Announcements: Winners are announced in the spring.
Award: First- through third-place winners in each category receive cash prizes ranging from $50 to $100. Winners also receive certificates.

CNW/FFWA Florida State Writing Competition
CNW/FFWA
P.O. Box A
North Stratford, NH 03590
www.writers-editors.com

Open to all writers, this annual contest awards outstanding works in the following categories: unpublished short story; previously published article or essay; unpublished children's story; and poetry.

Entry fees vary for each category but range from $3 to $25. Multiple entries are accepted under separate cover. Word count should not exceed 5,000 words. Do not staple manuscripts; use paper clips only.

Author's name should not appear on manuscript itself. Manuscripts will not be returned. Send an SASE or visit the website for further guidelines.

Deadline: March 15.

Representative winners: *Little Lessons*, Tina Twito; *A Gang of Meercats*, Denise Jordan; *The Stable Guests*, Jane B. Rawlings.

Announcements: Winners are announced by May 31.

Award: First- through third-place winners in each category receive cash prizes ranging from $50 to $100. Winners also receive honorary certificates.

Delacorte Dell Yearling Contest

Random House, Inc.
9th Floor
1745 Broadway
New York, NY 10019
www.randomhouse.com

Open to writers who have not yet published a contemporary or historical middle-grade novel set in North America, this annual competition is sponsored by Random House. The contest is open to writers living in the U.S. and Canada. Foreign-language manuscripts and translations are not eligible.

Entries should be between 96 and 160 pages and include a cover sheet listing author's name, address, phone number, and a brief plot summary. Accepts photocopies and computer printouts. Send an SASE or visit website for detailed guidelines.

Deadline: Manuscripts must be postmarked between April 1 and June 30.

Representative winners: *Prizefighter*, E. E. Charlton-Trujillo; *Some Kind of Pride,* Maria Testa.

Announcements: Winners are announced in the fall.

Award: Winner receives a book contract with $7,500 toward royalties and $1,500 in cash.

Delacorte Press Contest for a First Young Adult Novel

Random House, Inc.
9th Floor
1745 Broadway
New York, NY 10019
www.randomhouse.com

Awarding excellent young adult fiction for readers ages 12 to 18, this annual contest is open to English manuscripts by authors living in the U.S. and Canada. Eligible authors must not have published a young adult novel.

Entries should include a cover letter with author's name, address, telephone number, manuscript title, and brief synopsis. Manuscripts should be between 100 and 224 typewritten pages. Accepts photocopies and computer print-outs. Limit two entries per competition. Send SASE or visit the website for complete submission guidelines.

Deadline: Manuscripts must be postmarked between October 1 and December 31.

Representative winners: *Cal Cameron by Day, Spider-man by Night*, A. E. Cannon; *Squashed*, Joan Bauer; *Under the Mermaid Angel*, Martha Moore.

Announcements: Winners will be announced no later than April 30.

Award: Winners receive a book contract with $7,500 toward royalties and $1,500 cash prize.

Distinguished Achievement Awards

Suite 201
510 Heron Drive
Logan Township, NJ 08085
www.edpress.org

For 37 years, this award has honored quality and diversity among educational home and school materials. There are 64 contest categories including short story, nonfiction, and software for adults and children. Visit website for complete category list. All eligible submissions must have been published in the year preceding the contest.

Deadline: January.

Announcements: Winners are notified by mail in April.

Award: Winners are presented with a plaque at an awards banquet.

Margaret A. Edwards Award

Young Adult Library Services
  Association
50 East Huron
Chicago, IL 60611
www.ala.org/yalsa

This annual lifetime achievement award honors an outstanding author's contribution to young adult literature. It recognizes work that helps adolescents deal with relationships and their role in society.

Nominations are made by librarians and teenagers. Authors must be living at the time of nomination. All books must have been published in the U.S. no less than five years prior to the nomination.

Deadline: December 31.

Representative winner: *Weetzie Bat* books—*Weetzie Bat, Witch Baby, Cherokee Bat and the Goat Guys, Missing Angel Juan,* and *Baby Be-Bop,* Francesca Lia Block.

Announcements: Winner is announced in January during the American Library Association Midwinter Meeting.

Award: Winning author receives a cash award of $2,000.

Arthur Ellis Awards

Crime Writers of Canada
Box 113
3007 Kingston Road
Scarborough, Ontario M1M 1P1
Canada
www.crimewriterscanada.com

This annual competition for crime writers is sponsored by the

Crime Writers of Canada and awards several categories including best crime novel, best nonfiction (formerly best true crime), best first novel, best juvenile novel, best play, and best crime work in French.

All work must have been published in the year preceding the contest and be written by Canadian residents. Send an SASE or visit the website for details.
Deadline: January 31.
Representative winners: Howard Engel, Eric Wright, and Peter Robinson.
Announcements: Winners are announced in June at the annual awards dinner.
Award: Winners receive a hand-carved, wooden statue.

Empire State Award
Mendon Center Elementary School
110 Mendon Center Road
Pittsford, NY 14534
www.nyla.org

First presented in 1990, this award is sponsored by the Youth Services section of the New York Library Association. Open to all writers, it honors an author and illustrator of outstanding children's literature currently residing in New York State.

Send an SASE or visit the website for further information.
Deadline: November 30.
Representative winners: M. E. Kerr, Alice Provensen, Seymour Simon.
Announcements: Winner is announced in May.

Award: Winner is presented with an engraved medallion at the annual conference of the New York Library Association.

William Faulkner Creative Writing Competition
64 Pirate's Alley
New Orleans, LA 70116-3254
www.wordsandmusic.org

Sponsored by the Pirate's Alley Faulkner Society, a non-profit organization devoted to preserving the storytelling of the deep South, this contest awards prizes in seven divisions: novel; novella; novel-in-progress; short story; essay; poetry; and high school short story. Only original, unpublished work is accepted.

Entry fees range from $10–$35. Accepts photocopies and computer printouts. All submissions must include an entry form and cover letter including author's name, address, telephone number, category, and word count. Visit the website or send an SASE for a complete category list and entry form.
Deadline: April 30.
Representative winners: "The Grave Digger," Ron Magnuson Smith; "The Ice Garden," Moira Crone; "Jerusalem As a Second Language," Rochelle Distelheim.
Announcements: Finalists are announced in June; winners are announced in November.
Award: Winners in various categories receive cash awards ranging from $250–$7,500.

Shubert Fendrich Memorial Playwriting Competition

Pioneer Drama Service
P.O. Box 4267
Englewood, CO 80155-4267
www.pioneerdrama.com

In honor of the founder of Pioneer Drama Service, Shubert Fendrich, this annual contest is held to encourage the development of high-quality drama for educational and community theaters. It is open to writers who have not been published by Pioneer Drama Service. Any subject that is suitable for family viewing is accepted.

Entries should have a running time of 20–90 minutes. Include a cover letter with title, synopsis, cast list, proof of production, number of sets and scenes, and musical score or tape, if applicable. Accepts photocopies, computer printouts, disk submissions (text files or Microsoft Word) and e-mail submissions to editors@pioneerdrama.com.
Deadline: March 1.
Announcements: Winner is announced in June.
Award: Winner receives a contract for publication and a cash advance of $1,000.

Foster City International Writing Contest

Foster City Recreation Dept.
650 Shell Boulevard
Foster City, CA 94404
www.geocities.com/fostercity_writers

Open to all writers, this annual contest accepts original, unpublished entries in the categories of children's fiction; fiction; humor; poetry; and personal essay. Word lengths vary for each category.

Entry fee, $12. Multiple entries are accepted under separate cover. Accepts photocopies, computer printouts, and e-mail submissions to fostercity_writers@yahoo.com (RTF or Microsoft Word attachments). Send an SASE or visit the website for further information.
Deadline: December 17.
Representative winners: "Lost Language," Elizabeth Benton Appell; "Finding Monica," Yvette Irvin; "Orgy in Winter," Bruce Henderson; "Martin," Karen J. Stanton.
Announcements: Winners are notified in late January.
Award: First-place winners in each category receive a cash award of $100. Second-place winners receive a cash prize of $50. Several honorable mentions receive a ribbon.

H. E. Francis Award

Department of English
University of Alabama at Huntsville
Huntsville, AL 35899
www.uah.edu/colleges/liberal/english/whatnewcontest.html

Open to all writers, this annual contest is sponsored by the Ruth Hindman Foundation and the UAH English Department. It accepts previously unpublished work only.

Entry fee, $15. Author's name should not appear on manuscript. A cover letter should accompany all submissions with author's name,

address, and telephone number, title of work, and word count.
Deadline: December 31.
Representative winners: "At the Intersection of Heaven and Hell," Susi Klare; "Good Listener," Becky Hagenston.
Announcements: Winners are announced in March.
Award: First-place winner receives a cash award of $1,000.

Don Freeman Memorial Grant-In-Aid

Society of Children's Book Writers and Illustrators
8271 Beverly Boulevard
Los Angeles, CA 90048
www.scbwi.org

The Don Freeman Memorial Grant-In-Aid was established by the Society of Children's Book Writers and Illustrators to help writers further their training and work in the picture book genre.

The competition is open to full and associate members of the SCBWI who intend to make children's picture books their primary contribution to children's literature. Updated information is available at the website or with an SASE.
Deadline: Entries must be postmarked between February 1 and March 1.
Representative winners: Angela Cerrito, Emily M. Jiang.
Announcements: Grant winners are announced in August.
Award: Winner receives a cash award of $1,500. One runner-up

grant of $500 will also be awarded.

Friends of the Library Writing Contest

130 North Franklin Street
Decatur, IL 62523
www.decatur.lib.il.us

Previously unpublished and published work is accepted for this annual competition. Sponsored by the Friends of the Decatur Library, several categories are awarded including essay (to 2,000 words); fiction and juvenile fiction (to 3,000 words); and rhymed and unrhymed poetry (to 40 lines). Author's name should not appear on manuscript. Include a cover sheet with author's name, telephone number, and title of entry.

Entry fee, $3; limit 5 entries per person. Visit the website or send an SASE for further information.
Deadline: September 25.
Representative winners: "Mike," Mary Chandler; "The Desert Detective," Guy Belleranti.
Announcements: Winners are announced in December.
Award: First-place winners in each category receive a cash award of $50. Second- and third-place winners receive cash awards of $30 and $20, respectively.

Frontiers in Writing Contest

Panhandle Professional Writers
P.O. Box 19303
Amarillo, TX 79114
http://panhandleprowriter.org/Frontiers_in_Writing.htm

This annual competition is open to all writers and presents awards in several categories including juvenile/young adult novel; juvenile/young adult short story; historical novel; and screenplay. Only original, unpublished material is eligible.

Entry fees range from $10–$20. Accepts photocopies and computer printouts. Author's name must not appear on manuscript. Each entry must include an entry form with author's name, address, and telephone number. Check the website or send SASE for complete category list and word limits.

Deadline: March 1.

Award: The first-place entry judged "Best of Show" receives a cash award of $200. First-place winners in each category receive a cash award of $75. Second- and third-place winners in each category receive cash prizes ranging from $25–$50.

Paul Gillette Writing Contest

c/o Pikes Peak Writers
4164 Austin Bluffs Pkwy #246
Colorado Springs, CO 80918
www.ppwc.net

This annual contest looks to reward the work of emerging writers of various genres, including fiction, nonfiction, and children's and young adult literature. Entrants must certify that the submitted work has not been published prior to the contest. Multiple entries in more than one category are accepted when submitted separately.

Entry fee, $25. Include an SASE for return of manuscript. Author's name should not appear on manuscript or synopsis. Send an SASE or visit the website for complete guidelines.

Deadline: November 1.

Representative winners: *Zeke in Command*, Candace Paugh; *No Place Like Home*, Pamela Mingle.

Announcements: Winners are announced at the Pikes Peak Writers Conference in April.

Award: Winner receives a refund of conference fee, or cash prize of $100. Second- and third-place winners receive $50 and $25, respectively.

Danuta Gleed Literary Award

The Writers' Union of Canada
Suite 200
90 Richmond Street East
Toronto, Ontario M5C 1P1
Canada
www.writersunion.ca

The Writers' Union of Canada presents this award to foster writing in Canada and to "promote the rights, freedoms, and economic well being of all writers." Each year it presents an award for the best collection of short fiction by a Canadian author. Entries must have been published in the year preceding the contest. Submit four copies of entry. Visit the website or send an SASE for guidelines.

Deadline: January 31.

Representative winners: *Natasha and Other Stories*, David Bezmozgis; *So Beautiful*, Ramona Dearing; *Eyehill*, Kelly Cooper; *Off Centre*, Caroline Shepard.
Announcements: Winners are announced on Canada Day, April 23.
Award: First-place winner receives a cash award of $10,000. Second- and third-place winners receive a cash prize of $500.

The Golden Kite Awards
SCBWI Golden Kite Coordinator
8271 Beverly Boulevard
Los Angeles, CA 90048
www.scbwi.org

These awards are presented to members of the Society of Children's Book Writers and Illustrators for the most outstanding children's books published the year preceding the contest. The awards are presented in the categories of fiction, nonfiction, picture book text, and picture book illustration.

Publishers should submit four copies of each entry. Visit the website or send an SASE for further information.
Deadline: December 15.
Representative winners: *Bucking the Sarge*, Christopher Paul Curtis; *The Gift Moves*, Steve Lyon; *Apples to Oregon*, Deborah Hopkinson.
Announcements: Winners will be notified by March 1.
Award: Winners in each category are presented with Golden Kite Statuettes. Plaques are presented to honorable mentions.

Gold Medallion Book Awards
Evangelical Christian Publishers Association
Suite 101, 4816 South Ash Avenue
Tempe, AZ 85282
www.ecpa.org

Honoring excellence in evangelical Christian literature, these awards are presented in several categories including fiction, nonfiction, preschool, and biography/autobiography. Books must be submitted by publishers.

Entry fee, $125 per title for ECPA members; $275 for nonmembers. Send an SASE or visit the website for guidelines and a complete list of categories.
Deadline: December.
Representative winner: *Martin Luther, A Man Who Changed the World*, Paul L. Maier.
Announcements: Winners are announced at the Gold Medallion Book Awards Banquet in the spring.
Award: Plaques are awarded to the winner in each category.

Governor General's Literary Awards
The Canada Council for the Arts
Writing and Publishing Section
P.O. Box 1047
350 Albert Street
Ottawa, Ontario K1P 5V8
Canada
www.canadacouncil.ca

This annual award is presented to the most outstanding English-language book and French-language book in the categories of fiction, literary nonfiction, poetry, drama, children's literature (text), children's literature (illustration), and work of translation from French to English. Entries must be foreign or first Canadian edition trade books written, translated, or illustrated by Canadian citizens or permanent residents of Canada. For a work of translation, the original manuscript must be written in French by a Canadian author. Books with more than one author/illustrator are not eligible. Send an SASE or visit the website for further information.

Deadline: April.

Representative winners: *Airborn*, Kenneth Oppel; *Jabberwocky*, Stéphane Jorisch.

Announcements: Finalists are announced in October; winners are announced in November.

Award: The winner in each category receives a cash award of $15,000 and a specially bound copy of their book.

Lorian Hemingway Short Story Competition

P.O. Box 993
Key West, FL 33041
www.shortstorycompetition.com

This competition was founded in 1981 to promote the work of writers who have not yet reached major-market success. The annual competition is open to writers of short fiction whose work has not been published in a nationally distributed publication with a distribution that exceeds 5,000.

Original, unpublished fiction of 3,000 words or less is eligible. There are no restrictions on theme, but only entries of fiction will be considered. Entry fee, $10 for entries received by May 1, 2005; $15 for those postmarked between May 1 and May 15. Accepts photocopies and computer printouts. E-mail submissions are not accepted. Visit the website or send an SASE for complete guidelines.

Deadline: May 15.

Representative winners: *The Chemical Nature of Things*, Naomi Benaron; *Sushi's Armada/Kevin's Typewriter Too*, Rich Savastio; *Five Frames*, Lana Kyle.

Announcements: Winners are announced in July in Key West, Florida.

Award: First-place winner receives a cash award of $1,000. Second- and third-place winners each receive cash awards of $500.

Highlights for Children Fiction Contest

803 Church Street
Honesdale, PA 18431
www.highlights.com

This annual contest, open to all writers, follows a different theme each year. The 2006 theme is "stories that explore the true spirit of holiday celebrations."

No entry fee. Writers over the age of sixteen are eligible. Stories may not exceed 800 words; stories for beginning readers should not exceed 500 words. Indicate word count in upper right hand corner of first page. No crime, violence, or derogatory humor is accepted. Include an SASE for return of manuscript.

Deadline: February 28.

Representative winners: *Stinky Treasure*, Jacqueline Adams; *Fly on the Windshield*, Angela L. Fox; *Grandma's Purse*, Janice L. Tingum.

Announcements: Competition is announced in September; winners are announced in June.

Award: Winning entries are published in *Highlights for Children* and three cash prizes of $1,000 are awarded.

Insight Writing Contest

Insight Magazine
55 West Oak Ridge Drive
Hagerstown, MD 21740-7390
www.insightmagazine.org

This annual contest, sponsored by *Insight Magazine*, awards prizes for works with a strong spiritual message. It offers prizes in several categories including general short story, student short story, and student poetry.

Entrants in the student categories must be under the age of 22. Only previously unpublished work is accepted. The use of biblical text in entries is encouraged, but not required.

No entry fee. Entries should not exceed 7 typed pages for short stories and 1 page for poetry. Multiple entries are accepted. Author's name should not appear on manuscript. Include a cover sheet with author's name, address, telephone number, and entry title. Send an SASE or visit website for further information.

Deadline: June 1.

Announcements: Winners are announced in *Insight Magazine*.

Award: First- through third-place winners receive cash prizes ranging from $50–$250.

IRA Children's Book Awards

International Reading Association
Mary Cash
IRA Headquarters
800 Barksdale Road
Newark, DE 19714-8139
www.reading.org

This contest is sponsored by the International Reading Association and awards an author's first or second published book for children or young adults between the ages of preschool to seventeen. Fiction and nonfiction work intended for an audience of primary, intermediate, and young adults is considered. Books published during the year preceding the contest are eligible for this competition.

Works entered by author or publisher are accepted. Entries should encourage young people to read, and they should be free of racism and sexism. Guidelines and official application form is available with an SASE or at the website.

Deadline: November 1.

Representative winners: *Miss Bridie Chose a Shovel*, Leslie

Conner; *Eliza and the Dragonfly*, Susie Caldwell Rinehart.
Announcements: Winners are announced in January.
Award: Winners in each category receive a cash award of $500.

Barbara Karlin Grant

Society of Children's Book Writers
and Illustrators
8271 Beverly Boulevard
Los Angeles, CA 90048
www.scbwi.org

With the goal of recognizing and encouraging the work of aspiring picture book writers, this grant is awarded to members of SCBWI who have not yet published a picture book. Unpublished picture book manuscripts of fiction, nonfiction, or re-tellings of fairy tales, folktales, or legends are eligible. Length should not exceed 8 pages.

No entry fee. New applications and procedures are posted October 1 of each year. Instructions and complete guidelines accompany each application form. Visit the website for further information.
Deadline: Completed applications are accepted between February 15 and March 15.
Representative winners: Jerry Miller and Susan Anger.
Announcements: Winners are announced October 1.
Award: Winners receive a cash grant of $1,500. Runners-up receive cash grants of $500.

Coretta Scott King Award

American Library Association
50 East Huron Street
Chicago, IL 60611-2795
www.ala.org

This annual award is named after the widow of Dr. Martin Luther King, Jr., and recognizes distinguished literature written by African American authors whose work promotes an understanding of the "American Dream."

Send 3 copies of each entry. Visit the website or send an SASE for complete information.
Deadline: December 1.
Representative winners: *Remember: The Journey to School Integration*, Toni Morrison; *Ellington Was Not a Street*, Kadir Nelson.
Award: Winner receives a framed citation, an honorarium, and a set of Encyclopedia Brittanica, or World Book Encyclopedia.

Magazine Merit Awards

SCBWI
8271 Beverly Boulevard
Los Angeles, CA 90048
www.scbwi.org

This award is presented to members of SCBWI and recognizes outstanding magazine material published during the year of the contest. It seeks to honor excellence in writing and illustration that appeals to the interests of today's young readers. Categories include fiction, nonfiction, illustration, and poetry.

No entry fee. Submit 4 copies of the published work, showing proof of publication date. Include 4 cover sheets with member's name, address, telephone number, entry title, category, name of publication, and date of issue.
Deadline: December 15.
Announcements: Winners are announced in April.
Award: Winners in each category receive a plaque. Honor certificates are also awarded.

Maryland Writers' Association Novel Contest

P.O. Box 142
Annapolis, MD 21404
www.marylandwriters.org

This annual contest is sponsored by the Maryland Writers' Association in the interest of promoting the art, business, and craft of writing. Open to all writers, the competition accepts novel-length fiction in the categories of horror, fantasy, mystery, science fiction, romance, and historical fiction. Submissions should be a minimum of 50,000 words. All entries will receive constructive feedback.

Entry fee, $35. Accepts photocopies and computer printouts. Visit the website or send an SASE for complete contest guidelines.
Deadline: March 21.
Representative winners: *Sound of Silence,* Theresa Rizzo; *Scars on the Face of God*, Christopher G. Bauer; and *Silent Echoes,* Theresa Rizzo.

Announcements: Winners are announced in June.
Award: The overall contest winner receives a cash prize of $100. First-place winners in each category receive a cash prize of $50.

Mid-List Press First Series Award for the Novel

4324 12th Avenue South
Minneapolis, MN 55407-3218
www.midlist.org

Sponsored by Mid-List Press, this annual contest is open to all writers who have not yet published a novel. Entries must be at least 50,000 words.

Entry fee, $30. Limit one entry per competition. Accepts photocopies and computer printouts. Include an SASE for winners' list. Visit the website or send an SASE for complete details.
Deadline: Entries are accepted between October 1 and February 1.
Representative winner: *Escape: A Novel*, Dan Marshall.
Award: Winner receives publication by Mid-List Press and an advance against royalties.

Mythopoeic Society

Mythopoeic Society
P.O. Box 320486
San Francisco, CA 94132-0486
www.mythsoc.org

This annual contest honors a distinguished work of fantasy. Picture books for beginning readers to novels for young adults are considered. Books or collections by a single author, published in the year preceding the contest, are eligible.

The Mythopoeic Society nominates finalists and chooses winners. Send an SASE or visit the website for complete information and competition guidelines.

Deadline: February 28.

Representative winners: Arthur Trilogy, *The Seeing Stone; At the Crossing Places*; *King of the Middle March*, Kevin Crossley-Holland; *Sea of Trolls*, Nancy Farmer; *A Hat Full of Sky*, Terry Pratchett.

Announcements: 2005 announcements were made at the Tolkien conference in Birmingham, England.

Awards: Winners are presented with a statuette.

National Book Award for Young People's Literature

National Book Foundation
Suite 709
95 Madison Avenue
New York, NY 10016
www.nationalbook.org

In honor of excellence in children's literature, the National Book Foundation sponsors this annual competition. Fiction, nonfiction, and collections of single-author short stories and essays are eligible. E-books are also considered.

Entry fee, $100. Awards are given in the categories of fiction, nonfiction, poetry, and young people's literature. Translations and anthologies are not accepted. Entries must be submitted by publishers. Send an SASE or visit the website for further information.

Deadline: June 15.

Representative winners: *Arc of Justice*, Kevin Boyle; *Godless*, Pete Hautman; *Door in the Mountain*, Jean Valentine.

Announcements: Winners are announced in October.

Award: The winners in each genre receive a cash award of $10,000. Sixteen finalists recieve a cash prize of $1,000.

National Children's Theatre Festival

Actors' Playhouse at Miracle Theatre
280 Miracle Mile
Coral Gables, FL 33134
www.actorsplayhouse.org

The Actors' Playhouse presents this annual award to an original, unpublished musical script that targets children between the ages of three and twelve. Works that have received limited production exposure, workshops, or staged readings are encouraged. Musicals that appeal to children and adults have the best chance of winning.

Entry fee, $10. Cast size must not exceed 8 adults, who may play any number of roles. Entries should have a running time of 45–60 minutes. Accepts photocopies and computer printouts. Include an SASE for return of manuscript.

Deadline: June 1.

Announcements: Winners are announced in November.

Award: Winner receives a cash

award of $500 and a full production of the play (requires performance rights for a limited time).

The John Newbery Medal

Association for Library Services to
  Children
50 East Huron Street
Chicago, IL 60611
www.ala.org/alsc

Every year since 1921, the Newbery Medal has honored the most distinguished American children's book published in the year preceding the contest. Authors who are U.S. citizens or permanent residents are eligible. Genres may include fiction, nonfiction, or poetry. Reprints or compilations are not eligible. Books should target children up to the age of fourteen.

Nominations are accepted from ALSC members only.

Deadline: December 31.

Representative winners: *Kira-Kira*, Cynthia Kadohata; *Al Capone Does My Shirts*, Gennifer Choldenko.

Announcements: Winners are announced at the Midwinter Meeting.

Award: The Newbery Medal is presented to the winner at an annual banquet.

New Voices Award

Lee & Low Books
95 Madison Avenue
New York, NY 10016
www.leeandlow.com

This annual competition is sponsored by multicultural children's publisher Lee & Low and is open to writers of color who are residents of the U.S. and who have not previously published a children's book. Entries of fiction or nonfiction manuscripts for children between the ages of 2 and 10 that have not previously been submitted to Lee & Low are eligible.

Manuscripts should provide stories that children of color can relate to, and promote greater understanding of one another. Folklore and animal stories will not be considered. No entry fee. Entries should not exceed 1,500 words. Limit of 2 submissions per entrant; must be sent separately. Send an SASE or visit the website for complete guidelines.

Deadline: October 31.

Representative winner: *Fit Like Frankie*, Carmen Bogan.

Announcements: Winners are announced in January.

Award: Winner receives a publishing contract from Lee & Low and a cash award of $1,000. Honorable mention receives a grant of $500 and possible publication.

Ursula Nordstrom Fiction Contest

HarperCollins Children's Books
1350 Avenue of the Americas
New York, NY 10019
www.harperchildrens.com

Named for distinguished children's editor Ursula Nordstrom, this annual contest is open to U.S. citizens over the age of 21 who have not yet been published. It seeks to encourage new talent and innovation in middle-grade fiction. Material must be suitable for children between the ages of 8 and 12.

No entry fee. Manuscripts must be 100–300 pages in length. Entries are judged on the basis of originality, clarity of writing, development of plot and character, and suitability for publication. Accepts photocopies and computer printouts. Include an SASE for return of manuscript.
Deadline: Entries are accepted between March 15 and April 15.
Announcements: Winner is announced in June.
Award: Winner receives a book contract for a hardcover edition, a $7,500 advance, and a cash prize of $1,500.

NWA Nonfiction Contest
National Writers' Association
3140 South Peoria #295
Aurora, CO 80014
www.nationalwriters.com

This annual competition is sponsored by the National Writers' Association. Its purpose is to recognize and encourage the writing of excellent nonfiction. Only previously unpublished works are eligible and submissions are judged on originality, marketability, research, and reader interest.

Entry fee, $18. Multiple entries are accepted under a separate cover. Entries should not exceed 5,000 words. Accepts photocopies and computer printouts. All entries

must be accompanied by an official entry form, which is available with an SASE or at the website.
Deadline: December 31.
Announcements: Winners are announced in October.
Award: First-place winner receives a cash prize of $200. Second- and third-place winners receive $100 and $50, respectively.

NWA Novel Contest
National Writers' Association
3140 South Peoria #295
Aurora, CO 80014
www.nationalwriters.com

This annual novel contest seeks to encourage creativity and recognize outstanding ability in novel writing. The competition is open to all writers and accepts original, previously unpublished novels in any genre.

Entry fee, $35. Multiple entries are accepted under separate cover. Entries should not exceed 10,000 words and must be written in English. Accepts computer printouts. Include an SASE for return of manuscript. Guidelines are available at the website.
Deadline: April 1.
Announcements: Winners are announced in June.
Award: First-place winner receives $500. Second- and third-place winners receive $250 and $150, respectively. Fourth- through tenth-place winners receive a book and an honor certificate.

NWA Short Story Contest

National Writers' Association
3140 South Peoria #295
Aurora, CO 80014
www.nationalwriters.com

The purpose of this annual competition is to recognize potential in short story writing. Only original, previously unpublished material is accepted.

Entry fee, $15. Multiple entries are accepted when submitted with separate cover sheet. Author information must appear on first page. Entries should not exceed 5,000 words. Accepts photocopies and computer printouts. Copies of judges' evaluation sheets are available with an SASE.

Deadline: July 1.

Announcements: Winners are announced in the fall.

Award: First-place winner receives a cash award of $250. Second- and third-place winners receive $100 and $50, respectively.

Scott O'Dell Award for Historical Fiction

1700 East 56th Street
Chicago, IL 60637
www.scottodell.com

Established in 1982, this annual award strives to encourage new authors to focus on creating historical fiction for young readers that increases their interest in the genre. Only books published in the year preceding the contest are eligible.

No entry fee. Entries may be submitted by both authors and publishers. Stories must be set in either Canada, South or Central America, or the United States.

Deadline: December 31.

Representative winners: *Worth*, A. LaFaye; *A River Between Us*, Richard Peck; *Trouble Don't Last*, Shelley Pearsall.

Award: Winner receives a cash award of $5,000.

Once Upon a World Award

Museum of Tolerance
1399 South Roxbury Drive
Los Angeles, CA 90035-4709
www.wiesenthal.com

This annual contest is offered by the Simon Wiesenthal Center and Museum of Tolerance in an effort to promote and perpetuate tolerance, diversity, understanding, and social justice. It honors books that demonstrate the importance of history and the acceptance of social and personal responsibility written for children between the ages of 6 and 10.

No entry fee. All entries must have been published during the year preceeding the contest. A nomination form must accompany each entry. Forms are available with an SASE or at the website.

Deadline: April.

Representative winner: *Thank you, Sarah*, Laurie Halse Anderson.

Announcements: Winners are announced in June.

Award: Winner receives a cash award of $1,000.

Orbis Pictus Award for Outstanding Nonfiction for Children

Literacy & Teacher Education
School of Education
Husson College
1 College Circle
Bangor, ME 04401
www.ncte.org

This annual contest honors a previously published nonfiction book for children that appeals to their interests and has potential for classroom teaching.

Nominations may come from members of the NCTE as well as the general educational community. Books are judged on the following criteria: accuracy; organization; attractive design; interesting style; and enthusiastic writing. Submissions must be useful in kindergarten through eighth grade classrooms and should encourage independent thinking.

Nominations should include the author's name, book title, publisher, copyright date, and a brief explanation of why you liked the book. Visit the website for complete information.

Deadline: November 30.
Representative winner: *York's Adventures with Lewis and Clark*, Rhoda Blumberg.
Announcements: Winners are announced in April.
Award: Winners receive a plaque presented during the annual NCTE Convention. Five honor books will receive certificates of recognition.

Pacific Northwest Writers Literary Contest

P.O. Box 2016
Edmonds, WA 98020-9516
www.pnwa.org

The mission of this annual contest is to help new writers achieve recognition. Awards are presented in 10 categories including romance, adult genre novel, juvenile short story or picture book, and juvenile/young adult novel.

Entry fee, $35 for members; $45 for non-members. Limit one entry per category. Submit two copies of each entry. Author's name should not appear on manuscript. Include a 3x5 index card with author's name, address, telephone number, and title of entry. Visit the website or send an SASE for complete category list and guidelines.

Deadline: February 22.
Representative winners: *A Figure of Leaves*, Kathleen Snow; *The Porcelain Eagle*, Julie K. Casper.
Announcements: Winners are announced in July.
Award: Winners in each category receive cash prizes ranging from $100–$600.

PEN Center USA Literary Awards

PEN Center USA
Suite 41
672 South Lafayette Park Place
Los Angeles, CA 90057
www.penusa.org

Established in 1982, this annual

"Best of the West" contest is open to writers who live west of the Mississippi River. It recognizes literary merit in ten categories including fiction, nonfiction, poetry, children's literature, and translation. All entries must have been published in the year preceding the contest.

Entry fee, $35. Submit 4 copies of each entry. All entries must include a completed entry form. Send an SASE or visit the website for a complete list of categories and specific guidelines.
Deadline: December 31.
Representative winners: *Zipped*, Laura and Tom McNeal; *In the Shadow of Memory*, Floyd Skoot.
Announcements: Winners are announced in June.
Award: Winners in each category receive a cash award of $1,000.

PEN/Phyllis Naylor Working Writer Fellowship

PEN American Center
Suite 303
588 Broadway
New York, NY 10012
www.pen.org

Offered annually to an author of children's or young adult fiction, this fellowship is awarded to provide a writer with financial support. Authors who have published at least two books, and no more than five in the last ten years, are eligible.

Nominations must be made by an editor or fellow writer. The nominator should include a list of the candidate's published work and a description of the candidate's financial resources. Three copies of no more than 100 pages must be submitted. Send an SASE or visit the website for complete details.
Deadline: January 17.
Representative winners: Amanda Jenkins, Deborah Wiles, Franny Billingsley.
Announcements: Winner is announced in May.
Award: Winner receives a $5,000 fellowship.

Please Touch Museum's Book Awards

210 North 21st Street
Philadelphia, PA 19103
www.pleasetouchmuseum.org

This annual award has been presented to authors whose high-quality literature for children fosters a love of reading. A panel of experts consisting of librarians, professors, and children's literature consultants judge the entries. Awards are presented in two categories: books for ages 3 and under, and books for children ages 4 to 7.

Submit four copies of each entry. Entries are not returned. Send an SASE or visit the website for more information.
Deadline: September.
Representative winners: *Down on the Farm*, Merrily Kutner; *The Turn-Around, Upside-Down Alphabet Book*, Lisa Campbell Ernst.
Announcements: Winners are chosen in October.

Award: Winners receive a press release and are encouraged to hold a book signing at the museum. The winners are celebrated at an awards presentation dinner in May.

Pockets Annual Fiction Contest

Pockets Magazine
Box 340004
1908 Grand Avenue
Nashville, TN 37203-0004
www.pockets.org

Pockets Magazine sponsors this contest each year in search of new contributions to children's literature. Previously unpublished stories between 1,000 and 1,600 words are accepted. Biblical and historical fiction are not eligible.

No entry fee. Enclose an SASE for return of manuscript.
Deadline: August 15.
Representative winner: "Rule #2," Liza Gomez Maakestad.
Announcements: Winner is notified November 1.
Award: Winner receives a cash award of $1,000 and publication.

Edgar Allan Poe Awards

Mystery Writers of America
6th Floor
17 East 47th Street
New York, NY 10017
www.mysterywriters.org

The Mystery Writers of America sponsors this annual competition to enhance and promote the visibility of the mystery genre. It offers awards in 12 categories including best fact crime; best young adult mystery; best juvenile mystery; best first novel by an American author; and best motion picture screenplay.

No entry fee. All entries must have been published during the year preceding the contest. Submit one copy of entry to each member of the appropriate judging committee. Entry form and committee information available with an SASE or at the website.
Deadline: Varies for each category.
Representative winners: *Little Girl Lost*, Richard Aleas; *Chasing Vermeer*, Blue Balliett; *Story Time*, Edward Bloor.
Announcements: Winners are announced in April.
Award: An "Edgar" is presented to each winner. Cash prizes may also be awarded.

Michael L. Printz Award for Excellence in Young Adult Literature

American Library Association
50 East Huron
Chicago, IL 60611
www.ala.org/yalsa/printz

This prestigious award is presented to an outstanding work of young adult literature. Entries may be fiction, nonfiction, poetry, or an anthology. All entries must have been published in the year preceding the contest. Submissions should target young adults between the ages of 12 and 18.

ALA committee members may nominate any number of titles. Books are judged on their ability to get young people talking about the subject matter and excited about reading. Controversial topics are not discouraged.

Deadline: December 31.

Representative winner: *how i live now*, Meg Rosoff.

Announcements: Winners are announced at the annual ALA Midwinter conference.

Award: Winner is honored at an ALA awards ceremony.

Science Fiction/Fantasy Short Story Contest

Science Fiction Writers of the Earth
P.O. Box 121293
Fort Worth, TX 76121
http://home.flash.net/~sfwoe

Celebrating over 25 years, this annual contest is sponsored by Science Fiction Writers of the Earth and seeks to promote short story writing in the genres of science fiction and fantasy.

Entry fee, $5 for first entry; $2 for each additional entry. Manuscripts should be between 2,000 and 7,500 words in length. Accepts computer printouts. Visit the website or send an SASE for further guidelines.

Deadline: October 30.

Announcements: Winners are announced in February.

Award: First-place winner receives publication on the SFWoE website. First- through third-place winners

receive cash awards ranging from $50–$200. Special awards are also presented for outstanding work from younger authors.

Seven Hills Writing Contest

Tallahassee Writers' Association
P.O. Box 3428
Tallahassee, FL 32315
www.twaonline.org

Open to new writers, these contests are sponsored by the Tallahassee Writers' Association. Work in the categories of short story, memoir, and children's literature is accepted. Only previously unpublished material is eligible.

Entry fee, $10 for members; $15 for non-members. Multiple entries are accepted. Accepts photocopies and computer printouts.

Deadline: September 30.

Representative winner: *The Invisible Treasure of Knollwood Roost*, Jerry and Ada Forney.

Announcements: Winners are announced in April.

Award: First-place winners in each category receive $75. Second- and third-place winners receive $50 and $35, respectively.

Seventeen Magazine Fiction Contest

13th Floor
1440 Broadway
New York, NY 10018
www.seventeen.com

This annual fiction contest is open to writers between the ages of

13 and 21 and is sponsored by *Seventeen Magazine*. Material is judged on creativity, originality, and writing ability. Original, unpublished material on any subject of interest to young adults is eligible.

No entry fee. Entries should not exceed 2,000 words. Multiple entries are accepted. Accepts photocopies and computer printouts.
Deadline: December 31.
Representative winner: "Painting by Numbers," Dan Corkum.
Announcements: Winners are announced in spring.
Award: First-place winner receives a cash award of $1,000 and publication in *Seventeen Magazine*. Second- and third-place winners receive cash awards of $500 and $250, respectively.

Side Show Anthology Fiction Contest
Somersault Press
404 Vista Heights Road
El Cerrito, CA 94530
www.somersaultpress.com

The fiction anthology, *Side Show*, sponsors this annual contest to showcase the work of new authors. It accepts entries of literary fiction. Novels, essays, pornography, and genre fiction are not accepted. There are no restrictions on length or theme.

Entry fee, $12.50, which covers several manuscripts provided they are in the same envelope. Accepts photocopies and computer printouts. Submissions that include an SASE will be returned with a manuscript critique if requested.
Deadline: Ongoing.
Award: First-place winner receives publication in *Side Show* and a cash prize of $100. Second-place winner receives a cash award of $75 and third-place winner receives a cash prize of $50.

Skipping Stones Honor Awards
Skipping Stones
P.O. Box 3939
Eugene, OR 97403
www.skippingstones.org

These annual awards honor books that focus on ethnic diversity, globalism, and appreciation of cultural differences. Entries should promote understanding, compassion, non-violence, and an appreciation for the environment.

Entry fee, $50. Send 4 copies of each entry. Entries must have been published in the year preceding the contest. Send an SASE or visit the website for complete guidelines.
Deadline: January 15.
Representative winners: *The Raccoon Next Door*, Gary Bogue; *Chachaji's Cup*, Uma Krishnaswami.
Announcements: Winners are announced in April.
Award: Cash awards are given to the first- through fourth-place winners. Winning entries are reviewed in the summer issue of *Skipping Stones*.

Smart Publishing Winter Revelation Contest

11832 South Bishop
Chicago, IL 60643
www.geocities.com/smart_suzette/
smartpublishing.html

This annual contest awards writing that teaches readers of all ages the benefits of hindsight and offers them alternative solutions to problems in a fun-to-read format. Open to writers of all levels, its judges consider content and plot more important than a polished product. It accepts submissions in the categories of novels, novellas, short stories, and poetry for all reading levels. Manuscripts must be original and unpublished.

Entry fee, $10. Multiple entries are accepted. Accepts photocopies and computer printouts. All manuscripts must be bound. Visit the website or send an SASE for complete guidelines.

Deadline: May 2.

Announcements: Winners will be announced on June 1.

Award: Winner receives a publishing contract with Smart Publishing.

Kay Snow Writing Contest

Willamette Writers
Suite 5A
9045 SW Barbour Boulevard
Portland, OR 97219-4027
www.willamettewriters.com

Named for the founder of Willamette Writers, the purpose of these annual awards is to help writers reach their professional goals in a wide range of categories. Entries are accepted in several categories including juvenile short story or article, fiction, nonfiction, and student writer. Only original, unpublished material is accepted.

Entry fee, $10 for members; $15 for non-members. Word lengths vary for each category. Submit 3 copies of each entry. Author's name should not appear on manuscript. Include a cover letter with author's name, title of entry, and contact information. Send an SASE or visit the website for further information.

Deadline: May 15.

Representative winners: *The Big Brothers' Guide to Life with A New Baby*, Elizabeth Rusch; *The Comedian and the Bully,* Drew Lane.

Announcements: Winners are announced in August. Finalists will be notified by mail prior to the announcement of winners.

Award: Cash prizes ranging from $50 to $300 are awarded in each category. A Liam Callen award with a cash prize of $500 will also be presented to the best overall entry.

Society of Midland Authors Awards

P.O. Box 10419
Chicago, IL 60610
www.midlandauthors.com

Since 1915, the Society of Midland Authors has presented these awards to authors residing in the 12 Midwestern states. It accepts material in the categories of fiction, nonfiction, biography, poetry, and children's fiction and nonfiction.

No entry fee. All entries must be published in the year preceding the contest and book entries must be at least 2,000 words. Multiple submissions are accepted. Send an SASE or visit the website for complete competition guidelines.
Deadline: January 30.
Representative winners: *Ida B: . . . and Her Plans to Maximize Fun*, Katherine Hannigan; *Escape from Saigon*, Andrea Warren.
Announcements: Winners are announced in May.
Award: Winners in each category receive a cash award and a recognition plaque.

Southwest Writers Annual Contest
Southwest Writers Workshop
Suite A
3721 Morris Street NE
Albuquerque, NM 87111-3611
www.southwestwriters.org

This annual award honors distinguished original and unpublished writing in a wide array of genres. It accepts submissions in the categories of novel, short story, short nonfiction, book-length nonfiction, children's book, screenplay, and poetry. Send an SASE or visit the website for subcategories and complete category requirements.

Entry fee, $44 for non-members; $29 for members. Multiple entries are accepted under separate cover. Submit 2 copies of each entry.

Include a 9x12 SASE for return of manuscript.
Deadline: May 1.
Representative winners: *Cascabel*, Lynn Murray; "In the Face of Fear," Julie K. Casper.
Announcements: Winners are announced in the fall.
Award: Winners in each category receive cash awards ranging from $50 to $150. First-place winners in each category compete for a grand prize of $1,000.

The Spur Awards
Tracy L. Hutton, Awards Chair
5009 Justin Drive NW
Albuquerque, NM 87114
www.westernwriters.org

The Spur Awards are open to all writers and are given annually to the most distinguished writing about the American West. The following categories are awarded: Western novel (short novel), Western novel (long novel), short story, short nonfiction, contemporary fiction, biography, history, juvenile fiction and nonfiction, TV or motion picture drama, and first novel. Entries must have been published the year preceding the contest.

Send one copy of entry with a completed entry form; available with an SASE or at the website.
Deadline: December 31.
Representative winners: *Black Kettle: The Cheyenne Chief Who Sought Peace but Found War*, Thom Hatch; *Fire in the Hole!*, Mary Cronk Farrell.
Announcements: Winners are

announced in March.

Award: Winners in each category receive a cash award of $2,500.

Stanley Drama Award
Wagner College
Dept. of Theater and Speech
631 Howard Avenue
Staten Island, NY 10301
www.wagner.edu/stanleydrama.html

Open to aspiring playwrights, this contest accepts entries of original full-length plays, musicals, or series of two or three thematically related one-act plays that have not been professionally produced or received tradebook publication.

Entry fee, $20. Limit one submission per playwright. Musical entries must be accompanied by an audio cassette with all the music to be included in the play.

Deadline: October 1.

Announcements: Winners are announced approximately 60 days after the deadline.

Award: One first-place winner receives a cash prize of $2,000.

Tall Tales Press Hidden Talents Short Story Contest
20 Tuscany Valley Park NW
Calgary, Alberta T3L 2B6
Canada
www.talltalespress.com

Held annually, this contest is open to adult and young adult writers who want to gain experience. It accepts original, unpublished short stories (fiction or nonfiction) on a wide variety of topics.

Entry fee, $10 for adults; $5 for junior categories. Multiple entries are accepted if accompanied by a reading fee. Entries must not exceed 5,000 words. Send an SASE or visit the website for complete contest guidelines.

Deadline: May 31.

Representative winners: *Regular People*, Neil Naft; *Astray*, Richard Sarles; *Faith*, Robert Scott.

Announcements: Winners are announced after the contest deadline in *Writers' Journal* and on the website.

Award: Winners and honorable mentions receive cash awards ranging from $10 to $500 and possible publication.

Peter Taylor Prize for the Novel
Knoxville Writers' Guild
P.O. Box 2565
Knoxville, TN 37901-2565
www.knoxvillewritersguild.org

This annual contest is sponsored by the Knoxville Writers' Guild and is open to all writers residing in the U.S. Only full-length, unpublished novels are accepted. Short-story collections, translations, and nonfiction will not be considered.

Entry fee, $25. Entries should be a minimum of 40,000 words. Multiple and simultaneous submissions are accepted. Each entry should be accompanied by two cover sheets. Include an SASE for contest results. Manuscripts will not be returned.

Send an SASE or visit the website for complete details.

Deadline: Entries must be post-marked between February 1 and April 30.

Representative winner: *Fire on Mount Maggiore*, John Parras.

Announcements: Winners are announced in November.

Award: Winner receives a cash award of $1,000, publication of the novel by the University of Tennessee Press, and a standard royalty contract.

Sydney Taylor Manuscript Competition

Association of Jewish Libraries
315 Maitland Avenue
Teaneck, NJ 07666
www.jewishlibraries.org

Held annually, this contest seeks to honor high quality work in the genre of Jewish children's literature. It is open to authors who have not yet published a book of fiction and encourages submissions of Jewish material with universal appeal. Submissions should be previously unpublished and appropriate for children ages 8 to 11. Entries must be between 64 and 200 pages.

No entry fee. Limit one manuscript per competition. Manuscripts will not be returned.

Deadline: December 31.

Announcements: Winner is announced by April 15.

Award: Winner receives a cash award of $1,000.

Utah Original Writing Competition

617 East South Temple
Salt Lake City, UT 84102
www.arts.utah.gov/literature/comprules.html

Open to writers living in the state of Utah, this annual competition recognizes and rewards fine writing. It accepts previously unpublished work in several categories including young adult book, personal essay, short story, and general nonfiction and fiction.

No entry fee. Word lengths for each category vary. Limit one entry per category. Accepts photocopies and computer printouts. Manuscripts will not be returned. Send an SASE or visit the website for complete category list and contest guidelines.

Deadline: Entries must be post-marked by June 24.

Representative winners: *Not-A-Dr.-Logan's Divorce Book*, Sydney Salter Husseman; *Nicola*, Sara V. Olds.

Announcements: Winners are contacted in September.

Award: Winners in each category receive cash prizes ranging from $300 to $5,000.

Vegetarian Essay Contest

The Vegetarian Resource Group
P.O. Box 1463
Baltimore, MD 21203
www.vrg.org

The purpose of this annual contest is to educate and inform young people about vegetarian and vegan lifestyles. The contest is open to students in 3 categories: ages 14–18; 9–13; and 8 and under. Students do not need to be vegetarian to enter the contest. Material should be based on interviews, research, or personal opinion.

No entry fee. Entries should be between 2–3 pages in length. Limit one entry per competition. Accepts photocopies, computer printouts, and handwritten entries. Visit the website or send an SASE for complete guidelines.

Deadline: May 1.

Announcements: Winners are announced at the end of the year.

Award: Winners in each category receive a $50 savings bond and publication in *The Vegetarian Journal* (requires all rights).

Jackie White Memorial National Children's Play Writing Contest

Columbia Entertainment Company
309 Parkade Boulevard
Columbia, MO 65202
http://cectheatre.org/html/play_writing.html

The goal of this annual contest is to promote excellence in play scripts for enjoyment by children and families. Roles that challenge and expand the talents of actors are strongly encouraged. Entries should be full-length (1 to 1.5 hours running time) and include well-developed speaking roles for at least seven characters. Only previ-

ously unpublished and unproduced material is considered.

Entry fee, $10. Multiple entries are accepted. Include a 3x5 card with name of play, author's name, mailing address, telephone number, character descriptions, synopsis, résumé, and a cassette or CD of music, if appropriate.

Deadline: June 1.

Representative winners: *Five Frogs and a Prince*, Vicki Bartholomew; *The Patchwork Girl of Oz*, William S. Kilborne; *The Rose Slippers*, Rosa Soy and Sue Hadjopoulos.

Announcements: Winners are announced by August 31.

Award: Winner receives a $500 cash award and possible publication or staged reading of the winning entry.

William Allen White Children's Book Award

Emporia State University
Box 4051
1200 Commercial Street
Emporia, KS 66801
www.emporia.edu/libsv/waw-bookaward/index.htm

Founded in 1953, this annual competition looks to honor children's books that encourage boys and girls to read and enjoy books. Entries must have been published during the year preceding the contest, and are judged on clarity, factual accuracy, originality, and respect for the reader. One book for third- through fifth-grade students and one book for students in sixth through eighth grade is awarded.

The contest is open to North American residents only. Text-books, anthologies, and translations are not eligible. Visit the website for more information.

Deadline: May.

Representative winners: *Loser*, Jerry Spinelli; *Surviving the Applewhites*, Stephanie S. Tolan.

Announcements: Winners are announced in the fall.

Award: Winners receive a cash prize of $1,000 and a bronze medal.

Laura Ingalls Wilder Medal

Association for Library Services to
  Children
50 East Huron Street
Chicago, IL 60611
www.ala.org/alsc

This award is given by the Association for Library Services to Children every other year. It recognizes an author and illustrator who have made a lasting contribution to children's literature. All books must have been published in the U.S. The recipient is chosen by a committee of children's librarians. Nominations can only be made by ALSC members. Complete information about the medal is available at the website.

Deadline: Ongoing.

Representative winners: Laurence Yep, Milton Meltzer.

Announcements: Winners are announced in January.

Award: A medal is presented to the winners at an annual banquet.

Tennessee Williams One-Act Play Competition

UNO Lakefront
New Orleans, LA 70118
www.tennesseewilliams.net

Celebrating its twentieth anniversary, this annual competition recognizes excellence in one-act plays.

Entry fee, $15. Multiple entries are accepted under separate cover. Accepts photocopies and computer printouts. All entries must be typed and must include an entry form, which is available at the website or with an SASE. Send an SASE or visit the website for complete guidelines.

Deadline: Entries are accepted September 1 through December 15.

Announcements: Winners are announced by April.

Award: Winner receives a cash award of $1,000 and a staged reading at an annual literary festival.

Paul A. Witty Short Story Award

Kate Schlichting, Chair
Awards Subcommittee
333 Candee Avenue, Apt. 6-C
Sayville, NY 11782-3038
www.reading.org

The Paul A. Witty Short Story Award is presented to an author of an original short story that was published for the first time in a periodical during the year preceding the contest. This award was put in place to encourage children to read periodicals.

Authors and publishers may nominate a short story. Send entries to the designated Paul A. Witty Subcommittee Chair. No entry fee. Limit three entries per competition. Send an SASE or e-mail to exec@ reading.org for further information and guidelines.
Deadline: December 1.
Representative winner: "Free At Last! A Kurdish Family in America," Karen O'Connor.
Announcements: Winner is announced in the spring.
Award: Winner receives a cash award of $1,000 presented at the annual IRA convention.

Women in the Arts Annual Writing Contest
P.O. Box 2907
Decatur, IL 62524

The Women in the Arts Annual Writing Contest is open to all writers and accepts entries in the categories of essay; fiction and nonfiction for children (up to 1,500 words); plays (one-act); and rhymed and unrhymed poetry (up to 32 lines). All entries must be original work and may be previously published or unpublished.

Entry fee, $2. Multiple entries are accepted under separate cover. Entries are subject to blind judging. Author's name should not appear on manuscript. Include cover sheet with author's name, address, telephone number, e-mail address, title of entry, category, and word count. Do not staple entries. Manuscripts

will not be returned. Send an SASE for complete category information and further guidelines.
Deadline: November 1.
Announcements: Winners will be announced by March 15.
Award: First-place winners in each category receive a cash award of $50. Second- and third-place winners receive cash awards of $35 and $15, respectively.

Carter G. Woodson Book Awards
National Council for the Social Studies
Suite 500
8555 16th Street
Silver Spring, MD 20910
www.socialstudies.org

Established in 1974, these annual awards are given to the most distinguished social science books for young readers. The purpose of the awards is to encourage the writing and publishing of social science books that handle the topics of cultural and ethnic diversity with accuracy and respect.

All submissions must have been published during the year preceding the contest. Submit one copy of each nominated title to the full Carter G. Woodson Book Award Subcommittee, which ranges from 14 to 20 members. Send an SASE or visit the website for complete guidelines.
Deadline: February.
Representative winners: *Jim Thorpe's Bright Path*, Joseph

Bruchach; *The Voice that Challenged a Nation: Marian Anderson and the Struggle for Equal Rights*, Russell Freedman; and *The Civil Rights Act of 1964*, Rober H. Mayer.

Announcements: Winners are announced in the spring.

Award: Certificates and commemorative gifts are presented to two winners at the annual NCCS conference in November. Additional books will receive Honor awards.

Work-in-Progress Grants

Society of Children's Book Writers
and Illustrators
8271 Beverly Boulevard
Los Angeles, CA 90048
www.scbwi.org

These grants are awarded by the Society of Children's Book Writers and Illustrators to assist writers of children's literature with the completion of a project. Several categories are awarded including General Work-in-Progress; Contemporary Novel for Young People; Nonfiction Research; and Previously Unpublished Author. Requests for applications may be made beginning October 1 of each year. Instructions and complete guidelines will be sent with application forms. All applications should include a 750-word synopsis and writing sample of no more than 2,500 words from the entry.

Send an SASE or visit the website for complete information.

Deadline: Applications are accepted between February 1 and March 1.

Announcements: Winners of the grants are announced in September.

Award: Cash grants of $1,500 and $500 are awarded in each category.

Writers at Work Fellowship

P.O. Box 540370
North Salt Lake, UT 84054-0370
www.writersatwork.org

Sponsored by Writers at Work, this annual contest is open to all writers who have not yet published a book-length work. Original, unpublished material is eligible, including self-published material such as college essays or a self-printed novel that was distributed among friends. Previous winners may re-enter within a different genre. Categories include fiction and nonfiction (to 5,000 words), and poetry (to 6 poems).

Entry fee, $15. Multiple entries are accepted under separate cover. Accepts photocopies and computer printouts. Indicate category on outside envelope. Manuscripts will not be returned. Send an SASE or visit the website for further information.

Deadline: March 1.

Representative winners: "Mud Season," Lee Reilly; "The Decamerous Sisters Club," David G. Pace; "Exiled Girls of the Midwest," Alison Powell.

Announcements: Winners of the grants are announced in April.

Award: Winners in each category receive a cash prize of $1,500 and publication in *Quarterly West*. Honorable mentions are also awarded.

Writer's Digest Annual Writing Competition

4700 East Galbraith Road
Cincinnati, OH 45236
www.writersdigest.com

This contest is open to all writers and awards several categories including children's fiction, feature article, genre short story, memoir/personal essay, and stage play script. Only original, previously unpublished work is accepted.

Entry fee, $10. Multiple entries are accepted under separate cover. Accepts photocopies and computer printouts. Author's name, address, telephone number, and category should appear in the upper left corner of the first page. Manuscripts are not returned. Visit the website or send an SASE for complete category list, word length requirements, and additional guidelines.

Deadline: June 1.

Announcements: Winners are announced in the November issue of *Writer's Digest*.

Award: Grand-prize winner receives a cash award of $1,500. Cash prizes and books from *Writer's Digest* are also awarded to winners in each category.

Writers' Journal Writing Contests

P.O. Box 394
Perham, MN 56573-0374
www.writersjournal.com

Sponsored by *Writers' Journal,* these annual awards present prizes in several categories including short story, ghost story/horror, romance, travel, fiction, and poetry. Word lengths and guidelines vary for each contest.

All entries must be previously unpublished. Submit 2 copies of each entry. Accepts photocopies and computer printouts. Entry fees range from $5 to $10 depending on the category. Enclose a #10 SASE for winners' list.

Deadline: Varies for each category.

Representative winners: "Summerlake," Ken Wallin; "Roadkill," Timothy Charles Smith; "The Sound of the Sea," Steve Muscato; "A Potential Hero," Robbi Hess; "Alaska—America's Last Frontier," Lisa M. Yrizarry.

Announcements: Winners are announced in *Writers' Journal* and on the website after each contest deadline.

Award: Winners receive cash prizes and publication of their winning entry.

The Writing Conference Writing Contests

P.O. Box 664
Ottawa, KS 66067-0664
www.writingconference.com

This annual contest accepts entries from elementary, junior high, and high school students in an effort to encourage a love of writing. Submissions are accepted in the categories of short stories, short nonfiction, and poetry, and follow a yearly theme.

No entry fee. Limit one entry per competition. Accepts photocopies and computer printouts. Visit the website or send an SASE for further contest information.

Deadline: January.

Announcements: Winners are announced in February.

Award: Winners in each category receive publication in *The Writer's Slate*.

Writing for Children Competition

The Writers' Union of Canada
Suite 200
90 Richmond Street East
Toronto, Ontario M5C 1P1
www.writersunion.ca

Open to Canadian citizens and landed immigrants, this annual competition awards a writer who has not yet published a book, and does not have a book contract from a publisher. The contest was created with the purpose of discovering and promoting new writers of children's literature.

Entry fee, $15. Multiple entries are accepted. Entries should not exceed 1,500 words. Accepts photocopies and computer printouts. No fax or e-mail submissions. Manuscripts will not be returned. Send an SASE or visit the website for further information.

Deadline: April.

Representative winners: "Delroy's Present," Heather Beaumont; "Moon Belly Momma," Kari Jones;

"Snow Gophers," Kate Aley; "Tomatoes Please!" Margaret Angus.

Announcements: Winner is announced in July.

Award: Winner receives a cash prize of $1,500 and the Writers' Union of Canada will submit the winning entry to several children's publishers.

Paul Zindel First Novel Award

Hyperion Books for Children
114 5th Avenue
New York, NY 10011
www.hyperionchildrensbooks.com

This annual award is presented for a work of contemporary or historical fiction set in the U.S. that accurately reflects the cultural and ethnic diversity of our country. Submissions should be books intended for readers ages 8 through 12.

Submissions should be a book-length manuscript of between 100- and 240-typewritten pages. Manuscripts must be accompanied by an entry form (available at the website or with an SASE). Accepts photocopies and computer printouts. Limit two entries per competition.

Deadline: April 30.

Announcements: Winners will be notified after July 15.

Award: Winner receives a book contract with Hyperion Books for Children, covering world rights including but not limited to hardcover, paperback, e-book, and audio book editions with an advance against royalties of

$7,500. Winner also receives a cash prize of $1,500.

Zoo Press Award for Short Fiction

Zoo Press
P.O. Box 3528
Omaha, NE 68103
www.zoopress.org

Open to all writers, Zoo Press presents this award to a previously unpublished, original work of short fiction. Eligible collections of short stories must be a minimum of 40,000 words.

Entry fee, $25. Multiple entries are accepted. All entries must include a cover letter with author's name, address, telephone number, e-mail address, and manuscript title. Manuscripts will not be returned. Send an SASE or visit the website for complete guidelines and further information.

Deadline: February 14.

Announcements: Winners are announced in the late spring.

Award: Winning entry will be published by Zoo Press and winner receives a $5,000 advance against royalties.

Index

C

D

H

M

O